Economic Disasters of the Twentieth Century

Economic Disasters of the Twentieth Century

Edited by

Michael J. Oliver

Professor of Economics, École Supérieure de Commerce de Rennes, France

and

Derek H. Aldcroft

Fellow, University of Leicester, UK

Edward Elgar
Cheltenham, UK • Northampton, MA, USA

Published by
Edward Elgar Publishing Limited
The Lypiatts
15 Lansdown Road
Cheltenham
Glos GL50 2JA
UK

Edward Elgar Publishing, Inc.
William Pratt House
9 Dewey Court
Northampton
Massachusetts 01060
USA

Paperback edition 2008

A catalogue record for this book
is available from the British Library

Library of Congress Control Number: 2007925023

ISBN 978 1 84064 589 7 (cased)
ISBN 978 1 84844 158 3 (paperback)

Printed in Great Britain by the MPG Books Group, Bodmin and King's Lynn

Contents

Contributors

Derek H. Aldcroft is currently University Fellow in the School of History at the University of Leicester, formerly Research Professor in Economic History at Manchester Metropolitan University (1994–2001), Professor and Head of Department of Economic History at the Universities of Sydney (1973–76) and Leicester (1976–94). He is the author of many books and papers on British and European economic history including *From Versailles to Wall Street: The International Economy, 1919–1929* (Allen Lane, 1977), *The British Economy, Vol. I: The Years of Turmoil, 1920–1951* (Wheatsheaf, 1986) and *Studies in the Interwar European Economy* (Ashgate 1997). He has recently published a volume entitled *Europe's Third World* (Ashgate, 2006) and is currently working on Sub-Saharan Africa's growth failure since decolonization.

Michael Beenstock has been Professor of Economics at the Hebrew University of Jerusalem since 1989. He currently teaches macroeconomics, financial econometrics and time series econometrics. His current research interests include immigrant absorbtion, economics of the family, illicit drug consumption and macroeconometrics. In the past he took an interest in energy economics and has published a dozen papers in the area. His interest in OPEC began as a young economist at HM Treasury (London) where in 1971 he was a member of a working party on 'Vast Surpluses of Oil Producing Countries'. In October 1973 he wrote a paper predicting that by the end of the century oil prices would return to their 1972 level. Following this, he represented the Treasury in Whitehall and abroad on OPEC-related issues. He is currently advising the Monetary Policy Department at the Bank of Israel.

Forrest H. Capie is Professor of Economic History at the Cass Business School, City University, London. After a doctorate at the London School of Economics in the 1970s and a teaching fellowship there, he taught at the University of Warwick and the University of Leeds. He has been a British Academy Overseas Fellow at the National Bureau, New York, a Visiting Professor at the University of Aix-Marseille and at the London School of Economics, and a Visiting Scholar at the IMF. He has written widely on money, banking and trade and commercial policy. He was Head of

Department of Banking and Finance at City University from 1989 to 1992 and Editor of the *Economic History Review* from 1993 to 1999. He is currently a member of the Academic Advisory Council of the Institute of Economic Affairs. He is an Academician of the Academy of Social Sciences. He is currently on secondment at the Bank of England writing the next instalment in its history.

Niall Ferguson is the Laurence A. Tisch Professor of History at Harvard University. He is also a Senior Research Fellow of Jesus College, Oxford University and a Senior Fellow of the Hoover Institution, Stanford University. His books include *Paper and Iron: Hamburg Business and German Politics in the Era of Inflation 1897–1927* (Cambridge University Press, 1995), *The World's Banker: The History of the House of Rothschild* (2 vols, Penguin, 1998), *The Pity of War: Explaining World War One* (Basic, 1999), *The Cash Nexus: Money and Power in the Modern World, 1700–2000*.(Basic, 2001), *Empire: The Rise and Demise of the British World Order and the Lessons for Global Power* (Basic, 2003), and *Colossus: The Price of American Empire* (Penguin, 2004). He also edited *Virtual History: Alternatives and Counterfactuals* (Basic, 1999). His most recent, *The War of the World: Twentieth-Century Conflict and the Descent of the West*, was published by Penguin in September 2006. He is currently beginning work on a biography of Henry Kissinger.

W.R. Garside, formerly of the University of Birmingham, UK, is currently Professor of Economic History and Dean, University of Otago, New Zealand. He has written extensively on government economic policy in twentieth-century Britain with particular reference to industrial decline, unemployment and the political economy of structural change. Other published work embraces British fiscal policy in the 1930s, employers' industrial relations strategies, the British coal industry, the sources and validity of unemployment statistics since the mid-nineteenth century, European interwar economic policy and industrial rationalization in Britain between the wars. He is currently engaged on a revisionist study of the Japanese developmental state since 1945, building upon research first undertaken as Visiting Professor at the Institute of Economic Research, Hitotsubashi University, Tokyo. In addition, he collaborates with colleagues in Japan investigating the sources of Japanese growth and decline from the nineteenth century to present times and with others investigating business enterprise in twentieth-century New Zealand.

Steven Morewood is a lecturer in international history in the Institute of Archaeology & Antiquity, School of Historical Studies, University of

Birmingham. He is the co-author (with Derek Aldcroft) of *Economic Change in Eastern Europe since 1918* (Edward Elgar, 1995), which followed upon his initial foray into the region, a chapter, 'Eastern Europe in Transition, 1980–1990', for the third edition of D.H. Aldcroft's *The European Economy* (Routledge, 1990). For the fourth edition (2001) he provided an additional chapter, 'Towards a United Europe, 1990–2000'. He has also written 'Europe at the Crossroads 1974–2000' in D.H. Aldcroft and A. Sutcliffe (eds), *Europe in the International Economy 1500–2000* (Edward Elgar, 1999). He contributed 'Eastern Europe in the Twentieth Century' to M.J. Oliver (ed.), *Studies in Economic and Social History* in homage to Derek Aldcroft. On the Soviet Union he wrote 'Gorbachev and the Collapse of Communism' for *History Review*, No. 31, September 1998 and 'Mikhael Gorbachev and the Collapse of the Soviet Union', *History Teaching Review Year Book*, Volume 20 (2006). His research and teaching interests include the reasons for the fall of the Soviet Empire (part of Birmingham's 'End of Empire' first year survey course), the influence of the Great Powers on the Eastern Mediterranean region, especially the Balkans and Middle East, and the origins of the Second World War.

Michael J. Oliver is Professor of Economics at École Supérieure de Commerce de Rennes and a director of Lombard Street Associates, UK. He graduated in economic history at the University of Leicester and was awarded his PhD in economics and economic history from Manchester Metropolitan University. He has held posts at the universities of the West of England, Leeds, Sunderland and Bates College, USA and has been a Visiting Professor at Gettysburg College, Pennsylvania and Colby College, Maine. He is the author of several books including *Whatever Happened To Monetarism? Economic Policymaking and Social Learning in the United Kingdom Since 1979* (Ashgate, 1997); *Exchange Rate Regimes in the Twentieth Century* (with Derek Aldcroft, 1st edn, Edward Elgar, 1998) and *The Liquidity Theory of Asset Prices* (with Gordon Pepper, Wiley, 2006). He has contributed articles to *Economic History Review*, *Twentieth Century British History*, *Economic Affairs*, *Contemporary British History*, *Economic Review* and *Essays in Economic and Business History*. He is currently working on a reappraisal of the international monetary system between 1964 and 1972 and investigating the evolution of UK monetary policy since 1971.

John Singleton is Reader in Economic History at Victoria University of Wellington, NZ. He completed his PhD in economics at Lancaster University in England. After working at the London School of Economics and the Universities of Lancaster, York and Manchester, he moved to

Wellington, New Zealand in 1993. He is the author of *Lancashire on the Scrapheap: The Cotton Industry, 1945–70* (Oxford University Press, 1991) and *The World Textile Industry* (Routledge, 1997). He is also the principal author of *Innovation and Independence: The Reserve Bank of New Zealand 1973–2002* (Auckland University Press, 2006), the co-author (with Paul Robertson) of *Economic Relations between Britain and Australasia, 1940–1970* (Palgrave, 2002) and the joint editor (with Bob Millward) of *The Political Economy of Nationalisation in Britain, 1920–50* (Cambridge University Press, 1995). He has published many articles in journals such as the *Economic History Review*, *Business History* and the *Australian Economic History Review*.

Geoffrey E. Wood is Professor of Economics at Cass Business School, UK and Professor of Monetary Economics at the University of Buckingham. He went to the University of Warwick in 1968 as Lecturer in Economics and then spent two years as Visiting Economist with the Bank of England, where he was until recently a special advisor on financial stability. In 1975, he joined City University and since 1976 he has been Professor of Economics. He was Visiting Scholar at the Federal Reserve Bank of St Louis from 1977–78, has advised the New Zealand Treasury on a wide range of issues and has also been Visiting Scholar at the Federal Reserve Bank of New York and the Bank of Finland. Geoffrey Wood is also a Visiting Professorial Fellow in the Centre for Commercial Law Studies at Queen Mary and Westfield College, University of London and a Visiting Professor at the University of Athens.

Introduction

Michael J. Oliver and Derek H. Aldcroft

What epitaph should we give to the twentieth century? The philosopher and historian, Sir Isaiah Berlin, once described it as 'the most terrible century in Western history' while Eric Hobsbawm (1994) gave it the unpropitious title of 'the age of extremes'. Compared with the previous century, 'The Twentieth century . . . is a confusion of emergencies, disasters, improvisations, and artificial expedients. One passes in a few weeks of 1914 from a quiet stream, as it were, to white water' (Landes 1969, 359). A more unkind epitaph would be to label it 'the age of the common man'. This was the term used by Noel Coward in the mid-1950s to describe England, though for America he felt it was 'definitely the age of the crazy-mixed-up kid' (Payn and Morley 1998, 342, 351). One could go even further and describe it as 'the century of the common man and slob culture', epitomized surely by the way an insignificant corporal came for a time to dominate the continent of Europe and by the mass vulgarity and decline in social mores and family values of the latter half of the century.

Whatever one's personal predilection, few would dissent from view that it was a violent century: three super-monsters alone, Hitler, Stalin and Mao Tse-tung, were responsible, either directly or indirectly, for over 100 million deaths, while the frequent wars and military conflicts in the Third World together with the Great War may have accounted for another 50 million. To be sure, there were brighter interludes, notably the 'Belle Epoque' of the Edwardian era, and the 'Golden Age' of post-Second World War (the 1950s and 1960s) when economic growth surpassed that of any other period by a substantial margin (Bairoch 1976). Moreover, the century as a whole witnessed a big rise in living standards and in material and social progress generally, though there were exceptions, notably in Africa. Technological progress was also quite spectacular though not all of it was put to good account. Weapons of mass destruction and biological warfare are the evil products of this process, and even the mass consumerism generated by rapid technical change may be seen to have its downside (Geissler and van Courtland Moon 1999; de Grazia 2005).

This volume is concerned with another description for the twentieth century, namely, the age of economic disasters. This begs the obvious but difficult question of how we define an economic disaster. No doubt most centuries could claim they have had their share of disasters, but the twentieth century certainly seems to have been more prone to them than the previous one. Of course disasters are never purely economic; social and political factors loom large in events such as world wars, whereas oil price shocks are much more economic, though engineered by the machinations of an oil cartel. Others, the crisis in Eastern Europe from 1989 for example, may be politically determined but with huge economic implications.

These initial thoughts were in the minds of the editors after they were asked by Edward Elgar to prepare this volume, coupled to the realization that the selection of themes would be dictated by obvious disasters and conditioned by space and the availability of authors. After discussions with Elgar, the consensus that emerged was for a book that would have three aims. First, it would confine itself on the whole to a study of specific events or crises that had a finite time period, for example, the two World Wars and the Great Depression. Second, it would select one or two disasters that peppered the twentieth century, for example, financial crises and stock market crashes. Finally, it would have a macroeconomic slant. We are aware that these strictures will disappoint some readers who might be expecting a discussion on the global polarization of income between North and South, or between the First and Third Worlds (although tangentially this is referred to in the chapter on Africa). Similarly, the ever-present divide between rich and poor within societies, whether capitalist or otherwise, receives no treatment. For the same reason we have not touched upon the long-term prognosis favoured by the social historicists, who see the periodic crises and upheavals of the twentieth century as but one more nail in the capitalist coffin before societies revert to the systemic chaos from which they emerged some six or seven centuries ago (see Arrighi 1994). Some of our critics will also point to some notable omissions, for example, the existence of mass unemployment, although this topic is to some extent subsumed under other chapters, notably that on the Great Depression. Others that are excluded are more controversial, such as the rise of government spending and the welfare state, the breakdown of the family and social control, the increase in world population and the destruction of the resource base and environmental issues.

It is fair to say that in defining the events we are in a sense assuming that they were economic disasters of some magnitude, although we would add that contributors have had a free hand to decide the significance of their subject matter and so determine their severity. The problem with defining something as a 'disaster' from a macro standpoint is that the mere force of the word conjures up an image of all and sundry becoming embroiled in a sudden and violent maelstrom. In the case of war, it might seem obvious to associate such a word with the dreadful events that unfolded between 1914 and 1918 and again between 1939 and 1945. However, as John Singleton reminds us in his chapter on the First World War (Chapter 1), although there was death and destruction in Europe, the war had far less of an impact elsewhere in the world.

Clearly, the same cannot be said for the *economic* impact of the 'Great War'. Singleton carefully considers the individual costs, discussing the difficult concept of measuring the net loss of utility suffered by all who were directly or indirectly involved in the war. Singleton shifts the evidence to examine whether or not war was rational from an economic perspective, and he notes the lengths that main actors were ready to go to risk their wealth, crowns and even heads, as well as the lives and property of their underlings. The wider economic losses in Europe include destruction of property, social overhead capital and industrial capacity and, as he grimly notes, for the survivors, the psychological costs may have outweighed the material ones. However, even as war brought chaos to the European economies, as Singleton illustrates with a pithy quote from the vice-president of the Hudson Motor Car Company of Detroit, it is unsurprising that Europe's economic disaster was for the United States at least, 'the greatest business proposition since time began'. The impact on the rest of the world is striking: whereas Western Europe's real GDP fell by 11 per cent between 1913 and 1919 (and very much more in Eastern Europe and Russia), Latin America's real GDP rose by 4 per cent and Asia's real GDP rose by 13 per cent.

The legacies of economic disasters are frequently complicated to unravel, but Singleton manages to capture the controversy over the degree to which the First World War was responsible for the economic problems of the 1920s and early 1930s, including hyperinflation, deflation and the dislocation of the international monetary system. Rick Garside explores these themes in more detail in Chapter 2 on the Great Depression. Garside carefully traces how the global economic crisis of the early 1930s had its origins in the restoration of the gold standard from the mid-1920s and the policy regimes that emerged as a consequence. The mechanism through which cyclical depression was transmitted worldwide are explained in two stages: first, by an account of how the world economy developed in the 1920s to where it 'stood on a precipice' in 1929 and 1930, and, second, how the financial crisis in Europe in late spring and summer of 1931 proved to be the turning point of the Great Depression. Like other authors in this volume who comment on how economic disasters affect people, industries, regions and nations disproportionately, Garside offers us an account of how the Great Depression caused unemployment and industrial stagnation, the measures that some governments took to abate the consequences and how in others, 'limited pragmatism reigned'.

Are economic disasters avoidable? This is considered by Niall Ferguson in Chapter 3, who utilizes Churchill's famous assertion that the Second World War was 'the unnecessary war', to form the central thesis of his chapter. Conquest was not the solution to the economic problems of Germany, Japan and Italy and the economic arguments that led the Western powers to appease rather than to deter Germany and Japan were equally as spurious. As Ferguson discusses, both the Axis powers and Allies erred, a war was fought that cost governments $1 trillion, unquantifiable human suffering was inflicted during the conflict and yet, in spite of the disastrous impact of the Second World War, ultimately the vanquished were transformed into victors with the post-war 'miracle' of high and sustained growth over two decades.

Considering economic disasters of the twentieth century does not exclude comparative work with earlier centuries. This is particularly so for the monetary disasters that are covered in the volume, although, as Forrest Capie explains in Chapter 5, severe inflationary experiences belong in the twentieth century. To be sure, there were experiences of very rapid inflation in earlier times, for example, the American War of Independence in the late 1700s, the French Revolution of the 1790s or the Confederacy in the US Civil War of the 1860s, but these events were rare outside of the twentieth century. As Capie states, the fundamental cause of inflation is the scope given to governments for expanding the money supply and the fundamental reason for the extreme cases is serious social unrest and weak governments. Because of this, there are plenty of inflationary episodes to choose from in the twentieth century, whether it is Germany and Austria and for that matter much of Europe in the first half of the 1920s, China and Hungary in the 1940s, Israel in the 1980s, Indonesia in the mid-1960s, the Balkans in the 1990s and many Latin American and African countries from time to time during the century.

Concomitantly, as Michael Oliver (Chapter 6) points out quoting Charles Kindleberger, although there were financial crises in earlier centuries, they continued to occur in the twentieth century despite vigorous attempts to strengthen the international financial architecture. There were more currency crises during the Bretton Woods period than the interwar years and during the last quarter of the century there was a tendency for banking crises to spill over into the currency markets, creating what has become known as the 'twin crisis' problem. In the crisis periods of the twentieth century, emerging markets have suffered greater output losses than industrial countries, but because of differences in methodology, the evidence of how much growth has been reduced is mixed.

This thought does raise the question of whether there is a learning curve in economic matters. On the whole, the evidence does not fill one with confidence, whether it is because policy-making is often one step behind events, or whether it is impossible for decision-makers to agree on a coherent strategy or even if human nature prevents us from drawing lessons, as shown by the behavioural finance literature with its emphasis on heuristics, framing and prospect theory (see Kahneman and Tversky 2000). For instance, there is a high probability that whatever reforms continue to be made to the international financial architecture and however robust domestic financial systems are made, economists and policy-makers will still be dealing with financial crises 100 years hence. As Geoffrey Wood (Chapter 7) notes, stock markets have continued to have their fashion bubbles from the late 1920s onwards to the most recent IT euphoria, when market values lost all relevance to fundamentals so that the ensuing crash was all the more dramatic.

When we come to Africa it is difficult to find any benefits or the presence of a learning curve. As Derek Aldcroft (Chapter 9) shows, the new indigenous rulers in the post-colonial period eschewed the lessons of the past with disastrous consequences. Nor has there been much in the way of an enlightened policy in the West towards Africa. There is a lot of hot rhetoric but little substantive action that benefits the masses. International debt relief measures are often cosmetic, while the advanced nations continue to maintain trade barriers and gigantic subsidies to primary producers in their own countries to the detriment of African and Third World countries in general. However, Michael Beenstock's chapter (Chapter 4) on the rise and fall (and rise again) of OPEC does suggest a learning curve, at least insofar as OPEC III (which began at the start of the millennium) is concerned. Beenstock reminds us that the quadrupling of the price of oil in 1973/74 (OPEC I) led to panic in official circles with the sense of 'doom and hopelessness' only becoming worse when in 1979 OPEC further doubled the price of oil (OPEC II). The total cost of the OPEC I and II was about 15 per cent of world GDP. Per contra, following the five-fold increase in real oil prices since 2000, global stagflation did not break out during the first half of 2006 while world economic growth continued apace at about 3.5 per cent per year and stock markets remained strong. The difference between the 1970s and the 2000s is accounted for inter alia by sound macroeconomic policies and greater labour market flexibility. Like Ferguson, who argued that the Second World War was an avoidable economic disaster, Beenstock shows that the oil price explosion of the 1970s need not have turned into an economic disaster.

As Steven Morewood argues (Chapter 8), it is perhaps too early to reckon the full costs and benefits of the collapse of Eastern Europe. To be sure, the collapse of communism has begun a process (albeit a protracted one for several former Soviet bloc countries) towards full integration into the international economy. What is significant is that its disintegration and subsequent fragmentation of territories on ethnic or nationalistic lines is another Versailles only worse. The full implications of the post-First World War peace settlement were not immediately apparent at the time but the repercussions rumbled on throughout the twentieth century. The ethnic, religious and linguistic realities of the region only lay dormant under the new nation state structure that emerged after 1918. But as Hobsbawm (1994, 31) noted, 'The national conflicts tearing the continent apart in the 1990s were the old chickens of Versailles once again coming home to roost'. Perhaps the prospect of a decent future through joining the European Union will encourage many former Soviet bloc countries to quicken their pace of economic reform; although there will undoubtedly be some critics who argue that there should be a limit placed on the enlargement process.

If our assessment of each chapter has appeared unduly bleak and focused on the costs from the economic disasters, we should perhaps take a more positive approach and ask whether there were any benefits as well as the obvious costs from the economic disasters. The most obvious case of benefit arises from global warfare. Both World Wars gave rise to benefits in terms of new inventions and technologies (radar, nuclear power), as well as social progress and improved efficiency. Moreover, there is a marked contrast in the civil administration in wartime between the two World Wars, and a much better planned post-war reconstruction in the second case, which avoided many of the gross mistakes of interwar years and thereby laid the basis for the sustained prosperity of the Golden Age. The oil shocks of the 1970s led to concern about resources and fuel conservation measures, though long-term strategies for fuel conservation have been at best half-hearted and most consumers pay lip-service to them. If there is a serious long-term problem (both of supply and the environmental impact of energy consumption) the price of energy and fuel should be a good deal higher than it is, especially in countries such as the United States where energy is especially cheap. Similarly one can argue that a new economic policy ('Keynesianism') emerged out of the Great Depression, although it was unfortunately too late to do much to ease the situation in the 1930s, and when it did gain general acceptance, in the post-war period, it was of less relevance and less use in dealing with the economic problems of the 1970s and 1980s.

If one were to take a cynical view, one would acknowledge that economic disasters might sometimes produce benefits, but that more likely they give rise to more state interference, increased bureaucracy and the pursuit of power in the interests of the few (the elite) at the expense of the populace at large. The African experience of divide and rule and the concomitant increase in the power of the oligarchy is an excellent illustration. Perhaps what is remarkable given the number of large disasters that punctuated the previous century, is that economic progress was fairly robust taking the century as a whole. Growth was particularly strong in the Golden Age after the Second World War, and even with the slowing down of the last quarter of the century it was still higher than the long-term average in most regions of the world. Even the interwar years did not depart much from the long-term growth trend. All of which implies that economies are remarkably robust and resilient or adaptable to major shocks to their systems.

We would be foolish not to end this introduction by considering the one shock that the world might not be able to cope with in the twenty-first century, namely global warming. The majority of scientists now recognize that human activities are altering the concentration of the atmosphere (McCarthy et al. 2001, 24), although perhaps few would subscribe fully to James Lovelock's view that, unless we modify our behaviour, by the end of the present century the world will become 'Hell: so hot, so deadly that only a handful of the teeming billions now alive will survive' (Lovelock 2006, 147). The economic impact of such a scenario sits uncomfortably with the analysis in Mendelsohn and Neumann (1999) who instead point to the positive and beneficial effects of global warming. Where the truth lies has yet to be determined but Skene's (2006) recent admonishment that 'we must dispense with the notion that global warming is catastrophic and focus on maximizing its benefits' reminds us that, even if an environmental catastrophe were to strike in the twenty-first century, the resilience of human nature to adapt to disasters should not be underestimated.

REFERENCES

Arrighi, G. (1994), *The long twentieth century*, London: Verso.

Bairoch, P. (1976), 'Europe's gross national product: 1800–1975', *The Journal of European Economic History*, 5.

de Grazia, V. (2005), *Irresistible empire: America's advance through twentieth-century Europe*, Cambridge, MA: Harvard University Press.

Geissler, E. and van Courtland Moon, J.E. (eds) (1999), *Biological and toxin weapons: research, development, and use from the Middle Ages to 1945*, Oxford: Oxford University Press.

Hobsbawm, E. (1994), *Age of extremes: the short twentieth century 1914–1991*, London: Michael Joseph.

Kahneman, D. and Tversky, A. (eds) (2000), *Choices, values, and frames*, Cambridge: Cambridge University Press.

Landes, D.S. (1969), *The unbound Prometheus: technological change and industrial development in Western Europe from 1750 to the present*, Cambridge: Cambridge University Press.

Lovelock, J. (2006), *The revenge of Gaia: Why the earth is fighting back – and how we can still save humanity*, London: Allen Lane.

McCarthy, J.J., Canziani, O.F., Leary, N.A., Dokken, D.A. and White, K.S. (eds) (2001), *Climate change 2001: impacts, adaptation, and vulnerability, contribution of Working Group II to the Third Assessment Report of the Intergovernmental Panel on Climate Change*, Cambridge: Cambridge University Press.

Mendelsohn, R.O. and Neumann, J.E. (eds) (1999), *The impact of climate change on the United States economy*, Cambridge: Cambridge University Press.

Payn, G. and Morley, S. (1998), *The Noel Coward diaries*, London: Phoenix.

Skene, L. (2006), 'The foreseeable future', mimeo, London: Lombard Street Associates.

1.   'Destruction . . . and misery': the First World War[1]

John Singleton

During the winter of 1918–19, before Nature had cast her ameliorating mantle, the horror and desolation of war was made visible to sight on an extraordinary scale of blasted grandeur. The completeness of the destruction was evident. For mile after mile nothing was left. No building was habitable and no field fit for the plough. (John Maynard Keynes, quoted in Moggridge 1992, 286)

The First World War (1914–18), fought between the Allies, led by France and Britain, and the Central Powers, led by Germany, was the worst human-made catastrophe of the early twentieth century. As the distinguished Austrian economist, Ludwig von Mises, noted in 1919, 'not too much economic insight is needed to recognize that a war means . . . destruction of goods and misery' (von Mises 1983, 153). The 'Great War' brought death and destruction to Europe on a scale absent for centuries, though its impact on the rest of the world was relatively muted.

This chapter is primarily concerned with the immediate impact of the war on individuals, property, industrial and agricultural output, national income, technology and so on. It also examines the controversy over the degree to which the war was responsible for the economic problems of the 1920s and early 1930s, including hyperinflation, deflation and the dislocation of the international monetary system. We shall constantly keep in mind that events that are disastrous for some groups and individuals may not be disastrous for others.

THE FIRST INDUSTRIALIZED WAR

The First World War was more capital-intensive than any previous conflict. Rising capital intensity reflected the technical sophistication of modern weaponry and the massive industrial capacity of the belligerents. Artillery pieces, machine guns, rifles, bullets, shells, barbed wire, poison gas, military aircraft, submarines and even warships were manufactured in bulk. R.H. Mottram, a British officer on the Western Front, argued that warfare had

9

become an extension of industrial activity: 'There, stretched across the world, lay two gigantic factories, equipped with an inconceivable plant of all sorts and manned by whole nations, who were simply so many operatives, controlled by officers whose functions were those of foremen, or accountants'. Soldiers were 'the material on which the vast organisation worked, and the finished article made out of them was Death' (Mottram 1929, 129). Mines, factories and trenches were different stages in a gruesome production process (Ferguson 1999, 306).

WAS WAR CRAZY?

War, especially on the scale of 1914–18, has always presented mainstream economics with conceptual difficulties. Shortly after the war, A.C. Pigou, a central figure in welfare economics, seemed overwhelmed by its 'unimagined horror'. Pigou had been trained to explain 'the working of economic processes in normal conditions', or how people came to be 'clothed, fed, housed, and amused'. He conceded that economic rivalry had contributed to the outbreak of the war, but could not regard it as anything other than an irrational spasm of destruction. Over four 'fearful' years, 'the unconscious processes of normal life were abandoned, and Europe swung reeling to the conscious agony of war' (Pigou 1921, 1–2). War was an aberration.

Not all economists held war to be completely irrational. In a work published in 1915, Werner Sombart, a leader of the German historical school of economics, argued that war stimulated employment, technical change and economic development (Rotte 1997). From another perspective, the Marxist theoretician, V.I. Lenin, viewed war as an unavoidable aspect of the imperialist stage of economic development. He maintained that capitalist nations were compelled to build empires in order to establish secure and profitable outlets for surplus capital. Competition for territory inevitably led to war (Howard and King 1989, 243–66). Radical economists, such as J.A. Hobson, also remarked upon the self-interested role of arms producers in fomenting militarism (Hobson 1902).

Sombart's position seems otiose in retrospect, but in 1914 many Germans expected to win a spectacular victory. Lenin's thesis is weakened by the fact that no government went to war in 1914 in order to obtain more colonies (Kanya-Forstner 2000, 231). As for the wicked arms barons, they could not have made profits without enthusiastic customers. Many weapons are acquired for deterrent purposes and never used. The decision to go to war is separate and primarily political (Stevenson 1996).

Must we conclude that the war was an irrational spasm? Rationality, like beauty, is in the eye of the beholder. Did Europe's politicians, generals, kings and emperors suddenly become crazy in 1914? Curiously, they all imagined that they were acting in their own best interests and, presumably, in those of their nation or dynasty. Rationality is constrained (or bounded) by uncertainty and the intractability of complex problems. Game theory shows how both sides in an economic or non-economic contest may end up worse off, even though both act 'rationally' in pursuit of known objectives (Offer 1989, 15–16). Some historians regard the war as a tragic calamity, others as an episode in a vast power game (Smith 2000, 133–4); however, these interpretations are not mutually exclusive. In 1914, the main actors were ready to take huge risks with their wealth, crowns and even heads. They were prepared to take similar risks with the lives and property of their underlings.

GEOGRAPHICAL CHANGES

Literature on the economic impact of the First World War sometimes uses pre-war and sometimes post-war boundaries. Readers should note the main boundary changes after the First World War. France received the disputed region of Alsace-Lorraine from Germany. Poland was created out of land formerly belonging to the German, Russian and Austro-Hungarian Empires. The heartland of the Austro-Hungarian Empire was divided into the independent nations of Austria, Hungary and Czechoslovakia. Part of the Austro-Hungarian Empire, including Croatia, Slovenia and Bosnia was merged with the previously independent nation of Serbia, and other territories, to form the Kingdom of Serbs, Croats and Slovenes (later called Yugoslavia). Russia (the USSR after 1917) was stripped of Lithuania, Latvia, Estonia and Finland, which became independent countries, and temporarily lost parts of Central Asia and the Caucasus. Romania gained land at the expense of the Austro-Hungarian Empire. Turkey lost an empire in the Middle East and Germany was deprived of its overseas territories.

THE FIRST WORLD WAR COMPARED WITH OTHER DISASTERS

The First World War was less destructive than the Second World War, but the pace of economic recovery after 1918 was slower than after 1945 (Boltho 2001). It is much harder to make comparisons with earlier conflicts, such as the Thirty Years War in the seventeenth century, or the Revolutionary and Napoleonic Wars between 1792 and 1815. The First World War was shorter but more ferocious than either of those conflicts. By 1914, Western Europe had attained a comfortable surplus over subsistence, which provided a bigger cushion against famine and disease. The damage wrought by the Thirty Years War on the population of certain parts of the Holy Roman Empire was tremendous (Livi Bacci 2000, 86), but the rest of Europe was not seriously affected. By contrast, Spain, Holland, Switzerland and Scandinavia were the only parts of Europe to avoid military losses during the First World War. Comparisons between the economic impact of the First World War and other major economic tragedies are equally problematical. Taking into account falling birth rates, the First World War may have reduced the population of Europe, excluding Russia, by 22 million or 7 per cent. Inclusive of the Civil War, Russia's population may have fallen by 26 million, or 18.5 per cent (Notestein et al. 1944, 75). Though not human-made, the Black Death or bubonic plague, wiped out one-third of the European population in the mid-fourteenth century (Cameron 1993, 74–7).

Plagues and famines have at one time or another beset every major centre of world population (McNeill 1979). An influenza epidemic killed between 25 and 40 million people worldwide in 1918–19 (Winter 1988, 23), the economic aspects of which remain unknown. Although the war did not cause the influenza outbreak, it may have reduced people's resistance to disease. Some momentous historical events may be interpreted either as economic tragedies or signs of progress, according to one's perspective. The incorporation of non-European societies into the European orbit resulted in large-scale human, societal and environmental destruction. Indigenous economic structures were severely damaged, if not annihilated. Such invasions were disastrous for their victims, but some conquered regions, including North America and Australasia, went on to achieve high levels of prosperity. Even within Europe, economic historians have yet to give adequate thought to the environmental degradation caused by industrialization. Whether or not the First World War was the world's worst human-made economic disaster before 1939, it was certainly a calamity.

THE INDIVIDUAL COST OF WAR

Later sections emphasize the aggregate economic aspects of the war, but there is also value in considering its impact on the individual economic actor. Utility and opportunity cost – essentially two sides of the same coin – are subjective concepts (Kirzner 1986). The cost of the war was not so many billion pounds or dollars, or so many million tons of steel, but rather the net loss of utility suffered by all who were directly or indirectly involved.

Unfortunately, we have no adequate method of measuring an individual's utility, let alone of aggregating the utility of millions. As Offer (1996, 13) explains, the 'mental economy does not generate statistical yearbooks'. But we need not be silent about the war's economic impact on the individual. How might joining the army, as a conscript or volunteer, have affected the utility of the individual soldier? The key factors varied from case to case, and only a few are mentioned here. Most recruits were paid less in the army than in civilian life; they were separated from their friends and family; they risked mutilation and death. On the other hand, new recruits were embarking on an adventure. Serving their country gave many a sense of satisfaction. The possibility of glory may have inspired them. Mental states, whether transitory or otherwise, cannot be measured directly, though they are not completely hidden. Surveys of the reaction of French civilians and conscripts to the outbreak of war suggest that foreboding was more common than enthusiasm (Becker 1992). Offer (1993, 232) argues that Britons of all social classes derived psychic benefits from the 'status good' of Empire. Between 1914 and 1918, millions fought to protect such status goods.

Once soldiers had been in battle, their impressions of the utility/cost of war changed. No doubt many felt that they had underestimated the risks they were running, but some clearly found a sense of meaning in combat. Adolf Hitler had been a lonely and pathetic drifter before the war. As a dispatch runner in the German Army, he discovered a new sense of belonging and purpose. Hitler described the day on which he was decorated with the Iron Cross, Second Class, for having protected a wounded officer, as the 'happiest' of his life (Kershaw 1999, 92). Ferguson (1999, 357–66) argues that many soldiers enjoyed fighting and risking death. Comradeship provided some with compensation for the austerities of active service.

The First World War was experienced in radically different ways. Compare the writings of two German soldiers, Erich Maria Remarque (*All quiet on the Western Front, 1929*), and Ernst Junger (*Storm of steel, 1929*). Remarque dwelt upon the pointless suffering of the troops, while Junger focused on the exhilaration of warfare. More surprisingly, Annette Becker (1998) shows that some devout French Catholics regarded war service, and the prospect of death, as a way of sharing in Christ's suffering. Embracing rather than avoiding suffering turns economists' concept of rationality on its head.

How should the cost of wounds, whether psychological or physical, be assessed? There is evidence to suggest that some people who have undergone severe physical deprivation, such as the loss of a limb, soon regain former levels of contentment (Argyle 1996, 23). Whether or not this was also the case between 1914 and 1918 is impossible to tell. Perhaps many of the wounded felt lucky to be alive. But the treatment of mutilated servicemen after discharge from hospital was variable, and some were reduced to destitution (Bourke 1996, 31–75). British soldiers often expressed delight at receiving a 'blighty' wound, serious enough to merit a trip home, but not permanently incapacitating. Estimates of the cost of psychological wounds are equally problematical. Modern courts have awarded large amounts to sufferers of workplace stress. In 2000, Worcestershire County Council and its insurers agreed to pay a former employee £203 000 in compensation for ill health caused by stress at work (Aldred 2000). Fortunately for European governments, First World War soldiers could not sue their employer. Self-mutilation was common, indicating the willingness of some to pay a high price to escape battle. It is generally believed that experienced troops were the most prone to nervous disorders. The longer troops were on the front line, the more they understood the risks (Macdonald 1993, 231).

War imposed enormous costs on the families of soldiers and sailors. We could think of these costs as negative externalities of military service. Family incomes fell when adult males were at the war, although some firms made up the wages of former workers, and some state benefits were available to wives and families. Psychological costs, including anxiety and grief, were also felt by those left behind (Gregory 1997, 85–93), and may have outweighed any narrow financial costs. A culture of mourning pervaded Europe after 1918, and the fallen were commemorated in stone and stained glass in every town and village. Attempts were made to contact the dead through spiritualism. Such behaviour testifies to the magnitude of the psychological costs (Winter 1995). On the other hand, some women and children may have welcomed the absence, or even death, of a brutal or tiresome husband or father. Colonel Repington, war correspondent of *The Times*, joked that 'the ladies liked being without their husbands' (quoted in Ferguson 1999, 331). By the same token, many soldiers could have been glad of some respite from tiresome wives.

Enough evidence has been presented to show that the individual cost of the First World War is beyond calculation. It is impossible to attach money values to the impressions of utility/cost made in the minds of the men, women and children who experienced the war.

DEATH

Aggregating military and civilian fatalities, and reductions in births, the First World War and the Russian Civil War may have cost Europe 22 million and Russia 26 million lives, though the Russian figures should not be given much credence. Military deaths on both sides were high. France, Russia, Germany and Austria-Hungary all lost over 1 million men. The military fatalities of Serbia and Montenegro, though numerically smaller,

Table 1.1   Military losses during the First World War

Allied countries (pre-war boundaries)	1914 population	Military deaths	Central Powers (pre-war boundaries)	1914 population	Military deaths
France	39 600 000	1 327 000	Germany	67 800 000	2 037 000
French Colonies	52 700 000	71 000	Austria-Hungary	58 600 000	1 100 000
Britain & Ireland	45 221 000	723 000	Turkey	21 700 000	804 000
Canada	8 100 000	61 000	Bulgaria	4 700 000	88 000
Australia	4 900 000	60 000			
New Zealand	1 100 000	16 000			
South Africa	6 300 000	7 000			
India	321 800 000	54 000			
Belgium	7 600 000	38 000			
Italy	35 900 000	578 000			
Portugal	6 100 000	7 000			
Greece	4 900 000	26 000			
Serbia	4 900 000	278 000			
Romania	7 600 000	250 000			
Russia	167 000 000	1 811 000			
USA	98 800 000	114 000			
Allied total	812 521 000	5 421 000	Central Powers total	152 800 000	4 029 000

Source: Adapted from Winter (1985, 75).

were relatively the most severe. Britain (especially Scotland) and Italy also experienced significant military fatalities, but their combined losses were only slightly greater than those of France (Table 1.1). In addition to the 1.8 million Russian soldiers who died during the First World War, at least 1 million more were killed, counting both sides, in the ensuing Civil War (Wheatcroft and Davies 1994, 63). In the British case, for one historian, too few poets and too many skilled workers, were killed (Ferguson 1999, 269–70).

Recruitment and casualties were skewed towards the 15–49 age groups. In France, 79 per cent of men aged 15–49 in 1913 were called up and 13.3 per cent died in service. In Germany, 81 per cent were called up and 12.5 per cent lost their lives. In Britain, 49 per cent served and 6.2 per cent died. As for male Russians, aged 15–49, 39 per cent served and 4.5 per cent died (Gatrell and Harrison 1993, 430). Losses were heaviest among men aged between 20 and 30. Serbia's casualties were appalling. Almost one-quarter of the Serbian male population between the ages of 15 and 49 died in military service (Winter 1985, 75). Enemy action was not the only reason for military fatalities. Disease and poor medical services boosted losses, especially in Italy and Eastern Europe.

As always, the wounded outnumbered the dead. For instance, one in three British soldiers was wounded. Many injuries were slight, and 55 per cent of wounded British soldiers returned to active duty (Ferguson 1999, 296). Other wounds were more serious. Thousands were blinded. Over 41 000 British servicemen required the amputation of at least one limb, but multiple amputations were rare, accounting for less than 3 per cent of the total. Another 400 000 British troops caught venereal disease (Cooter 1993, 1541; Bourke 1996, 33, 161).

The First World War and related turmoil, including the Russian Civil War, caused huge numbers of civilian deaths from famine, disease, shelling, bombing and massacre. Civilian fatalities were highest in Eastern Europe where the front was more mobile, pre-war living standards were closer to subsistence and the war led to revolutionary upheaval. Traditional war-related diseases, such as typhus, smallpox and cholera, were major killers of civilians in Eastern Europe. Excluding Russia, the war may have caused over 5 million additional civilian deaths in Europe, and a deficit in births of over 12 million. Births fell because of the shortage of men and, in some countries, the deteriorating health of women. Undernourished women were less likely to conceive and bear a live child. In Russia, according to some estimates, the increase in civilian deaths was 14 million and the birth deficit 10 million. Two-thirds of these losses occurred in the Civil War, which saw crop failure, transport difficulties and famine, not to mention mass slaughter (Notestein et al. 1944, 75–7). Moreover, up to one-third of the 1.5 million Armenians living in the Ottoman Empire died of starvation, maltreatment and violence at the hands of Turks and Kurds (Yapp 1987, 269–70). According to one eyewitness, for 'a whole month corpses were observed floating down the River Euphrates hideously mutilated' (quoted in Bogart 1920, 280).

Conditions were better in the more advanced European economies. War interrupted, but did not reverse, the decline in mortality rates in London and Paris. Some marginal groups, including illegitimate children and the elderly, fared relatively badly, but their losses were cancelled out by the gains enjoyed by other children and adults. Mortality rates in Berlin rose between 1917 and 1919, but Germany did not starve as was claimed in later propaganda. The inadequacy and unfairness of the food distribution system in Germany may have caused almost as much distress as the absolute shortage of necessities (Winter 1997; Bonzon and Davis 1997).

Since the war did not stop all procreation, few countries suffered large reductions in population. On the basis of late twentieth-century boundaries, the population of Britain, the United States and Turkey actually increased between 1914 and 1918, whilst the population of Italy was constant. Austria, Belgium and Germany all experienced population falls of less than 2 per cent. Bulgaria and Hungary enjoyed population gains between 1913 and 1920, while Czechoslovakia, Romania and Russia recorded small declines. The main losers of population were France, which suffered a reduction of 7.1 per cent between 1914 and 1918, 'Yugoslavia' (including Serbia), which saw a fall of 8.6 per cent between 1913 and 1920, and Poland, which saw a fall of 10.3 per cent over the same period (Maddison 1995, 104–10). The German, Russian and Austro-Hungarian armies turned Poland into a battlefield, and both sides used Polish conscripts. To compound matters, the newly independent state of Poland plunged into a war with the Soviet Union.

On the basis of actuarial figures, Bogart (1920, 299) worked out that the capitalized value of military and civilian lives lost during the war was US$37 billion at pre-war prices. Bogart also produced an estimate of the overall cost of the war (US$338 billion), but his figures are too arbitrary to merit serious consideration. He attached a higher value to the lives of Americans than to the lives of soldiers of other nations, and justified this procedure on the basis of differences in earning power. Regardless of Bogart's questionable calculations, it is clear that the death or mutilation of millions of young men was a serious economic setback for Europe.

DESTRUCTION

The First World War devastated those areas of Eastern Europe, Belgium and France across which the armies fought. A heavy toll was also taken on shipping, which was attacked by surface vessels, submarines and mines. Strategic bombing was in its infancy, however, and direct damage to property behind the lines was slight on the Western Front. War also resulted in the depletion of stocks of raw materials and goods. Moreover, the value of fixed capital was eroded by the postponement of maintenance work and replacement investment.

Serbia lost up to half of its national wealth, or three times its national income, from wartime depredations. Enemy forces wrecked factories, farm buildings, railways and housing. Agricultural implements and livestock were destroyed or stolen, leaving Serbia with perhaps one-half of its pre-war stock of farm animals. Latvia also suffered greatly, as did Poland. Between 1914 and 1918, over 10 per cent of Poland's wealth was annihilated. Losses included 75 per cent of farm buildings, 1.7 million houses and millions of acres of farmland and forests. Entire villages were razed to the ground. Polish industrial production was 19 per cent of the pre-war level in 1919, as a result of thieving by the Germans, the destruction of plant and buildings and shortages of coal and other inputs. The coal shortage was exacerbated by the poor condition of the railways (Landau and Tomaszewski 1985, 22–4, 33–4; Aldcroft and Morewood 1995, 10–13).

During the First World War, the Russian government gave priority to the expansion of heavy industry and the improvement of the railway network. Investment in these strategic sectors occurred at the expense of light industry and agriculture, and the capital stock of Russian agriculture may in fact have fallen by 19 per cent between 1913 and 1921 (Gatrell 1994, 224). Southern and Western Russia suffered serious war damage between 1914 and 1917. Subsequent upheavals inside the former Russian Empire led to even greater physical losses. Marauding armies of Reds and Whites sacked the countryside, especially the grain-producing regions. Despite high wartime investment, the losses of the railways were severe. During the Civil War, 12 per cent of all railway bridges were destroyed, and 1885 km of track were wrecked. By September 1920, only 7296 of Russia's 17 577 locomotives were fit for service (Westwood 1964, 193, 200).

The area of destruction in Western Europe was smaller. Northern France, Belgium and Northern Italy bore the brunt. Most of Belgium fell into German hands in 1914, and for the next four years the front ran through its northwest corner before passing into France. Only 5 per cent of Belgian farmland suffered serious damage, but the invaders commandeered industrial machinery, animals and roofing materials. Just nine of Belgium's 60 blast furnaces survived intact. Under German direction, the mines were run to full capacity, but maintenance was neglected. The ports also suffered from lack of maintenance and the confiscation of equipment. In 1918, the retreating Germans wrecked as much of Belgian industry as they could, but the Spanish and Dutch representatives persuaded them not to flood the mines (Marks 1981, 171–6).

Germany occupied 38 850 km^2 of Northeast France between 1914 and 1918. The Northeast was vital to the French economy. As well as a productive farming area, it was an industrial powerhouse responsible for three-quarters of the coal, two-thirds of the iron and steel and most of the cotton and wool yarn produced in France. Scant regard was shown for private property. Mines were flooded and the shafts blown up as a precaution against underground enemy infiltration. Household goods, including bedding and underwear, were requisitioned. By far the most serious destruction occurred in the red and yellow zones on either side of the front line. These zones contained multiple lines of trenches, bunkers, shell holes and barbed wire thickets. Due to constant shelling, mining and digging, vast quantities of unexploded high explosive, shrapnel and gas shells, and the remains of countless men and horses, were churned into the mud. In 1919, 3.3 million hectares of land awaited clearance. A total of 293 000 private buildings were destroyed, and 500 000 damaged. In addition, 6525 public buildings including schools, town halls and churches were blown up. Some villages were completely destroyed. Many inhabitants of the red and yellow zones fled to other parts of France, and the devastated areas did not completely recover until the 1930s (Clout 1996; McPhail 1999). Buried shells were still inflicting casualties on French deminers in the 1990s (Webster 1994).

Fighting did not take place on British or, to any great extent, on German soil. But even these nations were unable to preserve their stock of fixed capital. Except for war-related industries and, particularly in Britain, agriculture, businesses were starved of resources for maintenance and replacement investment. Railways and mines became dilapidated. Merchant shipping losses were serious: over 2 million tons of shipping belonging to Germany and its allies were sunk or impounded, and nearly all of the remaining 4.5 million tons were seized as reparations (Sturmey 1962, 45). Germany sank over 12 million tons of Allied and neutral shipping. Two-thirds of the losses were British, representing 38 per cent of pre-war tonnage. Aided by a spurt in US shipbuilding, the Allies and neutrals had replaced their losses by November 1918, but the destruction of so many vessels during the war still amounted to a substantial loss of wealth (Salter 1921, 355–61). Real net domestic fixed capital formation was negative in Britain in 1916 and 1917, and only marginally positive in 1915 and 1918. Having risen by 7 per cent between 1910 and 1913, Britain's real net national wealth grew by a mere 0.4 per cent between 1913 and 1920 (Feinstein and Pollard 1988, 443, 469). In Germany, the real stock of capital, including houses, fell by 23 per cent between 1913 and 1920 (Sommariva and Tullio 1987, 226–7).

The burden of wartime destruction pressed most heavily on backward economies that were least able to cope. When farms and infrastructure were wrecked in Poland and Serbia, food shortages and famine soon followed. By comparison, in Western Europe the war was contained within a smaller area, and material losses were more affordable.

ECONOMIC ACTIVITY IN EUROPE AND THE UNITED STATES

In wartime, productive resources must be transferred from civilian industries and services into the munitions industries and armed forces.

Depending on the circumstances, this restructuring may be accomplished by market forces or by government fiat. Consumption must decline if the diversion of resources is substantial or imported necessities become scarce.

Producing munitions to hurl at an opponent may seem entirely wasteful, but that need not be the case. Defence is one of the few genuine public goods. It is conceivable that the inhabitants of Paris, fearing the arrival of German troops in 1914 and in 1918, would have preferred more guns to more butter. Waste is another subjective concept. In a volume on war finance, published in 1918, an American economist, J.L. Laughlin, wrote that:

> While laces, wines, or food are used up by those who consume them for personal pleasure or luxury, wealth to that amount is lost just as certainly as if they were war goods destroyed on the battle-line. . .Looked at from a purely economic point of view, we cannot regard the enormous destruction of wealth in war as something very different from what has been going on in peaceful days, through unproductive consumption. (Laughlin 1918, 48)

Economic statistics are scarcer and less reliable for the First World War than for the Second. Nevertheless, it is possible to obtain an indication of the scale of the war's impact upon heavy industry by calculating the number of standard gun units (SGUs)[2] produced by the major powers. During the First World War, Russia manufactured 63 600 SGUs, Germany 405 000, France 351 000, Britain 361 000, and the United States 117 000. The volume of munitions production continued to expand during the war, implying the progressive crowding out of civilian goods and services. Britain's output of artillery pieces increased from 91 units in 1914, to 3390 units in 1915, 4314 in 1916, 5137 in 1917 and 8039 in 1918 (Hardach 1977, 87; Adelman 1988, 45; Gatrell and Harrison 1993, 431). The Central Powers, especially Germany, were better than the Allies at killing, according to Ferguson (1999, 336). It cost the Allies over US$36 000 to kill an enemy soldier, whereas it cost the Central Powers just over US$11 000.

An attempt is made in Table 1.2 to calculate total war expenditure between 1914 and 1918 as a proportion of 1913 national income. These figures should be treated with extreme caution, especially for Russia, as they depend on sources of uneven reliability and consistency. Clearly, the burden of expenditure rose in the later stages of each country's involvement. Figures are given as reported and as adjusted for credit flows. France received credit from Britain and the United States; Italy and Russia obtained credit from Britain, the United States and France. Britain incurred large debts in the United States, and made even larger loans to the continental Allies. The burden of the war on the US economy was increased by the provision of credit to the Allies, which was spent on munitions and other essential goods. War expenditure was not restricted to the acquisition of

Table 1.2   War expenditure as a share of national income

	Total war expenditure in 1913 prices (US$ billion)		Total war expenditure as percentage of 1913 national income (%)	
		Adjusted for credits to (+) and from (−) allies		Adjusted for credits to (+) and from (−) allies
Russia (GDP)	6.7	4.8	42	30
Germany (NNP)	17.0	18.0	136	144
France (GDP)	11.0	10.0	115	105
UK (GDP)	16.5	18.5	144	162
USA (GNP)	8.8	13.6	22	34

Note: On the basis of pre-war boundaries.

Sources: Author's calculations using war expenditure data in Gatrell and Harrison (1993, 431–2); nominal national income estimates in Mitchell (1998a, 909, 910, 913 and 1998b, 766); and 1914 exchange rates in Gallarotti (1995, 43).

munitions, and included soldiers' pay and rations, pharmaceuticals, fuel for warships and military vehicles, and fodder for army horses. It would be unwise to draw too many conclusions from Table 1.2, but two findings stand out. First, the war imposed serious macroeconomic costs on all the leading belligerents. Secondly, Russia crumpled in 1917 under a burden that was apparently substantially lower than that borne by Germany, Britain and France. As real income per capita in Russia was initially less than half of the French or German levels, even a relatively small diversion of resources was hard to sustain (Gatrell and Harrison 1993, 430).

Table 1.3 shows what happened to real GDP in a number of countries, on the basis of late twentieth-century boundaries, between 1913 and 1919. Russian real national income, which is not shown in Table 1.3, may have fallen by one-quarter between 1914 and 1917 (Ferguson 1999, 250). Not surprisingly, most belligerents fared rather badly. Although the international economy was entering a cyclical downswing in 1914, the recession would not have been as severe or as prolonged as the impact of the war. The Italian economy grew strongly between the late nineteenth century and the mid-1920s, and apparently performed better than any other belligerent European economy during the war (Fratianni and Spinelli 1997, 108–9). But the Italian figures should be treated with particular caution. It should also be noted that Table 1.3 masks the full impact of war on the production of consumer goods and services, since a rising proportion of output was devoted to military

Table 1.3   Real GDP in 1919 as a percentage of 1913

Australia	94.7	Italy	111.0
Austria	61.8	Japan	140.9
Belgium	79.9	New Zealand	109.2
France	75.3	Sweden	89.4
Germany	72.3	UK	100.9
Hungary (1913–20)	82.6	USA	115.8

Note: Late twentieth-century boundaries.

Source: Maddison (1995, 148, 150, 154).

ends. European neutrals, including Sweden and Switzerland, also suffered falls in real GDP because of the interruption to commerce. Table 1.3 provides only lukewarm support for the hypothesis that a war fought on domestic territory results in a drop in output, whilst a war fought on foreign territory stimulates output (Caplan 2002).

The outbreak of war brought immediate disruption to business and employment in the most important European cities (Lawrence, Dean and Robert 1992). When industry had been put on a war footing, and millions of men absorbed into the armed forces, a shortage of labour developed. Women, old men, migrants and prisoners of war were encouraged into the labour force as substitutes. The Germans even pressed unemployed Belgians into war work in the Reich (Burchardt 1988, 10). Industrial production rose strongly in Italy and Russia between 1914 and 1915, but fell sharply in 1917. Britain, Germany and France did not experience an initial spurt in industrial production. Indeed war resulted in a significant decline in industrial production in the advanced European economies. Labour scarcity could not be eliminated in Britain, France and Germany. Raw material and fuel shortages constrained production in many industries (Singleton 1994, 614–17). Shortages were most acute in Germany and Austria-Hungary because of the blockade. Labour productivity usually dropped under wartime conditions, leading to further lost production. Output per worker hour fell by 14 per cent in Belgium between 1910 and 1921 (Cassiers and Solar 1990, 448). But industrial facilities with privileged access to essential inputs sometimes achieved significant productivity gains. For instance, output per worker rose by almost 60 per cent between 1913/14 and 1917/18 at one steel works owned by the German armaments giant Fried. Krupp AG (Burchardt 1988, 7–8). Productivity improvements were obtained under similar circumstances in other belligerent states.

The United States' role was principally that of a quartermaster and financier. Howard E. Coffin, vice-president of the Hudson Motor Car

Table 1.4   Real GDP per capita in 1919 as a percentage of 1913

Australia	87.9	Italy	111.0
Austria	65.2	Japan	131.8
Belgium	80.3	New Zealand	102.5
France	80.7	Sweden	86.2
Germany	72.1	UK	99.0
Hungary (1919–20)	81.5	USA	107.2

Note: Late-twentieth century boundaries.

Source: Maddison (1995, 194, 196, 200).

Company of Detroit, elegantly described the war as 'the greatest business proposition since time began' (Koistinen 1997, 148). War orders from Europe hastened the recovery of the US economy from the recession of 1914. Many of America's largest firms, including Du Pont (explosives and ingredients), Bethlehem Steel (shells, billets, forgings, etc.), US Steel (bars, forgings, wire, rope, railroad material, etc.) and Baldwin Locomotive Works (shells and components, locomotives and railroad parts) worked on these contracts (Koistinen 1997, 125). But the war was not responsible for America's global industrial domination, a phenomenon already firmly established by 1914 (Fearon 2000). Since the United States did not enter the war until April 1917, the diversion of labour into the armed forces was relatively modest.

As Table 1.4 shows, real GDP per capita fell in most countries directly affected by the war. Real GDP per capita is an indicator of productivity but not of living standards in wartime. Given that so much production was devoted to war purposes, living standards must have dropped by more than the fall in real GDP per capita.

IMPACT ON THE REST OF THE WORLD

The immediate effects of the war beyond Europe and the United States varied from country to country. Japan was arguably the main economic beneficiary of the European conflict. Though Japan was nominally a member of the Anglo-French coalition, its military contribution was neg-ligible. Instead, the Japanese capitalized on the decline in European exports to increase their own share of overseas markets for cheap manufactures, especially in Asia and Latin America. Temporary isolation from European competition also helped Japan's heavy industries to expand and gain a tighter grip over the domestic market. Even so, the war hastened rather than caused the maturation of Japan's industrial economy (Crawcour 1988, 436–44; Brown 2000).

After the initial confusion in international markets, war stimulated the production of many primary commodities in the Americas, Australasia, Africa and Asia. The interruption of intra-European agricultural trade, and the decline in commodity production in many European countries, generated an insatiable demand for strategic raw materials and essential foodstuffs from other parts of the world. Rising prices encouraged the expansion of productive capacity in the primary sector outside Europe. The subsequent outward shift in the supply curve was partly responsible for falling prices in the 1920s (Wrigley 2000a, 8, 26). As well as dislocating trade patterns, the war hampered the efforts of firms in other continents to raise short- and long-term capital in Europe. Consequently, US banks increased their presence in the developing world, especially in Latin America.

Despite the commodity boom, the prosperity of primary exporters should not be exaggerated, and was actually rather patchy. For instance, Australia's real GDP declined between 1913 and 1919. Shipping was in short supply, imported inputs were hard to obtain, and the dominions (Canada, Australia and New Zealand) put substantial forces into the field, leaving fewer hands at home. Countries that had relied on the German market were particularly unfortunate. Half of Nigeria's exports, including 80 per cent of its exports of palm kernels, had been sold to Germany in 1913, and alternative outlets had to be developed in Britain (Osuntokun 1979, 21–33). The demand for strategic raw materials and essential foodstuffs soared, but the demand for luxury and non-essential items dropped. Mexico (oil), Peru (copper), Bolivia (tin) and Chile (nitrates) all improved their net barter terms of trade during the war, but some banana and coffee producing countries in Central America and the Caribbean struggled, though their plight was somewhat alleviated by refocusing on the US market (Bulmer-Thomas 1994, 157).

Developing countries and the lands of white settlement could not obtain their usual volume of imports from Europe. The fall in the supply of European goods led to higher prices. American and Japanese firms offered substitutes, but the overall decline in imports tended to reduce consumer welfare. On the other hand, the shortfall of imports encouraged industrialization, not least in some Latin American countries. Manufacturing expansion was based on processing domestic raw materials (Bulmer-Thomas 1994, 184–8). India also saw some industrial growth, especially in textiles. Many industries that expanded during the war struggled after the revival of international competition in the 1920s.

The aggregate impact of the war outside Europe was modest. Maddison estimates that whereas Western Europe's real GDP fell by 11 per cent between 1913 and 1919, Latin America's real GDP rose by 4 per cent and Asia's real GDP rose by 13 per cent (Maddison 1995, 66). Asia and Latin America adjusted reasonably well to the disruption of international transactions, which suggests that they were not as dependent on Europe as had been imagined in 1913. If the impact of war had been greater, labour could have shifted from cash crops into the production of basic foodstuffs.

MAKING ENDS MEET ON THE HOME FRONT

How did the war affect the material welfare of civilians? How did they cope with shortages and inflation? The diversion of real resources into the war effort reduced the supply of goods and services available to consumers, and most groups faced a reduced standard of living.

Refugees from occupied territories, and families with a breadwinner at the war, often had to fall back on state relief payments, food subsidies, charity and rations. Many wives and daughters of servicemen eventually found employment, usually for meagre pay unless in munitions. Skilled (and even unskilled) munitions operatives were in high demand, but were expected to put in gruelling hours of overtime. Those seeking jobs in munitions works had to be prepared to commute or possibly move to a new district. Accommodation in munitions centres was frequently expensive and cramped (Bonzon 1997a, 1997b; Manning 1997).

Hardship, in relative or even absolute terms, was not confined to the working class and peasantry. The war disrupted many small businesses: patterns of demand shifted, fuel and other inputs became scarce, and skilled workers were conscripted into the forces or poached by munitions firms. Taxation and official borrowing covered only a fraction of war expenditure and all governments resorted to increasing the money supply. Middle and upper class rentiers who relied on income from fixed interest securities, and public employees whose salaries were controlled by the state, had no protection against inflation. Some were forced to consume capital, for example, by selling their homes (Lawrence 1997). By contrast, the owners of appreciating assets, such as stocks of food or engineering plants, were able to increase their real incomes and wealth.

The extent to which the war restricted the capabilities of the citizens of Paris, London and Berlin is discussed in a recent collaborative volume (Winter and Robert 1997). A capability is the freedom to achieve a certain functioning, such as being well nourished, working in an interesting job, being financially secure, or going on regular holidays (Stewart 1996, 52–6). War reduced the options of most families and limited their access to basic economic needs such as shelter, food and drink. Food shortages are an almost inevitable accompaniment of war. Throughout continental Europe the agricultural sector was made to release large numbers of men and horses for the war effort. Farmers had to forego deliveries of nitrogenous fertilizers, since nitrogen was a key ingredient in explosives. On the whole, the Western Allies managed to feed themselves more successfully than the Central Powers, the Russians or the Balkan Allies (Hardach 1977, 108–38).

Britain relied heavily on imports and was apparently the most vulnerable of the belligerents to food shortages. Between 1914 and 1918, however, the British government afforded a high priority to agriculture in the informal allocation of labour, horses, tractors and chemicals. More land was put under the plough, and the amount of calories produced rose by 24 per cent (Dewey 1989; Singleton 1993). The efforts of the Royal Navy, and later the US Navy, to protect Atlantic shipping enabled Britain to maintain a reasonable level of imports. British consumers may have eaten less beef and butter, stirred less sugar into their tea and grumbled more about prices and queues, but they did not go hungry. France and Italy also escaped serious food crises. Italians may have been better fed during than before the war. Food production declined when Northern France was invaded and men and horses left for the front, but increasing amounts of food were imported, especially from North America (Hardach 1977, 131–3; Zamagni 1993, 218).

The food crisis was more serious in Germany and Austria-Hungary (Lee 1975). Since the Central Powers were prevented from importing army horses from other continents, their farms had to be ruthlessly stripped of horses. Germany, which had been a large wheat importer before the start of the Allied blockade, began to experience bread shortages before the end of 1914. Wartime harvests were poor, and potatoes became the main bulk food of Germans. Though Germany did not starve, its people did suffer real deprivation, which undermined their morale and resistance to disease. Large increases occurred in the incidence of rickets and hunger oedema (Cooter 1993, 1549). The Central Powers would have coped more easily with food shortages had their rationing and distribution systems been better organized (Offer 1989, 22–38; Bonzon and Davis 1997). Civilian morale eventually crumpled. The number of German women convicted of theft rose significantly between 1916 and 1918. Women were reduced to snatching food from market stalls in broad daylight (Davis 2000, 223). Access to food was even more restricted in occupied Belgium and France. Germany did, however, allow the delivery of relief supplies via Holland, through an organization set up by the American philanthropist Herbert Hoover (McPhail 1999, 55–90).

Many parts of Eastern Europe faced outright famine. Russia's appalling food crisis was quite unexpected, given the large size of the agricultural sector. No other country in 1914 looked better placed to with-stand a long war (Gatrell 1994, 226). But food supplies soon broke down, especially in the urban areas. Shortages of inputs, regional harvest failure, transport difficulties and the reluctance of peasants to supply grain at low official prices were to blame. Lack of food in the cities hastened the onset of revolution. After the revolution, the food situation continued to dete-riorate, as peasants cut back on sowing in order to avoid levies by the Bolsheviks (Lih 1990). Russians were increasingly prone to enteritis, peptic ulcers, pyorrhoea and arteriosclerosis (Cooter 1993, 1549). When the grain crop failed in the Volga region in 1920 and 1921, there was no safety margin and famine ensued. In some places the population was reduced to cannibalism. Gangs roamed the streets in search of human prey, and parents killed their babies to feed themselves and older children (Figes 1996, 778)

War resulted in considerable inconvenience for consumers in Western Europe, serious deprivation in Germany and Austria-Hungary, and disas-ter in Russia.

TECHNOLOGICAL AND MEDICAL ADVANCES

The war was responsible for some technological advances, though these were scant recompense for four years of slaughter. In the medical sphere, the First World War saw the introduction of blood transfusions, the launch of aviation medicine, improvements in reconstructive and plastic surgery and advances in the design of artificial limbs (Cooter 1993, 1544).

But the main technological advances were in areas of marginal commer-cial relevance. Although technical progress was rapid in the aircraft indus-try, it would be many years before commercial air services were profitable. The only spin-off from the invention of the tank was improved caterpillar tracks for agricultural tractors (Singleton 1998). There was little demand for poison gas during the 1920s. New capacity for producing liquid chlo-rine, phosgene and ethylene was, however, converted to peaceful purposes. An improved form of tear gas was developed for use by police forces. But attempts to adapt poison gas technology for the production of insecticides were unsuccessful (Haber 1985, 149, 172, 314).

The war speeded up technological transfer and emulation. Japanese firms endeavoured to copy products that could no longer be imported from Europe. Britain, which had depended on Germany until 1914 to supply many chemicals and pharmaceuticals, including Salvarsan for treating syphilis, was compelled to manufacture substitutes (Robson 1988). Britain and France upgraded their scientific and optical instrument manufacturing industries when deprived of German supplies (Williams 1994). War orders boosted the French automobile and chemical industries, as well as the modern sector of the Italian economy. However, the expansion of the industrial North of Italy was partly at the expense of the impoverished South, which lost state aid during the war (Munting and Holderness 1991, 98–100, 154–5; Zamagni 1993, 217–29). When German competition revived in the 1920s, some of these new industries struggled to maintain momentum.

Serious power shortages early in the war encouraged the Tsarist government to embark on an accelerated programme of electrification (Coopersmith 1992, 99–120). Wartime needs and the unavailability of certain imports stimulated the growth of manufacturing in Bulgaria and Greece, and to a lesser extent in Poland, Rumania and Yugoslavia (Lampe and Jackson 1982, 338–41). In short, whilst the First World War hastened the diffusion of existing technologies, it did not give rise to many new products and processes with commercial applications. Against these limited benefits must be set the substantial losses to industrial capacity arising from neglect and enemy action.

THE WARTIME BALANCE SHEET

The First World War was catastrophic for those who were killed, seriously wounded or lost relatives or homes. For the survivors, the psychological costs may have outweighed the material ones. The overall cost of the war is inaccessible to economic enquiry. The bulk of Europe, except Spain, Switzerland and Scandinavia, was directly involved, as, towards the end, was the United States. Economic activity was dislocated when factors of production were diverted into the war effort. Some branches of the chemical and engineering industries were modernized during the war, but many other industries were starved of resources needed for maintenance and renewal. Agriculture also suffered, since horses were commandeered and farm capital was neglected.

THE ECONOMIC LEGACY OF 1914–18

Between 1913 and 1950, economic growth in most parts of the world was slower than it had been before 1913 or would be after 1950. The early 1930s witnessed the worst slump in history. Although the First World War was partly to blame for later economic turmoil, the complexity of the issues precludes a definitive assessment of its degree of responsibility.

Events in the 1920s were strongly influenced by the decisions of policy-makers at the end of the war (Aldcroft 1977). According to Aldcroft, the war was not the direct cause of the economic crises of the 1920s and 1930s. Rather, 'the actions of statesmen and policymakers in the aftermath of hostilities. . .were to blame for Europe's weakened state and. . .vulnerab[ility] to external shocks and. . .internal collapse' (Aldcroft 1991, 43). After the Armistice on 11 November 1918, millions of economic organizations, from the smallest family business to the nation state, faced a challenge no less daunting than that posed by the outbreak of war in 1914. Until normal conditions could be restored, the economies of the former belligerents would be highly fragile. Politicians, bankers, economists, businessmen, union leaders and workers had to make important decisions on the basis of incomplete or misleading information. They also had to operate within the constraints set by the economic reasoning of the time. Instead of working for the common good, many preferred to act in their own perceived best interests. Politicians sought re-election, bondholders campaigned for deflation, workers demanded higher wages and so on. Suffice it to say that the problems were immense and the actors poorly informed, confused and selfish.

Distributional struggles were intense in the aftermath of the war. Within each nation, the conflict was essentially over the retrospective reallocation of the financial burden. This was more than a question of class, indeed each class contained both winners and losers. At the international level, the struggles were over the redrawing of national boundaries, the payment of reparations and the settlement of inter-allied debt. Such disputes distracted attention from the arguably more fundamental objective of rapid economic recovery.

The following sections consider post-war economic growth, the reorganization of Central and Eastern Europe, reparations, inter-allied debt, post-war inflation and deflation, the implications of the war for the international monetary system, and distributional conflicts. Recovery was rather slow and hesitant. Even so, the record was not one of complete failure.

ECONOMIC GROWTH

Maddison portrays the period between 1913 and 1950 as a distinct phase in the growth of the world economy. This 'era [was] deeply disturbed by war [and] depression. . . It was a bleak age, whose potential for accelerated growth was frustrated by a series of disasters' (Maddison 1995, 65). By contrast, the periods before 1914, and from 1950 to 1973, saw comparatively high rates of growth and were marred by few serious crises. European real GDP per capita expanded by 1.4 per cent per annum between 1890 and

Table 1.5   Annual average growth rates of real GDP, 1913–29 (%)

Neutrals		Winners (European)		Losers	
Sweden	1.9	UK	0.7	Austria	0.3
Finland	2.4	Belgium	1.4	Germany	1.2
Denmark	2.7	Italy	1.7		
Switzerland	2.8	France	1.9		
Norway	2.9				
Netherlands	3.6	(extra-European)			
		Canada	2.5		
		USA	3.1		
		Japan	3.7		

Source: Feinstein et al. (1997, 13).

1913, and by 4.0 per annum during the 'Golden Age' between 1950 and 1973. By contrast, intensive growth was a mere 0.9 per cent per annum between 1913 and 1950 (Feinstein, Temin and Toniolo 1997, 9).

Maddison splits the period from 1913 to 1950 into sub-periods, of which 1913 to 1929 is of principal interest. Western Europe (including Austria, Belgium, Britain, France, Germany and Italy) did not regain its 1913 level of real GDP until 1924 (Maddison 1995, 66). In other words, extensive growth was set back by 11 years in Western Europe. Data problems prevent Maddison from making similar aggregate estimates for Eastern Europe. Nevertheless, he indicates that Czechoslovakia and Yugoslavia regained their 1913 levels of real GDP in 1923, followed by Hungary in 1925, Bulgaria in 1927 and Russia in 1929.

As Table 1.5 shows, between 1913 and 1929 the European neutrals experienced faster growth than the belligerents. Except for Britain, which was particularly vulnerable to the dislocation of international markets, the European Allies outperformed the former Central Powers. These findings accord with intuition: it is best to avoid war, but if war is unavoidable it is better to win.

That Western Europe and parts of Central Europe regained their pre-war levels of real GDP within six years of the Armistice was a creditable achievement. In the absence of war, however, real GDP would have grown by a considerable margin between 1913 and the mid-1920s.

Economic growth was not thwarted to the same extent in other parts of the world. The American and Japanese economies forged ahead in the 1920s, suggesting that they were relatively impervious to the difficulties in Europe. Levels of GDP in Latin America and Asia continued to expand in the 1920s, despite weaker commodity prices (Maddison 1995, 66–8). The developing world was not completely insulated from the after-effects of the war. For example, the price of Malaya's main export commodity, rubber, collapsed in the global recession of 1920–22, before recovering to a record high in 1925 (Brown 1997, 48). But the fortunes of the masses in the developing world depended more on the harvest than on the state of the international economy. When the price of an export crop, such as sugar, was low, land could be switched to rice production, thus limiting the impact on welfare. Relatively speaking, high-income primary producing countries, such as New Zealand, suffered the most from fluctuations in world demand and prices in the 1920s (Fleming 1999). Farmers who had bought land at inflated prices during the post-war boom repented when export prices fell in the early 1920s. Declining real capital outflows from the core European countries, including Britain (Cain and Hopkins 1993, 44), posed additional problems for peripheral countries, which were only partially relieved by increased supplies of American capital.

Did the First World War exercise a persistent or merely a short- or medium-term effect on growth (Mills 2000)? War imposed output losses on many countries, which were not reversed for a number of years. The capacity of real shocks to cause structural breaks in growth rates is a controversial topic, and the literature pays scant attention to the impact of the First World War. Ben-David and Papell (1995), however, argue that the First World War altered the long-term rate of growth in real GDP per capita in three cases: Finland (structural break in 1913), Sweden (1916) and Britain (1918). All three enjoyed higher growth rates after the structural break. Even so, it took them many years to overhaul the levels of real GDP per capita that would have prevailed by extrapolating pre-war growth rates – Britain did not catch up until 1940. The Second World War saw structural breaks in other European countries, including Austria, Belgium, France, Germany and Italy. Another article by the same authors identifies the following structural breaks in the growth of real GDP per capita: Germany (1913), Italy (1918), France (1921), Britain (1918) and Canada (1917). Except for Italy, which had slower growth after 1918, each country mentioned enjoyed an increase in the growth rate after the First World War (Ben-David and Papell 2000). Employing a different technique, Greasley and Oxley (1997) conclude that statistically significant events, affecting long-term growth rates of real GDP per capita, occurred in Finland (1913), Sweden (1918) and Britain (1918). They also find that the Second World War had a greater impact on growth rates than did the First World War. No structural breaks around the time of the First World War have been identified for Australia, the United States and Japan. Too much should not be read into any of these findings, which are hard to explain, although they are intriguing.

No consensus exists on the long-term implications of the First World War for economic growth. In the short and medium terms, however, the war clearly reduced growth. We now turn to the development of post-war economic and financial policy.

DISMEMBERING CENTRAL AND EASTERN EUROPE

One of the most momentous consequences of the First World War was the disintegration of the Austro-Hungarian Empire. Although politically moribund, the Habsburg Empire was not economically stagnant in the early twentieth century. Trade flourished within this Central European customs union. Its dismemberment after 1918 was an economically retrograde step, according to Komlos (1983). After 1918, trade between the former Habsburg states may have fallen by more than one-half (Frankel 1997, 119–20).

The successor countries were economically unbalanced. Czechoslovakia inherited the empire's most advanced industrial region, leaving Austria relatively underdeveloped. Hungary was cut off from its main sources of raw materials. High trade barriers were erected as each country sought to develop a distinct national economy. Hungary was on particularly bad terms with its neighbours because the peace settlement created new territorial grievances. Financial and commercial networks in Central Europe were shattered and the gains from regional specialization were lost. Intra-regional trade declined relative to trade with Western Europe (Aldcroft and Morewood 1995, 1–41).

Poland and what would become Yugoslavia faced problems of a different, but equally disruptive, character. Their task was to integrate regions, transport systems and business networks that had until recently been in separate states. Yugoslavia inherited five practically unrelated railway systems, and four gauges of track (Aldcroft and Morewood 1995, 7). Industry expanded quite rapidly in most parts of Central and Eastern Europe during the 1920s, artificially stimulated by protective measures. It is doubtful whether many new industries in this region, except in Czechoslovakia, were internationally competitive (Teichova 1985, 222–62). The new states of Central and Eastern Europe obtained relief and reconstruction loans from the Allies and the League of Nations, but the amounts involved were too small to have more than a moral effect (League of Nations 1945; Notel 1986). On the other hand, inflows of foreign investment were considerable, especially into extractive industries such as mining and oil production (Lampe and Jackson 1982, 428–32), and into the Czechoslovakian manufacturing sector.

The former Habsburg (and German) lands would have been more prosperous under pre-war political arrangements, but nationalists reckoned the material costs of self-determination as small compared with the emotional benefits of independence.

REPARATIONS

Strictly speaking, the war was paid for in real resources between 1914 and 1918. As von Mises (1983, 168) put it: 'War can be waged only with present goods'. Governments financed war-related expenditure by taxing, borrowing and printing money. All three methods imposed economic sacrifices on individuals. After the war, governments had to decide what to do about their vast accumulated debts. Higher taxes or levies, more inflation and default were the main options. Allied politicians contended that the defeated powers should reimburse the victors for at least some of the financial costs of the war, including war pensions (Kent 1989).

War debts and German reparations were central political and economic issues in the 1920s. Keynes, who attended the Versailles Peace Conference as a British Treasury official, predicted that demands for heavy reparations would lead to economic disaster in Germany and a lengthy period of international economic instability (Keynes 1920). But how onerous actually were reparations and war debts?

Under the 1921 London Schedule of Payments, Germany was required to make reparations of 132 billion gold marks, or about US$31 billion, to the European Allies. The rate of payment, including interest charges, was set at around 3 billion gold marks per annum. Some payments in kind were incorporated, but the bulk was to be in cash. It is doubtful whether the Allies really expected Germany to pay more than the first 50 billion gold marks, which was not an excessive sum even by the reckoning of Keynes's polemic against Versailles (Eichengreen 1992a, 131). Germany was also instructed to relinquish certain minor trophies; hence the skull of Sultan Mkwama of German East Africa was presented to Britain (Sharp 1991, 95). Germany's allies were treated leniently. The states of the former Austro-Hungarian Empire were asked for token reparations, and Turkey was pardoned.

Ferguson (1996, 656) suggests that the amount of reparations actually paid by Germany, during the first half of the 1920s, was equivalent to between 4 and 7 per cent of national income. This burden was not crippling, especially in comparison with the material losses borne by the

German population during the war itself. When Germany descended into hyperinflation, the Weimar government said that it could no longer meet the London Schedule of Payments. In 1924 Germany obtained the rescheduling of its financial obligations under the Dawes Plan. Subsequent German reparations payments were facilitated by a large inflow of US private capital, which Schuker rather facetiously describes as American reparations to Germany. Germany finally defaulted in 1932 during the Depression. Schuker (1988, 106–8) estimates that Germany paid reparations of approximately 17 billion gold marks in total – a fraction of the original bill.

The actual burden on Germany of reparations was not excessive compared with the reparations paid by France after 1815 and 1871. Germany was in any case richer in the 1920s than France had been in the 1810s or the 1870s (White 2001). Germany made no serious attempt to meet its total obligations (Ferguson 1999, 410). Reparations did, however, have a tremendous psychological impact on the German people, who hated being held to account for the war. Their festering resentment was a boon to the Nazis, and the principal cost of the Allies' demand for large reparations.

INTER-ALLIED SQUABBLING

For many years after the Second World War, the United States made generous amounts of economic aid available to the wartorn countries of Europe. By contrast, the years after 1918 saw a growing estrangement between the United States and the European Allies. Whereas the Second World War was the catalyst for greater international cooperation, the aftermath of the First World War witnessed considerable squabbling amongst the victors (Boltho 2001).

At the end of 1918 there was an urgent need for food and clothing in many parts of Europe, including the countries of the former Central Powers. The American Relief Administration, set up in early 1919, provided most of the $1250 million worth of relief supplies sent to Europe, 20 per cent of which was gratis. After the signing of the Treaty of Versailles in June 1919, however, the US relief programme was rapidly terminated, partly because the American government and taxpayers were understandably anxious to disentangle themselves from Europe, and partly because of inter-allied rivalry (Aldcroft 1999, 138–9). Wall Street had been willing to provide further credit for European recovery, but only on terms that were unacceptable to Britain and France, including that new credits be spent entirely in the United States, that US capital be allowed a half interest in British banks in the Far East and Latin America and that the Europeans make significant trade concessions (Schuker 1993). The Americans were perfectly entitled to limit their post-war commitment to Europe and to probe the weak bargaining positions of Britain and France. Perhaps they would have acted differently if they could have foreseen the events of the next two decades, but of course they could not. There was no precedent in 1919, but there would be one in 1945.

The future of inter-allied debt exercised policy-makers and journalists. Allied intergovernmental indebtedness stood at US$16.4 billion at the Armistice (Moulton and Pasvolsky 1932, 426). The European Allies, including Britain, were indebted to the United States to the tune of US$7 billion. Britain had lent more to the continental Allies than it had borrowed from the United States. The Americans made new loans to Europe in 1918–20, but inter-allied debt soured transatlantic economic relations until the 1930s. The European Allies said that they could not afford to repay the United States, and that any attempt to do so would intensify the post-war financial crisis. This was an exaggeration: indeed the amount involved, US$7 billion, was small in relation to the sum demanded of Germany.

European governments offered to cancel all intra-European war debt, and treat Germany more leniently, if Washington agreed to write off transatlantic debt. The United States proclaimed a three-year moratorium on interest charges in 1919, and later substantially scaled down demands for repayment, but for domestic political reasons declined to cancel inter-allied debt (Moulton and Pasvolsky 1932; Silverman 1982). Debt repayments finally ceased during the Depression.

Much has been made of inter-allied indebtedness, and the resulting discord among former Allies, but the economic aspects of this affair should not be exaggerated. Contemporaries believed that divisions among the Allies were responsible for an upsurge in protectionism and a lack of international monetary cooperation in the 1920s. Marrison (2000), however, finds no conclusive evidence of an overall increase in tariff protection between the pre-war and post-war eras. The controversial US tariff increases of 1921 and 1922 merely restored duties to their levels before the 1913 tariff cuts. As explained below, the reasons for the failure of monetary cooperation were complex, and could not have been overcome merely by a more harmonious approach to inter-allied indebtedness.

INFLATION, DEFLATION AND GOLD

The First World War ended sooner than had been expected in the first half of 1918. During 1919 and 1920 most governments were preoccupied with economic demobilization and the struggle against inflation. Before 1914 price stability had been the central goal of economic policy. Prices rose rapidly during the war, and after the Armistice the authorities were anxious to reverse the tide of inflation. Keynes viewed inflation as a threat to the survival of capitalism, because it discouraged saving and bred animosity towards entrepreneurs, who were branded as profiteers. Inflation was a serious threat to social cohesion (Moggridge 1992, 333).

The pre-war gold standard, involving the unlimited convertibility of major currencies into gold at fixed exchange rates, had been underpinned by the prior commitment of the leading powers to internal price stability (Gallarotti 1995; Eichengreen and Flandreau 1997; Bordo and Schwartz 1999, 153–60). Inflation, rising current account deficits and declining investor confidence forced European countries to restrict or suspend gold convertibility after 1914, in order to staunch the loss of gold reserves. During the war, news from the front, including casualty figures, exercised some influence over exchange rates, with the currencies of those countries that appeared to be winning appreciating relative to those that appeared to be losing (Hall 2004).

Wartime inflation was much higher in Europe than in the United States. Between 1914 and 1918, consumer prices rose by 69 per cent in the United States, compared with 100 per cent in Britain, 113 per cent in France, 204 per cent in Germany, 1063 per cent in Austria and 1334 per cent in Belgium (Maddison 1991, 300, 302). Moreover, inflation gathered pace in some countries in 1919–20. By the end of 1919, the US dollar was the only major currency still fixed against gold. European currencies floated and depreciated by substantial amounts against gold and the dollar.

Inflation was caused by the inability of governments to cover wartime expenditures with tax revenue, loans and asset sales. Attempts to raise tax rates were frustrated by opposition from sectional interests, whilst the appetite of domestic and foreign investors for government debt was limited. The Central Powers found it harder to borrow abroad than did Britain and France, but all belligerents resorted in some measure to the printing press or inflation tax (Balderston 1989; Horn 2002; Strachan 2004).

Inflation redistributed income and wealth. Despite apparent profiteering by some businesses, the outcome was a somewhat flatter distribution of income and wealth. The non-entrepreneurial middle class, including owners of fixed interest securities, did very badly. Working class households were partially cushioned by union bargaining power and state benefits.

Governments sold vast quantities of fixed interest securities, both domestically and abroad, between 1914 and 1918, but inflation eroded the growth in the real debt burden. The national plus state debt of Germany increased by the equivalent of US$15 billion between 1914 and 1919, whereas the national debts of Britain, France, Italy and the United States increased by $30 billion, $25 billion, $7 billion and $24 billion respectively (Ferguson 1999, 325). Servicing and repaying these debts would place great strain on government finances. Partial cancellation – a capital levy – was one possible solution (Eichengreen 1990). The other options were increased taxation, reduced social spending and the printing press (Makinen and Woodward 1990). Each approach had distributional implications.

What was to be done about inflation and war debt? Except in Germany, Austria, Hungary and Poland, there was little overt support for allowing inflation to continue, since inflation generated uncertainty for all sections of society. But it was difficult to build a political consensus for the stringent monetary and budgetary measures that would stabilize or reduce prices. Broadly speaking, the political left opposed deflation. It wished to maintain the levels of state benefits and wages, and was indifferent to the plight of holders of government debt. The political right advocated a period of sharp deflation, and contended that the pre-war distribution of income and wealth should be restored at the expense of the working class. Though it is tempting to say that bondholders could afford to take some punishment, not all bondholders were in fact wealthy. War debt had been sold in small packages to the middle classes and even skilled workers. Purchasers of debt had been promised repayment in full, and assured that prices would return to pre-war levels (Hughes 1988, 6–7). Any failure by the state to meet its commitments would weaken the legitimacy of capitalism.

Contemporary economic rhetoric was strongly supportive of deflation. Many economists argued that the price level should be deflated until the European currencies could safely rejoin the gold standard at the pre-war parities. They were confident that adjustments in wages and prices would occur smoothly, with little resistance from the unions, and minimal loss of output and employment. The benefits of returning to gold at the old parities were assumed to include financial stability and increased confidence. These points were repeated ad nauseam in the early 1920s. Johnson (1997, 71) quotes the psychoanalyst, Ernest Jones, who in 1917 asserted that belief in the gold standard was 'superstitious', and described gold coins as 'unconscious symbols for excrement, the material from which most of our sense of possession, in infantile times, was derived'. From another perspective, Eichengreen and Temin (1997) argue that faith in the gold standard and in the traditional parities was so ingrained that it constituted a gold standard *mentalité*. Support for a return to gold at the old parity was strongest in the City of London. Very few City firms, and no manufacturers, stood to gain from an appreciation in the external value of the pound (Pollard 1970, 17), but their owners would benefit in their capacity as bondholders from deflation. Thus contemporary economic dogma provided

convenient support for bondholders. British politicians either unhesitat-
ingly believed what they were told by their financial advisers or, like
Winston Churchill, the Chancellor of the Exchequer when Britain returned
to gold in 1925, swallowed their doubts.

Despite the assurance of most economists, it proved difficult for
European countries to go back to the gold standard at the pre-1914 parities.
Only Sweden (1922), the Netherlands (1924), Switzerland (1924), Britain
(1925), Denmark (1926) and Norway (1928) achieved this objective. All
except Britain had been neutrals. Moreover, 'success' was invariably the
result of a protracted campaign of budgetary retrenchment and monetary
restraint, which was responsible for high unemployment. After many vicis-
situdes, Finland (1926), Belgium (1926), Czechoslovakia (1923), France
(1926)[3] and Italy (1927) all returned to gold at much reduced parities
(Aldcroft and Oliver 1998, 5). France, Italy and Belgium had originally
aspired to the old parities. It was only in 1926 that the French 'Committee
of Experts' rejected that approach as unrealistic (Dulles 1929; Mouré 2002).
Clearly, opposition to deflation was much stronger in France and Belgium
than in Britain. The need for physical reconstruction also militated against
strict retrenchment in France and Belgium (Dulles 1929, 3). Creditors,
including official debt holders, bore more of the burden of post-war adjustment in France, whilst manufacturers and workers bore more of the burden
in Britain. Germany (1923),[4] Austria (1922) and the countries of Eastern
Europe returned to gold after much larger depreciations (Sargent 1982).

The glib assumption of economists that deflation would be relatively
painless was dramatically falsified, except in the United States. Between
1914 and 1920, excess demand for labour had encouraged unionization and
strengthened the resolve of labour leaders (Wrigley 2000b). Extension of
the franchise had also increased the political influence of the working class
in some countries. Workers negotiated higher wages, shorter hours and
increased social benefits in the aftermath of war. Political elites were initially reluctant to confront the unions, fearing the spread of Bolshevism.
Socialist parties complained about cuts in social spending, whilst trade
unions opposed reductions in money wages. During Britain's era of
deflation in the early 1920s, money wages fell by less than prices, so that
real wages increased and unemployment rocketed. Political and labour
market rigidities surprised and confused economists and policy-makers.
Deflationary policies were more muted in France, Belgium and Italy, all
three of which enjoyed higher economic growth than Britain between 1913
and 1929. Perhaps the British put too much emphasis on deflation, but at
least they took no risks with hyperinflation.

The relative merits of fixed and flexible exchange rates are still debated
(Bordo and Schwartz 1999, 203). Notwithstanding the gold standard

mentalité, support for the gold standard was not universal amongst economists in the early twentieth century (Laidler 1991; Cowen and Kroszner 1994, 121–72). But the gold standard was – if nothing else – familiar, and could have provided good service in the 1920s if realistic parities had been chosen after the war. With the best will in the world, however, it would have been almost impossible to identify stable gold parities for the major currencies in 1919. International markets were in flux and inflation was not yet under control. In any case, there are strong grounds for thinking that exchange rates chosen on scientific grounds would not have been politically acceptable. Britain's determination to return to the pre-war gold parity has already been mentioned. Even America had suffered inflation during the war, and in 1918 the US dollar was overvalued relative to gold. Some devaluation of the US dollar relative to gold would have helped to alleviate the international shortage of external reserves in the 1920s (Johnson 1997). But devaluation was out of the question, not least for reasons of national pride.

The uncoordinated rebuilding of the international monetary system was bound to lead to serious problems. Incoherent and misguided policies in the 1920s contributed to the onset and spread of depression in the early 1930s (Eichengreen 1992a, 1992b). Conflict between the advocates and opponents of deflation was settled in different ways in different countries, depending on the balance of political forces and the severity of the economic situation (Ferguson 1999, 423–4).

HYPERINFLATION

Several countries in Central and Eastern Europe, including Germany, Poland, Austria and Hungary, were plagued by hyperinflation in the early 1920s. Germany's hyperinflation has attracted the greatest interest from economists and historians (Balderston 2002), partly because of its possible connection to reparations. Many contemporaries attributed Germany's high post-war inflation to exchange rate depreciation or the runaway budget deficit. Since these phenomena were closely related, it is debatable which came first. A depreciating exchange rate raised the price of imports, and put the Weimar government under pressure to increase transfer payments and subsidies, so as to compensate adversely affected groups. The result was a wider budget deficit. Meanwhile, high budget deficits boosted demand for imports and shattered confidence in the paper mark on world markets (Eichengreen 1992a, 125–45). In order to pay reparations, the German authorities had to convert paper marks into hard currency, intensifying the spiral of depreciation. Industrialists believed that exchange rate depreciation would boost exports, and goaded the state into selling even more paper marks. But reparations, though an unwelcome burden, accounted for just one-third of the increase in German government spending as a share of net national product between the pre-war period and the early 1920s. The principal causes of the budget deficit were the increase in social spending on unemployment benefits, war pensions and food subsidies, and the financial losses of the rail and postal systems (Ferguson 1996). Political stalemate between the left, which would not accept cuts in spending, and the right, which vetoed large tax increases, produced chaos. Their intransigence reflected the widening of class divisions after Germany's defeat. Neither the middle class nor the working class would acquiesce in further economic sacrifices, and the government was too weak to pursue an independent policy (Feldman 1997).

Hyperinflation also broke out in Poland, although this country did not have to pay reparations. The Polish price level rose by over 1.5 million per cent between November 1918 and December 1923 (Landau and Tomaszewski 1985, 45). Austria and Hungary, which faced token demands for reparations, still underwent currency collapses. In some countries, post-war social and political dislocation was so severe that the government lost control over the budget. Possible solutions, including tax increases and cuts in spending, were rejected on sectional grounds. The Austrian example is particularly intriguing, because the eminent economist, Joseph Schumpeter, was Minister of Finance in 1919. Schumpeter proposed a large levy on property owners, but the right wing refused to countenance this scheme, whilst the left demanded a more radical policy of expropriation. Schumpeter's period as Finance Minister was brief, and Austria slipped into hyperinflation (Stolper 1994, 249–67, 288–93).

The German reichsmark was stabilized in 1924. But who had borne the brunt of hyperinflation? There were winners and losers across the social spectrum. Inflation redistributed income and wealth away from those living on fixed money incomes, including holders of government securities, towards those possessing bargaining power and appreciating real assets. Salaries of German university professors lagged behind inflation. In 1922, the professors warned the government that their health was being affected by 'aggravation, undernourishment, care, and indebtedness', and that they were losing the 'ability and willingness to work' (Feldman 1997, 547). Middle class savings were wiped out. But entrepreneurs and industrialists prospered if they could raise their prices faster than costs. Inflation reduced the cost of borrowing, and industrial investment grew strongly in the early 1920s. Hyperinflation was particularly advantageous to the printing industry: 133 firms were printing banknotes at the height of the crisis (Dornbusch 1987, 346–7). Workers achieved large nominal pay increases, but were not immune from the consequences of hyperinflation. Uncertain economic conditions increased the risk of redundancy, and wages often did not rise fast enough to keep pace with the cost of living. For example, the real wages of unskilled German chemical workers dropped from 114 per cent of the sum needed to maintain a small family in January 1922 to 69 per cent in December 1922 (Feldman 1997, 613).

Hyperinflation effectively annihilated Germany's internal or paper reichsmark government debt, eased the Weimar's budgetary troubles and reduced pressure on taxpayers (although many taxpayers were also bond-holders). Although between one-quarter and one-half of the German electorate were net paper reichsmark creditors, in most cases the net amounts were small. Only about 10 per cent of the electorate relied heavily on income from paper assets (Hughes 1988, 9–16). Dreading a Bolshevik revolution, and ranking the interests of producers above those of consumers, the Weimar paid little heed to the agitation of creditors. For the individuals and families ruined by hyperinflation this episode was a tragedy, and for many others it brought great anxiety. The legacy of hyperinflation cannot be examined in detail here, but it could have seriously weakened the banking system (Balderston 1991; Voth 2000). Economic turmoil in Germany was partly responsible for a succession of later disasters affecting Europe and the world. Disgruntled creditors, who claimed to have been swindled by the Weimar Republic, were amongst the most enthusiastic supporters of the Nazis (Hughes 1988, 181–8). The example of interwar Germany lends strong support to Keynes's thesis that runaway inflation leads to social breakdown.

REDISTRIBUTION

The overall distributional effect of the First World War was egalitarian in the major European economies. Four years of war had unleashed powerful social forces and caused massive economic disruption. Empires had fallen, whilst in Russia property rights had been overthrown. Money wages and benefits, but not real working class incomes, had risen substantially. After 1918, working class parties and trade unions fought attempts to transfer some of the financial burden of the war away from the holders of paper assets and onto the proletariat. Their resistance was relatively successful. Capitalism survived, but significant concessions were made to the working class in order to restore stability and safeguard the fundamental interests of property owners (Maier 1975).

Between 1911–13 and 1924, the share of the richest 5 per cent of adults in the aggregate net marketable worth of England and Wales fell from 87 per cent to 81.5 per cent (Lindert 2000, 181). The share of the poorest

60 per cent of taxpayer households in Germany's taxable income rose by 4.8 percentage points between 1913 and 1926, while the share of the top 10 per cent of households fell by 5.5 percentage points (Morrison 2000, 233). Earned income as a share of total income in Germany rose from 50 per cent to 65 per cent between 1913 and 1925 (Feldman 1997, 839; Kaelble and Thomas 1991, 36, 40–1). In France, dividends, interest and rent as a share of household primary income fell from 26.8 per cent in 1913 to 18.3 per cent in 1926 (Morrison 2000, 250). The war and economic downturn in the early 1920s also tended to have an egalitarian impact in the United States (Piketty and Saez 2003). But the levelling impact of the war might have been reversed if the fortunes of the rich had not been depleted in the Depression of the 1930s (Piketty 2003).

Modern readers are likely to view the redistribution of income and wealth in a positive light. However, the process by which the financial burden of the war was reallocated was intensely disruptive to economic activity. Currencies rose and fell, savings were destroyed, businesses collapsed and millions of jobs were lost. Failure to resolve the distributional questions arising from the war was a major cause of uncertainty and instability within nations and internationally.

CONCLUSION

The First World War was an economic disaster of the highest order, especially in Europe. Its greatest impact was felt at the level of the individual – millions were killed or wounded and others lost relatives, wealth and incomes. It is not possible to put a dollar figure on the 'cost' of the war. What level of compensation would have been adequate to satisfy those who suffered, whether materially or psychologically, as a result of the war? The war's effects were uneven. Beyond Europe and some of its offshoots (North America and Australasia) its impact was muted. Even within Europe, millions escaped relatively unscathed.

At the macroeconomic level, war disrupted the normal circuit of activity. Output declined in some countries, as men were pushed or pulled into the armed services. The structure of many economies changed, if only temporarily, between 1914 and 1918. In Europe and North America, resources were redirected into the armaments industries. Most economists would regard this process as wasteful, although it could be argued that munitions were 'goods' because they protected civilians from the depredations of a potential invader. War encouraged further industrialization and agricultural development in other continents. In particular, it accelerated Japan's emergence as a great economic power.

Research on the economic legacy of the war has been dominated, especially in recent years, by the tortured fate of the gold standard and the origins of the Great Depression. The First World War brought chaos into international monetary affairs, and policy-makers failed to reconstruct a durable mechanism after 1918. Their lack of success reflected the intensity of the distributional struggle both between and (especially) within nations. After the war, it was difficult for economic elites to re-establish their former mastery over the masses, and in most countries they had to make concessions. In Russia, however, the old economic elite was destroyed in 1917. Perhaps it was in Russia that the First World War had its most enduring economic impact

World economic growth was slow in the interwar period. It was some years before Europe had made up for the wartime interruption to economic growth. The First World War exerted the strongest challenge to modern capitalism before the Depression of the 1930s. Except in Russia, the market economic system did not collapse. The First World War was an economic disaster but, paradoxically, it also demonstrated the resilience of industrial capitalism.

NOTES

1. I am obliged to Derek Aldcroft, Gordon Boyce and Michael Oliver for comments on an earlier draft. All remaining errors are my own responsibility. I also wish to thank the staff of the Knowledge Centre of the Reserve Bank of New Zealand for finding certain books and articles. This chapter was written before the appearance of the superb collection of national studies edited by Broadberry and Harrison (2005).
2. SGUs are reckoned by weighting items as follows: rifles 0.01, machine guns 0.05, guns 1.00, tanks 5.00 and aircraft 5.00. Of course, this measure does not include certain important items such as ammunition and warships.
3. France stabilized de jure in 1926 and de facto in 1928.
4. Germany stabilized de jure in 1923 and de facto in 1924.

REFERENCES

Adelman, J.R. (1988), *Prelude to the Cold War: the Tsarist, Soviet, and U.S. armies in the two World Wars*, Boulder: L. Rienner.

Aldcroft, D.H. (1977), *From Versailles to Wall Street*, London: Allen Lane.

Aldcroft, D.H. (1991), 'Destabilizing influences in the European economy in the 1920s', in C. Holmes and A. Booth (eds), *Economy and society: European industrialization and its social consequences*, Leicester: Leicester University Press.

Aldcroft, D.H. (1999), 'The disintegration of Europe 1918–1945', in D.H. Aldcroft and A. Sutcliffe (eds), *Europe in the international economy 1500 to 2000*, Cheltenham, UK, Northampton, MA, USA: Edward Elgar.

Aldcroft, D.H. and Morewood, S. (1995), *Economic change in Eastern Europe since 1918*, Aldershot, UK and Brookfield, US: Edward Elgar.

Aldcroft, D.H. and Oliver, M.J. (1998), *Exchange rate regimes in the twentieth century*, Cheltenham, UK and Lyme, USA: Edward Elgar.

Aldred, C. (2000), 'Stress claims spur litigation', *Business Insurance*, 34.

Argyle, M. (1996), 'Subjective well-being', in A. Offer (ed.), *In pursuit of the quality of life*, Oxford: Oxford University Press.

Balderston, T. (1989), 'War finance and inflation in Britain and Germany, 1914–1918', *Economic History Review*, 42.

Balderston, T. (1991), 'German banking between the wars: the crisis of the credit banks', *Business History Review*, 65.

Balderston, T. (2002), *Economics and politics in the Weimar Republic*, Cambridge: Cambridge University Press.

Becker, A. (1998), *War and faith: the religious imagination in France, 1914–1930*, Oxford: Berg.

Becker, J.-J. (1992), ' "That's the death knell of our boys. . ." ', in P. Fridenson (ed.), *The French home front, 1914–1918*, Oxford: Berg.

Ben-David, D. and Papell, D.H. (1995), 'The great wars, the great crash, and steady state growth: some new evidence about an old stylized fact', *Journal of Monetary Economics*, 36.

Ben-David, D. and Papell, D.H. (2000), 'Some evidence on the continuity of the growth process among the G7 countries', *Economic Inquiry*, 38.

Bogart, E.L. (1920), *Direct and indirect costs of the Great World War*, New York: Oxford University Press.

Boltho, A. (2001), 'Reconstruction after two world wars – why the differences?', *Journal of European Economic History*, 30.

Bonzon, T. (1997a), 'The labour market and industrialization, 1915–1917', in J. Winter and J.-L. Robert (eds), *Capital cities at war: Paris, London, Berlin 1914–1919*, Cambridge: Cambridge University Press.

Bonzon, T. (1997b), 'Transfer payments and social policy', in J. Winter and J.-L. Robert (eds), *Capital cities at war: Paris, London, Berlin 1914–1919*, Cambridge: Cambridge University Press.

Bonzon, T. and Davis, B. (1997), 'Feeding the cities', in J. Winter and J.-L. Robert (eds), *Capital cities at war: Paris, London, Berlin 1914–1919*, Cambridge: Cambridge University Press.

Bordo, M. and Schwartz, A.J. (1999), 'Monetary policy regimes and economic performance: the historical record', in J.B. Taylor and M. Woodford (eds), *Handbook of macroeconomics*, Amsterdam: Elsevier, vol. 1A.

Bourke, J. (1996), *Dismembering the male: men's bodies, Britain and the Great War*, London: Reaktion.

Broadberry, S. and Harrison, M. (eds) (2005), *The Economics of World War I*, Cambridge: Cambridge University Press.

Brown, I. (1997), *Economic change in South-East Asia, c. 1830–1980*, Kuala Lumpur: Oxford University Press.

Brown, K.D. (2000), 'The impact of the First World War on Japan', in C. Wrigley (ed.), *The First World War and the international economy*, Cheltenham, UK and Northampton, MA, USA: Edward Elgar.

Bulmer-Thomas, V. (1994), *The economic history of Latin America since independence*, Cambridge: Cambridge University Press.

Burchardt, L. (1988), 'Between war profits and war costs: Krupp in the First World War', *German Yearbook on Business History*, 32.

Cain, P.J. and Hopkins, A.G. (1993), *British imperialism: crisis and deconstruction 1914–1990*, London: Longman.

Cameron, R. (1993), *A concise economic history of the world*, New York: Oxford University Press.

Caplan, B. (2002), 'How does war shock the economy?', *Journal of International Money and Finance*, 21.

Cassiers, I. and Solar, P. (1990), 'Wages and productivity in Belgium, 1910–60', *Oxford Bulletin of Economics and Statistics*, 52.

Clout, H. (1996), *After the ruins: restoring the countryside of northern France after the Great War*, Exeter: University of Exeter Press.

Coopersmith, J. (1992), *The electrification of Russia, 1880–1926*, Ithaca: Cornell University Press.

Cooter, R. (1993), 'War and modern medicine', in W.F. Bynum and R. Porter (eds), *Companion encyclopedia of the history of medicine*, London: Routledge, vol. 2.

Cowen, T. and Kroszner, R. (1994), *Explorations in the new monetary economics*, Oxford: Blackwell.

Crawcour, E.S. (1988), 'Industrialization and technological change, 1885–1920', in P. Duus (ed.), *Cambridge history of Japan*, Cambridge: Cambridge University Press, vol. 6.

Davis, B. (2000), *Home fires burning: food, politics, and everyday life in World War I Berlin*, Chapel Hill: University of North Carolina Press.

Dewey, P.E. (1989), *British agriculture in the First World War*, London: Routledge.

Dornbusch, R. (1987), 'Lessons from the German inflation experience of the 1920s', in R. Dornbusch, S. Fischer and J. Bossons (eds), *Macroeconomics and finance*, Cambridge MA: MIT Press.

Dulles, E.L. (1929), *The French franc 1914–1928*, New York: Macmillan.

Eichengreen, B. (1990), 'The capital levy in theory in practice', in R. Dornbusch and M. Draghi (eds), *Public debt management: theory and history*, Cambridge: Cambridge University Press.

Eichengreen, B. (1992a), *Golden fetters: the gold standard and the Great Depression, 1919–1939*, Oxford: Oxford University Press.

Eichengreen, B. (1992b), 'The origins and nature of the Great Slump revisited', *Economic History Review*.

Eichengreen, B. and Flandreau, M. (eds) (1997), *The gold standard in theory and history*, London: Routledge.

Eichengreen, B. and Temin, P. (1997), 'The gold standard and the Great Depression', NBER Working Paper 6060.

Fearon, P. (2000), 'Manufacturing industry in the United States during the First World War', in C. Wrigley (ed.), *The First World War and the international economy*, Cheltenham, UK and Northampton, MA, USA: Edward Elgar.

Feinstein, C.H. and Pollard, S. (eds) (1988), *Studies in capital formation in the United Kingdom*, Oxford: Clarendon Press.

Feinstein, C.H., Temin, P. and Toniolo, G. (1997), *The European economy between the wars*, Oxford: Oxford University Press.

Feldman, G.D. (1997), *The great disorder: politics, economics and society in the German inflation, 1914–1924*, New York: Oxford University Press.

Ferguson, N. (1996), 'Constraints and room for manoeuvre in the German inflation of the early 1920s', *Economic History Review*, 46.

Ferguson, N. (1999), *The pity of war*, New York: Basic Books.

Figes, O. (1996), *A people's tragedy: the Russian Revolution 1891–1924*, London: Jonathan Cape.

Fleming, G.A. (1999), 'Agricultural support policies in a small open economy: New Zealand in the 1920s', *Economic History Review*, 52.

Frankel, J.A. (1997), *Regional trading blocs in the world economic system*, Washington DC: Institute for International Economics.

Fratianni, M. and Spinelli, F. (1997), *A monetary history of Italy*, Cambridge: Cambridge University Press.

Gallarotti, G.M. (1995), *The anatomy of an international monetary regime: the classical gold standard, 1880–1914*, New York: Oxford University Press.

Gatrell, P. (1994), 'The First World War and war communism, 1914–1920', in R.W. Davies, M. Harrison and S.G. Wheatcroft (eds), *The economic transformation of the Soviet Union, 1913–1945*, Cambridge: Cambridge University Press.

Gatrell, P. and Harrison, M. (1993), 'The Russian and Soviet economies in two world wars: a comparative view', *Economic History Review*, 46.

Greasley, D. and Oxley, L. (1997), 'Shock persistence and structural change', *Economic Record*, 73.

Gregory, A. (1997), 'Lost generations: the impact of military casualties on Paris, London and Berlin', in J. Winter and J.-L. Robert (eds), *Capital cities at war: Paris, London, Berlin 1914–1919*, Cambridge: Cambridge University Press.

Haber, L.F. (1985), *The poisonous cloud: chemical warfare in the First World War*, Oxford: Clarendon.

Hall, G.J. (2004), 'Exchange rates and casualties during the First World War', *Journal of Monetary Economics*, 51.

Hardach, G. (1977), *The First World War 1914–1918*, London: Allen Lane.

Hobson, J.A. (1902), *Imperialism*, London: Allen & Unwin.

Horn, M. (2002), *Britain, France and the financing of the First World War*, Montreal: McGill-Queen's University Press.

Howard, M.C. and King, J.E. (1989), *A history of Marxian economics*, Basingstoke: Macmillan, vol. 1.

Hughes, M.L. (1988), *Paying for the German inflation*, Chapel Hill: University of North Carolina Press.

Johnson, H.C. (1997), *Gold, France, and the Great Depression, 1919–1932*, New Haven: Yale University Press.

Junger, E. (1929), *The storm of steel*, London: Chatto & Windus.

Kaelble, H. and Thomas, M. (1991), 'Introduction', in Y.S. Brenner, H. Kaelble and M. Thomas (eds), *Income distribution in historical perspective*, Cambridge: Cambridge University Press.

Kanya-Forstner, A.D. (2000), 'The war, imperialism, and decolonization', in J. Winter, G. Parker and M.R. Halbeck (eds), *The Great War and the twentieth century*, New Haven: Yale University Press.

Kent, B. (1989), *The spoils of war: the politics, economics, and diplomacy of reparations 1918–1932*, Oxford: Clarendon Press.

Kershaw, I. (1999), *Hitler, 1889–1936*, London: Allen Lane.

Keynes, J.M. (1920), *The economic consequences of the peace*, London: Macmillan.

Kirzner, I.M. (1986), 'Another look at the subjectivism of costs', in I.M. Kirzner (ed.), *Subjectivism, intelligibility and economic understanding*, Basingstoke: Macmillan.

Koistinen, P.A.C. (1997), *Mobilizing for modern war: the political economy of American warfare, 1865–1919*, Lawrence: University of Kansas Press.

Komlos, J. (1983), *The Habsburg monarchy as a customs union*, Princeton: Princeton University Press.

Laidler, D. (1991), *The golden age of the quantity theory*, London: Philip Allan.

Lampe, J.R. and Jackson, M.R. (1982), *Balkan economic history, 1550–1950*, Bloomington: Indiana University Press.

Landau, Z. and Tomaszewski, Z. (1985), *The Polish economy in the twentieth century*, London: Croom Helm.

Laughlin, J.L. (1918), *Credit of the nations: a study of the European War*, New York: Charles Scribner's Sons.

Lawrence, J. (1997), 'Material pressures on the middle classes', in J. Winter and J.-L. Robert (eds), *Capital cities at war: Paris, London, Berlin 1914–1919*, Cambridge: Cambridge University Press.

Lawrence, J., Dean, M. and Robert, J.-L. (1992), 'The outbreak of war and the urban economy: Paris, Berlin, and London in 1914', *Economic History Review*, 45.

League of Nations (1945), *The League of Nations reconstruction schemes in the inter-war period*, Geneva: League of Nations.

Lee, J. (1975), 'Administrators and agriculture: aspects of German agricultural policy in the First World War', in J.M. Winter (ed.), *War and economic development*, Cambridge: Cambridge University Press.

Lih, L.T. (1990), *Bread and authority in Russia, 1914–1921*, Berkeley: University of California Press.

Lindert, P.H. (2000), 'Three centuries of inequality in Britain and America', in A.B. Atkinson and F. Bourguignon (eds), *Handbook of income distribution*, Amsterdam: Elsevier, vol. 1.

Livi Bacci, M. (2000), *The population of Europe*, Oxford: Blackwell.

Macdonald, L. (1993), *The roses of no man's land*, Harmondsworth: Penguin.

Maddison, A. (1991), *Dynamic forces in capitalist development*, Oxford: Oxford University Press.

Maddison, A. (1995), *Monitoring the world economy 1820–1992*, Paris: OECD.

Maier, C.S. (1975), *Recasting bourgeois Europe: stabilization in France, Germany, and Italy in the decade after World War I*, Princeton: Princeton University Press.

Makinen, G.E. and Woodward, G.T. (1990), 'Funding crises in the aftermath of World War I', in R. Dornbusch and M. Draghi (eds), *Public debt management: theory and history*, Cambridge: Cambridge University Press.

Manning, J. (1997), 'Wages and purchasing power', in J. Winter and J.-L. Robert (eds), *Capital cities at war: Paris, London, Berlin 1914–1919*, Cambridge: Cambridge University Press.

Marks, S. (1981), *Innocent abroad: Belgium at the Paris Peace Conference of 1919*, Chapel Hill: University of North Carolina Press.

Marrison, A. (2000), 'Legacy – war, aftermath and the end of the nineteenth-century liberal trading order, 1914–32', in C. Wrigley (ed.), *The First World War and the international economy*, Cheltenham, UK and Northampton, MA, USA: Edward Elgar.

McNeill, W.H. (1979), *Plagues and peoples*, Harmondsworth: Penguin.

McPhail, H. (1999), *The long silence: civilian life under the German occupation of northern France, 1914–1918*, London: Tauris.

Mills, T.C. (2000), 'Recent developments in modelling trends and cycles in economic time series and their relevance to quantitative economic history', in C. Wrigley (ed.), *The First World War and the international economy*, Cheltenham, UK and Northampton, MA, USA: Edward Elgar.

Mitchell, B.R. (1998a), *International historical statistics: Europe, 1750–1993*, London: Macmillan.

Mitchell, B.R. (1998b), *International historical statistics: the Americas, 1750–1993*, London: Macmillan.

Moggridge, D.E. (1992), *Maynard Keynes: an economist's biography*, London: Routledge.

Morrison, C. (2000), 'Historical perspectives on income distribution: the case of Europe', in A.B. Atkinson and F. Bourguignon (eds), *Handbook of income distribution*, Amsterdam: Elsevier, vol. 1.

Mottram, R.H. (1929), 'A personal record', in R.H. Mottram, J. Easton and E. Partridge, *Three personal experiences of the war*, London: Scholartis.

Moulton, H.G. and Pasvolsky, L. (1932), *War debts and world prosperity*, New York: Century.

Mouré, K. (2002), *The gold standard illusion: France, the Bank of France, and the international gold standard, 1914–1939*, New York: Oxford University Press.

Munting, R. and Holderness, B.A. (1991), *Crisis, recovery and war: an economic history of continental Europe 1918–1945*, Hemel Hempstead: Philip Allan.

Notel, R. (1986), 'International credit and finance', in M.C. Kaser and E.A. Radice (eds), *The economic history of Eastern Europe, 1919–1975*, Oxford: Clarendon Press, vol. 2.

Notestein, F.W. et al. (1944), *The future population of Europe and the Soviet Union*, Geneva: League of Nations.

Offer, A. (1989), *The First World War: an agrarian interpretation*, Oxford: Clarendon Press.

Offer, A. (1993), 'The British Empire, 1870–1914: a waste of money?', *Economic History Review*, 46.

Offer, A. (1996), 'Introduction', in A. Offer (ed.), *In pursuit of the quality of life*, Oxford: Oxford University Press.

Osuntokun, A. (1979), *Nigeria in the First World War*, London: Longman.

Pigou, A.C. (1921), *The political economy of war*, London: Macmillan.

Piketty, T. (2003), 'Income inequality in France, 1901–1998' *Journal of Political Economy*, 111.

Piketty, T. and Saez, E. (2003), 'Income inequality in the United States, 1913–1998', *Quarterly Journal of Economics*, 118.

Pollard, S. (1970), 'Introduction', in S. Pollard (ed.), *The gold standard and employment policies between the wars*, London: Methuen.

Remarque, E.M. (1929), *All quiet on the Western Front*, London: Putnam.

Robson, M. (1988), 'The British pharmaceutical industry and the First World War', in J. Liebenau (ed.), *The challenge of new technology: innovation in British business*, Aldershot: Gower.

Rotte, R. (1997), 'Economics and peace-theory on the eve of World War I', in J. Brauer and W.G. Gissy (eds), *Economics of conflict and peace*, Aldershot: Avebury.

Salter, W.A. (1921), *Allied shipping control*, Oxford: Clarendon Press.

Sargent, T.J. (1982), 'The ends of four big inflations', in R.E. Hall (ed.), *Inflation: causes and effects*, Chicago: University of Chicago Press.

Schuker, S.A. (1988), 'American "reparations" to Germany, 1919–33', Princeton Studies in International Finance, 61.

Schuker, S.A. (1993), 'Origins of American stabilization policy in Europe: the financial dimension, 1918–1924', in H.-J. Schroder (ed.), *Confrontation and cooperation: Germany and the United States in the era of World War I, 1900–1924*, Oxford: Berg.

Sharp, A. (1991), *The Versailles settlement*, New York: St Martin's.

Silverman, D.P. (1982), *Reconstructing Europe after the Great War*, Cambridge MA: Harvard University Press.

Singleton, J. (1993), 'Britain's military use of horses 1914–1918', *Past & Present*, 139.

Singleton, J. (1994), 'The cotton industry and the British war effort, 1914–1918', *Economic History Review*, 47.

Singleton, J. (1998), 'The tank producers: British mechanical engineering in the Great War', *Journal of Industrial History*, 1.

Smith, L.V. (2000), 'Narrative and identity at the front: "Theory and the poor bloody infantry"' in J. Winter, G. Parker and M.R. Halbeck (eds), *The Great War and the twentieth century*, New Haven: Yale University Press.

Sommariva, A. and Tullio, G. (1987), *German macroeconomic history, 1880–1979*, New York: St Martin's.

Stevenson, D. (1996), *Armaments and the coming of war: Europe 1904–1914*, Oxford: Clarendon Press.

Stewart, F. (1996), 'Basic needs, capabilities, and human development', in A. Offer (ed.), *In pursuit of the quality of life*, Oxford: Oxford University Press.

Stolper, W.F. (1994), *Joseph Alois Schumpeter*, Princeton: Princeton University Press.

Strachan, H. (2004), *Financing the First World War*, Oxford: Oxford University Press.

Sturmey, S.G. (1962), *British shipping and world competition*, London: Athlone.

Teichova, A. (1985), 'Industry', in M.C. Kaser and E.A. Radice (eds), *The economic history of Eastern Europe, 1919–1975*, Oxford: Clarendon Press, vol. 1.

Von Mises, L. (1983), *Nation, state, and economy*, New York: New York University Press.

Voth, H.-J. (2000), 'German banking and the impact of the First World War', in C. Wrigley (ed.), *The First World War and the international economy*, Cheltenham, UK and Northampton, MA, USA: Edward Elgar.

Webster, D. (1994), 'The soldiers moved on. The war moved on. The bombs stayed', *Smithsonian*, 24.

Westwood, J.N. (1964), *A history of Russian railways*, London: Allen & Unwin.

Wheatcroft, S.G. and Davies, R.W. (1994), 'Population', in R.W. Davies, M. Harrison and S.G. Wheatcroft (eds), *The economic transformation of the Soviet Union, 1913–1945*, Cambridge: Cambridge University Press.

White, E.N. (2001), 'Making the French pay: the costs and consequences of the Napoleonic reparations', *European Review of Economic History*, 5.

Williams, M.E.W. (1994), *The precision makers: a history of the instruments industry in Britain and France, 1870–1939*, London: Routledge.

Winter, J. (1985), *The Great War and the British people*, Basingstoke: Macmillan.

Winter, J. (1988), 'Some paradoxes of the First World War', in R. Wall and J. Winter (ed.), *The upheaval of war: family, work and welfare in Europe, 1914–1918*, Cambridge: Cambridge University Press.

Winter, J, (1995), *Sites of memory, sites of mourning: the Great War in European cultural history*, Cambridge: Cambridge University Press.

Winter, J. (1997), 'Surviving the war: life expectation, illness, and mortality rates in Paris, London, and Berlin, 1914–1919', in J. Winter and J.-L. Robert (eds), *Capital cities at war: Paris, London, Berlin 1914–1919*, Cambridge: Cambridge University Press.

Winter, J. and Robert, J.-L. (eds) (1997), *Capital cities at war: Paris, London, Berlin 1914–1919*, Cambridge: Cambridge University Press.

Wrigley, C. (2000a), 'The war and the international economy', in C. Wrigley (ed.), *The First World War and the international economy*, Cheltenham, UK and Northampton, MA, USA: Edward Elgar.

Wrigley, C. (2000b), 'Organized labour and the international economy', in C. Wrigley (ed.), *The First World War and the international economy*, Cheltenham, UK and Northampton, MA, USA: Edward Elgar.

Yapp, M.E. (1987), *The making of the modern Middle East 1792–1923*, London: Longman.

Zamagni, V. (1993), *The economic history of Italy, 1860–1990*, Oxford: Clarendon Press.

2.   The Great Depression, 1929–33

W.R. Garside

The Great Depression of 1929–33 was such a major disruption to the stability and functioning of the principal industrial nations of the world and of the primary producing countries in their ambit that few observers of the twentieth century, be they economists, historians, political scientists or sociologists, can ignore it. The Depression spread worldwide though at an uneven pace. Quantitatively its effects were greatest in the United States where output during the period fell by 28 per cent and gross national product declined by around 10 per cent in real terms for three years running from 1930. In Europe, by contrast, output fell by 7 per cent overall, with falls of 15 per cent in Germany, almost as much in France though with lagged effects, and 5 per cent in the United Kingdom (Dow 2000, 157, 293). At its lowest point the economic collapse saw European trade fall to one-third of its 1929 value (Clavin 2000, 1).

It is the spectre of large-scale unemployment, however, that dominates images of the Great Depression. Even allowing for the uncertainty in international comparative unemployment data, the record is stark enough. In 1932 industrial unemployment averaged 36 per cent in the United States, 31 per cent in Denmark, 22 per cent in the United Kingdom and Sweden, 28 per cent in Australia and over 43 per cent in Germany. At its height in 1933 some six million people were registered unemployed in Germany and over 12 million in the United States (James 2002, 168). Although direct comparisons are difficult for those in countries less dependent upon industry, such as Poland, Bulgaria, Rumania and Czechoslovakia, theirs was a tail-spin experience of tumbling prices, high costs and indebtedness, rural over-population and restricted opportunities for emigration, with all the attendant hardships such circumstances implied.

Some indication of the comparative scale of industrial unemployment amongst the principal industrial nations during the interwar period is given in Table 2.1 to illustrate the magnitude and distinctiveness of the 1929–33 experience compared with the previous decade. The time series pattern of unemployment shows stable and relatively low unemployment in the 1920s followed by deep depression and then strong recovery in the United States, Canada and Australia. In Norway, the United Kingdom

Table 2.1 *Unemployment rates in industry for selected countries, 1920–39 (%)*

Year	Australia	Belgium	Canada	Denmark	France	Germany	Netherlands	Norway	Sweden	UK	US
1920	5.5	–	4.6	6.1	–	3.8	5.8	2.3	5.4	3.2	8.6
1921	10.4	9.7	8.9	19.7	5.0	2.8	9.0	17.7	26.6	17.0	19.5
1922	8.5	3.1	7.1	19.3	2.0	1.5	11.0	17.1	22.9	14.3	11.4
1923	6.2	1.0	4.9	12.7	2.0	10.2	11.2	10.7	12.5	11.7	4.1
1924	7.8	1.0	7.1	10.7	3.0	13.1	8.8	8.5	10.1	10.3	8.3
1925	7.8	1.5	7.0	14.7	3.0	6.8	8.1	13.2	11.0	11.3	5.4
1926	6.3	1.4	4.7	20.7	3.0	18.0	7.3	24.3	12.2	12.5	2.9
1927	6.2	1.8	2.9	22.5	11.0	8.8	7.5	25.4	12.0	9.7	5.4
1928	10.0	0.9	2.6	18.5	4.0	8.6	5.6	19.2	10.6	10.8	6.9
1929	10.2	1.3	4.2	15.5	1.0	13.3	2.9	15.4	10.2	10.4	5.3
1930	18.4	3.6	12.9	13.7	2.0	22.7	7.8	16.6	11.9	16.1	14.2
1931	26.5	10.9	17.4	17.9	6.5	34.3	14.8	22.3	16.8	21.3	25.2
1932	28.1	19.0	26.0	31.7	15.4	43.5	25.3	30.8	22.4	22.1	36.3
1933	24.2	16.9	26.6	28.8	14.1	36.2	26.9	33.4	23.2	19.9	37.6
1934	19.6	18.9	20.6	22.2	13.8	20.5	28.0	30.7	18.0	16.7	32.6
1935	15.6	17.8	19.1	19.7	14.5	16.2	31.7	25.3	15.0	15.5	30.2
1936	11.3	13.5	16.7	19.3	10.4	12.0	32.7	18.8	12.7	13.1	25.4
1937	8.4	11.5	12.5	21.9	7.4	6.9	26.9	20.0	10.8	10.8	21.3
1938	7.8	14.0	15.1	21.5	7.8	3.2	25.0	22.0	10.9	12.9	27.9
1939	8.8	15.9	14.1	18.4	8.1	0.9	19.9	18.3	9.2	10.5	25.2

Sources: Galenson and Zellner (1957, 455); Lebergott (1964, 512). The data are drawn from a variety of sources in each country varying from trade union reports, the operations of public agencies and private bodies and census statistics. For further discussion, including possible sources of bias and of over- and under-representation, see Eichengreen and Hatton (1988, 1–59).

and, to a lesser extent, in Sweden, a cyclical pattern was superimposed on an upward trend over the entire two decades. In France, Belgium and the Netherlands, unemployment, having been steady in the 1920s, rose to persistently higher levels after 1930. Germany was distinct in the sharp peak and dramatic fall of unemployment in the 1930s (Eichengreen and Hatton 1988, 11–14).

SEARCHING FOR STABILITY: THE GOLD STANDARD REGIMES OF THE 1920s

The origins of the global economic crisis of the early 1930s are often seen as a direct consequence of the First World War, which had imposed a major disruption to the financial and trading stability of Europe. Faced with deep uncertainty and with an ingrained fear of inflation and currency instability many countries sought in its wake to resurrect something of their previous financial and economic practices, almost in the belief that by doing so they would recover normality. Although much has been written about the symbolism of the Wall Street Crash in reflecting the important part American consumption, investment and national financial policy played in triggering the Great Depression, attention in recent years has focused more upon the endemic manner by which the restoration of the gold standard from the mid-1920s and the policy regimes that emerged as a consequence became the mechanism by which cyclical depression was transmitted worldwide (Choudhri and Kochin 1980; Temin 1989; Bernanke and James 1991; Eichengreen 1992a; Bernanke 1995).

In the wake of the destruction of trade and finance evoked by the First World War many countries hankered after the internationalization that they believed had underpinned the global economic stability of the late nineteenth-century industrialized world. Such a regime, it was believed, would resurrect a market-driven world, the free flow of goods, capital and people, and with it the security enjoyed before 1914 (James 2002). The restoration of currencies to a fixed exchange rate based on gold was critical to this endeavour. To Edwardian observers the gold standard represented the bedrock of stability. It was customarily thought, more as an article of faith than as an established fact, that the free movement of gold occasioned self-adjusting balance of payments equilibria. According to classical thinking any differences in foreign receipts and payments would induce changes in a country's stock of gold, thereby forcing an adjustment in monetary circulation. This would be sufficient through its effects on prices and incomes to alter the demand for imports and exports in the direction required to correct the balance of trade.

In truth, the success of the gold standard before 1914 had depended upon a number of fortuitous circumstances. These included the absence of divergent movements in imports, exports and interest rates and a marked degree of economic stability and price flexibility within the major industrialized nations, which had prevented serious disequilibrium within the international payments system. But when the dislocations of war and the pains of reconstruction appeared to threaten the viability of both the national and international economic order, it became the prime objective of many nations to seek the restoration of normality under a restored gold standard as soon as conditions would allow.

Most countries had emerged from war with their current account situations in disarray and were desperate for capital for reconstruction. The war had weakened Europe's capacity to export at the same time as international competition increased. As early as 1922 it was agreed at a conference in Genoa that trade expansion and the stabilization of currencies would best be achieved by resurrecting an international payments system based on a gold exchange standard (Boyce 1987). This was expected to provide an anchor between the extremes of inflation and deflation. Independent central banks would provide the institutional framework around which monetary policy would be framed according to the needs of the international economy. Pegged exchange rates, in other words, offered the prospect of debtor countries receiving transfers of financial resources, primarily from America. There investors would have less fear of exchange rate instability or reckless fiscal policies given that the external constraints of a fixed parity would impose fiscal orthodoxy and balanced budgets upon national governments (James 2001, 34–5).

The economic and financial stability allegedly provided by the gold exchange standard was expected to permit large international capital flows to develop between nations. That certainly happened. Capital flows of between $9 billion and $11 billion dollars occurred between 1924 and 1930 from the United Kingdom and France, but especially the United States. At the same time as lending in the form of long-term capital bonds was developing, major foreign inflows of short-term capital went to Germany, Britain and the United States from economically turbulent European countries and from Latin America (James 2002, 48–50).

The controlled monetary and fiscal policy expected under the gold standard regime was always going to be problematic when most industrialized countries were massively burdened with public debt as a consequence of financing the First World War. By the end of the hostilities the Russian Empire's public debt had increased by a factor of four, Italy's and France's by five, Germany's by eight, Britain's by 11 and the United States' by 19. (James 2001, 37). Nonetheless, economic adjustment in Britain, Italy,

France and Germany in the early 1920s was centred upon restoring fixed exchange parities. In Britain the Committee on Currency and Foreign Exchanges after the War (the Cunliffe Committee) argued in 1918 that the country should embark upon deflation in order to reduce prices towards US levels to enable a swift return to gold, advice that was slavishly followed down to 1925 (Parliament 1918, Cd. 9182). The Italians likewise prescribed deflation and reduced government expenditure. France, on the other hand, resisted cutting public expenditure and balancing the budget, normal pre-conditions for returning to gold, in order not to undermine its claim that German reparations were required to help finance the reconstruction of the French economy. As a consequence, France suffered high inflation and a rapidly depreciating currency, which served only to emphasize that the franc could only be stabilized ultimately by restoring the gold standard. In Germany there was a fear that stabilizing the currency and balancing the budget might be seen to reflect such financial probity that outsiders could consider the country better able to meet its reparations obligations than was customarily believed. Germany resorted instead to money creation but this merely fuelled inflation, wrecked consumer confidence, increased uncertainty and ensured a decline in industrial production. By 1924, stability was acknowledged to depend upon restoring the mark to its pre-war parity (Eichengreen and Temin 2000, 190–91).

Although the fixed exchange rates and adherence to the rules of classical orthodoxy to which the gold standard gave rise offered hope of a self-regulating mechanism to safeguard balance of payments and currency stability, it also imparted a deflationary bias to national economic policies. Governments routinely sought to maintain high interest rates and a tight fiscal stance for fear of losing reserves. Unilateral reflation was inhibited so long as fixed parities were in place. Any nation undertaking such action was likely to suffer rising imports, capital outflows, a loss of reserves, and an assault on its exchange rate. Outside of abandoning gold, a measure of internationally coordinated reflation would have been required to prevent a single country suffering the consequences of relaxing the external constraint (Eichengreen 1991, 1992b). Although the international monetary system provided arrangements for formal exchange rate management, it permitted a considerable degree of national autonomy in the conduct of policy. This put a premium on international policy coordination without providing any mechanism for bringing it about (Eichengreen and Sachs 1985).

Countries with low reserves were constrained by the obligations of the gold standard to follow movements in US interest rates if they were to preserve fixed exchange rates. The discipline of gold was seen, however, as an effective bulwark against inflation, the scourge of which had wreaked such havoc in post-war Germany. But the adjustment difficulties posed by stabilizing currencies at a fixed parity with gold were rarely considered in advance; they became apparent only in the aftermath. The gold standard was regarded as an externally imposed source of stabilization, providing constraints on the operation of sovereign monetary and financial policies. Thus reassured, South Africa and Britain returned to the gold standard in May 1925, Belgium in October 1925, Denmark and Italy in 1926 and France in 1928. By the end of that year the gold exchange standard had been adopted in 31 countries.

Britain's desire to restore its financial power and with it the strength of the City of London led it in 1925 to stabilize sterling at its pre-war parity of $4.86. This is generally recognized to have imposed upon the country a regime of high interest rates and worsening unemployment, given that sterling was overvalued by some 10 per cent. France, by contrast, avoided any risk of damaging industry, commerce and farming by choosing at the end of 1926 to peg the franc to gold at an exchange rate some 80 per cent lower than it had been in 1914. Belgium likewise stabilized below its pre-war parity in 1926 (Clavin 2000, 54–5). The stability of trade patterns and the viability of the gold standard in the later 1920s were directly influenced by the fact that Britain, Denmark, Norway and Italy stabilized their currencies on gold at an overvalued rate whilst France, Belgium and the United States undervalued theirs, thereby gaining an export advantage. Not that reduced exchange rates were necessarily easy to impose or live with. The experience of countries in Central and Eastern Europe (Czechoslovakia apart) show how Hungary, Poland and Rumania had to struggle against severe inflationary pressures and political turmoil before they were able to stabilize their currencies at a devalued rate. Without large gold reserves or a recovery in trade few such countries could protect their newly stabilized currencies save by imposing deflationary policies. Where currencies were overvalued in the wake of return to gold, as in Britain and Italy, governments had to adjust their prices and wages downwards to support their fixed parities, given that few governments were willing to contemplate a depreciation of their currency (Garside 1990; Boyce 1987).

Despite these strictures, it was the more fundamental weaknesses of the restored gold standard that were to have longer-term implications. Countries were limited in their capacity to embark upon expansionary policy. National and European economies were now more interconnected. It was open to particular countries to violate the rules of the game. Gold reserves were in short supply. Such factors proved to have a profound impact upon the transmission of economic depression internationally after 1929.

Although central banks were meant to control international monetary policy autonomously and thereby sustain confidence, they found their options limited. In many countries the enduring fear of inflation prevented such banks from influencing liquidity through the buying or selling of securities. Raising interest rates merely encouraged the flow of 'hot money' in search of immediate returns, thereby risking further financial instability. In the face of such limited orthodox control, commercial banking outside the United States grew vigorously during the 1920s as American capital exports and overseas bank deposits rose. Central bankers became increasingly concerned that the ideals of stabilization and reconstruction were giving way to financial disorder.

To make matters worse neither the French nor the American central banks behaved in a way supportive of the fixed-exchange system. France and the United States between them hoarded more than half of the world's total gold supply. Although most gold standard countries had to engage in restrictive fiscal policies to sustain the system, there was no obligation on the United States to counteract economic contraction by adopting expansionary policies. From 1928 the United States grew concerned over inflationary speculation in financial markets and began to tighten its monetary policy. With the American government and the Federal Reserve Board insistent on the preservation of price stability, pressure was transmitted to debtors abroad who were forced to deflate their economies. America refused to increase its money supply fearing that any resulting inflation would overstimulate economic activity by relieving the internal burden of debt. The French paid no heed to the sanctity of the parity, returning to gold in 1928 at one-fifth of the pre-war level. America and France, therefore, continued to enjoy the benefits of gold inflows but continued to violate the principles of the gold standard by refusing to lower interest rates or engage in open market operations to encourage gold to flow out again. They chose instead to hoard gold to protect their internal price levels, making conditions difficult both for countries with overvalued currencies based on gold and for those already short of gold (Aldcroft 1977; Clavin 2000, 62–3). The deliberate pursuit of such policies imposed deflationary pressures on the world economy, and especially on those countries with weak currencies (Eichengreen 1990, 246).

The drain on the national reserves of gold and foreign exchange in those European countries where investors feverishly sought French francs or US dollars made rising interest rates almost inevitable, with direct repercussions upon domestic investment and unemployment. Many countries in Central, Eastern and South Eastern Europe had only been able to sustain their gold standard obligations because of access to credit from the United States and Britain. Such credit enabled them to run current account deficits without having repeatedly to raise interest rates and impose deflationary policies. Once the operation of the gold standard came under severe pressure after 1928 the willingness of the principal central banks to continue to extend credit to countries carrying budget deficits withered. European banks were unwilling to stimulate domestic investment or to relieve debt burdens by lowering interest rates. That would have posed a direct threat to the gold standard by encouraging further gold outflows to France or America where interest rates were higher (Clavin 2000, 65–70, 98–9).

ON THE PRECIPICE: THE INTERNATIONAL ECONOMIC ORDER IN 1929–30

The complex network of loans and debts that had emerged in the 1920s fostered a measurable if patchy degree of growth and prosperity. European industrial production had risen 23 per cent beyond its 1925 level by 1929. Although economic growth was fairly rapid in Belgium, France and Sweden it was rather modest in Britain, Norway, Greece, Denmark and Austria. Europe by 1929 had even failed to raise its volume of trade to what it had been in 1913. International economic progress rested to a dangerous degree upon the continued economic health and largesse of the United States. The fundamental sources of disequilibrium had yet to become fully apparent. Whereas agricultural depression and the trading difficulties of heavy industry were common concerns within Europe, it was the excessive levels of international indebtedness that proved particularly worrying and ultimately most damaging.

European countries that had become overly dependent upon American credit to prop up their economies and balance of payments found the US authorities by 1929 preoccupied with national economic survival. The excessive speculative demand that had developed during the boom of the preceding years, fuelled by the confidence of consumers and firms that growth would continue, was checked in 1929, with the Wall Street Crash in October its most potent symbol. The decision by the Federal Reserve Board in August 1929 to raise the American discount rate to curb speculative fever had a dramatic effect in dampening the expectations of consumers and businesses at home. American investors by late 1929, moreover, were beginning to fear that tariffs, initially introduced to support agriculture, might give rise to ever-increasing protection at a time when consumer confidence and spending were already falling. Faced with a sudden loss of confidence, share prices fell by about 20 per cent between 1929 and 1930 as investment fell.

The 150 base point rise in US interest rates in 1928–29 plunged the world into recession by precipitating dramatic monetary contraction in those countries that had pyramided a large volume of liabilities upon a narrow base of reserves (Eichengreen 2002). When higher US interest rates made foreign investment less attractive, capital importing countries abroad developed serious balance of payments problems and were forced to tighten monetary policy. Faced with financial uncertainty a scramble broke out for the limited supplies of gold. Central banks in Germany, Italy and Britain raised bank rates in an effort to repatriate the much needed foreign investment upon which they had become so dependent. This merely exacerbated deflationary pressure within Europe. Unfortunately neither France nor, importantly, America, felt obliged to put the concerns of international finance above considerations of domestic economic stability. Hoover made a small concession by instituting a moratorium on the debt service of war debts but only for a short period. Although the Depression only struck France late in 1930 it immediately threatened to create demand for cheap money and reflation. Defence of the franc remained paramount within official circles and high interest rates were set to protect gold reserves, even if they discouraged investment and intensified deflation.

Policy-makers adhered to deflationary actions because defence of the global standard was integral to the ideology of central bankers and politicians both in Europe and the United States. The stability of the economy and of the exchange rate was assumed by bankers and politicians to be symbiotically intertwined. It proved easy for representatives of each group to rationalize their actions. It was not the duty of central banks to manipulate interest rates to influence economic prosperity. Their obligation was to protect parities by enforcing price and wage reductions where necessary in order to maintain the gold standard. This, they believed, would in turn restore and sustain employment.

Initially at least, governments were reluctant to raise taxes or to cut benefits to the increasing numbers of the unemployed purely for the sake of balancing their budgets. Raising interest rates and cutting relief expenditure threatened hunger marches, demonstrations and debt instability. Explanations of the Great Depression, therefore, that emphasize the shocks and structural developments of the 1920s alone pay insufficient attention to the policy choices that governments and central banks felt obliged to make in defence of a gold standard ideology. This dictated deflation, wage cuts and rising unemployment as a response to economic contraction. It was the gold standard, therefore, that ensured that the many contributing factors affecting the origins and course of the Depression were brought into an essential unity (Eichengreen and Temin 2000, 183–6). With supplies of money and credit dependent upon the quantity of gold and convertible foreign exchange held by central banks, the gold standard became the mechanism for spreading and deepening depression. In their efforts to obtain and retain gold reserves, central banks raised interest rates, destabilized commercial banks and depressed production and employment (Eichengreen 1992b).

The essential problem was that the gold standard was a gold exchange standard, with central banks holding reserves partly in gold and partly in foreign exchange. Countries losing gold because of deficits, for example, had little choice but to contract their money stock. But countries gaining reserves, such as the United States and France, could and did sterilize the inflow of gold, forcing the world money stock to decline. The corollary was that countries on gold could not expand their money supply to stimulate domestic demand for fear of raising prices, encouraging gold exports and weakening their currency.

With devaluation ruled out often on political as well as economic grounds the swiftest way to reduce prices in defence of a currency's parity was to attack labour costs. But the growth of trade unionism and institutionalized collective bargaining covering large numbers of workers preoccupied with relative wages (and often unwilling thereby to make the first concession toward adjustment) prevented wages being flexible enough to reduce costs to levels sufficient to restore external balance (Eichengreen and Temin 2000, 193–4). Few countries were able to impose any general reduction in costs (the exception being Germany where nominal hourly wages and earnings had risen substantially between 1925 and 1929 without any matching productivity gains). Most costs other than wages such as rents and mortgage payments were fixed for long periods and governments were generally reluctant to impose a general round of price reductions. In America, Hoover had preached that cutting wages in response to falling demand merely damaged consumer purchasing power and could only intensify the Depression. Resort to industrial rationalization, a means of squeezing out inefficiency and reducing prices, was an alternative approach. But it was a very problematic route. It depended on employer cooperation, a sound judgement of the anticipated links between reduced capacity and competitiveness and a willingness to await uncertain results. The option proved illusory (Garside and Greaves 1997).

The Depression in Germany graphically illustrated the emerging difficulties within the international economy. Germany had benefited from rising gross national product between 1925 and 1928, supported by a huge inflow of foreign investment during the second half of the 1920s, largely from the United States and most of it short-term. But little of the capital had been used for industrial rationalization or for raising productivity. When interest rates began to rise in America in 1928 in order to dampen speculation, Germany followed suit to lessen pressure on exchange reserves and to avoid devaluation. The official discount rate in October 1928 was 2 per cent higher at 7 per cent than it had been in early 1927. Output and investment began to decline. Businesses at home faced contemporaneous tax increases at the same time as existing tax concessions to foreign investors were being removed. Deficits appeared at state, regional and municipal levels. Although the reinstatement of tax concessions led to the renewal of foreign loans, they tended to be on a short-term basis offering only a temporary respite to Germany's deteriorating economic situation (James 2001). Germany's problems were those of Europe writ large. Foreign capital investment in Europe fell by over 1.2 billion dollars between 1928 and 1930 (Clavin 2000, 94).

With domestic economic policy sacrificed on a cross of gold European governments remained reluctant to jeopardize the credibility of their fixed exchange rates by engaging in reflationary policies to raise employment and consumption. Instigating public works in the face of mounting unemployment threatened budgetary stability. Collective memory of the inflations of the 1920s made politicians fearful of budget deficits. This made 'any kind of monetary and fiscal experimentation. . .politically, technically and psychologically very difficult, if not impossible' (Clavin 2000, 35). Discretionary monetary policy in France before 1927, for example, had prompted inflationary credit creation, predisposing officials to view monetary expansion as the route to financial and political chaos. German memories of inflation were, of course, more pronounced and haunted the policy-makers' psyche even in the midst of the Depression.

Expansionary policies were certainly debated. In Britain, Keynes had called as early as 1924 for coordinated action to distribute the flow of current savings towards schemes of national reconstruction in aid of the unemployed. The call was taken up by the Liberals in 1929 who deployed a crude multiplier analysis to argue for a deliberate unbalancing of the budget to stimulate purchasing power and employment. This 'radical alternative' served only to stiffen orthodoxy within the British establishment, not only because it upset the principle of minimum state interference within the economy, but also because it posed a threat to balanced budgets and London's already precarious international financial standing. It was far better to contain unemployment with a flexible system of insurance and discriminatory policies in favour of particular industries and regions than it was to tread the suspect path of deficit finance with all its attendant risks of inflation and balance of payments crises. This pragmatic approach was symptomatic less of a blatant denial of responsibility than it was of a deep-seated desire not to disturb capitalism's struggle for stability and survival. A consistent and deliberate absence of policy along radical lines, in other words, was itself a purposeful policy (Garside 1987).

Towards the end of the 1920s the French and Belgian authorities undertook an inventory of public works in an effort to increase the employment of unskilled workers, but by 1932 French Premier, Pierre Laval, was telling the National Assembly that although 'the government will never refuse to go as far as the resources of the country will permit' they should 'not ask it to commit acts that would unbalance the budget' (quoted in Garraty 1978, 207). Work creation was not directly discussed within the German cabinet before 1931. By deliberately deepening the crisis, the German government hoped to convince the Western powers that the schedule of reparations payments under which the country laboured was unviable from an economic and financial point of view. Thus the dismissal of work-creation programmes and the rigid adherence to balanced budgets were a product of both economic and foreign policy imperatives. Even so, the radical alternative of an active business cycle policy had been advocated by economists at the Institut für Konjunkturforschunin in the early 1930s. The German Trade Union Federation (ADGB) likewise called in 1932 for the immediate employment of one million workers over a one-year period on government-sponsored projects financed by long-term credits to the value of two billion reichsmarks. But neither pressure group managed to overcome the fear of German administrators that direct intervention to manage capitalism would destroy stability (Garside 1987).

The decline in trade and its impact on incomes and prices were equally effective in paralysing governments, enabling the transmission of depression via the gold standard to occur so virulently. Before 1914 the international economy had been integrated by the mobility of capital goods and people but the system came under severe strain during the post-war years. The growth of self-sufficiency, import substitution, technological change and the rise of tariff protection had severely reduced the opportunities of established manufacturing countries to secure anything like their pre-war shares of export markets. Caught between the twin blades of declining complementarity and rising competitiveness, many nations found previous export markets either more self-sufficient than in the past or supplied by nations such as the United States and Japan, which had earlier stolen a competitive march on those countries preoccupied with war. Protectionism and cartelization seemed obvious responses to falling commodity prices. But declining export demand made the financing of imports difficult. This reduced the demand for the products of primary producing countries, which were themselves suffering from falling prices and profits because of surplus production. Although foreign borrowing from the United States offered some immediate help, it merely increased levels of international indebtedness as countries, unable to earn the foreign exchange to pay previous debts, began to rely on capital imports to bolster weak balance of payments.

Some idea of the impact of the Depression in the United States on the rest of the world can be gained from Table 2.2. It offers a stylized indication of the reactions of a three-bloc trading system comprising the United States (US), Europe (EU) and the primary producing countries (PP),

Table 2.2   The pattern of world trade in 1929

	Trade to*				
	United States (US)	Europe (EU)	Primary producers (PP) ($ bn)	Total	Total excluding intra-trade
Trade from:					
US		2.5	2.8	5.3	5.3
EU	1.2	(10.5)	4.2	15.9	5.4
PP	2.8	5.4	(3.2)	11.4	8.2
Total	4.0	18.4	10.2	33.6	
Total excl. intra-trade	4.0	7.9	7.2		19.1

Note: * The value of the same trade flow is recorded differently by the exporting and importing countries. The differences arise because imports are recorded inclusive of carriage and insurance, which typically adds about 9 per cent to the value; and because of difference of timing and errors and omissions in the recording. Since the differences are not large enough to affect the argument, a simple average of two valuations is drawn.

Source: Dow (2000, 223).

defined as countries other than the United States and Europe. Over half of the United States' exports in 1929 were to the primary producing countries, with a third of its imports coming from them. Even US imports from the primary producers were significant, amounting to over one-third of primary producers' exports outside the area (Dow 2000).

By 1930 gross domestic product in the United States had fallen by 9 per cent. Over the period of the Depression, total US imports fell in volume by a third and in value by twice as much (Dow 2000, 159). The reduction of American imports from primary producing countries was especially serious as it prompted a substantial fall in world commodity prices and a growing inability of primary producers to service overseas debts or to buy essential products from America or Europe. This served in turn only to reduce output, imports and prices further in a vicious circle as Figure 2.1 illustrates (see Lee 1969; Dow 2000, 393).

The dramatic fall in prices of agricultural and manufactured products was not matched by any revival of international lending by wealthy nations such as Britain, the United States or France. Debtor nations in Europe suffering dramatic falls in the volume of their exports faced intensified balance of payments problems as they lost reserves from their central banks without being able to borrow as easily as they had done in the 1920s. Nations were now faced with a protracted decline in demand for all goods with most governments set against any significant relaxation of monetary

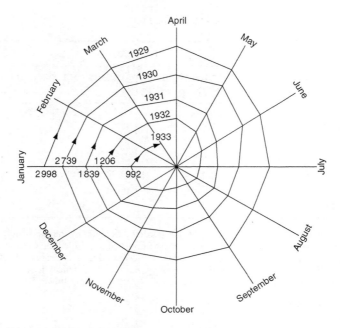

Source: Kindleberger (1973, 172).

*Figure 2.1   The contracting spiral of world trade, January 1929 to March
            1933: total imports of 75 countries (monthly values in terms of
            old US gold dollars (millions))*

policy. Fettered to gold, countries were unable to protect themselves against
the deflationary impact of restrictive monetary policy in the United States,
which had served only to induce similar restrictive monetary policies
throughout Europe. Nor did the collapse in primary producing prices
translate into a revival of demand for industrial products through a fall in
input costs. Demand in both sectors continued to decline; between 1929
and 1932 industrial output fell by one-third, with Germany, Austria,
Poland, Czechoslovakia and Yugoslavia the worst affected countries in
Europe (Clavin 2000, 108).

FINANCIAL CONTAGION AND THE EMERGENCE OF A GREAT DEPRESSION

Why was an economic recession in America transformed into a worldwide
depression? The key was the fragile operation of financial markets (James

2001, 29). Until the spring of 1931 the operation of the gold standard had obliged governments to react to declining prices and economic activity by imposing deflationary policies aimed at reducing aggregate demand and balancing the budget. This, however, had merely intensified the process of decline, allowing public policy to be a mechanism in the transmission of depression across nations. There was no consensus amongst national governments as to what appropriate domestic policy should be, except that it should externalize the adjustment costs as much as possible.

It was the financial crisis in Europe in late spring and summer of 1931 that proved to be the turning point of the Great Depression. Deflationary pressure, the deteriorating position of agriculture, the rising scale and value of indebtedness and the uncertain prospects of manufacturing industry threatened the solvency of many European banks. The collapse in Austria in May 1931 of the Creditanstalt, the country's largest bank, upon which some 60 per cent of Austrian industry was dependent, became symbolic of the difficulty banks faced in maintaining solvency in the face of continued depression. Losses of 140 million schillings were revealed. Depositors lost confidence and a run on the currency began. The Bank of England mounted a rescue operation but France, pursuing its national interest as in previous years, tried to stall two central loans organized by the Bank of International Settlements. In the end, financial aid proved to be too little and too late. To stave off economic collapse the Austrian government and the bank's creditors were left to service losses estimated at the end of 1931 to be around 923 million schillings. Increased spending on welfare and capital investments in the 1920s had already swollen the state budget; large deficits turned a financial crisis into a national emergency. The rescue of Creditanstalt alone cost around 9 per cent of Austria's GNP (James 2001, 53–6).

It was in Germany, however, that the most dramatic banking crisis occurred. Chancellor Bruning had attempted at the outset of the Depression to safeguard Germany's creditworthiness by imposing strict exchange controls and stemming any inflationary impulses. But by July 1931 it was clear that Germany's commercial banks were facing a crisis of confidence. Industrial debtors defected on their loans, which prompted German investors and companies to withdraw their money. But the seeds of decline had been sown before the Depression. Hyperinflation, political uncertainty, and a flight of domestic capital from Germany immediately after the war and during the later 1920s had increased the vulnerability of banks. By July 1931 German banks faced mounting short-term indebtedness. It was the Germans themselves, and later foreigners, who began withdrawing funds. The country was in dire need of foreign money and gold to stabilize its financial situation but although new loans became available from Britain, France and the United States in June 1931 they proved inadequate. Hoover announced a one-year truce on reparations and inter-allied debt payments in the same month. But in the absence of any more substantial help and with capital still in flight even from German nationals the Reichsbank was unable to stem the falling reserves of commercial banks (Clavin 2000, 125–7; James 2001, 60–61). Confidence and investment slumped as business and consumers anticipated further price falls in the immediate term. Germany was in a particular bind. Deflation persisted because of the important distinction at the time between a budget deficit per se and a budget deficit coupled with a chronic inability to finance it. Germany's cash reserve problem could not easily be resolved by recourse to the market via the tender of treasury bills or the issue of bonds. The country depended on recourse to the Reichsbank, which is why fiscal deflation was pushed to such severe limits. A counter-cyclical policy of reflation would have demanded a radical departure from accepted practice on the part of the central bank, necessitating a return to policies that threatened the spectre of inflation (Balderston 1982, 494–8).

The banking crises in central Europe in 1931 shattered international confidence. Capital had flowed across national frontiers, destroying already weak and vulnerable banking systems. The problems of the debtor countries spread the crisis to creditor nations. Britain and the United States were particularly vulnerable because of their substantial holdings of short-term debt, which was subject to panic withdrawal. Britain's situation provides a good example of the link between financial vulnerability, depression and the maintenance of the gold standard. Like other countries, Britain had imposed deflationary economic policies in an effort to keep the exchange rate stable but the problems of maintaining the fixed exchange rate were only part of the difficulty. The impact of financial weaknesses abroad was detailed in a Treasury memorandum on 27 July 1931 which read:

> We cannot control that we are in the midst of an unexampled slump nor the fact that Germany is bankrupt, that great assets of ours are frozen there, and that foreign nations are drawing their credits from there over our exchanges. Nor can we control the fact that foreign nations have immense sums of money in London and will try to get them away if distrust of the pound extends. . .the first thing at which foreigners look is the budgetary position. (Cited in James 2001, 70)

Britain was not faced with an intractable problem of banking but rather the freezing of assets in Central Europe. The German banking crisis had triggered a run on sterling as depositors grew fearful of mounting insolvency. Britain was finally forced to devalue in September 1931 primarily to halt even further losses of reserves given the dramatic reversal of expectations amongst investors and depositors.

Unlike small Central European or Latin American economies, America was not overly dependent on the international capital market nor did it have a major part of its assets, like Britain, invested in foreign countries. The traditional monetarist explanation of depression in America, as detailed by Freidman and Schwartz, is that the authorities failed to counter a substantial reduction in the money supply. The stock of money fell by one-third between 1929 and 1933. This (and the presumed causal direction is important to the case) invoked a fall in aggregate demand and output (Friedman and Schwartz 1963). The growth of the money supply had been checked earlier by restrictive monetary policy in 1928 and 1929 only for the economy to reel thereafter from the Wall Street Crash and a series of banking panics, first in 1930, then in late 1931, and during the winter of 1932–33. Bank failures (the number of banks in the United States declined from just over 24 000 at the end of 1929 to just fewer than 14 500 in 1933) and the public's subsequent determination to convert deposits into cash was met, not by an expansionary policy of open market operations, but by a perverse tightening of monetary policy by the Federal Reserve Board (the Fed) ensuring a deepening of depression (James 2001, 76). Moreover, many of the banks that were denied additional reserve funds from the Fed were concentrated in depressed rural and urban areas and were chronically insecure. They were unable to spread their losses and had no access to a lender of the last resort (Dow 2000, 394). Bank failures, argues Bernanke, increased the cost and availability of credit to households and firms from intermediary sources because defaults and failures increased lending risk. This merely forced additional cuts in consumption and production, thereby exacerbating depression (Bernanke 1983).

The first wave of bank failures in America during November/December 1930 and April 1931 are less significant than those that occurred after September 1931. As in Europe they were accompanied by a substantial loss of gold and by an immediate rise in interest rates. The monetarist explanation that focuses on the Fed's policy stance needs, however, to be viewed in a broader context. Members of the Fed knew little of the determinants of the money stock or the significance of the money supply. Moreover, the structure of the banking system was faulty; all banks were not required to become members of the Reserve system and many of those excluded proved to be those most in need during the Depression. What is significant in retrospect is the Fed's determination to reduce indebtedness. Rather than embark on a reflationary policy it actually reduced the money supply. Stabilization by monetary expansion (implied by Friedman and Schwartz's criticism) was ruled out by the policy-makers' fervent belief that already nervous markets would react adversely to signs of fiscal impropriety. The Fed's cautious if unhelpful policy was consistent with its previous practice and it cannot be readily assumed that, even if better quality economic intelligence had been available, the American monetary authorities would have seriously advocated a different policy.

The Fed lacked any cosmopolitan perspective on the issue of international finance and was unable to provide any leadership to central banks abroad. America was troubled less by an external current account problem than by the vulnerability of US banks to capital movements elsewhere. Whilst it is true that under Hoover the United States had engaged in expansionary fiscal spending, by the end of 1931 priorities had altered. Sustaining bond prices by cutting spending and the federal deficit were seen as the first steps in tackling depression. Foreign investors focused less on America's bank failures than Congress's failure to balance the budget and to embark upon the deflationary policies that Europe had undertaken (James 2001, 77–9). Hoover had in previous years supported public works expenditure as a means of stimulating recovery but had relied on states and local government rather than federal sources to finance such initiatives. By late 1931 he opted for deflationary tax rises, not because he had abandoned entirely his belief in creative budget accounting but because he was anxious to sustain the gold standard. Speculators were more likely to respond favourably to attempts to reduce the budget deficit rather than to increase it (Fearon 1993, 125). Although President Hoover established a Reconstruction Finance Corporation to provide loans to the ailing banking system, panics and banking failures continued. It took Roosevelt's promise in April 1933 to reduce federal expenditure, to balance the budget and to rescue the internal purchasing power of the currency by taking the dollar off gold to stem the tide.

Abandoning the parity regime became the way other countries, including France, the Netherlands, Switzerland and Belgium, rescued themselves from continued banking and fiscal strain (Eichengreen and Sachs 1985). Countries with high foreign debts and weak banking structures had proved unable to withstand deflationary shocks. The banking crises in late 1931, which transmitted depression from debtor to creditor countries almost as a contagious disease, paralysing policy initiatives in their wake, ended as countries broke their link with gold. Britain's abandonment of gold in September 1931 was a critical phase in the road to recovery given that some 15 other countries quickly left the gold standard. Portugal, the Scandinavian countries and the British colonies followed the 'floating pound'. The inflow of short-term capital to Sweden in 1930 and the early part of 1931 suffered a rebuff later in 1931 as capital sought refuge elsewhere in the wake of the bank and currency crises in Germany and Austria. The resulting internal currency crisis forced Sweden off the gold standard one week after Britain. South Africa devalued its currency in 1932 even though it possessed sufficient reserves to have retained a gold standard (Rothermund 1996, 8–9). Such countries were now free to countenance currency devaluation and to set interest rates and budgets in accordance with perceived national needs.

THE VARIABLE IMPACT OF THE DEPRESSION

The over-arching and international impact of the Great Depression should not disguise the fact that its effects were highly uneven across industries, regions and nations. In the United States, for example, some highly concentrated industries did well during the Depression, but they were not sufficiently numerous nor large enough in the national economy to have made a disproportionate impact (Bernstein 1987; Szostak 1995). Generally, most manufacturing industries lost employment but there were job increases in the beverages sector, in rayon, buttons and corsets, while physical output rose during the Great Depression years in each of the butter, cane sugar, chocolate and liquor sectors. And there were some business successes. By 1932 very large US corporations, public utilities and transportation were making profits, as were tobacco, chemicals and allied products and food and beverages (Heim 1998, 33–4).

Unemployment differentials among regions within the United States widened both as a consequence of the Depression and the lack of an effective regional policy. The Depression ultimately improved the economic position of the low-income South, even though this was an unintended outcome of New Deal policies. Average real per capita income in the United States fell by 28 per cent during 1929–33 with the sharpest drops in the Northwest, Central and far West regions. The Southeast and Southwest regions did relatively well with income falls of 24 per cent and 29 per cent respectively. The relative prosperity of tobacco manufacturers during the Depression partly explains the performance of some southern states, though the precise contribution of industrial composition (in terms of employment in the South being concentrated in industries that suffered relatively small employment declines during the Depression) is still a matter of debate. There is a suggestion that although New Deal expenditure did not particularly favour the southern states (being highest in wealthy western states), the Tennessee Valley Authority created in 1933 marked the nation's first comprehensive regional development programme. Moreover, New Deal agricultural policies discouraged share-cropping, encouraging a migration of labour to northern cities. This, together with minimum wage legislation, which applied to all states, ended the isolation of the South and linked it with the national labour market. With the low-wage plantation regime fast disappearing, the South welcomed outside flows of capital and government funding, all of which ultimately promoted industrialization (Heim 1998, 34–42).

In Britain it was clear to many politicians and outside observers by the end of the 1920s that competition and technological change had made industrial reconstruction imperative, either by the rationalization of the older trades or by a deliberate shift into a broader range of newer, expanding sectors, or both. The onset of the slump in 1930, however, dashed any lingering hopes of a spontaneous revival of the traditional export sectors. On the other hand, those in employment during the Depression years generally saw their purchasing power rise as prices fell. Even during the depths of the Depression some industries prospered. Although industrial production as a whole declined in the United Kingdom during 1929–32, output rose slightly in services and distribution. Capital goods industries and export-sensitive industries suffered relatively steep falls in output, shipbuilding declining by 90 per cent, mechanical engineering by 36 per cent, and ferrous and non-ferrous metals by 28 per cent, compared with an 11 per cent drop for all industry during the same period. But output increased during the Depression in paper and printing, leather and food, and gas, water and electrical engineering. At the same time there was a wide variation in annual profit rates amongst major manufacturing industry groups. Of 78 trade groups, 21 had profits in 1932 that were equal to or greater than their profits in 1927, while in six of the trade groups profits fell by more than 60 per cent and for half of the trade groups the drop was between 20 per cent and 50 per cent (Heim 1998, 30–31).

What the Depression illustrated clearly was that a relocation of the centre of activity had already occurred from the North or 'Outer Britain' (including mid-Scotland, Northumberland, Durham, Lancashire and South Wales) to the South or 'Inner Britain' (including London, the Southeast and the Midlands) and was solidifying with 'Inner Britain' escaping the worst ravages of the slump. Two of the most important factors influencing the location and pattern of growth of the newer industries between the wars were those of proximity to markets or distribution networks and the supply of a particular type of workforce better suited to the demands of a machine rather than to a trade. Spatial development, in other words, was more a product of a new set of industries with different locational determinants than of the relocation of existing firms or industries. The depressed areas had little to offer new and expanding industries that could not better be obtained elsewhere. New and expanding industries were more positively drawn towards the Midlands and the Southeast than to the mature industrial regions of Wales, Scotland and the North. In the former areas they drew increasingly upon a pool of juvenile and female labour with a background and aptitude best fitted to semi-skilled and unskilled work at the ruling wage. The conditions permitting the management of specialized branch plants of key industries had not yet emerged; branch expansion tended to be for the purposes of obtaining extra capacity rather than labour and such demands could often be met from within already prosperous areas.

The decline of the old industries and the rise of the 'new' were not, therefore, interdependent developments. The process was a largely disconnected one, with the result that structural adjustment, rather than converting capital and labour to fresh activities, simply left the depressed areas to decline. A more rapid growth of the developing sector could not be relied upon to solve the problems created by secular decline in a basic industry such as coalmining. Since the developing industrial sectors were growing in ways that did not depend crucially upon adjustments in the older sectors, industrial decline in the depressed regions was reinforced. At the same time those regions such as the Midlands, which had in earlier decades nurtured sectors destined to grow relatively quickly, such as motor cars and electrical goods, faced the Depression with a favourable balance of expanding as distinct from declining industries and were able to sustain a degree of relative prosperity even in the depths of the slump (Heim 1984; Garside 2000).

More generally, the Depression bore less heavily upon those countries that sought quickly to uncouple themselves from the international gold standard and to lessen their dependence on foreign countries in favour of greater import substitution and export promotion. The shock of the Great Depression, for example, encouraged some Latin American countries such as Brazil and Costa Rica, faced with further declines in export values and the cessation of capital inflows, to abandon any effort to sustain gold parity and the deflationary policies that accompanied it in favour of devaluation. In seven Latin American countries real import-exchange rates with respect to the dollar had by 1930–34 depreciated between 30 per cent and 90 per cent compared with 1925–29. This systematic devaluation was accompanied by higher tariffs and quantitative restrictions on imports, defaults on international debt payments, expansionary fiscal policy to sustain aggregate demand and other structural and reform policies including price regulation and wage flexibility.

Chile had returned to gold in 1926 but abandoned the standard in July 1931 before Great Britain. Its currency subsequently depreciated by some 40 per cent, a home-grown inflation, which aimed at increasing the money supply to fight unemployment (Rothermund 1996, 9). The outcome of such policy experimentation was a distinct shift in Latin America away from exports of primary products towards import substituting production of manufactured goods. Manufacturing growth rates down to 1939 grew faster than GDP. Elsewhere, countries under colonial control were less able to engage in trade and exchange controls, expansionary monetary and fiscal policies, or to default on debts. The British continued to defend over-valued currencies and deflation in India and Indonesia but as the terms of trade moved in favour of agriculture some parts of India, such as Madras, benefited from industrial investment in sugar refineries, cotton textile mills as well as in banks and insurance companies (Heim 1998, 43–7).

Japan is a classic example of a country whose determination to restore the gold standard in the 1920s ultimately wreaked economic havoc until government officials reversed their earlier priorities and disengaged from the global monetary system. Japan had abandoned the gold standard in September 1916 but the government began to prepare for a return to gold at the pre-war parity as early as 1922. However, the policy stalled. Opposition within the banking establishment and the costs imposed upon Japan by the Great Kanto earthquake in 1923 necessitated a gold export embargo and the expatriation of overseas gold reserves to help sustain the exchange rate. This put paid to any early return to a fixed parity. The sub-sequent depreciation of the yen boosted exports but also fuelled inflation and a tight macroeconomic policy. Efforts to restore gold resumed in late 1926. The yen appreciated as domestic prices fell and exports declined. Recession followed amidst efforts in 1927 to tackle bad debts in the banking sector. Public fears about the viability of bank deposits led to a financial panic, again postponing an early return to gold.

The new Japanese government returned in 1929 was committed to bal-anced budgets and orthodox deflationary economic policy in preparation for a return to gold, almost as an act of national honour. The embargo on gold exports was removed on 11 January 1930, which immediately linked Japan to the global monetary system. The decision could not have been made at a worse time. The Japanese authorities had regarded the reversals in America in 1929 as a temporary setback. Once on gold, however, they were faced with substantial outflows of reserves, a sharp drop in the price of silver (which reduced Japanese exports to China from already existing low levels), a rise in Indian tariffs on cotton goods, and a fall in the prices of silk and cotton goods in the United States. Wage cuts became a common occurrence in 1930. Labour disputes increased both in number and dur-ation whilst the agricultural sector witnessed a collapse in prices and a rise in farm indebtedness.

Having returned to gold in 1930 Japan stuck to the standard with a vengeance. The government tried to support the currency by an intensification of deflation but suffered a haemorrhage of gold reserves, the more so once Britain abandoned gold. Altogether Japan lost some 700 million yen in gold, an amount that exceeded the net amount of gold-backed dollars borrowed from the United States since 1924 (Metzler 2002, 298). Speculators had decided that the yen was destined to leave the gold standard. Defending gold meant restricting fiscal expenditure but this conflicted with Japan's growing military ambitions. The ruling party found it impossible to engage in such retrenchment and collapsed in December 1931. Almost immediately Japan opted for radical devaluation. By insulating itself from global monetary pressure after only a year on gold the country ensured that its depression was short and relatively mild.

Had there been international agreement earlier for coordinated devaluation followed by reflation the economic history of the early 1930s might have been markedly different (Eichengreen and Sachs 1985). But for most of the Depression years the faith of national officials in monetary and fiscal orthodoxy and the stabilization of the international order via a system of fixed exchange parities remained largely undimmed, whatever stark signs of domestic economic and financial turmoil surrounded them. It was only when the linkages operating through financial markets spread crisis from debtor to creditor nations that the shock to confidence spurred countries – Japan but notably America – to disengage with the international monetary order. Britain, France, the Netherlands and Switzerland ultimately chose to do likewise, free thereafter to pursue deliberate policies of national economic recovery.

REACTING TO DEPRESSION

The Great Depression pushed countries increasingly towards economic autarky destroying any expectation that the world economy would be controlled by international institutions. As James puts it, the fragility of the international financial mechanism 'Brought back all the resentments and reactions of the nineteenth century but in a much more militant and violent form. Instead of a harmonious liberal vision of an integrated and prosperous world, beliefs about the inevitability of conflict and importance of national priorities gripped populations and politicians' (James 2001, 29).

Policy responses to the Depression in the majority of industrialized nations were as myopic as they were common. They emphasized protection of the domestic economy through raised tariffs and the creation of economic blocs through the use of import quotas, exchange control and bilateral trade agreements. As early as 1930, America had introduced the Hawley Smoot tariff, which raised US import duties to record levels, triggering retaliation elsewhere. Such actions served only to reduce the overall level of international trade and to foster the political and trading dependence of one set of producers upon another, be it Britain's or France's preferential treatment of their Empires, or Germany's outreach to South-Central European producers (Garside 1998; James 2002, 69, 70). Whereas, for example, the share of US trade with Germany and Britain (both of which formed economic blocs) as a proportion of total world exports between 1926 and 1930 stood at 5.7 per cent it had fallen to 3.5 per cent by 1934 (James 2001, 164). Countries denied access to markets they had previously supplied or only on more onerous terms merely retaliated by restricting imports to their own domestic markets, setting nation against nation in a 'beggar-thy-neighbour' mentality.

The 'death' of international liberalism in the face of clearing and barter arrangements, protectionism and controls over emigration and immigration strengthened moves towards state-centred regulation and planning. The costs of economic adjustment in the wake of the Depression, in other words, were increasingly imposed upon those outside one's own national community. The devaluation of the US dollar in 1933 was a deliberate attempt to import inflation as a means of reflating the domestic economy (and the agricultural sector in particular). Domestic considerations clearly transcended concerns over international stability. Roosevelt was aware that a vigorous programme of deficit spending was likely to sap the confidence of investors and the business community at home. The New Deal was an essentially political rather than avowedly economic programme. It was pragmatic, fluid and geared towards internal rather than external considerations, paying scant regard to the fate of the gold standard, war debts or the stability of other currencies. Roosevelt wanted to reverse the deflation of the Depression years but with greater freedom of action than would ever be provided under a fixed exchange rate system.

It is no coincidence either that the Japanese 'developmental state' was born in the ruins of the global economic order. Japan's notable economic recovery in the 1930s was due in large part to expansionary public expenditure ('Keynesian policies. . .without a Keynes' Kindleberger 1973, 17, Hadley 1989), relaxed monetary policy and a revival of export competitiveness following depreciation of the yen. It was only when the gold standard mentality was dropped in favour of domestic revival on the back of a depreciated currency that expansionary fiscal and monetary policies were able to be pursued, giving rise to an economic recovery that outstripped that of France, Germany, the United Kingdom and the United States down to 1937 (Heim 1998, 47; Cha 2003).

Elsewhere those countries that devalued or imposed exchange control in the wake of the Depression recovered more quickly than those that clung to gold. Abandonment of fixed exchange rates enabled countries to implement expansionary monetary policies, reduce interest rates and adopt deliberate strategies to boost exports and investment. Sweden is often regarded as being in the forefront of enlightened policy-making in the aftermath of the slump because of its ready acceptance of unbalanced budgets. After abandoning gold in 1931 the country set firm to raise domestic purchasing power, exports and employment financing increased public expenditure from loans. This active counter-cyclical fiscal policy was significant if only because it stood in stark contrast to experience in other countries. But it did not get under way until strong external forces helped to boost confidence. Exports in particular benefited from the significant devaluation of the crown against other currencies. New Zealand's early and unusually fast recovery from depression was associated with a fundamental shift in its monetary regime. This was underpinned by a deliberate choice to devalue the currency (which quickly redistributed income to the beleaguered farm sector) and by a doubling of the money supply between 1932–37, which lowered real interest rates (Greasley and Oxley 2002). Not all currency depreciations, however, were associated with early or sustained economic recovery. The distinguishing factor appears to be whether the devaluation was freely undertaken and linked to an inflationary regime, as in New Zealand and Argentina, or whether, as in the case of Brazil, Mexico and Australia, depreciations were forced upon the countries (della Paolera and Taylor 1999).

There were few more vivid contrasts between pre- and post-Depression policies than in Germany. We have already noted that plans to increase public works expenditure to break the grip of deflation were afoot during the Bruning, von Papen and Schleicher administrations but they foundered in the prevailing climate. The arrival of full employment during 1933 to 1936 is traditionally associated with the economic miracle achieved by Nazi deficit spending and state intervention on an unprecedented scale. Although many of the Nazi spending plans were merely pragmatic improvisations of measures initiated by previous administrations, they were now made subject to the primacy of political and social goals as defined by the national leadership. For Hitler, economic problems were not insuperable constraints; they were issues to be overcome by political will. Production, consumption and the distribution of income were thereby dictated by a form of organized capitalism under which participants could accumulate profits so long as they accepted the primacy of politics and control from above in the interests of national power and stability (Barkai 1990). During its first year the Nazi regime conformed to fairly orthodox views of finance, viewing public expenditure for the creation of jobs as little more than a temporary expedient necessary until such time as the 'natural' recovery provided work for all. Only when the regime was politically secure did Hitler countenance ambitious state spending plans and only then in a command economy embracing controls over prices, wages, the money market, foreign exchange and overseas trade (Overy 1982). The dramatic fall in unemployment from the mid-1930s, therefore, has to be seen in light of the overriding characteristics of the Nazi regime. Autarkic policies were a natural outgrowth of the political premises of Nazism. Deficit spending was but one component of a whole set of economic and institutional measures, which rejected regulation of the economy by market forces in favour of the dictum of state supremacy in the pursuit of rearmament and an expansionist war.

If abandoning gold freed most countries from the grip of deflationary policies, it was France's stubborn determination to cling to gold that soured its economic performance for much of the 1930s. French officials believed that convertibility was a necessary social discipline and until 1936 pursued contractionary fiscal policies with ghoulish fervour. Public expenditure was cut and taxes raised in order to suppress domestic spending and to defend convertibility. But although government spending was reduced by nearly six million francs during 1931 to 1935, it proved insufficient to secure a balanced budget or to restore confidence (Mouré 1991, 45, 189–90). If the authorities had let the franc float in the second half of 1933 the economic climate might have been transformed but reducing prices and costs via devaluation was never an option in the official mind. The desire to recapture budgetary balance was powerful, fed by memories of the inflationary actions of bankers and politicians in the 1920s. It was only when the franc was devalued in October 1936 that systematic thought was given to a recovery strategy. Even that proved painful and protracted requiring a further devaluation and a muted stimulus from rearmament expenditure.

Britain realized after the autumn of 1931 that liberal internationalism was in retreat. This posed particular problems for a country whose economic growth and industrial structure had long been geared to world patterns of demand. Attention became focused, therefore, not on seeking industrial and export competitiveness through competitive devaluation but on managing and supporting sterling to make it attractive as a reserve and transaction currency. Both the City and the Treasury worked to ensure that the external orientation of economic and financial policy remained as intact as it had been in the 1920s. Capital exports were promoted to develop Empire markets, mechanisms put in place to iron out fluctuations in sterling's international value and tariffs retained for their likely positive effect on revenue and the currency (Garside 1990). This went hand in hand, however, with a resurgence of orthodox fiscal policy. Resistance to budget deficit spending stiffened in Britain after 1933 given the authorities' desire to sustain the domestic-based economic recovery, which was based in part upon a rise in real consumption amongst the unemployed, a housing boom and the stimulus provided by investment and employment in new industries geared to the home market. No one wanted to court a collapse of confidence by engaging in deficit finance.

Limited pragmatism reigned. A more rapid decline of older industries is only conducive to re-employment in more productive activities if a continuous adjustment process can be assumed. It will only spur more rapid growth overall if a slower decline would impede the growth of the developing sectors sufficient to counterbalance the positive demand effects of keeping workers in the declining industries employed. British officials in the 1930s, therefore, struck by the continued secular decline of key industries in regions with few immediate sources of re-employment, acted to sustain industrial activity therein rather than face the political consequences of deepening unemployment from any enforced shake-out of labour. The National Government was more prepared to prop up the existing industrial structure and to curtail competition to prevent instability than it was to seek reforms that lowered costs. Officials were aware by the early 1930s of how little industrial reconstruction was actually occurring within coal and other staple trades. By then, however, government attention had shifted from the pursuit of efficiency and competitiveness towards cartelization and output and price control in an effort to limit the spread of unemployment. Officials were prepared to act only when the particular problems of an industry outweighed the general objections to government intervention in business. In truth the Depression had neither devastated the British economy sufficiently nor altered the balance of power amongst industrial capital, the City and government to provide any tangible basis upon which any radical alternative economic policy could be formulated (Booth and Pack 1985; Garside 1985).

CONCLUSION

Although there is a growing consensus that both monetary and non-monetary factors account for the Great Depression, it is clear that the contraction in monetary policy in America in the late 1920s provided the initial impulse towards a recession that was then superimposed upon other countries. Other nations had to varying degrees failed to adjust to the changing international competitive environment and had become overly dependent upon foreign, largely American, borrowing. This merely heightened the fragility of their external position 'allowing the shift towards contraction in US policy to elicit an even more dramatic shift abroad' (Eichengreen 1992b, 223). As we have seen, the traumatic effects of depression were transmitted rapidly because of the widespread adoption of the gold standard, which fixed exchange rates internationally, thereby circumscribing national policies of reflation.

The scale of the ensuing economic crisis put paid to the dominant liberal economic doctrine of economies possessing self-healing powers. Although the measures taken to combat the Depression varied from country to country, it was the shift to national, political and economic autarky rather than international cooperation that was so marked. The paucity of coordinated action reflected the manner in which beleaguered nations blamed others for the condition in which they found themselves. It reflected, too, the limited extent to which the Depression had weakened inherent fears of inflation and instability.

Initial responses to the Depression in America, Britain, Germany, France, Eastern Europe and Australasia focused on budgetary balance and the sustenance of confidence, and a rejection of currency devaluation, which in turn merely reinforced internal deflation as countries slavishly avoided low interest rates or deficit spending for fear of encouraging gold outflows. Mechanistic gold standard arrangements may have perished during the early 1930s but it was the political economy of fiscal experimentation thereafter that was revealing. Two examples must suffice. The de facto policy of budget deficits that emerged in America was not part of an explicit commitment to government spending as the leading edge of national recovery. Roosevelt's adoption of Keynesian-type policies in 1938 secured an important political advantage; only two years before he had reduced government expenditure and raised taxes in a determined effort to balance the budget. Nowhere was the influence of politics more apparent than in Germany. Hitler's fiscal programme was more conservative than is commonly supposed. Many of the preoccupations and prejudices of the previous administrations lingered, especially concern over the stability of the mark. What emerged was the determination of the Nazi regime to subordinate workers, producers and investors to the supremacy of the state rather than regulation by market forces. The Nazis forged highly politicized policies with the benefit of isolationism. Full employment was a direct result but the principal stimulus to deficit spending came as in Japan from rearmament, itself a direct expression of the overriding philosophical and political goals to which the country was subjected.

If tight money had exacerbated economic conditions in countries such as Sweden, New Zealand and the United States during the early years of the Depression, it was the expansion of their monetary base that was crucial to recovery in later years. That said, the gap between those countries that could contemplate currency depreciation and those that could not was clearly exposed. Central and Eastern European countries, bedevilled by exchange and balance of payments difficulties and faced with rising protectionism abroad and falling capital imports, reacted by imposing tariff quotas and exchange controls rather than contemplate the inflationary consequences of currency depreciation (League of Nations 1944; Eichengreen 1992b).

In hindsight, the analysis of the origins, course and outcome of the Great Depression must remain an exercise in 'historical political economy'. Although the proximate causes and effects of the economic downturn require detailed examination of the national economies thus affected, the economic ideas and responses revealed must be regarded, in Maier's words, 'not as frameworks for analysis, but as beliefs and actions that must themselves be explained. They are contingent and problematic; that is they might have been different and they must be explained within particular political and social contexts' (Maier 1987). To the graphic data of industrial production, unemployment, gold stocks and fiscal policy, therefore, have to be added the less tangible but important issues of the power of vested interest groups, the significance of the political setting in which public policy was formulated, the impact on policy of nationalism and the drive towards self-determination (as in Germany and Eastern Europe), and the symbiotic relationship between policy activism and a country's perception of what needed to be resurrected from the past, whatever the change in circumstance.

And there is an additional factor. If economic orthodoxy ruled for so long during the turbulent years of the Great Depression and for periods after it, it did so because the voices of economic radicalism were both few and readily circumscribed and because there was a stoic acceptance of contemporary conditions amongst many of the affected populations. Images of dole queues and of weary souls lined up at soup kitchens remain vivid but, on the whole, unemployment did not generate widespread protest, least of all revolutionary outburst. The international character of the Depression made it difficult for many to believe that any single government could be held to account, whilst the lack of intellectually convincing suggestions of how unemployment might be significantly reduced across nations, to say nothing of the threat that the jobless posed to those clinging to any employment, however fragile, sustained the belief that conditions could only improve in due course (Garraty 1978).

But perhaps the lasting legacy of the Great Depression belongs to another era. When the 'Golden Years' of post-war economic reconstruction and recovery faltered on an international scale in the mid-1970s, economists and politicians, faced with the unnerving spectacle of rising unemployment and searing inflation, were forced to re-examine the 'certainties' of prevailing orthodoxies in their search for remedial policies. They had little choice. However sophisticated economic reasoning and the administrative machinery of governments had become, officials knew what the populace expected: there was to be 'no return to the 1930s'.

REFERENCES

Aldcroft, D.H. (1977), *From Versailles to Wall Street, 1919–1929*, London: Allen Lane.

Balderston, T. (1982), 'The origins of economic instability in Germany 1924–1930: market forces versus economic policy', *Vierteljahrschrift für Sozial und Wirtschaftsgeschichte*, 69.

Barkai, A. (1990), *Nazi economics. Ideology, theory, and policy*, Oxford: Berg.

Bernanke, B. (1983), 'Nonmonetary effects of the financial crisis in the propagation of the Great Depression', *American Economic Review*, 73.

Bernanke, B. (1995), 'The macroeconomics of the Great Depression, 1919–39', *Journal of Money, Credit and Banking*, 27.

Bernanke, B. and James, H. (1991), 'The gold standard, deflation, and financial crises in the Great Depression: an international comparison', in R. Glen Hubbard (ed.), *Financial markets and financial crises*, Chicago, IL: Chicago University Press.

Bernstein, M.A. (1987), *The Great Depression: delayed recovery and economic change in America, 1929–1939*, Cambridge: Cambridge University Press.

Booth, A. and Pack, M. (1985), *Employment, capital and economic policy Great Britain 1918–1939*, Oxford: Blackwell Publishers.

Boyce, R.W.D (1987), *British capitalism at the crossroads*, Cambridge: Cambridge University Press.

Cha, M.S. (2003), 'Did Takahashi Kockiyo rescue Japan from the Great Depression?', *Journal of Economic History*, 63.

Choudhri, E.U. and Kochin, Levis A. (1980), 'The exchange rate and the international transmission of business cycle disturbances: evidence from the Great Depression', *Journal of Money, Credit, and Banking*, 12.

Clavin, P. (2000), *The Great Depression in Europe, 1929–1939*, New York: St Martin's Press.

della Paolera, G. and Taylor, A.M. (1999), 'Economic recovery from the Argentine Great Depression: institutions, expectations, and change in macroeconomic regime', *Journal of Economic History*, 59.

Dow, C. (2000), *Major recessions. Britain and the world, 1920–1995*, Oxford: Oxford University Press.

Eichengreen, B. (1990), *Economic stability. Essays in the history of international finance*, Cambridge: Cambridge University Press.

Eichengreen, B. (1991), 'Relaxing the external constraint: Europe in the 1930s', in G. Alogoskofis, L. Papdemos and R. Portes (eds), *External constraints on macroeconomic policy: the European experience*, Cambridge: Cambridge University Press.

Eichengreen, B. (1992a), *Golden fetters: the gold standard and the Great Depression*, New York: Oxford University Press.

Eichengreen, B. (1992b), 'The origins and nature of the Great Slump revisited', *Economic History Review*, 45.

Eichengreen, B. (2002), 'Averting a global crisis', in H. James (ed.), *The interwar depression in an international context*, Munich: R. Oldenbourg.

Eichengreen, B. and Hatton, T.J. (1988), 'Interwar unemployment in international perspective: an overview', in B. Eichengreen and T. Hatton (eds), *Interwar unemployment in international perspective*, London: Kluwer Academic Publishers.

Eichengreen, B. and Sachs, J. (1985), 'Exchange rates and economic recovery in the 1930s', *Journal of Economic History*, 45.

Eichengreen, B. and Temin, P. (2000), 'The gold standard and the Great Depression', *Contemporary European History*, 9.

Fearon, P. (1993), 'Hoover, Roosevelt and American economic policy', in W.R. Garside (ed.), *Capitalism in crisis: international responses to the Great Depression*, London: Pinter Publishers.

Friedman, M. and Schwartz, A.J. (1963), *Monetary history of the United States, 1867–1960*, Princeton: Princeton University Press.

Galenson, W. and Zellner, A. (1957), 'International comparison of unemployment rates', in National Bureau of Economic Research, *The measurement and behaviour of unemployment*, Princeton: Princeton University Press.

Garraty, J. (1978), *Unemployment in history. Economic thought and public policy*, New York: Harper & Row.

Garside, W.R. (1985), 'The failure of the "radical alternative": public words, deficit finance and British interwar unemployment', *The Journal of European Economic History*, 14.

Garside, W.R. (1987), 'Public works and mass unemployment: Britain's response in a European perspective 1919–1939', *Archiv für Sozialgeschichte*, XXVII.

Garside, W.R. (1990), *British unemployment, 1919–1939: a study in public policy*, Cambridge: Cambridge University Press.

Garside, W.R. (1998), 'Party politics, political economy and British protectionism, 1919–1932', *History*, 83.

Garside, W.R. (2000), 'The political economy of structural change: Britain in the 1930s', in C. Buchheim and R. Garside (eds), *After the slump. Industry and politics in 1930s Britain and Germany*, Berlin: Peter Lang.

Garside, W.R. and Greaves, J.J. (1997), 'Rationalisation and Britain's industrial malaise: the interwar years revisited', *The Journal of European Economic History*, 26.

Greasley, D. and Oxley, L. (2002), 'Regime shift and fast recovery on the periphery: New Zealand in the 1930s', *Economic History Review*, 55.

Hadley, E.M. (1989), 'The diffusion of Keynesian ideas in Japan', in Peter A. Hall (ed.), *The political power of economic ideas: Keynesianism across nations*, Princeton: Princeton University Press.

Heim, C.E. (1984), 'Structural transformation and the demand for new labor in advanced economies: interwar Britain', *Journal of Economic History*, 44.

Heim, C.E. (1998), 'Uneven impacts of the Great Depression: industries, regions, and nations', in Mark Wheeler (ed.), *The economics of the Great Depression*, Kalamazoo, MI: W.E. Upjohn Institute for Employment Research.

James, H. (2001), *The end of globalization: lessons from the Great Depression*, Cambridge, MA: Harvard University Press.

James, H. (2002), 'Economy', in J. Jackson (ed.), *Europe 1900–1945*, Oxford: Oxford University Press.

Kindleberger, C. (1973), *The world in depression 1929–1939*, London: Allen Lane.

League of Nations (1944), *International currency experience: lessons of the interwar period*, Geneva: League of Nations.

Lebergott, S. (1964), *Manpower in economic growth*, New York: McGraw-Hill.

Lee, C.H. (1969), 'The effects of the Depression on primary producing countries', *Journal of Contemporary History*, 4.

Maier, C. (1987), *In search of stability. Explorations in historical political economy*, Cambridge: Cambridge University Press.

Metzler, M. (2002), 'American pressure for financial internationalization in Japan on the eve of the Great Depression', *Journal of Japanese Studies*, 28.

Mouré, K. (1991), *Managing the franc Poincaré: economic understanding and political constraint in French monetary policy, 1928–1936*, Cambridge: Cambridge University Press.

Overy, R. (1982), *The Nazi economic recovery, 1932–1938*, London: Macmillan.

Parliament, United Kingdom (1918), *First interim report of the Commission on Currency and Foreign Exchanges After the War*.

Rothermund, D. (1996), *The global impact of the Great Depression, 1929–1939*, London: Routledge.

Szostak, R. (1995), *Technological innovation and the Great Depression*, Boulder, CO: Westview.

Temin, P. (1989), *Lessons from the Great Depression*, Cambridge, MA: MIT Press.

3. The Second World War as an economic disaster[1]

Niall Ferguson

On 20 April 1949, the *New York Times* carried three items about Japan. The most arresting headline was: 'Japan's War Cost Is Put at $31 Billion; 2,252,000 Buildings Razed, 1,850,000 Dead'. Similar figures were produced in the post-war period for nearly all the combatant countries. In four countries – China, Germany, Poland and the Soviet Union – the death toll was even higher, or five countries if the mortality of the 1943 Bengal famine is attributed to the war. Altogether, the best available estimates suggest, somewhere in the region of 60 million people lost their lives as a result of the Second World War. In some countries the mortality rate was higher than one in ten. In Poland it approached one in five (Harrison 1998a, 3,7).[2] No other previous war had been so catastrophic in relative, much less in absolute, terms. Nor was Japan unique in the scale of destruction its capital stock had suffered. Although the bombing of Hiroshima and Nagasaki represented the logical culmination of Anglo-American strategy – two entire cities laid waste by just two atomic bombs – comparable devastation had already been wreaked in other cities by conventional weaponry. In the aggregate, according to the US Strategic Bombing Survey, 40 per cent of the built-up areas of 66 Japanese cities had been destroyed; nearly a third of the urban population had lost their homes. In Germany a similar proportion of the housing in 49 cities had been destroyed or seriously damaged. Of course, although they lacked the Allies' bombing capability, the Germans and Japanese had meted out their share of destruction before suffering this explosive 'payback'. Around 30 per cent of Polish buildings had been destroyed, and comparable proportions of the country's agricultural property, mines and industry. More than a fifth of Yugoslavian housing had been wrecked. The story was much the same in Ukraine and Byelorussia (Belarus), which had borne the brunt of the Nazi occupation. Eastern China was in a state of unquantifiable chaos thanks in large measure to the depradations of Japanese rule. Nor had Western Europe escaped unscathed. In Great Britain about 30 per cent of the homes were destroyed or damaged; in France, Belgium and the Netherlands about

20 per cent. The exactions of German occupation had reduced gross domestic product in France and the Netherlands to below 60 per cent of the 1938 level; Italy had fared little better. According to the *Encylopaedia Britannica*, the cost of the war 'to governments' – meaning, presumably, its aggregate fiscal costs – amounted to $1 trillion. Given the unquantifiable human suffering that lies behind all such statistics, it seems almost bathetic to call the Second World War an *economic* disaster. It was, quite simply, the greatest human-made disaster of any kind in modern history.

Yet the two other items about Japan in that same day's *New York Times* told a contrasting story: one of rapid economic recovery. Not only were Japanese farmers achieving a record post-war harvest, more significantly, the paper published a remarkable photograph under the headline: 'Japanese Items Ready for Export'. The caption below the picture read: 'Samples of paper umbrellas, table tennis balls, textiles and fish nets which will be flown to the United States to encourage American firms to place orders with Japanese manufacturers.' This was just the beginning of an explosive growth of Japanese exports, the composition of which would soon change from such low-value products to sophisticated industrial manufactures. Herein lay one of the great ironies of the Second World War. Out of the ashes it left in its wake, grew phoenix-like, the economies of the defeated powers.

Any interpretation of the Second World War as an economic disaster has to take account of both sides of this strange coin. On one side, the quintessence of disaster: six years of systematic destruction of people and capital. On the obverse, the prelude to economic miracles unprecedented in human history.

Economic historians have done less than might have been expected to resolve this seeming paradox. For example, the two pre-eminent English-language journals of economic history have published surprisingly little on the subject of the Second World War since 1949. There have been 17 articles about the war in the *Journal of Economic History* and just four articles in the *Economic History Review*. By comparison, the *Journal of Economic History* published no fewer than 30 articles about the Great Depression in the same period. Yet the Depression, though it left millions idle, killed few people. While it certainly emptied many buildings and left them to decay, it destroyed no cities. It is not as if the war had nothing to do with economics. Those who began it, both in Europe and in Asia, explicitly averred their economic motivations. Behind the rhetoric about 'living space' and 'Asian co-prosperity' were cold calculations about Germany's and Japan's need to acquire by force strategic raw materials that they could not acquire by trade. At the same time, economics played a central role in the debates about how far to 'appease' rather than confront the dictators. And, needless to say, once the war began it was economics as much as grand strategy that decided its outcome. The economic spin-offs of the war are also well known, not least in accelerating technological innovations that lay the foundations of post-war growth.

There are, it is true, distinguished exceptions to the rule of relative neglect. Building on their earlier researches on the Nazi economy, Alan Milward (1987) and Richard Overy (1996) have both addressed the central economic questions about the war's origins and course. Mark Harrison (1998b), too, has done much to illuminate the economic foundations of the Soviet war effort. Thanks to Hugh Rockoff (1998) and others, we now know much more than we did about the workings of American war economy. J.R. Vernon (1994) demonstrated more than a decade ago that 'half or more' of the US recovery from the Depression occurred in 1941 and 1942, and that most of the increase in real GNP in those years was attributable to the war-induced fiscal stimulus. More recently, Robert Higgs (2004) has cast doubt on the enduring economic value, in terms of capital formation, of wartime government investment. There is also an important literature on the insti-tutional consequences of the war, which allowed 'fresh starts' for Germany and Japan, but reinforced institutional deficiencies in Britain (Olson 1982; Barnett 1986). Yet it was striking that, when a group of historians recently co-authored a new economic history of the war, their contributions were quite different in terms of approach and methodology, making any kind of comparative reading distinctly difficult (Harrison 1998c).

The most alluring avenue of inquiry at present is to use financial market data to draw inferences about contemporary investors' views of the war. Here, more or less standard methods of identifying structural breaks in bond price series are used to illuminate the attitudes of investors in various markets, notably Zurich, Stockholm, Paris and London (see Frey and Kucher 2000, 2001; Brown and Burdekin 2002; Oosterlinck 2003; Waldenström and Frey 2003). It is nevertheless symptomatic that these papers essentially concern themselves with the reactions of financial markets to war, treating military and political events, once again, as exo-genous shocks that investors could anticipate and discount, or be (pleas-antly or unpleasantly) surprised by.

In this chapter I will argue that the economics of the Second World War can be understood under four headings: the economic motivations of its instigators; the economic arguments that prevented their being deterred from going to war; the economic reasons for their ultimate but very costly and hard-fought defeat; and the economic consequences of the Allied victory. I hope to show that the war was an economic disaster in more than one sense; not only in terms of the death and destruction that it caused, but also because from an economic point of view it was unnecessary. Conquest was not the solution to the economic problems of Germany, Japan and Italy that the leaders of those countries claimed it would be. Equally spurious were the economic arguments that led the Western powers to appease rather to deter Germany and Japan. Because both sides erred, a war ended up being fought that the Axis powers stood no realistic chance of winning, but which the Allied powers nevertheless found extremely expensive to win. Post-war economic growth, which saw the vanquished transformed into victors, in large measure vindicated Winston Churchill's famous assertion that the Second World War ought to be known as 'the unnecessary war'.

ECONOMIC MOTIVATIONS FOR WAR

The Depression caused radical changes in economic policy in most countries, but radical changes in political and legal arrangements in only some countries and the adoption of expansionist foreign policies in fewer still. Most countries in fact responded to the crisis as Britain and the United States did; by seeking as far as possible to avoid external conflicts. This was as much out of parsimony as altruism; the assumption was that the cost of fighting unemployment at home ruled out further expenditures on small wars abroad. Even the majority of authoritarian regimes were quite content to persecute internal enemies and bicker with their neighbours over borders. Only three countries aspired to territorial expansion and war as a means to achieve it. They were Japan, Italy and Germany. Their dreams of empire were the proximate cause of the multiple conflicts we know as the Second World War.

Why did only these three authoritarian regimes adopt and act upon aggressive foreign policies aimed at the acquisition of empires? A conventional answer might be that they were in thrall to anachronistic notions of imperial glory. Yet there was nothing anachronistic about the idea of empire in the 1930s. In a world without free trade, empires offered all kinds of advantages to those who had them. It was undoubtedly beneficial to the United Kingdom to be at the centre of a vast sterling bloc with a common currency and common tariff. And what would Stalin's Soviet Union have been if it had been confined within the historic frontiers of Muscovy, without the vast territories and resources of the Caucasus, Siberia and Central Asia? The importance of empire became especially obvious to the self-styled 'have not' powers when they adopted rearmament as a tool of economic recovery. For rearmament in the 1930s – if one wished to possess the most up-to-date weaponry – demanded copious supplies of a variety of crucial raw materials. Neither Italy, Germany nor Japan had these commodities within their own borders other than in trivial quantities. By contrast, the lion's share of the world's accessible supplies lay within the borders of one of four rival powers: the British Empire, the French Empire, the Soviet Union and the United States. Thus, no country could aspire to military parity with these powers without substantial imports of commodities whose supply they all but monopolized. For three reasons, it was not possible for the 'have nots' to rely on free trade to acquire them. First, free trade had been significantly reduced by the mid-1930s, thanks to the imposition of protectionist tariffs. Second, Italy, Germany and Japan lacked adequate international reserves to pay for the imports they required. Third, even if their central banks' reserves had been overflowing with gold, there was a risk that imports might be interdicted by rival powers before rearmament was complete. There was therefore an attractive logic to territorial expansion.

The concept of *Lebensraum* (literally, 'living space', the concept of imperial expansionism) had been originated in the late 1890s by Friedrich Ratzel, Professor of Geography at Leipzig, and developed by the Orientalist and geopolitical theorist Karl Haushofer, whose pupil, Rudolf Hess, may have introduced the term to Hitler in the early 1920s. We can now see that the argument was based on an excessively pessimistic view of economic development. Since 1945, gains in both agricultural and industrial productivity have allowed 'haves' and 'have nots' alike to sustain even larger populations than they had in 1939. By the end of the twentieth century, Italy's population density was 17 per cent higher than 60 years before, Britain's 28 per cent higher, France's 42 per cent higher, Germany's 64 per cent higher and Japan's 84 per cent higher. As a result of decolonization, all these countries had been 'have nots' (in the interwar sense) for most of the intervening years, yet their economies had grown significantly faster than in the periods when some or all of them had been 'haves'. Clearly, 'living space' was not as indispensable for prosperity as Haushofer and his disciples believed. Yet in the interwar context the argument had a powerful appeal – and particularly in Germany, Italy and Japan. In the late 1930s, as Figure 3.1 shows, Germany had the fourth-highest population density of the world's major economies (363 inhabitants per square mile), after the United Kingdom (487), Japan (469) and Italy (418). Under the Treaty of Versailles, however, Germany had been deprived of its relatively few colonies, whereas Britain had added to its already vast imperium, as had France. If, as Hitler had learned from Haushofer, 'living space' was essential for a densely populated country with limited domestic sources of food and raw materials, then Germany, Japan and Italy all needed it. Another way of looking at the problem was to relate available arable land to the population employed in agriculture. By this measure, Canada was ten times better endowed than Germany, and the United States six times better. Even

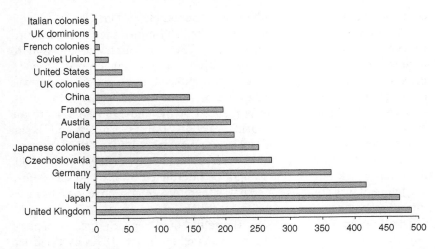

Source: Epstein (1938).

Figure 3.1   Population per square mile, 1938

Germany's European neighbours had more 'farming space': the average Danish farmer had 229 per cent more land than the average German; the average British farmer 182 per cent more and the average French farmer 34 per cent more. To be sure, farmers in Poland, Italy, Romania and Bulgaria were worse off; but further east, in the Soviet Union, there was 50 per cent more arable land per agricultural worker (Tooze 2006, Table 4).

Living space had a secondary meaning, however, which was less frequently articulated but in practice much more important. This was the need that any serious military power had for access to strategic raw materials. Here changes in military technology had radically altered the global balance of power – arguably even more so than post-1918 border changes. Military power was no longer a matter of 'blood and iron', or even coal and iron, as it had been in Bismarck's day. Just as important were oil and rubber. The production of these commodities was dominated by the United States, the British Empire and the Soviet Union or countries under their direct or indirect influence. American oilfields alone accounted for just under 70 per cent of global crude petroleum production; the world's next largest producer was Venezuela (12 per cent). The Middle Eastern oilfields did not yet occupy the dominant position they enjoy today: between them, Iran, Iraq, Saudi Arabia and the smaller gulf states accounted for less than 7 per cent of total world production in 1940. The critical point was that oil production in all these countries was in the hands of British or American firms, principally Anglo-Persian, Royal Dutch/Shell and the successors to

Standard Oil (Yergin 1991). Nor was modern warfare solely a matter of internal combustion engines and the rubber tyres. Modern planes, tanks and ships – to say nothing of guns, shells, bullets and the machinery needed to make all these things – required a host of sophisticated forms of steel, which could be manufactured only with the admixture of more or less rare metals like antimony, chromium, cobalt, manganese, mercury, molybdenum, nickel, titanium, tungsten and vanadium. Here too the situation of the Western powers and the Soviet Union was dominant, if not monopolistic. Taken together, the British Empire, the French Empire, the United States and the Soviet Union accounted for virtually all the world's output of cobalt, manganese, molybdenum, nickel and vanadium, around three-quarters of all chromium and titanium, and half of all tungsten. The former German colony of Southwest Africa, now securely in British hands, was practically the only source of vanadium. The Soviet Union, followed distantly by India, accounted for nearly all manganese production. Nickel was virtually a Canadian monopoly; molybdenum an American one (*Economist* 1938, 25ff.).

The case that Germany, Italy and Japan lacked 'living space' was therefore far from weak. Germany had abundant domestic supplies of coal and the biggest iron and steel industry in Europe, but before the 1930s needed to import all its rubber and oil (Tooze 2006, App. 2). Rearmament necessarily increased Germany's appetite for both these commodities; at the same time, however, diverting resources into armaments reduced the amount that Germany could export – and, in the absence of ample hard currency reserves and foreign credit lines, it was only through exporting that Germany could earn the money to pay for imports. There was thus a clear and recurrent conflict between Hitler's military ambitions and the economic resources at his disposal. There had already been one foreign exchange crisis in 1934, which had forced a sharp reduction in imports. Hitler's Four Year Plan memorandum of August – September 1936 was intended to overcome this constraint on his military ambitions. As Hitler made clear, his priority remained the confrontation and defeat of 'Bolshevism', meaning Soviet communism. The paramount objective of the German government must therefore be 'developing the German Army, within the shortest period, to be the first army in the world in respect to training, mobilization of units [and] equipment'. Yet Hitler proceeded to enumerate the difficulties of achieving this within Germany's existing borders. First, an 'overpopulated' Germany could not feed itself because 'the yield of our agricultural production can no longer be substantially increased'. Second, it was 'impossible for us to produce artificially certain raw materials which we do not have in Germany, or to find other substitutes for them'. Hence, Hitler reasoned, 'the final solution' could be found only 'in an extension of our living space, and/or the sources of the raw materials and food supplies of our nation'.

Yet Germany was not yet in a military position to win 'living space' through conquest. Rearmament would therefore only be possible through a combination of increased production of domestically available materials (e.g., low-grade German iron ore), further restriction of non-essential imports (e.g., coffee and tea) and substitution of essential imports with synthetic alternatives (e.g., ersatz fuel, rubber and fats). The core of the Four Year Plan was therefore a huge investment in new technologies capable of producing synthetic raw materials using domestically available commodities such as coal, as well as the creation at Salzgitter of a vast new state-owned factory designed to manufacture steel from low-quality German iron ore.

Hitler's memorandum should be understood primarily as a repudiation of the earlier 'New Plan' favoured by the Reichsbank President and Economics Minister Hjalmar Schacht, which had aimed at replenishing Germany's depleted hard currency reserves through a complex system of export subsidies, import restrictions and bilateral trade agreements. Hitler dismissed brusquely Schacht's arguments for a slower pace of rearmament and a strategy of stockpiling raw materials and hard currency. The memorandum was also an explicit threat to German industry that state control would be stepped up if the private sector failed to meet the targets set by the government. However, the most important point in the entire report was the timetable for war that it established. Hitler's two conclusions could not have been more explicit:

1. The German armed forces must be ready for combat within four years.
2. The German economy must be fit for war within four years (Treue 1955).

By decisively sanctioning an acceleration in the pace of rearmament and overriding Schacht's warnings of another balance of payments crisis, Hitler's Four Year Plan memorandum significantly increased the likelihood that Germany would be at war by 1940. In the words of Major General Friedrich Fromm of the army's Central Administrative Office: 'Shortly after completion of the rearmament phase, the Wehrmacht must be employed, otherwise there must be a reduction in demands or in the level of war readiness' (Tooze 2006, Ch. 7). Indeed, the Four Year Plan made it quite likely that war would come even sooner than that. By the time Hitler addressed his senior military leaders on 5 November 1937 – a meeting famously summarized by Colonel Friedrich Hossbach – it had become apparent that the enormously expensive mobilization of internal resources envisaged in the Four Year Plan could not possibly deliver the level of rearmament the service chiefs regarded as necessary until, at the earliest, 1943. It was for this reason that Hitler turned his attention to the possibility that 'living space' – and the resources that came with it – might be acquired sooner rather than later, beginning with Austria and Czechoslovakia. From early 1938 onwards Hitler embarked on a policy of territorial expansion and accelerated rearmament, which made war in Europe increasingly probable. Such was the circular quality of the ideology of *Lebensraum*: a country needed a large and well-equipped military in order to acquire additional space; but such a military could be built only by conquering additional space.

The Japanese need for 'living space' seemed even more acute. The collapse of global trade after 1928 had dealt Japan's economy a severe blow – a blow made more painful by the ill-timed decision to return to the gold standard in 1929 (the very moment it would have made sense to float the yen) and by Finance Minister Inoue Junnosuke's tight budgets. The terms of trade turned dramatically against Japan as export prices collapsed relative to import prices. In volume terms, exports fell by 6 per cent between 1929 and 1931. At the same time, Japan's deficits in raw materials soared to record heights (see Figure 3.2). Unemployment rose to around one million. Agricultural incomes slumped.

There were, it is true, alternatives to territorial expansion as a response to this crisis. As Finance Minister from December 1931, Takahashi Korekiyo cut Japan's economy loose from the deadweight of orthodox

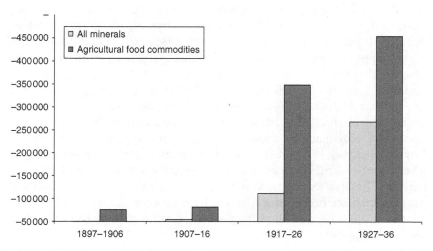

Source: Yasuba (1996, Table 3).

Figure 3.2   Japan's raw materials deficit, 1897–1936 (thousands of yen)

economics, floating the yen, boosting government spending and monetizing debt by selling bonds to the Bank of Japan. These proto-Keynesian policies worked as well as any tried elsewhere during the Depression. Between 1929 and 1940 gross national product rose at a real rate of 4.7 per cent per annum, significantly faster than in the Western economies in the same period. Export volumes doubled. In theory, Japan might have carried on in this vein, reining in the budget deficit as the recovery gathered pace, exploiting her comparative advantage as a textile manufacturer at the heart of an Asian trading bloc. As a percentage of total world trade, intra-Asian trade doubled between 1913 and 1938 (Sugihara 1997, 260). By 1936 Japan accounted for 16 per cent of total Chinese imports, a share second only to that of the United States (Endicott 1975, 186).

Yet the proponents of military expansion forcefully argued against the option of peaceful commercial recovery. Japan's principal export markets were neighbouring Asian countries; could those markets be relied upon to remain open in an increasingly protectionist world? There was, in any case, good reason to suspect the Western powers of preparing to abandon the so-called 'unequal treaties' with China in response to Chinese nationalist pressure. In 1929 the British had restored tariff autonomy to China and ended its embargo on arms shipments. The following year, it restored the North China naval base of Weihaiwei to Chinese control. This boded ill for Japan, which saw the subjugation of China as indispensable to its trade policy. At the same time, Japan was heavily reliant on imports of Western machinery and raw materials (Boyd 1988, 143). In 1935 it depended on the British Empire for half its imports of jute, lead, tin, zinc and manganese, nearly half its imports of rubber, aluminium, iron ore and cotton and one-third of its imports of pig iron (Neidpath 1981, 136). Around a third of Japan's imports came from the United States, including copious quantities of cotton, scrap iron and oil. Around 80 per cent of Japanese oil was imported from the United States in the 1930s and 10 per cent from the Dutch East Indies; the nearest other source was the Soviet-controlled island of Sakhalin (Coox 1988a, 19). Her dependence on American heavy machinery and machine tools was greater still. Japan also needed the English-speaking economies as markets for its exports, around a fifth of which went to British imperial markets. In the words of Freda Utley, the left-wing English journalist and author of *Japan's feet of clay* (1936), a liberal Japan seemed doomed to 'oscillate between the Scylla of dependence on the USA and the Charybdis of dependence on British empire markets' (Sugihara 1997, 267).

Territorial expansion was the alternative to such insecurity. In the short term, the militarists reasoned, the increased military expenditure caused by a shift to formal imperialism would stimulate Japan's domestic economy, filling the order books of companies like Mitsubishi, Kawasaki and Nissan, while in the long term, it was argued, the appropriation of resource-rich territory would ease the country's balance of payments problems – for what use is an empire if it does not guarantee cut-price raw materials? At the same time, Japan would acquire desperately needed 'living space' to which its surplus population could emigrate. In the words of Lieutenant General Ishiwara Kanji, one of the most influential proponents – and practitioners – of a policy of territorial expansion:

> Our nation seems to be at a deadlock, and there appears to be no solution for the important problems of population and food. The only way out . . . is in the development of Manchuria and Mongolia. . . . [The] natural resources will be sufficient to save [Japan] from the imminent crisis and pave the way for a big jump (cf. Hata 1988, 292; Yasuba 1996, 553n.).

In one respect this argument was not wholly spurious. That Japan faced a Malthusian crisis seemed all too clear when famine struck some rural areas in 1934. Imperialism addressed this problem. Between 1935 and 1940 around 310 000 Japanese emigrated, mostly to the growing Japanese empire in Asia; this certainly eased the downward pressure on domestic wages and consumption (Yasuba 1996, 555 and Table 5). In another respect, however, the case for expansion was deeply suspect. Quite simply, expansion exacerbated precisely the structural problems it was supposed to solve, by requiring increased imports of petroleum, copper, coal, machinery and iron ore to feed the nascent Japanese military-industrial complex. As the Japanese Marxist, Nawa Toichi, put it, 'the more Japan attempted to expand the productive capacity of her heavy and military-related industries as a preparation for her expansion policy. . . the greater her dependence on the world market and the imports of raw materials' became (Sugihara 1997, 275). These arguments applied with equal force to Italy, which manifestly lacked the domestic economic resources to conduct more than small-scale wars against technologically inferior foes (Zamagni, 1998).

DETERRENTS VERSUS APPEASEMENT IN EUROPE

The Second World War was an economic disaster partly because it was, from a strictly economic point of view, avoidable. The ambitions of what became the Axis powers to rearm and acquire living space by conquest could have been resisted far more effectively than they were had the Western powers, Britain, France and the United States, adopted strategies aimed at deterring rather than appeasing the 'have nots'. This is not the place to discuss the military, diplomatic and domestic political arguments for and against appeasement. But it is germane to consider the economic arguments since these played an arguably decisive role, particularly in the British case.

The main argument advanced against more rapid rearmament in 1930s Britain was economic. All that accelerated arms spending would achieve, it was objected by the mandarins of the Treasury, would be to undermine Britain's precarious economic recovery. Better to proceed at a moderate pace and to play for time. The key question is whether this argument was correct.

Fighting the First World War had, to be sure, increased the British national debt by a factor of 12. By 1927 it was equivalent to a crushing 172 per cent of gross domestic product. The interest on the debt accounted for more than two-fifths of public expenditure in the late 1920s.[3] Budget surpluses and an overvalued exchange rate – following Churchill's decision, as Chancellor of the Exchequer, to return to the gold standard in 1925 – were attained at the expense of jobs in manufacturing. The staple British industries of the late Victorian era – coal, iron, ship-building and textiles – had now been replicated all over the world; export markets for such British products inexorably shrank. 'Invisible' earnings from Britain's still immense overseas investments, financial services and shipping were also under pressure (Kennedy 1981, 226–30). Less obvious but in some ways more profound was the damage that the war had done to the labour force. Under the system of volunteering that had been used to recruit the new divisions needed in the first half of the war, a great many skilled workers had been drawn into the armed forces, of which a substantial proportion were either killed or incapacitated (Greasley and Oxley 1996). The official solution to post-war problems was essentially Victorian in conception: budgets should be balanced, the pound should return to gold and free trade should be restored. In the name of 'retrenchment', defence expenditure was reined in, so that as a share of total public spending it fell from nearly 30 per cent in 1913 to just over 10 per cent 20 years later (Kennedy 1981, 239f.). The Ten-year Rule amounted to a spending freeze for the armed services. Even when it was dropped in 1932, the Treasury insisted that 'financial and economic risks' militated against significant increases in the defence budget (Howard 1972, 98).

As Chancellor of the Exchequer, Neville Chamberlain was one of the driving forces behind the creation of the Defence Requirements Committee (DRC), in the belief that a clear ordering of military priorities would make his life easier at the Treasury. He welcomed the identification of Germany as the biggest potential danger (Dilks 1978, 109–12). Yet it was also Chamberlain who ruled out as 'impossible' the additional £97 million that would have been needed to create and maintain an adequate expeditionary force for use on the continent. His preference for a deterrent strategy based on bombers was motivated in large measure by the fact that it looked cheaper than the alternative (Howard 1972, 108f.). When the DRC proposed in November 1935 that its 'Ideal Scheme' of rearmament be financed by a Defence Loan, there was consternation in the Treasury; again Chamberlain insisted on cutting the spending bids for the navy and the army (Newton 1996, 67f.). Soon the air force, too, started to look expensive. As one Treasury official put it after Munich, 'We think that we shall probably not be able to afford it [the Air Ministry's latest proposals] without bringing down the general economy of this country and thus presenting Hitler with precisely that kind of peaceful victory which would be most gratifying to him' (Kennedy 1976, 233; see also Peden 1979). The Treasury gave even shorter shrift to the requests of the army and navy for additional funds (Shay 1977, 282f.). As for Churchill's demands for much larger defence expenditures, which he first advanced in 1936, Chamberlain dismissed these out of hand. Only in 1937 was new borrowing undertaken to finance rearmament, to the tune of £400 million, and even then Chamberlain had initially tried to cover the increased costs by raising taxes (Coghlan 1972, 213; Dilks 1978, 117; Thomas 1983, 560; Newton 1996, 304). His successor at the Treasury, Sir John Simon, insisted that total defence spending from April 1937 to April 1942 should be capped at £1500 million (Parker 1981, 312).

In any case, it was hoped that a policy of economic engagement with Germany might serve to divert the Nazi regime from aggression. On the one hand, officials at the Bank of England and the Treasury, supported by influential firms in the City of London, wanted to preserve trade with Germany and avoid a total German default on money owed to Britain. On the other, they deprecated the kind of economic controls that would undoubtedly be required if large-scale rearmament was to be undertaken without domestic inflation and a widening current account deficit (see Wendt 1971; Shay 1977; Newton 1996). Traditional financial strength was supposed to be the 'fourth arm' of British defence, in Inskip's phrase; hence the Treasury's perennial preoccupation with the balance of payments and the exchange rate. The great fear was that in the event of a prolonged war Britain's credit abroad would prove far weaker than between 1914 and 1918, for the current account deficits of the later 1930s were eating away at Britain's net creditor position, her gold reserves and the strength of sterling (cf. Parker 1975, 637ff.; Peden 1984). For all these reasons it was not until 1938 that defence expenditure exceeded 4 per cent of gross domestic product and not until 1939 that the same could be said of the government's deficit (see Figure 3.3).

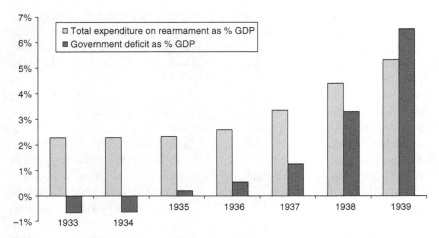

Source: Thomas (2006, Table 1); Feinstein (1972, Table 3); Bank of England.

Figure 3.3   UK defence expenditure and government deficit, 1933–39 (percentage of GDP)

The economic arguments for appeasement reflected British economic strength as much as weakness. Compared with what had happened in Germany and the United States, the Depression in the United Kingdom had been mild. Once Britain had gone off gold in September 1931 and interest rates had been cut to 2 per cent by the Bank of England, recovery came quite swiftly – not, certainly, to the old industrial regions of the North, but to the Midlands and the Southeast, where new industries and services were springing up. Cheap money also fuelled a construction boom in England south of the Trent. But for precisely these reasons, it was argued, significantly higher expenditure on rearmament would have created problems of over-heating in the British economy, in the absence of matching tax increases or cuts in other government programmes (Coghlan 1972, 205–9). Keynes (1940) himself was to argue that, in the event of large-scale defence expenditures, inflation and balance of payments problem could be avoided only if the economy were much more strictly controlled than it had been in the First World War, with severe taxation of consumption. Such an illiberal regime was inconceivable in peacetime. In April 1939 Keynes spelt out the constraints on pre-war rearmament: 'The first is the shortage of labour; the second is the shortage of foreign resources' (Parker 1981, 317). For once he was articulating the conventional wisdom.

Yet these concerns were surely exaggerated. With the annual rate of growth in consumer prices peaking at just under 7 per cent in September

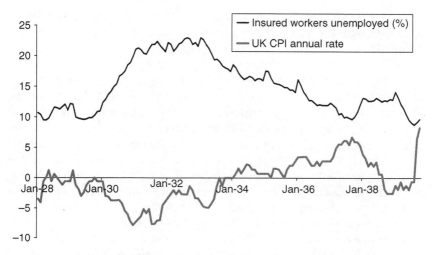

Source: Http://www.nber.org/data/ and http://www.globalfinancialdata.com.

Figure 3.4   UK unemployment and inflation, 1928–39

1937 and then rapidly declining (see Figure 3.4), and with long-term interest rates below 4 per cent until the outbreak of war itself, the Treasury had
far more room for manoeuvre than it admitted. With so much slack in the
system – with good reason, contemporaries feared a recession in 1937 –
higher levels of borrowing would not have 'crowded out' private sector
investment. On the contrary, they would probably have stimulated growth
(Thomas 1983, 571). As for skilled labour, that was only an issue because,
for originally economic reasons, Chamberlain had committed Britain to a
sophisticated airborne deterrent that turned out not to worry Hitler; and
because the government was almost superstitiously nervous of antagoniz-
ing the bloody-minded leadership of the Amalgamated Engineering Union
by 'diluting' the skilled labour force (Parker 1981, 328–43). In practice, the
rearmament programme stimulated staple industries as well as the infant
aeronautical engineering sector; even on limited budgets the navy needed
ships and the army needed guns, tanks and uniforms, so the iron, coal and
textile sectors all benefited. Wages for skilled labourers did not jump
upwards, as the Treasury pessimists had feared; on the contrary, wage
differentials narrowed (Thomas 1983, 564f., 567, 570). A more rational
policy, both economically and strategically, would have been to build more
ships and more tanks and to conscript the unemployed – who still
accounted for 14 per cent of insured workers as late as January 1939 – and
prepare a British Expeditionary Force the Germans could not have

ignored. Chamberlain was simply wrong to fear that Britain lacked the personnel 'to man the enlarged Navy, the new Air Force, and a million-man Army' (Howard 1972, 135; Dunbabin 1975, 598).

Finally, fretting about Britain's financial 'fourth arm' of defence presupposed that foreign powers would lend to Britain in a war only if it were financially attractive to do so, whereas both the United States and the Dominions would have powerful strategic and economic incentives to lend to Britain if the alternative was a victory for the dictators and an interruption to Atlantic export shipments. In any case, the current account deficits of the later 1930s were trivial – equivalent to around 1 per cent of GDP a year, compared with net overseas earnings of at least 3.5 per cent on a total stock of overseas assets worth £3.7 billion ($17 billion).[4] Britain was not broke in 1938. The crucial point was that by 1939 it might well be if its hard currency reserves continued to diminish. The fatal error was the assumption – first enunciated by the Permanent Under-Secretary at the Foreign Office, Sir Robert Vansittart – that Britain gained by waiting (Schmidt 1983, 103–8; Parker 1993, 68). As he observed in December 1936, 'Time is the very material commodity which the Foreign Office is expected to provide in the same way as other departments provide *other* war material. . . . To the Foreign Office falls therefore the task of holding the situation until at least 1939' (Dunbabin 1975, 597). In reality, the 'policy of caution' gave Hitler just as much time to build up his military forces and was positively disadvantageous to Britain from an economic point of view, since with each passing month of political uncertainty British hard currency reserves were further depleted.

British decision-makers failed to appreciate how much weaker Germany's position was than their own in the decisive summer of 1938, when Hitler might very well have been confronted and humiliated if not actually defeated over Czechoslovakia. It was not just in military, diplomatic and political terms that Germany was vulnerable in 1938.[5] Of equal importance was its acute economic vulnerability. The Four Year Plan could not possibly have improved the German position much by September 1938, barely two years since Hitler's memorandum had been drafted. Domestic iron ore production had certainly been boosted, but the increment since 1936 was just over a million tons, little more than a tenth of imports in 1938. No more than 11 000 tons of synthetic rubber had been produced, around 12 per cent of imports (Tooze 2006, Table 6). The rationale of annexing Austria and Czechoslovakia was precisely to address the shortages of raw materials that were continuing to hamper German rearmament (Overy 1999, 194–200). Had war come in 1938, the journalist Ian Colvin (1965, 273) had it on good authority that Germany had only sufficient stocks of petroleum for three months. In addition, the German economy was by now suffering from acute labour shortages, not least as a result of the upsurge in arms spending that had been set in train by the Four Year Plan (Tooze 2006, Ch. 8). As Colvin's testimony suggests, Germany's economic problems were no secret. Indeed, its financial symptoms were highly visible. Schacht's resignation as Economics Minister – which he submitted in August 1937, though it was not accepted until November – was widely seen as a blow to the regime's fiscal credibility, although he stayed on as Reichsbank President (Smelser 1983, 38f.; Brown and Burdekin 2002, 665). Aside from his objections to the Four Year Plan, Schacht had two concerns: the mounting inflationary pressure as more and more of the costs of rearmament were met by printing money, and the looming exhaustion of Germany's hard currency reserves.

These problems did not go away. German exports were a fifth lower in 1938 than the year before. In July, Germany had to give in when Britain insisted on a revision of the Anglo-German Payments Agreement and continued payment of interest due on the Dawes and Young bonds (issued to help finance reparations) (MacDonald 1972, 115ff.). The anti-appeasing commercial attaché in the British Embassy in Berlin had a point when he argued for cancelling the Anglo-German Payments Agreement. By further reducing Germany's access to hard currency, that would have struck at the German economy's Achilles heel (MacDonald 1972, 121). Small wonder the German stock market slumped by 13 per cent between April and August 1938; the German Finance Minister Count Schwerin von Krosigk warned that Germany was on the brink of an inflationary crisis. In a devastating Reichsbank memorandum, dated 3 October 1938, Schacht said the same. When Schacht and his colleagues repeated their warnings of inflation Hitler fired them (Tooze 2006, Ch. 9).

As we have seen, British officials worried a great deal about Britain's shortages of labour and hard currency. But in both respects the German position was far worse in 1938, just as it was worse militarily, diplomatically and domestically. Had Chamberlain resisted the temptation to fly off to Germany in pursuit of 'peace in our time', but had instead held firm to the maintenance of Czechoslovakia's territorial integrity, the pressure on Germany would have far exceeded that on Britain. Even after Hitler's bad faith became apparent, he and key officials in the Treasury and the Foreign Office clung to the notion that time was on Britain's side and that it was better to fight later than sooner. But this was wrong. Time – not to mention the free gift of Czechoslovakia – enabled Hitler to improve Germany's strategic position, particularly by concluding the Nazi-Soviet Pact. In terms of military and economic preparedness, it was the Germans not the British who gained the most from the last 12 months of peace. In economic terms Munich was a disaster, for the simple reason that a relatively small war over Czechoslovakia would have been so much less costly than the war that began with the partition of Poland in 1939.

Appeasement meant that Germany was undeterred by subsequent British commitments to other Central and East European countries. 'Our enemies are little worms', he remarked, two days before the Nazi-Soviet Pact was signed; 'I saw them at Munich' (Overy 1999, 191). Slow rearmament also meant that Germany was undeterred by the diminutive forces Britain had at her disposal to send to Europe even as late as 1940.

THE JAPANESE CASE

The Japanese case was different. Here, it is true, the British offered even less reason for concern than they did in Europe. It was not difficult for Japanese decision-makers to work out that the British Empire in Asia was as enfeebled by 1941 as the Dutch and French. Even had the Europeans adopted more confrontational policies, they would have lacked credibility given the magnitude of the setbacks they had suffered in Europe in 1940. The sole obstacle to Japanese hegemony in Southeast Asia was therefore America (Kinhide 1973). On the one hand, it was clear that the United States had scant appetite for war, in Asia or anywhere else. On the other, Americans had little desire to see Japan as sole master of China, let alone the whole of East Asia. But those who ran US policy in the Pacific believed they did not need to take up arms to prevent this because of Japan's dependence on trade with the United States and hence its vulnerability to economic pressure (Barnhart 1987,178f.). Even if the Americans did not intervene militarily, they had the option to choke the Japanese war machine to death, especially if they cut off oil exports to Japan (Scalapino 1980, 117). This was precisely what made it so hard for American diplomats and politicians to foresee the Japanese attack on Pearl Harbor. As normally risk-averse people, they could not imagine the Japanese being so rash as to gamble on a very swift victory when the economic odds were stacked so heavily against them (Graebner 1974, xvi–xvii). They assumed that the partial sanctions imposed after the Japanese invasion of Indo-China would send a clear enough signal to deter the Japanese. Their effect was precisely the opposite.

The origins of the war in the Pacific were in large measure economic. The Japanese-American Commercial Treaty of 1911 was abrogated in July 1939. By the end of the year, Japan (along with other combatants) was affected by the Roosevelt's 'moral embargo' on the export of 'materials essential to airplane manufacture', which meant in practice aluminium, molybdenum, nickel, tungsten and vanadium (Barnhart 1984, 179f.). At the same time, the State Department applied pressure on American firms to stop exporting technology to Japan that would facilitate the production of aviation fuel (Lu 1961, 150; Barnhart 1987, 180f.). With the National Defense Act of July 1940 the President was empowered to impose real prohibitions on the exports of strategic commodities and manufactures. By the end of the month, after a protracted wrangle between the State Department and the Treasury, it was agreed to ban the export of high-grade scrap iron and steel, aviation fuel, lubricating oil and the fuel blending agent tetraethyl lead. On 26 September the ban was extended to all scrap; two months later the export of iron and steel themselves became subject to licence (Lu 1961, 144; Barnhart 1987, 182–97; Coox 1988b, 326). No one knew for sure what the effect of these restrictions would be. Some, like the State Department's 'Advisor on Far Eastern Affairs', Stanley Hornbeck, said they would hobble the Japanese military; others, like the US Ambassador in Tokyo, Joseph Grew, that they would provoke it. Neither view was correct. The sanctions had in fact been imposed too late to deter Japan from contemplating war, since the Japanese had been importing and stockpiling American raw materials since the outbreak of war in China (Lu 1961, 244f.). Only one economic sanction was regarded in Tokyo as a *casus belli* and that was an embargo on oil. That came in July 1941, along with a freeze on all Japanese assets in the United States – a response to the Japanese occupation of southern Indo-China (Barnhart 1987, 263ff.). From this point, war in the Pacific was inevitable.

For a long time the Japanese Foreign Ministry had found it hard to imagine the United States taking up arms against a victorious combination of Germany, Italy and Japan – especially if the Soviet Union were on friendly terms with that combination (Lu 1961, 109–13). A guiding assumption was that the American public was staunchly isolationist, and that the victories of Japan and its allies would reinforce rather than reverse that sentiment (Barnhart 1984, 440, 446f.). The army was also reluctant to confront the United States, hoping that the conquest of European possessions in Asia could somehow be achieved without precipitating American intervention (Akira 1973, 191; Coox 1988b, 325). Until September 1941 Japan's naval strategists were the only ones prepared to contemplate a war with America. However, they ultimately could see no other way of winning it than to deal a knockout blow to the US navy at the outset (Kiyoshi 1982, 129ff.). By April 1941 Admiral Yamamoto Isoroku had convinced himself that the ships stationed at Pearl Harbor could be sunk in one fell swoop. On 1 November Lieutenant-General Suzuki Teiichi assured the participants at a ministerial-military Liaison Conference that supplies from the territories to be occupied would be sufficient to meet Japan's material needs. 'In 1943', he declared, 'the material situation will be much better if we go to war' (Kiyoshi 1982, 132; Barnhart 1984, 449).

This was not in fact the same as saying that Japan's material situation was equal to the challenge of war against the British Empire, the Dutch East Indies and the United States (for more realistic assessments of Japan's economic position, see Coox 1988b, 333ff.). All Suzuki meant was that Japan's material situation was bound to deteriorate the longer war was postponed. The navy alone was consuming 400 tons of oil an hour, just idly waiting; after 18 months it would all be gone (Jansen 1975, 404f.). It therefore followed that it was better to strike now rather than to wait. This rationale was sufficient to commit Japan to such a war if no diplomatic breakthrough had been achieved by midnight on November 30, 1941.

It is sometimes suggested that the decision-makers in Tokyo were succumbing to some kind of irrational Oriental fatalism – an impression heightened by Tōjō's assertion on 14 October that 'a man sometimes must dare to leap boldly from the towering stage of Kiyomizu Temple' (Coox 1988a, 14). Links have been drawn between the decision for war against the United States and the samurai code, or a specifically Japanese 'siege mentality', if not collective hysteria. Yet in many ways this way of thinking was more Western than Eastern in its provenance. Unknowingly, Tōjō was echoing Bethmann Hollweg's arguments for a German war against Russia in 1914 and Hitler's arguments for a German war against the Western powers in 1939. Even the timeframe was similar:

> Two years from now [1943] we will have no petroleum for military use; ships will stop moving. When I think about the strengthening of American defences in the south-western Pacific, the expansion of the U.S. fleet, the unfinished China Incident, and so on, I see no end of difficulties. We can talk long about suffering and austerity but can our people endure such a life for long?. . .I fear that we would become a third class nation after two or three years if we merely sat tight. (Coox 1988b, 336)

Thus, when Tōjō spoke of 'shutting one's eyes and taking the plunge' he was making a very German argument: to gamble on immediate war rather than submit to relative decline in the near future; to put to use military assets that would certainly bankrupt the country if they continued to sit idle (Jansen 1975, 405–8; Buruma 2003, 96). In the words of a High Command policy paper presented to the Imperial Conference of 6 September 1941, the American aim was 'to dominate the world'; to this end the United States aimed 'to prevent our empire from rising and developing in East Asia'. Japan was in 'a desperate situation, where it must resort to the ultimate step – war – to defend itself and ensure its preservation'. The alternative was to 'lie prostrate at the feet of the United States' (Coox 1988b, 329).

The Japanese were not fantasists. For Foreign Minister Matsuoka Yōsuke, Pearl Harbor was the disastrous culmination of a strategic miscalculation. He had assumed that the combination of the Tripartite Pact with Germany and Italy and the Neutrality Treaty with the Soviet Union would deter the United States from resisting Japanese expansion in Asia (Lu 1961, 119). Nomura Kichisaburo, the last pre-war ambassador to Washington, had favoured a more moderate policy, seeking a return to the Open Door regime in China, rather than risk war with the United States (Graebner 1974, xii). Nor were all Japan's senior naval officers persuaded by Yamamoto's plan. Nagano Osami, Chief of the Navy Staff, argued that Japan was 'bound for self-destruction and. . .destined for national extinction' – though he regarded this, somewhat paradoxically, as true to 'the spirit of defending the nation in a war' (Kimitada 1975, 119). In the summer of 1941 the Economic Mobilization Bureau produced a report that concluded that after two years of hostilities, Japan's economic resources would probably not suffice to sustain air and naval operations. Nagano expected that 'the situation [would] become increasingly worse' as early as the second half of 1942 (Coox 1988a, 13). Tōjō himself admitted that he did not know what Japan would do if war continued after 1943 (Coox 1988b, 333ff.). It was not hubris that led to Pearl Harbor, but a conviction that it was preferable to take the chance of defeat in war than 'to be ground down without doing anything' (Coox 1988a, 14).

Perhaps the real fantasists were the Americans, who adopted a remarkably confrontational stance in the final pre-war months, given the vulnerability of their own military installations in the Pacific, particularly the Philippines. The British were markedly more conciliatory, even temporarily closing the Burma Road between July and October 1940 in response to Japanese pressure (cf. Lowe 1974, 44ff.; Lowe 1977, 284–7). For reasons that are not easy to fathom, Roosevelt consistently exaggerated the future economic and strategic importance of China and underestimated the perils of war with Japan (Clayton 1986, 709f.). He declined an invitation from Konoe to attend a summit conference in the summer of 1941. Secretary of State Cordell Hull wanted complete withdrawal of Japanese troops from China and Indo-China; he would not hear of any suspension of US aid to Chiang, which the Japanese demanded. In his fateful note of 26 November, Hull even proposed a mutual surrender of extraterritorial rights in China – an end, in effect, to the old system of unequal treaties – and recognition of the Kuomintang government (Coox 1988b, 337). With some justification, the policy of the United States towards Japan in this period has been likened to its policy towards the Soviet Union during the Cold War, with the difference that the United States failed to appreciate the very grave danger of a Japanese first strike (Iriye 1981, 1).

ECONOMIC DETERMINANTS FOR DEFEAT

Could the Axis powers have won the Second World War? By the summer of 1942, Hitler's soldiers had reached the banks of the River Don, the gateway to the Caucasus, and were pressing on towards the Volga. The Soviet oilfields at Maykop were captured; the swastika flew on the peak of Mount Elbruz. Poland, the Baltic States, the Ukraine and Byelorussia: all were in German hands. By this stage in the war, Germany and its allies controlled virtually all of Western and Central Europe too, with the exception of a handful of neutral countries (Eire, Portugal, Sweden, Switzerland and Spain). As one Russian commentator put it, 'Paris, Vienna, Prague and Brussels had become provincial German cities' (Grossman 1985, 195). The Balkans had yielded to German arms, as had Crete. In North Africa it was very nearly the same story. On 17 June 1942, Rommel's Afrika Korps captured the British stronghold of Tobruk and thrust into Egypt to within 50 miles of Alexandria. Intoxicated by victory, Hitler contemplated the future German conquest of Brazil, of Central Africa, of New Guinea. The United States, too, would ultimately be 'incorporated . . . into the German World Empire' (Burleigh 1999, 341f.). Japan, meanwhile, had achieved no less astonishing victories in Asia and the Pacific. Already by 1941 the greater part of Eastern China was in Japanese hands. The six-month onslaught that began with Pearl Harbor created a vast 'Greater East Asia Co-prosperity Zone', embracing modern-day Malaysia, Myanmar, Indonesia, Thailand and Vietnam, to say nothing of a huge arc of Pacific islands. By the summer of 1942, then, as Richard Overy has observed, only an incurable optimist could be certain that the Allies would win the war. 'We have already lost a large proportion of the British Empire', lamented Alan Brooke, Chief of the Imperial General Staff, in 1942, 'and are on the high road to lose a great deal more of it'. Britain seemed to be 'a ship. . .heading inevitably for the rocks' (Alanbrooke 2001, 243f.). 'Would we be able to save India and Australia?. . .Egypt was threatened. . . . Russia could never hold, [the] Caucasus was bound to be penetrated'. The Germans might even reach the Gulf oilfields ('our Achilles heel') (Alanbrooke 2001, 249, 280–83, 355).

Military historians have long debated the strategic options open to Germany and Japan, in search of alternative decisions that might have tipped the war Hitler's and Hirohito's way. The difficulty with all the counterfactuals that have been proposed is that virtually none of them suggests a way in which the Axis powers could have overcome the overwhelming economic odds against them once they had taken on simultaneously the British Empire, the United States and the Soviet Union. To be sure, the Blitzkrieg campaigns of 1939–42 narrowed the economic gap between the Axis powers and their foes. The Germans very successfully sucked resources out of occupied Western Europe; at their peak in 1943 unrequited transfers from France amounted to 8 per cent of German gross national product – equivalent to a third of pre-war French national income (Milward 1987, 140, Tables 21, 22). Germany all but monopolized the exports of the West European countries it occupied. The former Czechoslovakia, too, was a substantial net contributor to the German war effort (for trade figures for Central and Eastern Europe see Kaser and Radice 1986, 523–9). So deep did Operation Barbarossa and subsequent German offensives penetrate that they captured a huge proportion – more than half – of Soviet industrial capacity.[6] Moreover, the Germans were able to treat their empire as a bottomless reservoir of cheap labour. Foreign workers accounted for a fifth of the active civilian labour force by 1943 (Noakes and Pridham 1988, 908ff.). After being put in charge of German armaments production, Albert Speer galvanized the Third Reich's economy, almost trebling German weapons production between 1941 and 1944 by imposing standardization on the manufacturers and achieving startling improvements in productivity (Overy 1996, 198f., 201–4, 242ff.; though see Budrass, Scherner and Streb 2005, which seeks to diminish Speer's contribution). The Japanese also performed feats of economic mobilization, increasing aircraft production by a factor of 5.5 between 1941 and 1944.

Yet it was nowhere near enough. The Big Three Allies had vastly superior material resources. In 1940, when Germany and Italy had faced Britain and France, the latter combination's total economic output had been roughly two-thirds that of the other side's. The defeat of France and Poland increased the odds against Britain, but the German invasion of the Soviet Union restored the economic balance. With the entry of the United States into the war, the scales tipped the other way; indeed, they all but toppled over. Combined Allied GDP was twice that of the principal Axis powers and their dependencies in 1942. It was roughly three times as large in 1943, and the ratio continued to rise as the war went on, largely as a result of the rapid growth of the US economy (see Figure 3.5). Between 1942 and 1944, American military spending was nearly twice that of Germany and Japan combined (Goldsmith 1946). It is difficult to see how different strategic decisions could have prevented this disastrous lengthening of the economic odds on an Axis victory. So much of the increment in Allied production simply lay beyond the reach of Axis arms, in the United States and beyond the Urals. Moreover, the additional oilfields that might have come within Hitler's reach had he fought the war differently were still far too modest in their output to have narrowed the petroleum gap between the two sides significantly.

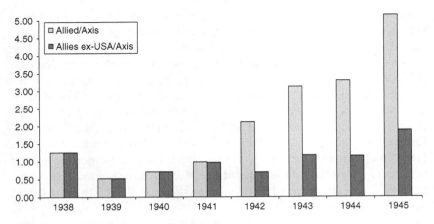

Note: This chart calculates the ratio of Allied to Axis combined gross domestic product. The bars to the right not only remove US GDP from the calculation, but also the value of American aid to the United Kingdom and the Soviet Union.

Source: Harrison (1998a, 10).

Figure 3.5   Ratio of Allied to Axis GDP, with and without the United States, 1938–45

Moreover, the Axis powers were fighting not only against the British, Russians and Americans; they were fighting against the combined forces of the British, Russian and American empires as well. The total numbers of men fielded by the various parts of the British Empire were immense. All told, the United Kingdom itself mobilized just under six million men and women. But an additional five million came from India, Canada, Australia, New Zealand and South Africa (Ellis 1993, 227f.). Victories like El Alamein and even more so Imphal were victories for imperial forces as much as for British forces; the colonial commitment to the Empire proved every bit as strong as in the First World War (see, for example, McKernan 1995, 37–48).[7] Especially remarkable was the fact that more than 2.5 million Indians volunteered to serve in the British Indian army during the war – more than 60 times the number who fought for the Japanese. The rapid expansion of the Indian officer corps provided a crucial source of loyalty – albeit loyalty that was conditional on post-war independence (details can be found in Prasad and Char 1956, App. 13–16 and see also Chenevix-Trench 1988 and Barkawi 2006). The Red Army was also much more than just a Russian army. In January 1944 Russians accounted for 58 per cent of the 200 infantry divisions for which records are available, but Ukrainians accounted for 22 per cent, an order of magnitude more than fought on the German side, and a larger proportion than their share of the pre-war Soviet population (cf. Rakowska-Harmstone 1990; Alexiev and Wimbush 1993, 432f., 441; Gorter-Gronvik and Suprun (2000)).[8] Half the soldiers of the Soviet 62nd Army at Stalingrad were not Russians (Beevor 2002, 170).

The American army, too, was ethnically diverse. Although they were generally kept in segregated units, African Americans accounted for around 11 per cent of total US forces mobilized, and fought in all the major campaigns from Operation Torch onwards (Hargrove, 1985, 3–5; Buckley 2001, 262–318). Norman Mailer's reconnaissance platoon in *The naked and the dead* includes two Jews, a Pole, an Irishman, a Mexican and an Italian. Two of the six servicemen who raised the Stars and Stripes on Iwo Jima were of foreign origin (Davie 1947, 195).[9] More than 20 000 Japanese-Americans served in the US army during the war (Myer 1971, 146–53).

The Germans, it is true, had made some efforts to mobilize other peoples in occupied Europe, as had the Japanese, but these were dwarfed by what the Allies achieved. Indeed, the abject failure of the Axis empires to win the loyalty of their new subjects ensured that Allied forces were reinforced by a plethora of exile forces, partisan bands and resistance organizations. Even excluding these auxiliaries, the combined armed forces of the principal Allies were already just under 30 per cent larger than those of the Axis in 1942. A year later the difference was more than 50 per cent. By the end of the war, including also Free French and Polish forces, Yugoslav partisans and Romanians fighting on the Russian side, the Allies had more than twice as many men under arms (based on the various figures in Harrison 1998c; for the end of the war see Ellis 1993, 227f.).

The best measure of the Allied advantage was in terms of military hardware, however, since it was with capital rather than labour – with machinery rather than personnel – that the Germans and the Japanese were ultimately to be defeated. In every single category of weapon, the Axis powers fell steadily further behind with each passing month. Between 1942 and 1944, the Allies out-produced the Axis in terms of machine pistols by a factor of 16 to one, in naval vessels, tanks and mortars by roughly five to one, and in rifles, machine guns, artillery and combat aircraft by roughly three to one (Harrison 1998a, 17). Blitzkrieg had been possible when the odds were just the other way round. Once both sides were motorized – one of the defining characteristics of total war – the key to victory became logistics, not heroics. The four-fold numerical superiority of British armour was one of the keys to victory at El Alamein (Ellis 1993, 228, 230). The average ratio of Soviet to German armour at the beginning of the offensives of 1944 and 1945 was just under eight (Ellis 1993, 14, 230). The ratio in terms of combat aircraft on the Eastern Front rose from three in July 1943 to ten by January 1945 (Ellis 1993, 233). Likewise, Allied dominance of the skies ensured the success of D-Day and guaranteed the ultimate defeat of the Germans in Western Europe.

In the Pacific, meanwhile, the United States simply swamped Japan with a tidal wave of mass-produced armaments. American submarines reduced the Japanese merchant marine by three-quarters, cutting off the supply of indispensable imports. American anti-aircraft guns shot down Japanese planes faster than Japanese factories could build them. American shipyards built and repaired battleships while Japan's sat idle for want of materials (Willmott, 1983, 521f.; Coox 1988b, 377f.; Nalty 1999). By 1944 the United States was producing 26 times as much high explosive as Japan (Coox 1988a, 21). In terms of tanks and trucks the Japanese were in the same second-class league as the Italians. In terms of medical provision – an area where the Allies made major advances during the war – they were in the nineteenth century (Clayton 1986, 717; Harrison 2004). Again, it is impossible to imagine any alternative Japanese strategy after Pearl Harbor that could have compensated for this immense economic imbalance (for a survey of the literature see Peattie 1998). In putting their faith in increasingly suicidal tactics, Japanese commanders revealed themselves as (in Alvin Coox's apt phrase) 'medieval samurai warriors masquerading as practitioners of modern military science' (Coox 1988a, 39). The Americans, by contrast, were the masters of overkill, whose first principle was: 'always have on hand more of everything than you can ever conceivably need' (Cozzens 1948, 12).

The sheer scale of American economic capabilities had been underestimated by both the Japanese and the Germans. The Axis leaders deluded themselves into believing that, with the Great Depression, the American economic model had disintegrated. Yet American corporations led the world in the techniques of mass production and modern management. Despite the sluggish growth of aggregate demand in the mid-to late 1930s, firms like General Motors had been taking major strides forward in efficiency, exploiting those economies of scale that were unique to the huge American market. Exports to Britain and the Soviet Union had given GM and its peers a foretaste of what was to come. With the American entry into the war, they were inundated with government orders for military hardware. In the First World War, the result had been a mess: production bottlenecks, chronic waste and inflationary pressure. In 1942 the opposite happened. 'The real news', as Charles E. Wilson (1943) of General Motors put it, 'is that our American methods of production, our know-how about the business, could be applied to mass production of all these war things. . .and that is the one factor that I think our Axis enemies overlooked'.[10] Here, too, a compromise was involved. With astonishing speed the big corporations converted themselves from the champions of a consumer society to the servants of a command economy. As John Hancock and Bernard Baruch observed: 'With the coming of war a sort of totalitarianism is asserted. The government tells each business what it is to contribute to the war program . . .' (Nelson 1946, 393).

In macroeconomic terms the results were startling enough. By 1942 US gross national product was more than 60 per cent higher than it had been in 1938. By 1944 it was more than double its pre-war level. Between 1940 and 1943, five million new jobs were created (Vatter 1985, 16). This was the result of an immense fiscal stimulus, which saw federal deficits rise above 20 per cent of GNP, and an attendant surge in both private investment and personal consumption (Vernon 1994; Rockoff 1998). Though some raw materials did have to be rationed, the United States was, as Wilson of GM put it, the first country to work out how to have both guns and butter in wartime.[11] Much of the credit for this success must go to the corporate executives – the so-called 'dollar-a-year men' like Philip Reed of General Electric – who gave their services effectively gratis to the government during the war, and facilitated the remarkably smooth cooperation between the War Department and the big manufacturers, hitherto staunch opponents of Roosevelt (Nelson 1946; cf. McQuaid 1994, 13f; on business opposition to the New Deal see Stromberg 1953). Never before or since has the federal government intervened on such a scale in American economic life, building and sometimes also owning a vast number of new industrial facilities (Smith 1959, 477ff.). Agencies like the National Defense Advisory Commission, the Office of Production Management, the War Production Board and the Office of War Mobilization transformed the regulatory landscape (Koistinen 2004).

It was at the microeconomic level, however, that the output war was really won. For the biggest wartime advances in mass production and management were made in vast factories like Ford's mile-long bomber assembly line at Willow Run, Boeing's B-29 plant at Seattle or General Motors' aero-engine factory at Allison. At peak Boeing Seattle was churning out 16 B-17s a day and employing 40 000 men and women on round-the-clock shifts (cf. Redding and Yenne 1983; Rodgers 1996, 65). Never had ships been built so rapidly as the Liberty Ships, 2700 of which slid down the slipways during the war years. It was at wartime General Motors that Peter Drucker (1946, 31–81) saw the birth of the modern 'concept of the corporation', with its decentralized system of management.[12] And it was during the war that the American military-industrial complex was born; over half of all prime government contracts went to just 33 corporations (Vatter 1985, 60). Boeing's net wartime profits for the years 1941 to 1945 amounted $27.6 million; in the preceding five years the company had lost nearly

$3 million.[13] General Motors Corporation employed half a million people and supplied one-tenth of all American war production. Ford alone produced more military equipment during the war than Italy (Overy 1996, 193–7). Small wonder some more cerebral soldiers felt they were risking their necks not in a 'real war. . .but. . .in a regulated business venture' (Jones 1962, 35; Heller 1962, 292, 298). It was strange indeed that the recovery of the American economy from the Depression should owe so much to the business of flattening other people's cities. Tokyo's economic disaster was Seattle's economic boom.

Though much more reliant than the Western Allies on pitting men directly against enemy fire, the Soviet Union also out-produced Germany in military hardware. From March 1943 onwards, the Russians had consistently been able to field between twice and three times as many tanks and self-propelled guns as the Germans. This was remarkable, given the relative backwardness of the Russian economy and the enormous challenge of relocating production eastwards after the German invasion (Harrison 1981, 182–91; Overy 1996, 181). Magnitogorsk, Sverdlovsk and Chelyabinsk became the heartland of a new military-industrial complex, the defining characteristic of which was increased productivity through standardization and economies of scale (Overy 1996, 182, 185f.). The T-34 battle tank was one of the great triumphs of wartime design. Simple to build but easily manoeuvrable, protected with innovative sloped armour and packing a hefty punch, it was the very antithesis of the notoriously inadequate American Sherman M4 (Nye 2002). The later IS-1 and IS-2 'Josef Stalin' tanks were a match even for the German Panther and the Tiger I and II, which were also vulnerable to the giant SU-152 anti-tank gun (Overy 1997, 190–93). The volumes produced of these and other weapons were large. Soviet production accounted for one in four Allied combat aircraft, one in three Allied machine guns, two-fifths of Allied armoured vehicles and two-thirds of Allied mortars (Barber and Harrison 2006).

Nevertheless, the Soviet economic achievement should not be seen in isolation from the American. It is well known that the system of 'lend lease' provided a vital multi-billion pound economic lifeline to Britain. Net grants from the United States totalled £5.4 billion between 1941 and 1945, on average around 9 per cent of UK gross national product (Broadberry and Howlett 1998, 51). Less well known are the vast quantities of material that the Americans made available to the Soviets. All told, Stalin received supplies worth 93 billion rubles, between 4 and 8 per cent of Soviet net material product (Harrison, 1998b). The volumes of hardware suggest that these official statistics understate the importance of American assistance: 380 000 field telephones, 363 000 trucks, 43 000 jeeps, 6000 tanks and over 5000 miles of telephone wire were shipped along the icy Arctic supply routes to Murmansk, from California to Vladivostok, or overland from Persia. Thousands of fighter planes were flown along an 'air bridge' from Alaska to Siberia (Forsyth 1992, 354). Nor was it only hardware that the Americans supplied to Stalin. Around 58 per cent of Soviet aviation fuel came from the United States during the war, 53 per cent of all explosives and very nearly half of all the copper, aluminium and rubber tyres, to say nothing of the tons of tinned spam – in all, somewhere between 41 and 63 per cent of all Soviet military supplies (Overy 1997, 195f.; Burleigh 2001, 734). American engineers also continued to provide valuable technical assistance, as they had in the early days of Magnitogorsk. The letters 'U.S.A.' stencilled on the Studebaker trucks were said to stand for *Ubit Sukina syna Adolf* – 'to kill that son-of-a-bitch Adolf' (Overy 1997, 197). The Soviets would have struggled to kill half so many Germans without this colossal volume of American aid. It was not an aspect of the 'Great Patriotic War' that Stalin was particularly eager to publicize. But without this vast contribution of American capital – as both Zhukov and Stalin's successor Nikita Khrushchev privately conceded – the Soviet Union might conceivably have lost the war or would, at least, have taken much longer to win it (Overy 1997, 195).

That total war would ultimately be decided by material rather than moral factors was not lost on all Germans. 'The first essential condition for an army to be able to stand the strain of battle', wrote Rommel, 'is an adequate stock of weapons, petrol and ammunition. In fact, the battle is fought and decided by the quartermasters before the shooting begins. The bravest men can do nothing without guns, the guns nothing without plenty of ammunition; and neither guns nor ammunition are of much use in mobile warfare unless there are vehicles with sufficient petrol to haul them around' (van Creveld 1977, 200). By the final year of the war, an active US army division was consuming around 650 tons of supplies a day. Because a single army truck could carry just five tons, this posed a formidable logistical challenge. Indeed, as supply lines were stretched from 200 to 400 miles in the months after D-Day, deliveries to the advancing armies slumped from 19 000 tons a day to 7000 tons (van Creveld 1977, 216 – 30 and 23n.). The last phase of the war revealed the importance (consistently underrated by both the Germans and the Japanese) of assigning ample numbers of men to the task of supply rather than combat. The ratio of combatants to non-combatants in the German army was two to one; but the equivalent American ratio in the European theatre was one to two. In the Pacific, the Japanese ratio was one to one; the Americans had 18 non-combatants for every man at the front (Overy 1996, 319).

It is no doubt entertaining to imagine how Hitler might have used a Nazi atomic bomb to negate these disadvantages (Gill 1995; Lindsey 2002) but the reality is that Werner Heisenberg and the German scientists came nowhere near devising one. Even had the Germans achieved more rapid improvements in their air defences – for example, developing and deploying jet-powered fighters earlier – material constraints would have limited the number of these that could have been built (Price 1995; Isby 2002). In the unmanned rockets, the V-1 and V-2, the Germans did produce remarkable new weapons that inflicted heavy casualties and dented civilian morale in London; but they were not the war-winning innovations of Hitler's dreams (on increasingly desperate German hopes that new weapons could avert defeat, see Speer 1970, 412). The Japanese were even further away from a decisive technological breakthrough (Coox 1988a, 26).

In short, while they might well have been able to defeat the British Empire had it fought unassisted – while they might even have defeated Britain and the Soviet Union, had the United States remained neutral – those were not wars Hitler and his confederates chose to fight. They staked their claim to world power against all three empires: the British, the Russian and the American. If anything was inevitable in the history of the twentieth century, it was the victory of this overwhelming combination (Levine 1985). Neutral investors certainly thought so, to judge by the wartime performance of German bonds traded in Switzerland, which plunged 39 per cent on the outbreak of war, rallied during 1940, then declined again in response to the aftermath of Operation Barbarossa, plunging at the time of the Yalta Conference to roughly the same low point they had first touched in September 1939 (Frey and Kucher 2000). Different outcomes in particular military engagements – for example, the battles of Coral Sea, Midway, Guadalcanal or even Leyte Gulf – would have done no more than delay the unavoidable collapse (Ambrose 1992; Arnold 2001; Cook 2001; Lindsey 2001; Burtt 2001; Anderson 2001). Even if the Germans had succeeded in repelling the Allied landings in Italy and France – which is not inconceivable, given the inherent riskiness of Operation Overlord – or in checking for longer the Allied advance through the Ardennes, they would still not have been in a position to win the war (Ruge 1965; Ambrose 1992, 2002; Klivert-Jones 1995; Anderson 2004; Campbell 2004; Prados 2004; Tsouras 2004a, 2004b). Indeed, diverting German forces westwards in 1944 merely served to hasten the collapse in the East (Manteuffel, 1965).

THE ECONOMIC IMPACTS OF ALLIED BOMBING

One of the most vexed economic questions of the Second World War is how far the policy of bombing German and Japanese cities hastened its end. Britain had already committed itself to building bombers during the 1930s in the misguided belief that they might deter German aggression. Since German fighting forces were quite widely dispersed for much of the war, the obvious targets for aerial bombardment were economic – the factories that were supplying Hitler's forces with weapons and the infrastructure that allowed these to be transported to the various fronts. However, most of these economic targets were, by their very nature, located in densely populated areas like the Ruhr. Moreover, British bombers were very far from accurate. In October 1940 the British ruled that, in conditions of poor visibility, their airmen could drop their bombs in the vicinity of targets, in so-called 'free fire zones'. This made it more likely that German civilians would be hit – a necessity that Churchill sought to make into a virtue. As he put it on October 30, 'The civilian population around the target areas must be made to feel the weight of war' (Lindqvist 2002, paragraph 181).

Throughout 1941, Churchill repeatedly emphasized the need for Bomber Command to target the morale of ordinary Germans. The strategy of 'area bombing' – the aim of which was in fact to incinerate urban centres – was thus in place even before Air Marshal Arthur 'Bomber' Harris took over Bomber Command (Overy 1996, 112f.). Nine days before Harris's appointment, on St Valentine's Day, 1942, Air Vice-Marshal N.H. Bottomley, Deputy of the Air Staff, wrote to Bomber Command to convey the decision 'that the primary object of your operations should now be focused on the morale of the enemy civil population and in particular, of the industrial workers', and that these operations should take the form of 'concentrated incendiary attacks'. The letter was accompanied by an annexe listing 'selected area targets', at the top of which was Essen. By attacking it first, 'the maximum benefit should be derived from the element of surprise'. Like the other prime targets, Duisberg, Düsseldorf and Cologne, Essen was without question an industrial city. Yet the criteria listed for calculating the 'estimated weight of attack for decisive damage' were the size and population of the built-up area. Attacks on factories and submarine building yards were to be considered 'diversionary', and were to be undertaken preferably 'without missing good opportunities of bombing your primary targets'.[14] What this meant was that a rising proportion of first British and then American resources were diverted into the destruction of German and Japanese cities – in other words, the slaughter of civilians. According to Overy (1996, 129), 7 per cent of Britain's total war effort in terms of production and combat-man hours went into strategic bombing, rising to 12 per cent in the last two years of war.

This was precisely the policy the US State Department had denounced as 'unwarranted and contrary to principles of law and humanity' when the Japanese had first bombed Chinese cities (Dower 1986, 38). It was precisely the policy that Neville Chamberlain had once dismissed as 'mere terrorism' – a policy to which 'His Majesty's government [would] never resort' (Lindqvist 2002, paragraph 177).

What made the concept of strategic bombing so appealing? Air war was not necessarily cheaper, since the planes themselves were expensive to produce and the crews expensive to train. Mortality rates were among the highest in the war; the life expectancy of a Lancaster was estimated at just 12 missions, while the average odds of survival for bomber crews were worse than one in two. To civilian politicians, however, strategic bombing was preferable to relying on ground troops because of the comparatively small numbers of men involved. Air war was in large part about the substitution of capital for labour – of machinery for men. A single crew of trained fliers could hope to kill a very large number of Germans or Japanese even if they flew only 20 successful missions before being killed or captured themselves. Revealingly, Churchill spoke of 'pay[ing] our way by bombing Germany' when he visited Moscow in 1942; the currency he had in mind was German not British lives (Harriman and Abel 1975, 153). The more Stalin pressed the Western powers to open a Second Front in Western Europe, the more Churchill extolled the virtues of strategic bombing, promising attacks that would 'shatter the morale of the German people' (Overy 1996, 102f.). He was equally sanguine about the benefits of bombing Italy, arguing that 'the demoralization and panic produced by intensive heavy air bombardment' would outweigh 'any increase in anti-British feeling' (Grigg 1999, 152). In such views he was greatly encouraged by his scientific adviser and head of the wartime Statistical Department, the physicist Frederick Lindemann (see Fort 2004). As so often in war, inter-service rivalry played its part too. In appointing Sir Charles Portal, Commander-in-Chief of Bomber Command, to the post of Chief of the Air Staff in October 1940, Churchill ensured that a dogmatic proponent of area bombing would have a seat at Britain's strategy-making high table. Alan Brooke was sceptical about Portal's insistence that 'success lies in accumulating the largest air force possible in England and that then, and then only, success lies assured through the bombing of Europe'. But he could not prevent the diversion of substantial resources to Portal's squadrons (Alanbrooke 2001, 332, 409, 411).

Similar calculations persuaded Roosevelt to invest in strategic bombing: first, wild exaggeration of what German bombers could do to America, then a somewhat smaller exaggeration of what American bombers could do to Germany (Overy 1996, 100). To be sure, the American approach was in other respects different from the British. While the British favoured night area bombing, the Americans prided themselves on the greater accuracy of their planes. Equipped with the Norden bomb sight, the Flying Fortress was almost certainly a better machine than its British counterpart. But it was still far less precise than had been hoped, even with the benefit (though also the cost, in terms of greater vulnerability) of attacking during the day. By the time of the Casablanca Conference of January 1943, the Americans had come round to the Churchillian notion that their aim should be 'the progressive destruction and undermining of the morale of the German people to a point where their capacity for armed resistance is fatally weakened' (Overy 1996, 116). Roosevelt's confidant, Harry Hopkins, was among those who firmly believed this.

The effects of the Allied bombing campaigns against Germany and Japan were, as is well known, horrendous. What the RAF and USAAF did dwarfed what the Luftwaffe had been able to inflict on Britain during the Blitz. Beginning on the night of 24–25 July 1943, vast swathes of the city of Hamburg were destroyed in a raid codenamed 'Operation Gomorrah'. Sheltered from detection by the new device known as 'Window' (a shower of aluminium strips that smothered German radar), 791 RAF bombers rained down high explosive and incendiary bombs, creating a devastating firestorm that raged far beyond the control of the German emergency services. Around three-quarters of the city was laid waste in the succeeding days, as the initial bombardment was followed up by both American and British raids. At the very least, 45 000 people were killed and nearly a million rendered homeless. The flames were visible more than 100 miles away (Overy 1996, 118ff.). The author Hans Nossack (2004), who had left his Hamburg home for a few days in the country, returned to find flies and rats feasting on – and, incongruously, geraniums sprouting from – the charred human remains of his fellow citizens. Inhabitants of the smart suburbs along the Elbe to the West of the city saw their gardens turn grey with ash. All this was achieved at a remarkably low cost to Bomber Command, whose losses amounted to less than 3 per cent of the planes involved. Nor did the Allies relent as the war drew to a close. Around 1.1 million tons of the total 1.6 million tons of explosives dropped by Bomber Command and the 8th US Air Force – some 71 per cent – were dropped during the last year of the war (calculated from figures in Ellis 1993, 22f.). Once the Allies had developed a long-range fighter escort (in the form of the P-51 Mustang), they were in a position to bomb Germany with something approaching impunity (Overy 1996, 122ff.). The firestorm unleashed on Dresden in February 1945 engulfed 95 000 homes. At the very least, 35 000 people died, including those who sought safety in the city's fountains only to see them boil dry and others who were asphyxiated in the bomb shelters underneath the main railway station.

Was the strategy of area bombing in any sense justifiable? For many years it was fashionable to deny that Bomber Command made any significant contribution to the Allied victory. Much continues to be made by critics of the inaccuracy as well as the cruelty of strategic bombing (Lindqvist 2002, paragraph 207). Even some RAF personnel on occasion expressed concern that they were being asked, in effect, to 'do in. . .children's homes and hospitals' (Rolfe 2000, 53). It has been argued that they would have been better employed bombing the approaches to Auschwitz (Wyman 1984; Rubinstein 1997; Breitman 1999). It has even been suggested that an offer to stop the bombing could have been used as a bargaining chip to save the Jews destined for the death camps (Lindqvist 2002, paragraphs 192, 193). In the case of Dresden, doubts have been expressed about the official justification for the raid, namely that the Soviets had requested the attacks after a batch of Enigma decrypts revealed German plans to move troops from Dresden to Breslau, where the Red Army was encountering fierce resistance.[15] In fact, the main railway links out of the city survived more or less unscathed; trains were running again within a few days (Hastings 2004, 386). It is difficult to avoid the conclusion that the aim of the mission was quite simply to devastate one of the few major German cities that had not yet been hit. In denouncing the bombing war, one German writer has consciously applied the language normally associated with the crimes perpetrated by the Nazis: this was *Vernichtung* (annihilation) perpetrated by flying *Einsatzgruppen* (task forces), who turned air raid shelters into gas chambers (Friedrich 2003; Stargardt 2004).

To be sure, the effect of such attacks on German morale was far less than the pre-war strategists had predicted. Sir Hugh Trenchard's pre-war assertion that the moral effect of bombing was 20 times greater than material effect proved to be nonsense (Overy 1996, 105). If anything, the indiscriminate character of the air attacks aroused more defiance than defeatism. While it undoubtedly served to undermine the credibility of the Nazi regime in the minds of some Germans, it simultaneously enhanced its credibility in the minds of others. One woman, Irma J., wrote an unsolicited letter to Goebbels, demanding 'on behalf of all German women and mothers and the families of those living here in the Reich' that '20 Jews [be] hanged for every German killed in the place where our defenseless and priceless German people have been murdered in bestial and cowardly fashion by the terror-flyers'. Georg R. wrote from Berlin in a similar vein. 'Having been burned out once and bombed out twice', he indignantly demanded: 'No extermination of the German People and of Germany but rather the complete extermination of the Jews' (Stargardt 2004, 67).

There can be no doubt that a campaign aimed at crippling military and industrial facilities would have been preferable. As early as 1942, in his book *Victory through air power*, Alexander de Seversky enunciated the principle that 'Destruction of enemy morale from the air can be accomplished only by precision bombing'. Economic assets, not populous conurbations, were 'the heart and vitals of the enemy' (de Seversky 1942, 16). The Allies achieved far more with their focused attack on the German V-2 base at Peenemünde on 17 August 1943 than they had achieved the previous month by laying waste to Hamburg (Rolfe 2000, 16). Their attacks on oil refining facilities were also very successful.

On the other hand, precision attacks could go wrong precisely because the Germans could work out where to expect them – as the Americans discovered to their cost when they attacked Schweinfurt, a centre of ball-bearing production in Northern Bavaria, on 17 August and 14 October 1943. In the first raid, 36 B-17s were shot down out of an initial strike force of 230; 24 bombers were lost the same day in a similar attack on Regensburg. In the October attack – the 8th US Air Force's 'Black Thursday' – 60 out of 291 B-17s were shot down and 138 badly damaged (cf. Bendiner 1981, 172f.; Overy 1996, 122; Arthur 2004, 277). Comparable costs might have been incurred for no military benefit by bombing Auschwitz, significantly further east. The 186 missions flown (at Churchill's insistence) to drop supplies to the Poles during the Warsaw Rising suffered losses at a rate of 16.8 per cent, three times the casualty rate over Germany (Rolfe 2000, 114, 123). For all its indiscriminate character, there is no denying that strategic bombing inflicted significant damage on the German war effort. It diverted air cover away from the strategically vital Eastern Front. In the spring of 1943, 70 per cent of German fighters were in the Western European theatre, leaving German ground forces in the East increasingly vulnerable to Soviet air attacks. Lack of air support was one of the reasons the German tanks were beaten at Kursk. By April 1944 there were only 500 single-engine fighters left on the Eastern Front, facing around 13 000 Soviet aircraft (Overy 1996, 124). No fewer than two million men were tied down in air defence; valuable forces that might have been productively employed. Moreover, as Speer later noted, 'the nearly 20,000 anti-aircraft guns stationed in the homeland could almost have doubled the anti-tank defenses on the Eastern Front' (Grigg 1999, 154). The situation on the Eastern Front was, indeed, the principal rationale for the bombing of Dresden. 'In the midst of winter', the RAF crews who flew the mission were told in their briefing notes, 'with refugees pouring westwards and troops to be rested, roofs are at a premium':

> Dresden has developed into an industrial city of first-class importance. . .its multiplicity of telephones and rail facilities is of major value for controlling the defence of that part of the front now threatened by [the Soviet] offensive. The intentions of the attack are to hit the enemy where he will feel it most, behind an already partially collapsed front. . .and incidentally to show the Russians when they arrive what Bomber Command can do (Hastings 2004, 387).

That illustrates how difficult it was to distinguish military from civilian targets by this stage in the war; although the aim was partly to render German civilians homeless (and dead, though that was not made explicit) as well as to impress the Soviets, bombing Dresden was also designed to weaken German command and control capabilities. The relentless pressure exerted by the bombing raids also helped the British and American armies by eroding the Germans' fighter strength on the Western Front. At the time of D-Day, the Germans had barely 300 serviceable planes available to repel the invaders, as against 12 000 on the British and American side (Overy 1996, 118, 124; for detailed figures see Ellis 1993, 238).

Furthermore, strategic bombing greatly hampered Speer's considerable efforts to mobilize Germany's economy for total war. In May 1944, for example, the Germans were still producing 156 000 tons of aviation fuel, but bombing of their oil installations, which began in that month, cut production to 17 000 tons in August and just 11 000 tons in January 1945 (Grigg 1999, 155). Not all the available statistics are, it is true, so impressive. As we have seen, the Allies dropped around 1.6 million tons of explosives and incendiaries on Germany and North West Europe, more than 20 times the amount the Germans dropped on Britain throughout the entire war, including the V-1 and V-2 rockets (Ellis 1993, 236). The impact on German armaments production was, at first sight, minimal. As Figure 3.6 shows, the major raids of July 1943 merely slowed the growth of arms production, which resumed its upward trend by March 1944. It was not until after July 1944, as the Allied raids reached their devastating climax, that output from Speer's factories declined. Even then, production in January 1945 was merely reduced to the level of December 1943; it was still more than double what it had been in 1941. A breakdown of the main components of German arms output suggests that bombing hampered only some sectors of the economy (see Table 3.1). The production of vehicles, ships, gunpowder and explosives were all substantially reduced between June 1943 and January 1945. Yet the production of rifles and pistols rose by a fifth and that of tanks by nearly two-thirds. Production of aircraft and ammunition was virtually unchanged.

Nevertheless, the best measure of the impact of strategic bombing is not actual output, but the difference between actual and potential output. In January 1945 Speer and his colleagues sought to calculate the damage done by Allied bombing in the previous year. The figures are impressive: 35 per cent fewer tanks than planned, 31 per cent fewer aircraft and 42 per cent fewer trucks (Overy 1996, 128–33, 204f.). We cannot know exactly what wonders Speer might have worked with the German economy in the absence of sustained bombardment. What we do know is that Speer himself called the air war 'the greatest lost battle on the German side' (Hastings 1979, 241).

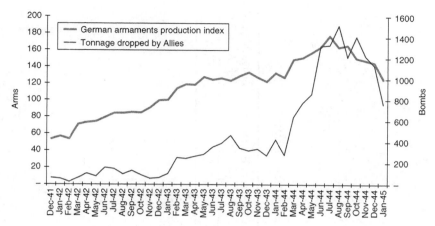

Source: Ellis (1993, 22f.); Tooze (2006, App. 6).

Figure 3.6 *The impact of bombing, January 1942–January 1945 (January 1943 = 100)*

CONCLUSIONS

How are we to reconcile the self-evidently disastrous impact of the Second World War with the post-war 'miracle' of high and sustained growth over more than two decades? One possible answer is that the Second World War was not as global as its name suggests. Violence was in fact relatively localized, a great deal of it concentrated in a triangle of territory between the Baltic, the Balkans and the Black Sea. In absolute terms, as is well known, many more Soviet citizens died violently between 1939 and 1945 than people of other nationalities – perhaps as many as 25 million, if not more. This suggests that more than one in ten Soviet citizens was a victim of the war, though it might be more accurate to say that one in ten was a victim of totalitarianism between 1939 and 1945, given the number of lives lost to Stalin's domestic policies.[16] In percentage terms Poland was the country hardest hit by the war (see Figure 3.7). The Polish mortality rate (total military and civilian fatalities as a percentage of the pre-war population) amounted to just under 19 per cent, of whom a large proportion were Polish Jews killed in the Holocaust. Among other combatants, only Germany (including Austria) and Yugoslavia suffered mortality rates close to 10 per cent.[17] The next highest rates were for Hungary (8 per cent) and Romania (6 per cent). In no other country for which figures have been published did mortality rise above 3 per cent of the pre-war population, including a number of Central

Table 3.1 The impact of Allied bombing (percentage change between June 1943 and January 1945)

German armaments production index	Weapons	Tanks	Vehicles	Aircraft	Ship-building	Ammunition	Powder	Explosives	Tonnage dropped by Allies
0	+19	+64	−63	−1	−21	−2	−19	−36	+116

Source: Ellis (1993, 22f.); Tooze (2006, App. 6).

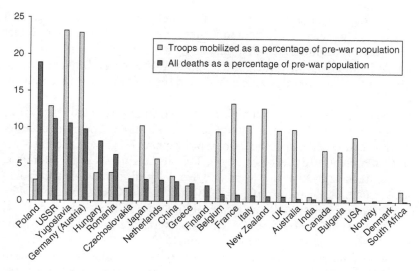

Source: Ferguson (2006).

Figure 3.7   Mobilization and mortality rates in World War II

and Eastern European countries, Czechoslovakia (3 per cent), Finland (2 per cent) and Bulgaria (0.3 per cent). For four of the principal combatants, France, Italy, the United Kingdom and the United States, total wartime mortality was less than 1 per cent of the pre-war population. For the three Western European countries, the First World War was, at least by this measure, a more disastrous conflict. It is also worth noting that Japan's mortality rate during the Second World War (2.9 per cent) was significantly lower than Germany's, as was China's (at most, 5 per cent). The total death toll of the war, though huge in absolute terms was in fact modest in relative terms, amounting to less than 3 per cent of the pre-war world population, a loss very swiftly made up by high post-war birth rates.

Yet this argument is not wholly persuasive. For among the most successful economies in the post-war era were precisely those countries that had been worst affected by the war. Average per capita growth rates for the period 1950–73 were higher than those for 1913–50 in almost every major economy except India's. The biggest improvements were registered in Germany and Austria (just under 30 times higher); in Japan (nine times higher) and in Italy (six times higher). Only fascist Spain's margin of improvement was higher. The communist economies of the Eastern Bloc also fared well; Stalinist planning proved a remarkably effective way of reconstructing economies ruined by war. Hungarian growth was eight times higher in the 1950s and 1960s than it had been in the era of world wars and depression; Eastern Europe as a whole enjoyed per capita growth of nearly 3.8 per cent, more than four times the pre-1950 figure. The Soviet Union achieved annual growth of just under 3.4 per cent – nearly a full percentage point higher than the United States (2.4 per cent). Ironically, some of the highest growth rates were achieved in the vanquished Axis countries (see Figure 3.8).

A second explanation is that high growth was simply a consequence of the low base from which so many countries began in 1945. The more destruction they had experienced, the more rapidly countries grew in the post-war era as they engaged in reconstruction. This argument was given an important refinement by the late Mancur Olson. By disrupting dysfunctional social structures, he argued, particularly the vested interests represented by pre-war labour unions, the war created a kind of political-economic *tabula rasa* (clean state), allowing new 'encompassing interests' to become the social basis for policy and action (Olson 1982). But here, too, there are difficulties. There is no question that German trade unions were weaker in 1949 than they had been in 1929 and that as their power recovered they acted differently in the context of a new 'politics of productivity'. On the other hand, it is difficult to sustain the claim that the structures of corporate organization on the side of capital were radically altered, despite the initial ambitions of the occupying Allied powers, in either Germany or Japan. This argument looks most persuasive in the British case, where the war tended to entrench both incompetent managements and quarrelsome trade unions

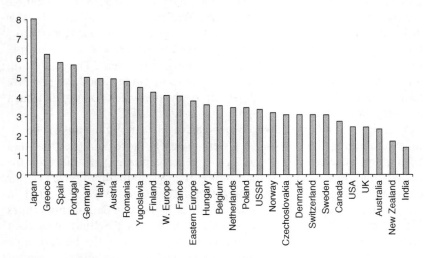

Source: Maddison 2001, Table A1-d.

Figure 3.8   GDP growth rates for selected countries, 1950–73 (per capita)

(Barnett 1986). It offers little explanation for the success of the American economy in the 1950s, which stands in such marked contrast to the 1930s despite the manifest continuities in terms of political economy.

Perhaps the best explanation for the contrast between the war and the post-war experience is that policy-makers had learned from both the errors of the Depression and the successes of the war. The general acceptance of Keynes's critique of procyclical fiscal and monetary policies, the partial acceptance of his design for a post-war international monetary order and the partial (to be precise, American and German) rejection of his earlier arguments for autarkic trade policies formed the basis for a new global order based on domestic demand management, pegged exchange rates, restricted cross-border capital mobility and trade liberalization. If, despite the fears of contemporaries, history did not repeat itself in the form of a post-war slump, that was in large measure a result of this policy paradigm shift. This line of argument has long appealed to economists, not least because it gives much of the credit for post-war prosperity to advances in their own discipline.

An equally important role may nevertheless have been played by changes in another field, namely that of military strategy. The Second World War had, as we have seen, come about for two reasons: because the Axis powers believed empire would enrich them and because the Western powers believed appeasement would avert war. Devastating defeat had taught the losers that 'living space' soon turned into killing space; that they lacked the wherewithal to make their empires endure, much less pay. Conversely, the high cost of victory had persuaded the Allies of the folly of appeasement. In the Cold War that ensued both sides adopted the maxim *si vis pacem, para bellum* (if you want peace, prepare for war), with the result that high levels of capital-intensive defence spending were maintained. The consequences were twofold: both superpowers were deterred from resorting to open conflict (though numerous proxy wars were fought) while at the same time their economies were stimulated in precisely the way the US economy had been during the preceding war. The American way of warfare – whereby productivity could soar without the impediment of falling bombs and the disasters took place far from centers of employment – became generalized in the northern hemisphere.

Thus the Second World War was at once an economic disaster and an economic boon. False economic assumptions led the Axis powers to start the war and prevented the Western powers from effectively deterring them. Yet the economic successes of the Allied war economies – and particularly that of the United States – ensured that the new empires created by Japan, Italy and Germany did not endure for long. Moreover, the substitution of capital for labour in Allied warfare inflicted a terrible retribution on Axis cities, while at the same time bringing unprecedented prosperity to American cities. Two new models of state-led production – the American and the Soviet – were put to the test of total war and passed it with flying colours. Those new models were then exported around the northern hemisphere, generating major improvements in economic performance nearly everywhere they were adopted or imposed. Economic historians have for too long failed to appreciate that in these and other respects the 'defining moment' of the twentieth century was not the Great Depression, but the Great Conflagration that followed it.

NOTES

1. This paper draws heavily on Ferguson (2006). Full acknowledgements for assistance have been provided in the book.
2. On the Soviet figures, see Overy (1997, xvi, 287); for German mortality, see Overmans (1999) and for China see Ho (1959, 250–53).
3. Figures for the national debt kindly supplied by Professor Charles Goodhart. Figures for gross domestic product are taken from Feinstein (1972, Table 3). Debt service is from Flora et al. (1983, 4448ff.).
4. Calculated from Mitchell (1976, 333ff.).
5. For the non-economic aspects of the problem, see Ferguson (2006, Chs. 9 and 10).
6. To be precise, 71 per cent of the Soviet Union's iron ore mines, two-thirds of its aluminium, manganese and copper, 63 per cent of its coal mines, 57 per cent of its rolled steel production, 40 per cent of its electricity generating capacity and a third of its rail network. See Overy (1996, 82) and Burleigh (2001, 498).
7. 70 per cent of Slim's 14th Army were Gurkha, African or Burmese.
8. Central Asians and Caucasians were, however, under-represented. Indeed, more of them fought for the Germans.
9. The total number of aliens in the army and navy was 125 880.
10. 'Looking ahead', Testimony of C.E. Wilson, President of General Motors Corporation, before the Special Committee of the United States Senate to Investigate the National Defense Program (Truman Committee), 24 November 1943, pp. 28f.
11. General Motors Corporation, *Press conference by C. E. Wilson, President of General Motors, October 19, 1945* (New York), p. 3.
12. It should nevertheless be noted that total factor productivity growth slackened during the war, an inevitable consequence of the conversion from peacetime to wartime products. See Field (2005).
13. Calculated from figures in Boeing Airplane Co. and Subsidiary Companies, *Reports to Stockholders* (Washington, 1936–1950). Note, however, that the war was less profitable for the chemical conglomerate DuPont, which had fared better in the 1930s, because of the costs of switching production to explosives and steep wartime taxation (see Carpenter 1946).
14. National Archives, London, S.46368/D.C.A.S, Air Vice-Marshal Bottomley to Air Officer Commanding-in-Chief, Bomber Command, 14 February 1942.
15. Compare Lindqvist (2002 paragraphs 214, 216, 217) with Arthur (2004, 403). The literature is very extensive and the controversy bitter (see McKee 1982; Garrett 1993). For a vivid evocation of the aftermath of the raid, see Vonnegut (2003).
16. The Soviet figures are famously problematic. Total Soviet demographic losses have been put as high as 43–47 million by some recent scholars (i.e., including thwarted normal reproduction). The *Times atlas of world history*'s total of 21.5 million includes around

seven million deaths of Soviet citizens deported to the gulag and one million Soviet citizens deported as members of 'suspect' nationalities. The official Soviet figure for total excess mortality was 26.6 million, but this may include 2.7 million wartime and post-war emigrants as well as normal natural mortality. On the other hand, it may underestimate the number of Soviet prisoners who died in German captivity.

17. Overmans (1992) has substantially revised upwards the estimates for German military losses. Note that his total figure for losses of 5.3 million includes just under 400 000 men who did not have German citizenship in 1939 but nevertheless were recruited or conscripted into the Wehrmacht or SS.

REFERENCES

Akira, F. (1973), 'The role of the Japanese military', in D. Borg and S. Okamoto (eds), *Pearl Harbor as history: Japanese-American relations, 1931–1941*, New York: Columbia University Press.

Alanbrooke, A.F.B. (2001), *War diaries, 1939–1945* (A. Danchev and D. Todman eds), London: Weidenfeld & Nicolson.

Alexiev, A. and Wimbush, S.E. (1993), 'Non-Russians in the Red Army, 1941–1945', *Journal of Slavic Military Studies*, 6.

Ambrose, S.E. (1992), 'The secrets of Overlord', in R. Cowley (ed.), *The experience of war*, London: Norton.

Anderson, C.J. (2001), 'There are such things as miracles: Halsey and Kurita at Leyte Gulf', in P.G. Tsouras (ed.), *Rising sun victorious: the alternate history of how the Japanese won the Pacific War*, London: Greenhill Books.

Anderson, C.J. (2004), 'The race to Bastogne: Nuts!' in P.G. Tsouras (ed.), *Battle of the Bulge: Hitler's alternate scenarios*, London: Greenhill Books.

Arnold, J.R. (2001), 'Coral and purple: the lost advantage', in P.G. Tsouras (ed.), *Rising sun victorious: the alternate history of how the Japanese won the Pacific War*, London: Greenhill Books.

Arthur, M. (2004), *Forgotten voices of the Second World War: a new history of World War Two in the words of the men and women who were there*, London: Ebury.

Barber, J. and Harrison, M. (2006), 'Patriotic war, 1941 to 1945', in R.G. Suny (ed.), *The Cambridge history of Russia*, vol. III: *the twentieth century*, Cambridge: Cambridge University Press.

Barkawi, T. (2006), 'Combat motivation in the Colonies: The Indian army in the Second World War', *Journal of Contemporary History*, 41.

Barnett, C. (1986), *The audit of war: the illusion and reality of Britain as a great nation*, London: Macmillan.

Barnhart, M.A. (1984), 'Japanese intelligence before the Second World War: "best case" analysis', in E.R. May (ed.), *Knowing one's enemies: intelligence assessment before the two World Wars*, Princeton, NJ: Princeton University Press.

Barnhart, M.A. (1987), *Japan prepares for total war: the search for economic security, 1919–1941*, Ithaca, NY: Cornell University Press.

Beevor, A. (2002), *Berlin: the downfall, 1945*, London: Viking.

Bendiner, E. (1981), *The fall of fortresses: a personal account of one of the most daring and deadly air battles of the Second World War*, London: Souvenir Press.

Boyd, C. (1988), 'Japanese military effectiveness: the interwar period', in A.R. Millett and W. Murray (eds), *Military effectiveness, vol. ii: the interwar period*, Boston, MA: Allen & Unwin.

Breitman, R. (1999), *Official secrets: what the Nazis planned, what the British and Americans knew*, London: Allen Lane.

Broadberry, S. and Howlett, P. (1998), 'The United Kingdom: "Victory at All Costs"', in M. Harrison (ed.), *The economics of World War II: six great powers in international comparison*, Cambridge: Cambridge University Press.

Brown, W.O. and Burdekin, R.C.K. (2002), 'German debt traded in London during the Second World War: a British perspective on Hitler', *Economica*, 69.

Buckley, G. (2001), *American patriots: the story of blacks in the military from the Revolution to Desert Storm*, New York: Random House.

Budrass, L., Scherner, J. and Streb, J. (2005), 'Demystifying the German "armament miracle" during World War II: new insights from the annual audits of German aircraft producers', Yale University Economic Growth Center Discussion Paper, 905.

Burleigh, M. (1999), 'Nazi Europe: what If Nazi Germany had defeated the Soviet Union?', in Niall Ferguson (ed.), *Virtual history: alternatives and counterfactuals*, New York: Basic Books.

Burleigh, M. (2001), *The Third Reich: a new history*, London: Pan.

Burtt, J. (2001), 'Guadalcanal: the broken shoestring', in P.G. Tsouras (ed.), *Rising sun victorious: the alternate history of how the Japanese won the Pacific War*, London: Greenhill Books.

Buruma, I. (2003), *Inventing Japan: from empire to economic miracle, 1853–1964*, London: Phoenix.

Campbell, K.H. (2004), 'Holding Patton: Seventh Panzer Army and the Battle of Luxembourg', in P.G. Tsouras (ed.), *Battle of the Bulge: Hitler's alternate scenarios*, London: Greenhill Books.

Carpenter, W.S. (1946), *The Du Pont Company's part in the National Security Program, 1940–1945: Stockholder's Bulletin*, Wilmington, DE: E.I. du Pont de Nemours and Company, Inc.

Chenevix-Trench, C. (1988), *The Indian army and the King's enemies, 1900–1947*, London: Thames and Hudson.

Clayton, J.D. (1986), 'American and Japanese strategies in the Pacific War', in P. Paret (ed.), *Makers of modern strategy from Machiavelli to the nuclear age*, Princeton, NJ: Princeton University Press.

Coghlan, F. (1972), 'Armaments, economic policy and appeasement: the background to British foreign policy, 1931–7', *History*, 57.

Colvin, I. (1965), *Vansittart in office: an historical survey of the origins of the Second World War based on the papers of Sir Robert Vansittart*, London: Gollancz.

Cook, T.F. Jr. (2001), 'Our Midway disaster', in R. Cowley (ed.), *What if?: the world's foremost military historians imagine what might have been*, London: Macmillan.

Coox, A. (1988a), 'The effectiveness of the Japanese military establishment in the Second World War', in A.R. Millett and W. Murray (eds), *Military effectiveness, vol. ii: the interwar period*, Boston, MA: Allen & Unwin.

Coox, A. (1988b), 'The Pacific war', in P. Duus (ed.), *The Cambridge history of Japan, vol. vi: the twentieth century*, Cambridge: Cambridge University Press.

Cozzens, J.G. (1948), *Guard of honor*, New York: Harcourt, Brace and Company.

Davie, M.R. (1947), *Refugees in America: Report of the Committee for the Study of Recent Immigration from Europe*, New York: Harper & Bros.

de Seversky, A.P. (1942), *Victory through air power*, New York: Simon and Schuster.

Dilks, D. (1978), ' "The unnecessary war"? military advice and foreign policy in Great Britain, 1931–1939', in A. Preston (ed.), *General staffs and diplomacy before the Second World War*, London: Croom Helm.

Dower, J.W. (1986), *War without mercy: race and power in the Pacific War*, London: Faber.

Drucker, P.F. (1946), *The concept of the corporation*, New York: The John Day Company.

Dunbabin, J.P.D. (1975), 'British rearmament in the 1930s: a chronology and review', *Historical Journal*, 18.

Economist (1938), 'Munition Metals', pp. 25–7, 1 October.

Ellis, J. (1993), *The World War II databook: the essential facts and figures for all the combatants*, London: Aurum.

Endicott, S.L. (1975), *Diplomacy and enterprise: British China policy, 1933–1937*, Manchester: Manchester University Press.

Epstein, M. (ed.) (1938), *The statesman's yearbook: statistical and historical annual of the states of the world for the year 1938*, London, Macmillan.

Feinstein, C.H. (1972), *National income, expenditure and output of the United Kingdom, 1855–1965*, Cambridge: Cambridge University Press.

Ferguson, N. (2006), *The war of the world: history's age of hatred*, London: Allen Lane.

Field, A.J. (2005), 'The impact of World War II on US productivity growth', unpublished paper, Santa Clara University, September.

Flora, Peter et al. (eds) (1983), *State, economy and society in Western Europe, 1815–1975: a data handbook in two volumes*, Frankfurt: Campus Verlag.

Forsyth, J. (1992), *A history of the peoples of Siberia: Russia's North Asian colony, 1581–1990*, Cambridge: Cambridge University Press.

Fort, A. (2004), *'Prof.': the life and times of Frederick Lindemann*, London: Pimlico.

Frey, B.S. and Kucher, M. (2000), 'History as reflected in capital markets: the case of World War II', *Journal of Economic History*, 60.

Frey, B.S. and Kucher, M. (2001), 'Wars and markets: how bond values reflect the Second World War', *Economica*, 68.

Friedrich, J. (2003), *Der Brand: Deutschland im Bombenkrieg, 1940–1945*, München: Propyläen.

Garrett, S.A. (1993), *Ethics and airpower in World War II: the British bombing of German cities*, New York: St Martin's Press.

Gill, J.H. (1995), 'Operation Greenbrier: defusing the German bomb', in K. Macksey (ed.), *The Hitler options: alternate decisions of World War II*, London: Greenhill Books.

Goldsmith, R. (1946) 'The power of victory', *Military Cultures*, 19.

Gorter-Gronvik, W.T. and Suprun, M.N. (2000), 'Ethnic minorities and warfare at the Arctic Front, 1939–1945', *Journal of Slavic Military Studies*, 13.

Graebner, N.A. (1974), 'Introduction', in R.D. Burns and E.M. Bennett (eds), *Diplomats in crisis: United States-Chinese-Japanese relations, 1919–1941*, Oxford: EBC-Clio.

Greasley, D. and Oxley, L. (1996), 'Discontinuities in competitiveness: the impact of the First World War on British industry', *Economic History Review*, 99.

Grigg, J. (1999), *1943: The victory that never was*, London: Penguin.

Grossman, V. (1985), *Life and fate: a novel*, New York: Harper & Row.

Hargrove, H.B. (1985), *Buffalo soldiers in Italy: black Americans in World War II*, Jefferson, NC: McFarland.

Harriman, W.A. and Abel, E. (1975), *Special envoy to Churchill and Stalin, 1941–1946*, New York: Random House.

Harrison, M. (1981), 'Resource mobilization for World War II: the USA, UK, USSR and Germany, 1938–1945', *Economic History Review*, 41.

Harrison, M. (ed.) (1998a), 'The economics of World War II: an overview', in M. Harrison (ed.), *The economics of World War II: six great powers in international comparison*, Cambridge: Cambridge University Press.

Harrison, M. (1998b), 'The Soviet Union: the defeated victor', in M. Harrison (ed.), *The economics of World War II: six great powers in international comparison*, Cambridge: Cambridge University Press.

Harrison, M. (ed.) (1998c), *The economics of World War II: six great powers in international comparison*, Cambridge: Cambridge University Press.

Harrison, M. (2004), *Medicine and victory: British military medicine in the Second World War*, Oxford: Oxford University Press.

Hastings, M. (1979), *Bomber Command*, London: Joseph.

Hastings, M. (2004), *Armageddon: the battle for Germany, 1944–45*, London: Macmillan.

Hata, I. (1988), 'Continental expansion, 1905–1941', in P. Duus (ed.), *The Cambridge history of Japan*, vol. vi: *the twentieth century*, Cambridge: Cambridge University Press.

Heller, J. (1962), *Catch-22*, London: Cape.

Higgs, R. (2004), 'Wartime socialization of investment: a reassessment of US capital formation in the 1940s', *Journal of Economic History*, 64.

Ho, P. (1959), *Studies on the population of China, 1368–1953*, Cambridge, MA: Harvard University Press.

Howard, M. (1972), *The continental commitment: the dilemma of British defence policy in the era of two world wars*, London: Maurice Temple Smith Ltd.

Iriye, A. (1981), *Power and culture: the Japanese-American war, 1941–1945*, Cambridge, MA: Harvard University Press.

Isby, D.C. (2002), 'Luftwaffe triumphant: the defeat of the bomber offensive, 1944–45', in P.G. Tsouras (ed.), *Third Reich victorious: the alternate history of how the Germans won the war*, London: Greenhill Books.

Jansen, M.B. (1975), *Japan and China: from war to peace 1894–1972*, Chicago, IL: Rand McNally College Publishing Company.

Jones, J. (1962), *The thin red line*, New York: Scribner.

Kaser, M.C. and Radice, E.A., (eds) (1986), *The economic history of Eastern Europe, 1919–1975*, 2 vols, Oxford: Clarendon Press.

Kennedy, P. (1976), 'The tradition of British appeasement', *British Journal of International Studies*, 2.

Kennedy, P. (1981), *The realities behind diplomacy: background influences on British external policy, 1865–1980*, London: Fontana.

Keynes, J.M. (1940), *How to pay for the war: a radical plan for the Chancellor of the Exchequer*, London: Macmillan.

Kimitada, M. (1975), 'Japanese images of war with the United States', in A. Iriye (ed.), *Mutual images: essays in American-Japanese relations*, Cambridge, MA: Harvard University Press.

Kinhide, M. (1973), 'The structure of Japanese-American relations in the 1930s', in D. Borg and S. Okamoto (eds), *Pearl Harbor as history: Japanese-American relations, 1931–1941*, New York: Columbia University Press.

Kiyoshi, I. (1982), 'Japanese strategy and the Pacific war, 1941–1945', in I. Nish (ed.), *Anglo-Japanese alienation, 1919–1952: papers of the Anglo-Japanese Conference on the history of the Second World War*, Cambridge: Cambridge University Press.

Klivert-Jones, T. (1995), 'Bloody Normandy: the German controversy', in K. Macksey (ed.), *The Hitler options: alternate decisions of World War II*, London: Greenhill Books.

Koistinen, P.A.C. (2004), *Arsenal of World War II: the political economy of American warfare*, Lawrence, KE: University Press of Kansas.

Levine, A.J. (1985), 'Was World War II a near-run thing?', *Journal of Strategic Studies*, 8.

Lindqvist, S. (2002), *A history of bombing*, London: Granta.

Lindsey, F.R. (2001), 'Nagumo's luck: the Battles of Midway and California', in P.G. Tsouras (ed.), *Rising sun victorious: the alternate history of how the Japanese won the Pacific War*, London: Greenhill Books.

Lindsey, F.R. (2002), 'Hitler's bomb, target: London and Moscow', in P.G. Tsouras (ed.), *Third Reich victorious: the alternate history of how the Germans won the war*, London: Greenhill Books.

Lowe, P. (1974), 'Great Britain and the coming of the Pacific War, 1939–1941', *Transactions of the Royal Historical Society*, 24.

Lowe, P. (1977), *Great Britain and the origins of the Pacific War: a study of British policy in East Asia, 1937–1941*, Oxford: Clarendon Press.

Lu, D.J. (1961), *From the Marco Polo Bridge to Pearl Harbor: Japan's entry into World War II*, Washington, DC: Public Affairs Press.

Manteuffel, H. von (1965), 'The battle of the Ardennes 1944–45', in H.-A. Jacobsen and J.Rohwer (eds), *Decisive battles of World War II: the German view*, transl. E. Fitzgerald, New York: Putnam.

McKee, A. (1982), *Dresden 1945: the devil's tinderbox*, London: Souvenir.

McKernan, M. (1995), *All in! Fighting the war at home*, London: Allen and Unwin.

McQuaid, K. (1994), *Uneasy partners: big business in American politics, 1945–1990*, Baltimore, MD: Johns Hopkins University Press.

Maddison, A. (2001), *The world economy: a millennial perspective*, Paris: OECD.

Milward, A.S. (1987), *War, economy and society 1939–1945*, London, Penguin.

Mitchell, B.R. (1976), *Abstract of British historical statistics*, Cambridge: Cambridge University Press.

Myer, D.S. (1971), *Uprooted Americans: the Japanese Americans and the War Relocation Authority during World War II*, Tucson, AZ: University of Arizona Press.

Nalty, B.C. (1999), 'Sources of victory', in B.C. Nalty (ed.), *The Pacific War: the story of the bitter struggle in the Pacific theater of World War II*, London: Salamander.

Neidpath, J. (1981), *The Singapore naval base and the defence of Britain's Eastern empire, 1919–1941*, Oxford: Clarendon.

Nelson, D.M. (1946), *Arsenal of democracy: the story of American war production*, New York: Harcourt, Brace and Company.

Newton, S. (1996), *Profits of peace: the political economy of Anglo-German appeasement*, Oxford: Clarendon.

New York Times (1949), 'Japan's farmers exceed rice quota', 20 April.

Noakes, J. and Pridham, G. (eds) (1988), *Nazism, 1919–1945, vol. III: foreign policy, war and racial extermination: a documentary reader*, Exeter: University of Exeter Press.

Nossack, H.E. (2004), *The end: Hamburg 1943*, Chicago, IL: University of Chicago Press.

Nye, J.V.C. (2002), 'Killing Private Ryan: an institutional analysis of military decision making in World War II', Washington University in St Louis, draft prepared for the ISNIE conference in Boston.

Olson, M. (1982), *The rise and decline of nations: economic growth, stagflation and social rigidities*, New Haven, CT: Yale University Press.

Oosterlinck K. (2003), 'The bond market and the legitimacy of Vichy France', *Explorations in Economic History*, 40.

Overmans, R. (1992), 'German historiography, the war losses and the prisoners of war', in G. Bischof and S. Ambrose (eds), *Eisenhower and the German POWs: facts against falsehood*, London: Louisiana State University Press.

Overmans, R. (1999), *Deutsche militärische Verluste im Zweiten Weltkrieg*, München: R. Oldenbourg.

Overy, R. (1996), *Why the Allies won*, London: Pimlico.

Overy, R. (1997), *Russia's war*, London: Penguin.

Overy, R. (1999), 'Germany and the Munich crisis: a mutilated victory?', in I. Lukes and E. Goldstein (eds), *The Munich Crisis, 1938: prelude to World War II*, London: Frank Cass.

Parker, R.A.C. (1975), 'Economics, rearmament, and foreign policy: the UK before 1939 – a preliminary study', *Journal of Contemporary History*, 10.

Parker, R.A.C. (1981), 'British rearmament 1936–9: Treasury, trade unions and skilled labour', *English Historical Review*, 96.

Parker, R.A.C. (1993), *Chamberlain and appeasement: British policy and the coming of the Second World War*, London: Macmillan.

Peattie, M.R. (1998), 'Japanese strategy and campaigns in the Pacific War, 1941–1945', in L.E. Lee (ed.), *World War II in Asia and the Pacific and the war's aftermath, with general themes: a handbook of literature and research*, Westport, CT: Greenwood.

Peden, G.C. (1979), *British rearmament and the Treasury, 1932–1939*, Edinburgh: Scottish Academic Press.

Peden, G.C. (1984), 'A matter of timing: the economic background to British foreign policy, 1938–1939', *History*, 69.

Prados, J. (2004), 'Operation Herbstnebel: smoke over the Ardennes', in P.G. Tsouras (ed.), *Battle of the Bulge: Hitler's alternate scenarios*, London: Greenhill Books.

Prasad, S.N. and Char, S.V. Desika (1956), *Expansion of the Armed Forces and Defence Organization, 1939–1945*, Calcutta: Combined Inter-Services Historical Section (India & Pakistan).

Price, A. (1995), 'The jet fighter menace, 1943', in Kenneth Macksey (ed.), *The Hitler options: alternate decisions of World War II*, London: Greenhill Books.

Rakowska-Harmstone, T. (1990), ' "Brotherhood in Arms": The ethnic factor in the Soviet armed forces', in N.F. Dreisziger (ed.), *Ethnic armies: polyethnic armed forces from the time of the Habsburgs to the age of the superpowers*, Waterloo, Ontario: Wilfrid Laurier University Press.

Redding, R. and Yenne, B. (1983), *Boeing: planemaker to the world*, London: Arms and Armour.

Rockoff, H. (1998), 'The United States: from ploughshares to swords', in Mark Harrison (ed.), *The economics of World War II: six great powers in international comparison*, Cambridge: Cambridge University Press.

Rodgers, E. (1996), *Flying high: the story of Boeing and the rise of the jetliner industry*, New York: Atlantic Monthly Press.

Rolfe, M. (2000), *Looking into hell: experiences of the Bomber Command war*, London: Cassell.

Rubinstein, W.D. (1997), *The myth of rescue: why the democracies could not have saved more Jews from the Nazis*, London: Routledge.

Ruge, F. (1965), 'The invasion of Normandy' in H.A. Jacobsen and J. Rohwer (eds), *Decisive battles of World War II*, London: André Deutsch.

Scalapino, R.A. (1980), 'Southern advance: introduction', in J.W. Morley (ed.), *The fateful choice: Japan's advance into Southeast Asia, 1939–1941*, New York: Columbia University Press.

Schmidt, G. (1983), 'The domestic background to British appeasement policy', in W.J. Mommsen and L. Kettenacker (eds), *The fascist challenge and the policy of appeasement*, London: Allen & Unwin.

Shay, R.P. (1977), *British rearmament in the thirties: politics and profits*, Princeton, Princeton University Press.

Smelser, R.M. (1983), 'Nazi dynamics, German foreign policy and appeasement', in W.J. Mommsen and L. Kettenacker (eds), *The fascist challenge and the policy of appeasement*, London: Allen & Unwin.

Smith, E.R. (1959), *The army and economic mobilization*, Washington, DC: Office of the Chief of Military History, Dept. of the Army.

Speer, A. (1970), *Inside the Third Reich: memoirs*, London: Macmillan.

Stargardt, N. (2004), 'Victims of bombing and retaliation', *German Historical Institute London, Bulletin*, 26.

Stromberg, R.N. (1953), 'American business and the approach of war, 1935–1941', *Journal of Economic History*, 13.

Sugihara, K. (1997), 'The economic motivations behind Japanese aggression in the late 1930s: perspectives of Freda Utley and Nawa Toichi', *Journal of Contemporary History*, 32.

Thomas, M. (1983), 'Rearmament and economic recovery in the late 1930s', *Economic History Review*, 36.

Tooze, A.J. (2006), *The wages of destruction: the making and breaking of the Nazi Economy*, London: Allen Lane.

Treue, W. (1955), 'Hitler's Denkschrift zum Vierjahresplan 1936', *Vierteljahreshefte für Zeitgeschichte*, 3.

Tsouras, P.G. (2004a), *Disaster at D-Day: the Germans defeat the Allies, June 1944*, 2nd edn, London: Greenhill Books.

Tsouras, P.G. (2004b), 'Ardennes disaster: the Iron Curtain falls on the White House', in P.G. Tsouras (ed.), *Battle of the Bulge: Hitler's alternate scenarios*, London: Greenhill Books.

van Creveld, M. (1977), *Supplying war: logistics from Wallenstein to Patton*, Cambridge: Cambridge University Press.

Vatter, H.G. (1985), *The US economy in World War II*, New York: Columbia University Press.

Vernon, J.R. (1994), 'World War II fiscal policies and the end of the Great Depression', *Journal of Economic History*, 54.

Vonnegut, K. (2003), *Slaughterhouse-five: or the children's crusade: a duty-dance with death*, London: Vintage.

Waldenström, D. and Frey, B.S. (2003), 'How government bond prices reflect wartime events: the case of the Stockholm market', SSE/EFI Working Paper in Economics and Finance No. 489, Stockholm School of Economics.

Wendt, B.-J. (1971), *Economic appeasement: Handel und Finanz in der britischen Deutschlandpolitik, 1933–1939*, Düsseldorf: Bertelsmann Universitätsverlag.

Willmott, H.P. (1983), *The barrier and the javelin: Japanese and Allied Pacific strategies, February to June 1942*, Annapolis, MD: Naval Institute Press.

Wyman, D.S. (1984), *The abandonment of the Jews: America and the holocaust, 1941–1945*, New York: Pantheon Books.

Yasuba, Y. (1996), 'Did Japan ever suffer from a shortage of natural resources before World War II?', *Journal of Economic History*, 56.

Yergin, D. (1991), *The prize: the epic quest for oil, money and power*, London: Simon & Schuster.

Zamagni, V. (1998), 'Italy: how to lose the war and win the peace', in M. Harrison (ed.), *The economics of World War II: six great powers in international comparison*, Cambridge: Cambridge University Press.

4. The rise, fall and rise again of OPEC

Michael Beenstock

No event of the period following the Second World War had so sharp and pervasive an impact on the world economy as the series of shocks to the oil market that followed closely on the outbreak of the Arab-Israeli war on 6 October 1973. (Fried and Schultze 1975, 1)

DISASTER STRIKES

When OPEC (the Organization of Petroleum Exporting Countries) quadrupled the price of oil in 1973/74 it was immediately regarded as an unmitigated disaster. It was as if a bolt of lightning had struck out of a clear blue sky. There was panic in official circles. The world appeared to be hostage to OPEC's whim and fortune. Indeed, this sense of doom and hopelessness only seemed to fulfil itself when in 1979 OPEC further doubled the price of oil. The rapid and even unprecedented economic growth enjoyed by the world economy during the post-war period came to an abrupt end in 1973, and a new age of stagflation had dawned. The lights appeared to be going out over the world economy. We had taken for granted that such anti-social behaviour could never happen. But the unthinkable had occurred.

The OPEC price revolution spawned a great deal of muddled and even stupid thinking. The 'doomwatchers' thrived. Suddenly, it was claimed that the world was running out of oil as well as other natural resources (the so-called Club of Rome school as formulated by Meadows et al. 1972). Economic development based on hydrocarbons and other non-renewable resources was deemed to be no longer sustainable. Indeed, as the Shah of Iran smugly pointed out at the time, by raising the price of oil OPEC was simply conserving oil for future generations. It was assuming responsibility for intergenerational equity by checking the profligacy of the present generation of oil consumers for the benefit of our children and grandchildren, who otherwise would be deprived of scarce oil. Many academic economists gave credence to this view, even as late as the start of the 1990s

(Heal and Chichilnisky 1991). They interpreted the oil price revolution as a belated manifestation of Hotelling's Rule,[1] according to which the price of exhaustible resources should rise over time. OPEC was not behaving as an exploiter, but was simply obeying the inevitable dictates of some deep economic logic beyond its control.

The oil price explosion had geopolitical implications too. Although they had to pay larger oil import bills the Indian-led Non-aligned members at the United Nations, which were predominantly poor, cheered from the sidelines at OPEC's audacity to inflict economic hurt on the rich countries. The World Bank and similar institutions saw OPEC's behaviour as a long-waited redressing of the balance of economic power between the rich North and the poor South, to be emulated in other areas of North–South economic relations. Since 1950 the terms of trade of the developing countries had steadily deteriorated because the price of raw materials, including crude oil, had fallen in world markets (Spraos 1980). Attempts to reverse this trend by commodity pricing agreements in raw materials such as tin, copper and coffee had signally failed. By contrast, OPEC had succeeded. Encouraged by the World Bank, the United Nations commissioned Willy Brandt, a former West German Chancellor, to carry out an independent inquiry into international economic relations. The Brandt Report (Independent Commission on International Development Issues 1980) called for the creation of a 'New International Economic Order', in which the rich countries would act to benefit the developing countries.

Because OPEC initially failed to consume its newfound wealth, the international capital market became flooded with petrodollars. The Petrodollar Problem was a direct corollary of the Oil Price Problem. Petrodollars could be used to destabilize international capital markets, and to gain control over strategic economic assets in the West. By 1975 the world seemed to be unrecognizable economically and politically from what it was only two years before. Sheikh Yamani, the ubiquitous and urbane Saudi Minister for Oil, had become an international celebrity. Commentators hung onto his every utterance.[2] All sorts of new buzzwords entered the lexicon of the 'chatterati', such as conservation, non-renewability, unsustainable development, North–South dialogue, New International Economic Order and stagflation.

For their part, key oil consuming countries tried to coordinate their actions and share their misery by establishing the International Energy Agency (IEA) in November 1974. However, apart from collecting statistics, the IEA did not succeed in finding a reply to OPEC's power. It could have retaliated by acting as an oil monopsony,[3] but IEA members were not prepared to be so confrontational. Indeed, IEA stood as a monument to the helplessness of the oil consuming countries.

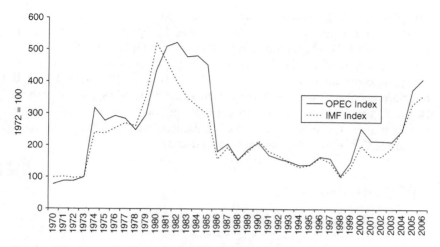

Source: The data until 2004 are taken from OPEC (2004). Data for 2005 and 2006 have been calculated from the nominal oil price as published in OPEC (2006) and estimates of world inflation and the multilateral value of the US dollar.

Figure 4.1 Real oil prices, 1970–2006

But it all came to an abrupt end in 1986 when the price of oil collapsed as shown in Figure 4.1. The figure plots two measures of the real price of oil (the difference between them is discussed below, in the section on the political economy of oil). So-called experts were as confounded by the fall in oil prices as they had been surprised by its rise. In the early 1980s Stanford's Energy Modeling Forum (EMF) (Sweeney 1981) had predicted that real oil prices would continue to rise by about 4 per cent per annum. This conventional wisdom was unceremoniously and rapidly refuted. But so had been the conventional wisdom that had previously been voiced by Adelman (1972): that oil prices would continue to fall (between 1955 and 1970 real oil prices had fallen on average by 6.5 per cent per year). Indeed, it turned out that the handful of sceptics and doubters had been right after all (Friedman 1974; Griffin and Teece 1982; Beenstock 1983). OPEC's grip on oil prices and the world economy was a passing phenomenon. The world economy had returned to business as normal, in which the oil crisis had been replaced by the debt crisis. However, the seeds of this new crisis were partly planted in 1973 when the oil price crisis broke out.

By 1998, real oil prices were almost back to where they were in 1972. Subsequently, however, OPEC staged a comeback and the real price of oil is currently (April 2006) back to where it was at its peak in the early 1980s.[4]

So we can now talk of OPEC III in reference to the almost five-fold increase in real oil prices that has occurred since 2000. The increase and pace of oil prices in OPEC III are similar to what they were in OPECs I and II, yet disaster has not struck. Global stagflation has not broken out. The ability of the world economy to weather OPEC III proves that OPECs I and II need not have been so disastrous. Crises, such as oil price hikes, do not have to turn into tragedies. Sound macroeconomic policy combined with greater labour market flexibility and OPEC's enhanced absorptive capacity have prevented OPEC III from turning into a disaster.

OPEC OIL PRICING

Historical Background[5]

OPEC was established in 1960 by Venezuela, Iran, Iraq, Saudi Arabia and Kuwait with the explicit purpose of counterbalancing the economic power of the Seven Sisters (Exxon, Mobil, BP, Shell, Texaco, Gulf and Socol) and governments in the oil-consuming countries. The economic rents from oil production had largely been captured by the oil companies and Treasuries in the oil-consuming countries. The oil companies coordinated their activities to sign lucrative contracts for oil extraction concessions in what eventually became OPEC, while Treasuries taxed oil consumption to final users by imposing heavy excise duties especially on petroleum. A key original objective of OPEC was to recover as much as possible of these lost rents.

During the 1960s OPEC membership expanded, and by 1970 OPEC had gained sufficient power to halt the decline in real oil prices, which had occurred since 1950 (Figure 4.2) and before. During the early 1970s the real price of oil rose by about 20 per cent, having declined by about 50 per cent during 1950–70. OPEC intended to adhere to this policy of achieving modest increases in real oil prices during the 1970s. OPEC had never intended to bring about the oil price explosions of 1973/74 and 1979. Indeed, subsequent events surprised OPEC as much as they surprised oil consumers.

Angered by US support for Israel in the Yom Kippur War, Arab members (excluding Iraq) of OPEC (OAPEC) imposed an oil embargo on the United States and Holland. The shortage of oil that resulted raised oil prices in world markets. OAPEC had not consciously intended to create such a large increase in oil prices. Surprised by its success, OPEC rapidly internalized its market power, and during 1974 it officially quadrupled oil prices by establishing production quotas among its members.

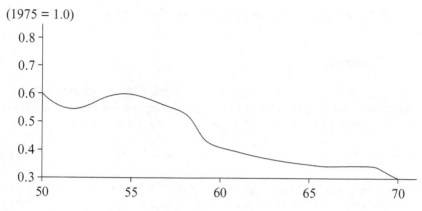

Source: Beenstock and Willcox (1981, 229)

Figure 4.2   The real oil price, 1950–70

Whereas before 1974 market forces had determined the price of oil, OPEC subsequently decided it. Had it not been for the Yom Kippur War, OPEC would most probably not have discovered its enormous power, and the international economic history of the last quarter of the twentieth century would have looked quite different.

In the aftermath of what became to be known as OPEC I, real oil prices began to decline (Figure 4.1). This was partly the result of world inflation triggered by the increase in oil prices, as well as the weakness of the US dollar, in which oil prices were set. However, OPEC II changed all this following the Iranian Revolution in 1979. Partly to punish the West, OPEC doubled oil prices. In doing so OPEC had over-extended itself and had sown the seeds of its demise.

To gain some analytical understanding into OPEC's pricing policy during this period I present two models, which explore different aspects of the economics involved. The first model examines the behaviour of a monopolist faced with a downward sloping demand curve where the demand response to price is greater in the long run than in the short run. This model is motivated by the fact that in the short run there was little the consuming countries could do in the face of higher oil prices. However, in the longer run consumers are more able to consume less energy and produce more substitutes to OPEC oil. OPEC should have taken into account that consumers may have little sovereignty in the short run, but this sovereignty grows over time. Whereas the first model is dynamic, the second model is static and recognizes that OPEC is a cartel rather than a monopolist. The second model explores the tensions within the cartel and the constraints that these tensions imply for oil pricing.

Dynamic Monopoly

In what follows, Q denotes OPEC oil production, P the price of oil, C its (fixed) unit cost of extraction, t time and r the rate of interest on petrodollars. The demand for OPEC oil is assumed to be linear in its price:

$$\dot{Q}_t = \lambda(\alpha - \beta P_t - Q_t) \tag{4.1}$$

where β denotes the long-run sensitivity of demand to price, and λ measures the exponential speed of adjustment. The greater is λ the more rapidly demand adjusts to price. Equation (4.1) assumes a first-order adjustment process of demand. The long-run demand for OPEC oil implied by equation (4.1) is $Q = \alpha - \beta P$. The term α captures scale effects on the demand for OPEC oil, which will grow over time if the world demand for energy grows more rapidly than non-OPEC supply of energy. Here, however, we simplify by assuming that α is constant, implying that the demand for OPEC oil grows in line with the supply of non-OPEC energy.

In each period OPEC's profit is $(P - C)Q$. OPEC's problem is to set oil prices over time so as to maximize the present value of its profits. Its maximand is therefore:

$$V = \int_0^\infty (P_t - C)Q_t e^{-rt} dt \tag{4.2}$$

where r is the rate of discount. For simplicity, oil reserves are assumed to be infinite over the relevant planning horizon. For all practical purposes this is a realistic approximation to the situation in the Arabian Gulf, which is massively endowed low-cost reserves.

The Hamiltonian (dropping t subscripts for convenience) is:

$$H = (P - C)Qe^{-rt} + \mu\lambda(\alpha - \beta P - Q)$$

where μ is a costate variable.

The first-order conditions are:

$$\frac{\partial H}{\partial P} = Qe^{-rt} - \mu\lambda\beta = 0$$

$$-\dot{\mu} = \frac{\partial H}{\partial Q} = (P - C)e^{-rt} - \mu\lambda$$

The optimal pricing policy generated by these conditions may be shown to be:

$$P^* = \frac{(\lambda + r)\alpha + \lambda\beta C}{(2\lambda + r)\beta} \tag{4.3}$$

Note that despite the fact that the underlying optimization problem is dynamic, equation (4.3) is static. This arises because the distributed lag in demand is exponential and the rate of discount is, of course, exponential. According to equation (4.3) OPEC immediately raises the oil price to P^* from what it was before the oil price revolution (P_0). If the oil market was previously perfectly competitive the price of oil would have been determined by its marginal cost of extraction in which case $P_0 = C$. It is easy to prove that $P^* > P_0$ since from equation (4.3) $P^* - P_0 = (r + \lambda)(\alpha - \beta C)$. Since $Q_0 = \alpha - \beta C > 0$ it has to be the case that $P^* > P_0$.

As expected, equation (4.3) implies that OPEC will set a higher price the greater is demand (α), and the cost of extraction (C) and the smaller is the long-run price sensitivity of demand (β). It may be shown that equation (4.3) implies that the price varies directly with the discount rate. A higher rate of discount implies that future profits are less important. Since there is a lag in demand, OPEC exploits the lag by charging more. Finally, it may be shown that P^* varies inversely with λ, the speed of adjustment in demand. OPEC faces more consumer sovereignty in the short run the more rapid the speed of adjustment, which reduces OPEC's monopoly power. The average lag of demand to price is equal to $1/\lambda$. Therefore, if half the adjustment of demand to price took five years $\lambda = 0.2$.

Equation (4.3) establishes that if there is an exponential lag in demand to price, P^* is independent of time. This result does not generalize to other lag structures so that P^* will generally be time dependent. This is the case when, for example, equation (4.1) is replaced by:

$$\ddot{Q} = \lambda_1\lambda_2(\alpha - \beta P - Q) - (\lambda_1 + \lambda_2)\dot{Q} \tag{4.4}$$

Equation (4.4) implies that if the price of oil were fixed, its demand is equal to:

$$Q_t = B_1 e^{-\lambda_1 t} + B_2 e^{-\lambda_2 t} + \alpha - \beta P \tag{4.5}$$

where B_1 and B_2 are arbitrary constants. According to equation (4.5) the demand for oil adjusts over time to its long-run demand of $\alpha - \beta P$ with a doubly exponentiated lag. If the roots of equation (4.4) happened to be complex the adjustment process may be non-monotonic.

In this case it may be shown that the counterpart to equation (4.3) is:

$$P_t^* = A_1 e^{-\rho_1 t} + A_2 e^{-\rho_2 t} + P^* \tag{4.6}$$

where ρ_1 and ρ_2 are the roots of the characteristic equation:

$$\rho^2 - (1 - \lambda_1 - \lambda_2)\rho + 2\lambda_1\lambda_2 + r = 0 \tag{4.7}$$

and where:

$$P^* = \frac{C + \frac{\alpha}{\beta}(1 + \frac{r}{\lambda_1\lambda_2})}{2 + \frac{r}{\lambda_1\lambda_2}} \tag{4.8}$$

Note that when $r = 0$, $\rho_1 = \lambda_1$ and $\rho_2 = \lambda_2$. Note also that the partial derivatives of equation (4.8) are qualitatively similar to their counterparts in equation (4.3).

The important point being made here is that it may be optimal for OPEC to change oil prices over time. For example, OPEC I and II followed by the price fall in the mid-1980s might have been part of an optimal policy.

Cartel Theory

OPEC is not a monopoly but a cartel comprising N heterogeneous members. They are heterogeneous because each member faces different production costs. C_j denotes the cost of production in member j. There are low-cost producers such as Saudi Arabia and high-cost ones such as Venezuela. Heterogeneity no doubt assumes other forms too in terms of economic structure, political interests etc., but we ignore these here. The demand for OPEC oil is assumed to be static and is represented by $Q = \alpha - \beta P$, where $Q = \Sigma_j Q_j$ and the profits of member j are $\pi_j = (P - C_j)Q_j$. Since oil is a homogeneous product there is a common global price for oil (P). Cartel members are assumed to be selfish and sell oil to maximize their individual profit. There are no side-payments between OPEC members. If there were, OPEC would be able to be more exploitative than it is here.

The simplest natural solution to the cartel's problem is the Cournot–Nash equilibrium. The first-order conditions are:

$$\frac{\partial \pi_j}{\partial Q_j} = P - C_j + Q_j \frac{\partial P}{\partial Q_j} = P - C_j + \frac{Q_j}{\beta} = 0 \tag{4.9}$$

Equation (4.9) implies that member j produces $Q_j = \beta(P - C_j)$. Since the sum of the member's output is equal to Q, equation (4.9) implies that the equilibrium price is:

$$P = \frac{\alpha + \beta N \bar{C}}{\beta(1 + N)} \qquad (4.10)$$

Equation (4.10) states that the price of oil varies inversely with number of cartel members. Indeed, as N tends to infinity the price tends to its competitive solution, which is equal to average cost. Apart from this the cartel price varies directly with demand (α) and inversely with β.

Since N is constant, equation (4.10) implies that OPEC would only change the price of oil if costs or their assessment of α and β happened to change. For example, the fall in oil prices in the mid-1980s could only be interpreted as a rational response according to the model if OPEC raised its assessment of β or lowered its assessment of α.

The Cournot–Nash solution misses an important ingredient to OPEC behaviour, and perhaps cartel behaviour in general, in that it assumes that members do not cheat. To introduce cheating into the model we define:

$$\phi_j = \sum_{k \neq j}^{N} \frac{\partial Q_k}{\partial Q_j}$$

which is member j's assessment of how other members are likely to respond if it raises production. If each member has the same assessment of its rival's response to cheating, that is, $\phi_j = \phi$, it may be shown that equation (4.10) becomes:

$$P = \frac{\alpha(1 + \phi) + \beta N \bar{C}}{\beta(1 + \phi + N)} \qquad (4.11)$$

Equation (4.11) reverts to equation (4.10) when $\phi = 0$. Note that if $\phi = -1$, equation (4.11) implies that the cartel price equals average cost, that is, it mimics the competitive price. If each member believes that its rivals will produce one barrel less when it produces one barrel more, the cartel price mimics the competitive price. If, however, the opposite applies and each member believes that if it cheats so will its rivals cheat, then $\phi > 0$ and equation (4.11) implies that the cartel price will be higher. This is because it may be shown that equation (4.11) implies that P varies directly with ϕ. The irony is that if every member expects every other member to cheat, each member takes this into consideration in advance, and prices are higher than otherwise.[6]

Equation (4.11) states that oil prices depend upon the cartel culture as captured by ϕ. If ϕ happens to fall because the cartel is more disciplined then its members agree to lower oil prices. Since ϕ may vary independently of cost and demand parameters, it serves as a factor in its own right in the determination of oil prices. In short, the price of oil set by the cartel may change even if costs and demand conditions remain unchanged. According to this 'Cournot Model with Cheating' the price collapse in 1985 might not have been demand induced, but may have been induced by a decrease in ϕ. A change in the cartel culture induced OPEC to lower prices independently of demand.

Saudi Arabia, the Swing-producer Model

So far OPEC has been treated as a price fixing cartel in which each member of the cartel plays a similar role. However, Saudi Arabia is by far the dominant member because its oil reserves are so vast. The interests of Saudi Arabia are quite different from those of members such as Venezuela whose reserves are dwindling. Saudi Arabia must consider the more distant future, which Venezuela can afford to ignore. As Sheikh Yamani remarked in 2003 in reference to the Oil Age, 'The Stone Age did not end because the world ran out of stone'. The Oil Age could end as a result of the discovery of substitutes for hydrocarbons leaving Saudi Arabia stranded with worthless reserves of crude oil. It is not surprising that Saudi Arabia has been a voice of moderation within OPEC.

One way of modelling the dominant role of Saudi Arabia is to assume that it behaves as a monopolist, which is constrained by OPEC and non-OPEC producers alike. In such a model Russia and the United Kingdom are just as much price-takers as Venezuela and Indonesia. Saudi Arabia behaves as a swing-producer, which varies its output in order to keep prices at a level that serves Saudi interests. The swing-producer model is essentially the same as the model presented above, except that it is for Saudi Arabia instead of OPEC as a whole. As a monopolist, Saudi Arabia is obviously more constrained than OPEC as a whole because it has to contend with supply competition from other OPEC members. Hence, the price it can set will be generally below the price that OPEC as a whole can set.

This way of modelling Saudi Arabia's dominant role is too extreme because it implies that OPEC has no independent role. It is also in Saudi interests to buy the cooperation of other OPEC members so that it can limit competition. An alternative is to model OPEC negotiations as a Nash bargain in which Saudi interests are pitted against the interests of other members of OPEC. The Saudi threat point is to go-it-alone as an independent monopolist. It is in this way that Saudi Arabia disciplines the cartel, but the interests of other members of the cartel get reflected.

There can be little doubt that the oil price revolution in the 1970s was a direct result of OPEC's concerted action. The causes of the price collapse in the mid-1980s are more obscure. Three different theories have been suggested to account for the collapse of oil prices. The first sees OPEC as a cynical monopolist, which sharply raises oil prices on a one-off basis in the knowledge that it would eventually lower them. The second sees OPEC as underestimating consumer sovereignty in the oil consuming countries. It got too greedy in 1979 and eventually paid the price. The third attributes the oil price collapse to a change in the cartel culture. Of course, all three phenomena might have been at work; the three theories are not mutually exclusive.

I attach particular importance to the second of these theories. OPEC underestimated the effect of its own greed; the world demand for primary energy fell and the supply of primary energy from outside OPEC increased. Since OPEC oil exports are equal to the balance between the former and the latter, OPEC's oil market contracted because demand fell and competing supply increased. By the mid-1980s OPEC oil exports seemed to be on the way to disappearing completely. Figure 4.3 shows that during 1950–70 the energy intensity of GDP in the developed market economies was broadly trend-free despite the fact that real energy prices had been falling. Figure 4.4 shows that following the increase in oil prices in the 1970s the world began to reduce its use of energy relative to GDP. By 2000 the ratio of primary energy use to GDP had fallen by 20 per cent, although this trend was not uniform, for example, in the USSR this ratio increased. There can be no doubt that this was a direct result of higher energy costs. Whereas before 1973 world demand for energy grew roughly at the same rate as world GDP, subsequently world energy demand grew more slowly than GDP. Indeed, world consumption of primary energy was more or less static during the first half of the 1980s (Figure 4.5).

Also, the production of primary energy outside OPEC rose (Figure 4.5) from about 2000 MTOE (million tons of oil equivalent) in 1972 to 6000 MTOE 15 years later. Caught in the closing scissors between falling demand and rising non-OPEC energy supply, OPEC's oil exports began to fall in the late 1970s, and by the mid-1980s this trend had turned into a rout. They declined from 4000 MTOE in the late 1970s to only 1500 MTOE in 1985 (Figure 4.5).

Saudi Arabia had assumed the role of 'swing-producer' inside OPEC. By the mid-1980s this role had become untenable. As the market for OPEC oil dwindled, the pressure to cheat on oil export quotas grew, and Saudi Arabia could no longer hold the oil price. So the price collapsed. This would have happened sooner but for the Iran–Iraq War, which broke out in 1981. As a result of hostilities the supply of oil from Iran and Iraq fell from

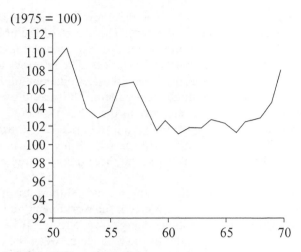

(1975 = 100)

Source: Beenstock and Willcox (1981, 226).

Figure 4.3 *The ratio of total energy consumption to GDP in developed market economies, 1950–70*

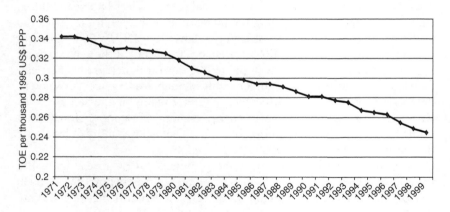

Source: *Energy balances of non-OECD countries, 1998–1999*, International Energy Agency.

Figure 4.4 *Total world primary energy use relative to GDP, 1971–99*

6.645 million barrels per day (mbd) in 1979 to only 2.462 in 1981. Indeed, since 1980 political developments in the Persian Gulf have persistently helped to bolster oil prices. The Gulf War of 1991 followed on the heels of the Iran–Iraq War. Sanctions applied to Iraq reduced Iraq's oil production from around 3 mbd before the Gulf War War to only 0.66 mbd in 1993. It was hoped that oil production would recover in Iraq following the fall of

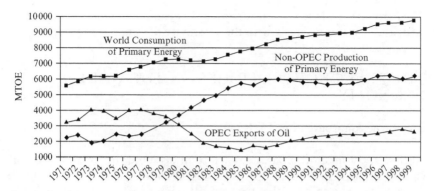

Source: *Energy balances of non-OECD countries, 1971–1999*, International Energy Agency.

Figure 4.5   World energy balances, 1971–99

Saddam Hussain in 2003. However, political instability in Iraq has prevented this. Finally, in 2006 the threat of UN sanctions on Iran in the context of the latter's nuclear policy has further created uncertainty regarding the supply of oil from the Gulf.

The OPEC Roller Coaster

We raised the possibility that a rational monopolist might increase prices and then lower them to exploit the lag in the response of demand to price. Suppose that this has happened; prices were jacked-up and then fell. What is to stop the monopolist from repeating the exercise? Once consumers have got used to the lower price there is an obvious incentive for the monopolist to exploit them all over again by raising the price once more. The luckless consumers will be exploited again before the price gradually falls back to P^*. Indeed, if nothing changes OPEC can keep up this policy indefinitely and the price of oil will roller-coast.

This roller-coaster will come to a standstill if consumers anticipate that OPEC will repeatedly try to exploit them. In this case, consumers will be influenced by 'permanent' oil prices, and they will not increase their consumption when OPEC lowers its price. This will prevent OPEC from repeatedly exploiting them. If OPEC expects consumers to be influenced by permanent oil prices rather than current oil prices, the problem becomes static rather than dynamic as mentioned previously. In this case the optimal permanent oil price is simply:

$$\tilde{P} = \frac{\alpha}{2\beta - C}$$

The permanent oil price varies directly with demand and the cost of extraction, and it varies inversely with the sensitivity of demand to price.

THE EFFECT OF OIL PRICES ON THE WORLD ECONOMY

The Keynesian Conventional Wisdom

At first, most macroeconomists failed to understand the long-term implications of higher oil prices for the world economy (oil consumers, OC). Their Keynesian thinking led them to believe that after a period of recession and cost-push inflation, business would return to normal. Output, employment and related real variables would eventually return to what they otherwise would have been. However, because OPEC had raised the price at which they sold oil to OC, the latter suffered a terms of trade loss equal to OPEC oil exports multiplied by the increase in oil prices. Since OPEC exported about 30 mbd and the price of oil had risen by $9/bl the terms of trade loss was close to $100 billion in 1974. In today's prices, this is considerably higher. This loss was OPEC's gain.

This conventional wisdom is well summarized by Fried and Schultze (1975, 5–6):

> Assuming that the real price of imported oil remains the same, therefore, the next few years should see a transition phase in which the problems associated with the unemployment- and inflation-creating aspects of the oil price rise will gradually give way to problems associated with the transfer of resources to the oil-exporting countries and to domestic energy producers. The higher oil prices will lead to a slightly reduced rate of growth in living standards, not because output and employment are still curtailed but because each unit of energy consumed will cost more in terms of economic resources.

In 1974 the design of macroeconomic policy was still Keynesian in conception too. Governments related to the recession as a temporary phenomenon, which required no long-term fiscal adjustment. Once the recession was over there was no need to cut public spending. But the conventional wisdom was wrong. Business did not return to normal. Output, employment and investment suffered permanently and not just temporarily. The failure to understand the longer-term macroeconomic implications of higher oil prices lulled governments into a false sense of security. Because they failed to cut public expenditure in time, fiscal deficits increased to levels that destabilized inflation. Stagflation turned out to be more than just a passing phenomenon. Indeed, it took almost a decade before a deeper understanding of the macroeconomic implications of higher oil prices was reached. But by then oil prices were on their way down.

Supply-side Economics[7]

Whereas the Keynesian conventional wisdom focused on the demand side, the macroeconomic thinking that replaced it focused on the supply side. Real GDP in OC is denoted by V and its deflator by P_v. Gross output is denoted by Y and its deflator by P_y. Under the simplifying assumption that oil is OC's only imported input, which is used to produce V, we have the identity: $YP_y = VP_v + EP_e$. Nominal gross output is identically equal to nominal GDP plus the value of intermediate inputs. Alternatively, value added is gross output minus intermediate inputs.

The production function for gross output is assumed to be $Y = F(K, L, E)$, where K and L denote capital and labour. This recognizes the fact that production involves the use of energy. In the gross output production function energy may either complement or substitute other factors of production. Substitution occurs when, for example, energy is used to replace labour. Complementarity occurs when energy raises the productivity of labour. For simplicity we assume that the product market in OC is perfectly competitive. Real profits are defined as $\pi = (YP_y - LW - EP_e)/P_v$ where W denotes wages.

The first-order conditions for profit maximization are:

$$\frac{\partial \pi}{\partial L} = \frac{\partial Y}{\partial L}\frac{P_y}{P_v} - \frac{W}{P_v} = 0$$

$$\frac{\partial \pi}{\partial E} = \frac{\partial Y}{\partial E}\frac{P_y}{P_v} - \frac{P_e}{P_v} = 0$$

Assuming for convenience a Cobb–Douglas technology for gross output: $Y = AL^\alpha E^\beta K^{1-\alpha-\beta}$, these first-order conditions imply the following factor demands for energy and labour:

$$\ln E = \frac{(\alpha - 1)[\ln \frac{P_e}{P_y} - \ln (\beta A K^{1-\alpha-\beta})] - \alpha[\ln \frac{W}{P_y} - \ln (\alpha A K^{1-\alpha-\beta})]}{1-\alpha-\beta}$$

$$(4.12)$$

$$\ln L = \frac{(\beta - 1)[\ln \frac{W}{P_y} - \ln (\alpha A K^{1-\alpha-\beta})] - \beta[\ln \frac{P_e}{P_y} - \ln (\beta A K^{1-\alpha-\beta})]}{1-\alpha-\beta}$$

$$(4.13)$$

Equation (4.12) states, not surprisingly, that the demand for energy varies inversely with its relative price (deflated by the deflator for gross output) because $0 < \alpha < 1$. Equation (4.13) states that the demand for labour also varies inversely with the relative price of energy because $0 < \beta < 1$. The elasticity of demand for labour with respect to the price of energy is $-\beta/(1-\alpha-\beta)$.

What does this imply about GDP $= V$? The elasticity of gross output with respect to the real price of energy is equal to:

$$\frac{d \ln Y}{d \ln \frac{P_e}{P_y}} = \psi = \frac{\beta(\alpha - 1) + \alpha(\beta - 1)}{1 - \alpha - \beta} < 0 \tag{14.14}$$

which is negative because $\alpha + \beta < 1$. National income accounting theory implies the following relationship between GDP and gross output:

$$V = \left(Y - E\frac{P_e}{P_y}\right)\frac{P_y}{P_v} \tag{4.15}$$

According to equation (4.15) the elasticity of GDP with respect to the relative price of energy comprises four components: (1) the contribution of gross output is negative and is equal to $\psi Y/V$. (2) According to equation (4.12) the elasticity of energy demand (E) with respect to the relative price of energy is $-(1-\alpha)/(1-\alpha-\beta)$. This increases GDP ($V$) given gross output ($Y$) through equation (4.15). (3) On the other hand the relative price of energy has risen, which directly reduces GDP. The total contribution of energy to GDP is therefore negative and is equal to $-\beta/(1-\alpha-\beta)$ times E/V. (4) When the relative price of energy increases the gross output price deflator naturally increases relative to the GDP deflator, which raises GDP (V) in equation (4.15). The elasticity of P_y/P_v with respect to the relative price of energy is equal to E/Y.

The theory of production that has been presented implies that the elasticity of real GDP with respect to the relative price of energy is:

$$\varepsilon = \psi\frac{Y}{V} - \frac{\beta}{1 - \alpha - \beta}\frac{E}{V} + \frac{E}{Y} \tag{4.16}$$

The first two terms in equation (4.16) are negative, but the final term is positive. However, $\varepsilon < 0$ as may be seen in the following numerical example: $\alpha = 0.5$, $\beta = 0.1$, $Y/V = 1.11$, $E/Y = 0.1$. These assumptions are realistic given the share of energy in GDP. The first term is equal to -1.25, the second is -0.0044, and the final term is 0.1, in which case $\varepsilon = -1.1544$. In the nature of things, it is the first term that is dominant.

The previous discussion establishes the following important results regarding the effect of higher energy prices:

- Equation (4.16) establishes that aggregate supply falls permanently.
- Equation (4.13) establishes that unless real wages fall, employment falls and unemployment increases permanently.
- Profitability decreases. As a result the capital stock is likely to fall. Equations (4.12) and (4.13) show that this will further reduce the demand for energy and labour such that equation (4.13) understates the fall of GDP.

Table 4.1 illustrates the empirical orders of magnitude of these effects obtained for the UK economy. Higher oil prices tip the economy into a recession, which bottoms out after two years. During the recession, employment falls by 1.2 per cent and the demand for energy falls by even more. Year 7 in Table 4.1 represents the long run, in which GDP falls permanently by 0.5 per cent, implying a long-run elasticity of GDP with respect to oil prices of −0.1. Energy demand falls permanently by 2 per cent, employment by 0.2 per cent and the capital stock by 0.3 per cent. The economy becomes less energy intensive[8] (the ratio of energy to GDP falls by 1.5 per cent) but more labour intensive (the ratio of employment to GDP rises by 0.3 per cent) so that labour productivity decreases. The productivity of capital decreases too by 0.2 per cent. Table 4.1 serves to illustrate the point that the recessive effects of higher oil prices are permanent and not merely temporary as predicted by the conventional wisdom. However, these recessive effects are greater in the short run than they are in the long run.

A quintupling of real oil prices induces a less dramatic increase in energy prices to consumers because primary energy accounts for only about 60 per cent of the cost of final energy consumption. The remainder is accounted for by specific taxes and duties, and the cost of energy transformation and delivery. The quintupling of oil prices therefore induces a doubling of

Table 4.1   Supply-side effects of 5 per cent increase in oil price

Year	Energy	Employment	Capital	GDP
1	−0.9	−0.9	0.2	−0.3
2	−3.2	−1.2	−0.1	−0.8
3	−2.6	−1.1	−0.4	−0.8
4	−1.9	−0.8	−0.4	−0.7
7	−2.0	−0.2	−0.3	−0.5

Source: Beenstock et al. (1986, Table 11).

energy prices, which implies that GDP falls by about 8 per cent in the
long run.

Stagflation Theory

Figure 4.6 illustrates the market for GDP in OC. Before the increase in oil
prices the aggregate demand schedule is D_0 and the long-run aggregate
supply schedule is S^*_0. To simplify matters there is no initial inflation. The
initial price level is P_0 and at A the rate of unemployment is equal to the
natural rate, therefore the short-run aggregate supply schedule S_0 intersects
its long-run counterpart at A. The increase in oil prices initially shifts the
aggregate demand schedule to the left for several reasons. As mentioned,
the terms of trade loss lowers permanent income in OC. Permanent income
rises in OPEC, but OPEC's absorptive capacity is lower than OC's, hence
world consumption falls. So does world investment demand, because
although investment in energy and energy substitutes increases in OC,
profitability as a whole has decreased. The new aggregate demand schedule
is represented by D_1.

The long-run aggregate supply schedule also shifts to the left to S^*_1. The
reasons have been presented in the previous section. S^*_1 is drawn under the
assumption that the capital stock remains at K_0. We assume that real wages
remain unchanged in the short run. Therefore the short-run aggregate
supply schedule associated with S^*_1 is S_1. The new equilibrium is therefore
at B, where GDP has fallen, the price level has risen, and unemployment

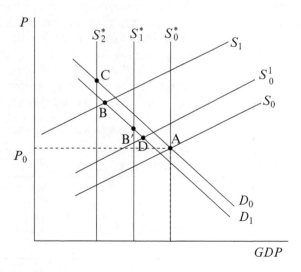

Figure 4.6   Stagflation in the oil consuming countries

has increased. Had wages been flexible, the new equilibrium would have been at B'. The rates of unemployment at A and B' are the same.

Subsequently, aggregate demand recovers as OPEC learns to absorb more, and increases its consumption. For argument's sake we assume it eventually recovers to D_0. The long-run aggregate supply schedule shifts further to the left because, as discussed in the previous section, the capital stock falls. It eventually settles down to S^*_2 so that the new equilibrium is at C. During the transition from A to B to C prices rise and output falls. In short, the transition from A to C is stagflationary. It may take several years before C is reached. However, once it is reached stagflation comes to an end. At C output, the capital stock, employment and real wages are permanently lower. So is energy consumption.

This analysis may be contrasted to the conventional Keynesian wisdom according to which the economy moves from A to D in the short run and then back to A in the long run. The transition from A to D reflects two phenomena. First, aggregate demand has fallen from D_0 to D_1. Second, because workers wish to be compensated for higher energy prices, there is cost-push inflation and the short-run aggregate supply schedule becomes S'_0. Note that S'_0 must lie to the right of S_1 because the Keynesian model assumes that the demand for labour does not depend upon the price of energy. The Keynesian recession is less deep than the one described above, because it ignores the supply side of the economy, which has been adversely affected. It is also less persistent because it ignores the contraction in aggregate supply, induced by the higher price of energy.

Some of these effects have been illustrated in Table 4.1. Table 4.2 provides supplementary estimates of the empirical orders of magnitude of the effects of higher oil prices for the Industrialized Countries (IMF definition) as a whole. After three to four years GDP is about 1 per cent lower and cumulative inflation is about 1 per cent, that is, there is worldwide stagflation. The modest increase in inflation stems from the fact that the simulation assumes that governments do not accommodate the inflationary effects of oil prices. This explains why interest rates rise sharply, and then fall. Non-oil commodity prices rise but by less than the increase in oil prices. This outcome reflects the balance of a number of countervailing forces. The fall in GDP reduces the world demand for raw materials, which lowers commodity prices. The initial increase in interest rates raises the cost of holding stocks of raw materials, which lowers commodity prices. However, energy is used in the production of raw materials, which raises the price of commodities. The net effect is to raise commodity prices, but by more in the short run than in the longer run.

These estimates imply that a quadrupling of oil prices lowers GDP in the industrialized countries by about 13 per cent after about four years. Table 4.2

Table 4.2   The effects of a 10 per cent increase in oil prices on Industrialized Countries

Year	GDP	Prices	Commodity prices	Interest rates
1	0	0.41	6.09	6.04
2	−0.77	0.94	4.46	5.11
3	−1.04	1.13	2.76	−5.17
4	−1.07	1.2	3.66	−2.62

Source: Beenstock (1988, Table 3.1).

refers to the Industrialized Countries. The Oil Importing Developing Countries (IMF definition) also suffer the consequences of higher oil prices. Beenstock (1995) estimates that the long-run elasticity of GDP with respect to real oil prices is −0.065, which suggests that a quadrupling of oil prices lowers GDP in these countries by about 9 per cent. The bottom line may be summarized as follows. The quadrupling of real oil prices adversely affected world GDP by about 12 per cent. In addition it created a terms of trade transfer to OPEC of about 3 per cent of world GDP. The total cost of the OPEC oil price disaster was therefore about 15 per cent of world GDP. This effect was fortunately temporary because in 1986 oil prices collapsed.[9]

The International Capital Market

OPEC's limited absorptive capacity in the 1970s meant that OPEC savings increased. What happens to OC savings is not clear. The fiscal deficit in OC increases, either because the government fails to understand that its permanent tax revenue has fallen, or because it takes its time to cut back public expenditure. This will reduce OC saving. What happens to private savings in OC? Figure 4.6 implies that during the transition from A to C, permanent income falls by more than current income. The permanent income hypothesis implies that private savings increase under such circumstances. So OC savings may either increase or decrease. OC investment definitely decreases.

Figure 4.7 represents the international capital market, where r denotes the world rate of interest. The world demand for investment is initially (before the increase in oil prices) represented by schedule I_0. For simplicity we assume that OPEC investment is zero. The initial world savings schedule is represented by S_0, of which OC savings are represented by C_0. OPEC savings are measured by the horizontal difference between S_0 and C_0. Because OPEC does not invest, this difference is equal to OPEC's current

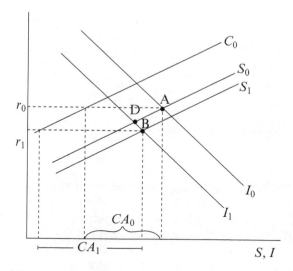

Figure 4.7   The international capital market

account surplus (CA_0) and OC's current account deficit. The world rate of interest in determined at A and is equal to r_0.

In the immediate aftermath of an oil price rise we assume for simplicity that the OC savings schedule does not change because although the fiscal deficit in OC increases, this is offset by an increase in private savings. OC investment contracts, and the new investment schedule is I_1. OPEC savings increase, so that the new world savings schedule is S_1. The new equilibrium in the international capital market is at B, at which the world rate of interest falls to r_1 and OPEC's current account surplus increases to CA_1 from CA_0. The placement of petrodollars in the world capital market depresses world interest rates. Subsequently, OPEC raises its consumption and runs down its petrodollars, as it learns to absorb, so that the world saving schedule reverts to S_0. Investment remains lower. The next equilibrium is therefore at D. This analysis implies that the world interest rate falls in the short term and recovers partially in the medium term. In the very long term the rate of interest must, of course, return to r_0.

During the 1960s, world real interest rates averaged about 2 per cent per year. Subsequently they began to fall, and by 1973 they were about zero. During the mid-1970s they were negative, bottomed out at −3.5 per cent in 1975 and became positive once more in 1981. During the 1980s they averaged 3 per cent. There can be little doubt that the sharp fall in world interest rates during the 1970s was the direct result of petrodollar recycling as predicted by the theory that has been presented.[10] In the early 1980s OPEC's current account balance turned from positive to negative, and it

Table 4.3   The effects of a $50 billion increase in petrodollars

Year	GDP	Commodity prices	Real interest rates
1	0	0	−0.89
2	0.39	1.15	−1.04
3	0.74	3.21	−1.19
4	1.00	4.03	−1.39

Source: Beenstock (1988, Table 3.5).

began to draw down its petrodollars. It was this that restored world interest rates to a more normal level during the 1980s.

Table 4.3 reports the results of a simulation in which OPEC holds an additional $50 billion in the international capital market. The effect is to lower world interest rates by about 1 per cent per annum, which has the effect of raising GDP by about 1 per cent after four years in the Industrialized Countries and of raising the prices of non-oil raw materials by 4 per cent. Table 4.3 shows that some of the adverse effect of higher oil prices on oil consumers was mitigated by the lowering of world interest rates resulting from petrodollar recycling. Indeed, because the cost of international borrowing became so cheap in the 1970s, much of the recycling went to the Non-oil Developing Countries. This laid the foundations for the international debt crisis, which broke out in the 1980s.

POLITICAL ECONOMY

Islamic Resurgence

The oil price revolution of the 1970s had political consequences too, some of which have been long-lasting. According to Huntington (1996, 116):

> The Saudi, Libyan, and other governments used their oil riches to stimulate and finance the Muslim revival, and Muslim wealth lead Muslims to swing from fascination with Western culture to deep involvement in their own and willingness to assert the place and importance of Islam in non-Islamic societies.

It is difficult to imagine the force of Islam in international relations today had OPEC not raised oil prices in the 1970s. Indeed, OPEC I and OPEC II had distinct Islamic dimensions. OPEC I was a direct consequence of the Yom Kippur War between Israel, Egypt and Syria, and OPEC II was a direct consequence of the Iranian Revolution.

The oil price revolution also has a deeper psychological significance. Bernard Lewis (2002), among others, points out that, for centuries, Islamic civilization had been superior to Western and other civilizations. Islam led the world in science, culture and the arts in an age in which the Western world was relatively backward. Moreover, conscious of their superiority, Muslims looked down upon Christian and other heathen civilizations, on cultural as well as religious grounds. However, this leadership was gradually lost to the West after the Middle Ages. This period coincides with the Industrial Revolution, the spread of democracy, the rise of individualism, the separation of church and state, and the consolidation of other values, which form the backbone of Western civilization. By the twentieth century the West had become the dominant civilization. According to Lewis (2002), Muslims grew increasingly embittered as their civilization lost ground to its Western rival. What had been a superiority complex turned into a profound inferiority complex. As a result of this bitterness the Muslim Brotherhood was established in Egypt in the 1920s, and so Islamic fundamentalism was born.

Western superiority was founded upon dispatchable energy. Indeed, as Jevons (1865) observed, without coal, modern economic growth was not sustainable. During the nineteenth century the main source of primary energy was coal. During the twentieth century, oil became increasingly important as a source of primary energy. It is one of nature's greatest ironies that the world's largest reserves of crude oil are in the Arabian Gulf, the birthplace of Islam. The key to Western superiority and the eclipse of Islam just happened to be buried under the ground where the Prophet Muhammad first stepped. The West was vulnerable.

OPEC proved this vulnerability in the 1970s. In doing so, it helped to restore Islamic pride. For a while it seemed that the key to Western superiority lay in the hands of Saudi Arabia and other Gulf states. If Muslims could not become like the West, then at least they could cut the West down to size. The longer-term failure of the oil weapon to threaten the economic superiority of the West has most probably aggravated Muslim frustration with the West.

International Economic Diplomacy

The United Nations Conference on Trade and Development (UNCTAD) first convened in 1964 to discuss economic relationships between the developed and developing countries. The original intentions of UNCTAD[11] were sensible, focusing on such matters as free trade, official development assistance and international investment. However, UNCTAD rapidly turned into a politically fractious fault line between the rich North and the poor South. The North was accused of exploiting the South and was responsible for its economic backwardness. The most important changes demanded by the developing countries at UNCTAD were the extensive use of commodity agreements to stabilize and raise commodity prices. Such agreements would stem and even reverse the secular decline in the real price of raw materials, which were largely produced in the South and consumed by the North. Whereas European and other developed countries were prepared to entertain the extension of commodity price agreements, the US government flatly refused.

In this context OPEC's success in raising oil prices in the 1970s was perceived by other Southern countries as a major political victory of the South over the North, and especially over the United States. The oil-importing developing countries turned a blind eye to the fact that OPEC's price revolution impoverished them. Instead, OPEC's boldness caught their imagination and provided them with a role model to copy. As a result, the UN General Assembly was convened in April 1974 and the Declaration and Program of Action of the New International Economic Order was adopted. Thus did the New International Economic Order (NIEO) become part of the vernacular. In December 1974 the General Assembly formally threw down the gauntlet to the Industrialized Countries by approving the Charter of Economic Rights and Duties of States.

This Charter might have been stillborn, like so many other UN initiatives, but for Henry Kissinger, who as Secretary of State was concerned by the potentially destabilizing effects of higher oil prices in the Third World. Kissinger might also have believed that NIEO could be used as a political lever to get OPEC to lower oil prices. His judgement could not have been more wrong. In December 1975 the Conference on International Economic Cooperation was established to consider fundamental reforms in such areas as trade, finance, energy and commodity markets. The South pressed for various types of commodity agreements, but most Northern countries refused to cooperate. In June 1977 the Conference was wound up, having settled nothing and having spread a cloud of acrimony between North and South.

This might have been the end of the matter. However, the President of the World Bank, Robert McNamara, was instrumental in setting up the Independent Commission on International Development Issues under the chairmanship of Willy Brandt. The Brandt Commission reported in 1980. Despite a distinct lack of enthusiasm on the parts of President Reagan and Prime Minister Thatcher, in October 1981 a summit was held in Cancun, Mexico to discuss the Brandt Report. The summit failed to come to any substantial agreement, and so the politics of NIEO more or less ran into the ground. Shortly afterwards oil prices collapsed, and NIEO died.

OPEC III

Since the turn of the millennium the oil price history of the 1970s has more or less repeated itself. Figure 4.1 plots two real oil price series. One is calculated by OPEC and one is based on the IMF's methodolology (IMF 2006).[12] The latter is simply the nominal oil price deflated by the US consumer price index. The former is a multilateral index in that it takes account of the changing value of the US dollar against a basket of currencies, and it deflates oil prices by consumer price indices in countries apart from the United States. If the real value of the US dollar increases, OPEC's measure of real oil prices will increase whereas the IMF's index will not change. In Figure 4.1 the index calculated by the OPEC secretariat is denoted by the 'Global' index, while the IMF-type index is denoted by the 'United States'.

Because the real value of the US dollar was not constant the two series in Figure 4.1 often behaved quite differently. For example, during the first half of the 1980s real oil prices were considerably higher according to the 'Global' index than they appeared from a parochial US perspective. OPEC's measure is superior because it expresses real oil prices globally rather than parochially. However, OPEC's real oil price index is not global enough because it refers to the major industrialized countries and ignores developing countries. According to the IMF, in early 2006 the real oil price was about 60 per cent of its OPEC II peak. According to OPEC it stood at 90 per cent of its OPEC II peak.

In 1998/99 real oil prices were at their level as on the eve of OPEC I. By April 2006 real prices were close to their peak of OPEC II. What triggered OPEC III was not a dramatic decision to raise prices as in the 1970s, but a decision to restrict OPEC production in the face of growing demand, especially from China and India, the two Asian giants. During the first half of the 2000s, world consumption of crude oil grew by 8.5 per cent, or by 6.5 mbd, of which China accounted for 1.8 mbd of the increase. This increase was considerably less than the 20 per cent increase in world GDP over the same period. During this period OPEC crude oil production rose by only 1.9 mbd to 29.9 mbd, and OPEC exports of crude rose by even less from 27.4 mbd in 2000 to 28.6 mbd in 2005. The gap between OPEC supply and world demand was closed by an 11 per cent increase in non-OPEC supply of crude oil.

Had OPEC allowed oil production to increase by more than it did, oil prices would not have risen so steeply, and world oil consumption would have grown more rapidly. Even without the growth in demand for oil by China the price of oil would have increased but less dramatically. One cannot blame China or India for the increase in oil prices, as did the IMF (2006). Had OPEC raised its oil production to about 34 mbd, which it could easily have done, oil prices would not have risen. OPEC engineered the oil price increase by passive resistance; by limiting supply rather than actively raising prices. Such a policy is maybe less confrontational but the result is the same.

During the first half of the 2000s the IMF's non-fuel commodity price index rose by 35 per cent and its price index for metals rose by 70 per cent. Indeed, the latter increase occurred during 2004–05 and coincided with the increase in oil prices. It is tempting to argue that there was nothing insidious to the increase in oil prices, which simply followed the general increase in commodity prices. This argument echoes similar claims concerning OPEC I, that the general increase in commodity prices that began in 1970 eventually expressed itself in oil prices. This argument is not convincing for several reasons. First, oil prices in OPEC III began increasing ahead of the prices of other commodities. Second, not all commodity prices increased during OPEC III. For example, the prices of agricultural raw materials remained flat. Third, special factors have been responsible for the increase in the prices of metals, especially in the cases of copper and gold. Just as OPEC I cannot be understood as a commodity price phenomenon, so OPEC III cannot be understood in these terms.

The transfer of income in OPEC III from the oil-consuming countries to OPEC was massive, about $500 billion per year at 2005 prices. This is roughly similar in absolute terms to the transfer during OPEC I and II, but is less in relative terms because the world economy has grown since the 1970s.[13] However, whereas this caused stagflation in the 1970s, the world economy has taken OPEC III in its stride. Indeed, during the first half of 2006 world economic growth continued apace at about 3.5 per cent per year, rates of inflation continued to remain low and stock markets remained strong. These favourable developments prove that the stagflation of the 1970s was not inevitable.

OPEC III has not caused stagflation for several reasons:

- The main reason is that since the 1970s the design and conduct of macroeconomic policy had greatly improved. In the 1970s there was much uncertainty about the effects of oil prices on inflation. Most countries accommodated cost-push inflation giving rise to nominal instability. By contrast, in OPEC III the public did not expect oil prices to be accommodated. This firm belief meant that there would be no stagflation in OPEC III. The increase in oil prices raised relative prices, but not absolute prices.
- OPEC had greater absorption problems in the 1970s than in the 2000s. In 2004–05 OPEC imports have been about 80 per cent of oil exports, whereas in 1974–75 the corresponding proportion was only

38 per cent. This has meant that OPEC III is less deflationary in terms of world aggregate demand than OPEC I and II.

- Although the absolute size of OPEC III is similar to OPEC I and II, the relative size is only 40 per cent of what it was, because the world economy had grown.
- The adverse effect of OPEC I and II on permanent world income was greater than in OPEC III. In the 1970s there was fear that OPEC might raise prices by more than it did. OPEC III occurred after the oil price crash in the mid-1980s. Consumers in OPEC III were therefore more sanguine than they were a generation before. In absolute terms permanent income was less affected in OPEC III, and in relative terms the effect was even smaller.
- The terms of trade loss induced by higher oil prices and the empirical complementarity between labour and energy mean that real wages must fall in equilibrium. The more flexible the labour market the speedier and less painful the transition. In the 1970s labour markets were relatively inflexible. Union power was most probably much greater then than a generation later. Therefore, in OPEC I and II the real wage contraction induced more unemployment than in OPEC III.

The increase in energy cost in OPEC III obviously reduced profits in the consuming countries. No doubt economic growth in the 2000s would have been more favourable than it was had OPEC III not occurred. All this goes to prove that the oil price explosion of the 1970s need not have turned into an economic disaster. The oil price explosion that occurred in the 2000s did not turn into a disaster. The world has learnt to cope better.

NOTES

1. Hotelling (1931) argued that the competitive price of exhaustible resources will increase over time at a rate equal to the relevant rate of discount.
2. They still do. On 25 October 2003 in an article in the *Economist*, Yamani was predicting the end of the Oil Age.
3. OPEC would have had to compete to sell oil to IEA members.
4. According to the IMF (2006), real oil prices in early 2006 were only 60 per cent of their peak. According to OPEC they were much higher. Unlike OPEC, the IMF fails to take account of changes in the real exchange rate of the US dollar against a broad basket of currencies. An increase in the real value of the US dollar will increase OPEC's index of real oil prices, but not the IMF's.
5. Danielsen (1982) provides a comprehensive history of OPEC and the world oil market.
6. This is similar to the result obtained according to the theory of conjectural variations. For example, see Varian (1993).
7. This section draws on Bruno (1980) and Beenstock and Dalziel (1986).

8. US energy consumption per 1996 dollar of GDP fell from 18.1 thousand BTUs (British thermal units) in 1973 to 10.5 thousand in 2002.
9. Brown and Yücel (2002) provide a useful review of the literature. They also discuss the apparent asymmetry where the fall in oil prices had less of a beneficial effect than did the increase in oil prices have a harmful effect.
10. Surprisingly the IMF (2006, 89–91) finds no effect of petrodollars on interest rates.
11. The early history of UNCTAD has been reviewed by Johnson (1967).
12. The author wishes to thank Patrick Minford for supplying data so that the IMF figures can be reconstructed.
13. In 2005 world GDP was $61 trillion at PPP exchange rates (IMF 2006, 177), so the terms of trade loss from OPEC III was about 0.8 per cent of world GDP.

REFERENCES

Adelman, M. (1972), *The world petroleum market*, Baltimore, MD: Johns Hopkins University Press.

Beenstock, M. (1983), *The world economy in transition*, London: George Allen & Unwin.

Beenstock, M. (1988), 'An aggregate model of output, inflation and interest rates for industrialised countries', *Review of World Economics*, 124.

Beenstock, M. (1995), 'An econometric model of the oil importing developing countries', *Economic Modelling*, 12.

Beenstock, M. and A. Dalziel (1986), 'The demand for energy in the UK: a general equilibrium analysis', *Energy Economics*, 7.

Beenstock, M. and P. Willcox (1981), 'Energy consumption and economic activity in industrialized countries', *Energy Economics*, 3.

Beenstock, M., Warburton, P., Lewington, P. and Dalziel, A. (1986), 'A macroeconomic model of aggregate supply and demand for the UK', *Economic Modelling*, 4.

Brandt Commission (Independent Commission on International Development Issues) (1980), *North–South: a programme for survival*, London: Pan Books.

Brown, S.P.A. and Yücel, M.K. (2002), 'Energy prices and aggregate economic activity: an interpretive survey', *Quarterly Review of Economics and Finance*, 42.

Bruno, M. (1980), 'Import prices and stagflation in industrialized countries', *Economic Journal*, 90.

Danielsen, A.L. (1982), *The evolution of OPEC*, New York: Harcourt Brace Jovanovich.

Fried, E.R. and Schultze, C.L. (eds) (1975), *Higher oil prices and the world economy*, Washington, DC: The Brookings Institution.

Friedman, M. (1974), 'FEO and the gas lines', *Newsweek*, 4 March, 71.

Griffin, J.M. and Teece, D.J. (eds) (1982), *OPEC behavior and world oil prices*, London: George Allen & Unwin.

Heal, G. and Chichilnisky, G. (1991), *Oil and the international economy*, Oxford: Clarendon Press.

Hotelling, H. (1931), 'The economics of exhaustible resources', *Journal of Political Economy*, 39.

Huntington, S.P. (1996), *The clash of civilizations and the remaking of world order*, New York: Simon & Schuster.

IMF (2006), *World economic outlook*, Washington, DC: IMF.

Jevons, W.S. (1865), *The coal question: an inquiry concerning the progress of the nation, and the probable exhaustion of our coal mines*, London, Macmillan.

Johnson, H.G. (1967), *Economic policies towards less developed countries*, London: George Allen & Unwin.

Lewis, B. (2002), *What went wrong*, Oxford: Oxford University Press.

Meadows, D.H., Meadows, D.L., Randers, J. and Behrens, W.W. (1972), *The limits to growth*, New York: Universal.

OPEC (2004), *Annual statistical bulletin*, http://www.opec.org/library/Annual%20 Statistical%20Bulletin/asb2004.htm.

OPEC (2006), *Bulletin*, March-April, http://www.opec.org/library/OPEC%20 Bulletin/2006/OB03042006.htm.

Spraos, J. (1980), 'The statistical debate on the net barter terms of trade between primary commodities and manufactures', *Economic Journal*, 90.

Sweeney, J. (1981), *Energy Modeling Forum VI*, Palo Alto, CA: Stanford University.

Varian, H. (1993), *Intermediate microeconomics*, New York: Norton.

5. Inflation in the twentieth century

Forrest H. Capie

In August 1993 inflation in Serbia was running at an annual rate of 363 000 000 000 000 000 per cent. It is difficult to grasp quite what life would be like under these conditions. And yet there were several experiences in the twentieth century of a similar kind. Inflation of this kind is almost exclusively a twentieth-century phenomenon. Almost all the severe inflationary experience belongs in the twentieth century. There were some isolated instances before 1914, but not many. The obvious explanation is that when the world was tied to metallic currency there was much less scope for expanding the money supply – the fundamental cause of inflation. Paper money, more obviously a technological possibility in the twentieth century, and the appeal it had for weak governments, combined to produce the inflation that characterized the world after 1914. The fundamental reason for the extreme cases is serious social unrest and weak governments. Grave social unrest or actual disorder provokes large-scale spending by the established authority in an attempt either to suppress or placate the rebellious element. And this is readily possible with a printing press. Social unrest is also likely to produce a sharp fall in tax revenues. The government then prints money. As Keynes (1923, 41) put it, inflation 'is the form of taxation which the public find hardest to evade and even the weakest government can enforce when it can enforce nothing else'.

It was in the late twentieth century that inflation reached its most devastating heights. In the years 1960 to 1992 world prices (insofar as they can be measured) rose 17-fold. In the developed OECD world it was obviously much less than that but nevertheless it still suffered its worst ever aggregate inflation rates. These years produced the worst experience ever for the world as a whole. In the same period in Latin America prices rose 14 000 000-fold. In Brazil it was even worse at 22 000 000 000-fold; and Argentina worst of all at 1 200 000 000 000-fold. These countries struggled to make economic headway at a time when the world was generally prospering. Many other countries and regions also suffered very high inflation at different points within this period: Israel for example in the 1980s; Indonesia in the mid-1960s; much of Africa across the period; and the

Balkans in the 1990s. Inflation of these magnitudes destroys savings and economic incentives and of course any confidence in governments. In monetary matters reputation is of key importance and countries without reputable government and monetary and financial institutions have suffered as a consequence.

DEFINITIONS

Inflation is a long-run process. We have all become accustomed to inflation in recent times as if it were one of the great constants in life. Yet there was a time when there was no inflation. It is worth distinguishing between the kind of inflation to which we have become accustomed and the more serious and frequently devastating kind that has appeared in several places. Hyperinflation has been defined by Cagan (1956, 25) as 'beginning in the month the rise in prices exceeds 50 percent and as ending in the month before the monthly rise in prices drops below that amount and stays below for at least a year'. That definition is now widely accepted but another in a dictionary of economics suggests that hyperinflation means prices rising at the rate of at least 1000 per cent per month (and the rises might be as fast as 100 000 per cent per month), though this source does not say how many months the rises should last in order to qualify (Pearce 1981). If this definition were taken to mean average rate of price rise over the period, then of the seven hyperinflations Cagan examined, only one would remain – that of Hungary in 1945–46 where the average monthly rate of price rise was 19 800 per cent.

If Cagan's precise numerical definition is adhered to, then only the cases of the 1920s and 1940s remain, and as far as can be established no other hyperinflation has occurred anywhere at any time. The recent experience in Latin America, and in a handful of other countries in Africa and the Middle East fade away in comparison. However, since one purpose of this chapter is to place twentieth-century experience in some perspective and so in relation to the more striking historical cases, Cagan's definition could be relaxed. What might be called 'very rapid inflation' could be defined for those cases when price rises reach an annual rate of, say 100 per cent, in any one year. Some justification for the round figure can be found in Cagan, who argues that note issuers seek to maximize revenue. The elasticity of the demand for money curve meant that for the seven hyperinflations he examined, the maximum constant revenue was reached when the inflation rates were over 100 per cent per annum (Cagan 1972, 14).

INFLATION IN THE LONG RUN

A brief survey of world price history illustrates just how rare the twentieth-century experience of very rapid inflation has been. In the whole course of human history the number of bursts turns out to be very few. Indeed there are only a handful outside the twentieth century, with the principal ones being those of the American War of Independence in the late 1700s, the French Revolution of the 1790s and the Confederacy in the US Civil War of the 1860s (Lerner 1954, 1955). There are accounts in history books of fearful episodes of price rises in ancient times but the inflation rates appear to be low by modern standards. For example, the declining Roman Empire was said to be beset with inflation (Mitchell 1947); it was supposedly the major ill of the third century AD. But the price data available suggest a rise from a base of 100 in 200 AD to 5000 by the end of the period. There are also accounts of 'catastrophic' inflation under conditions of primitive money, but there must be a touch of hyperbole here. While the quantity theory is invoked on most occasions, the idea of producing sufficient cows (or observing their increasing velocity of circulation!) or tobacco or even cowrie shells is not consistent with what is meant by hyperinflation. In any event there are seldom reliable data to peruse let alone to examine these experiences. Indeed, even for the twentieth century the data are less than robust and should be treated with extreme caution.

The experience of the twentieth century, of course, is better known and is entirely different. The first major burst of genuine hyperinflation followed or was coterminous with the First World War. The shock of that hyper-inflationary experience is thought to have helped produce the political climate and policies that led to stable or falling prices until the Second World War. The second major burst of hyperinflation affected Hungary, Greece and China at the end of the Second World War. The experience since then around the world has been unremitting inflation, with price increases reaching rates previously unseen in many OECD countries, and of high and accelerating rates in several developing countries. These latter have reached or are at the present time reaching rates in excess of 100 per cent per annum and, at their most rapid, over 1000 per cent per annum.

INFLATION IN THE 1920s

The early 1920s are well-known for the exceptional rates of inflation experienced in several countries in Central and Eastern Europe. There were five countries that at some points between 1919 and 1925 suffered extremely severe bursts of inflation. They were Austria, Hungary, Poland, Russia and

Germany, and the respective rates of price rises from the beginning to the end of the hyperinflation were: 14 000, 23 000, 2.5 million, 4 million and 1000 million. Most of the rest of Europe suffered some inflation but only in these five cases did inflation soar into these astronomical regions.

Some see the fundamental cause of these inflations as the overwhelming pressure to restore (leaving aside Russia for the moment) some resemblance of the standard of living that had prevailed before the First World War. The important point stressed in this argument is the extent of the devastation and the sense of exhaustion that hung over most of Europe at the end of the war. The need to rebuild was urgent and the governments who embarked on reconstruction programmes faced massive expenditures and little prospect of raising revenue (Aldcroft 1977). This is not to say that the inflations were inevitable.

Apart from the strong desire for reconstruction, there were several additional burdens and difficulties faced by these countries. Poland was at war with Russia until 1921. All of the countries faced huge reparation payments and the German burden for all practical purposes proved impossible. In Austria and Hungary there was the problem of huge numbers of administrative personnel left over from the Empire (Notel 1984).

In the face of these actual and desired expenditures, taxation was inadequate and the tax system in any case was inefficient. The League of Nations reported that their technical advisers were powerless to address the inefficient accountancy, the slowness with which arrears of taxes were collected, and even the wholesale corruption. Even where there was good intent there quickly came a point where real taxes yielded less than the cost of collection.

In addition to the domestic pressures there was an external one in the form of a growing deficit, as imports replaced domestic production and exports were negligible. This put additional pressure on the foreign exchanges, and while the depreciating currency might in normal circumstances have worked to restore equilibrium, in these times there was an inelastic demand for imports and inelastic supply of exports. One slightly offsetting factor at least initially was that the depreciated currency attracted a capital inflow as long as there was a prospect of return to the pre-war parity. As soon as the expectation of return to pre-war parity became remote the capital inflow was reversed, the exchange rate weakened further and this added to pressure on prices. In these circumstances, it is not surprising that weak or inexperienced governments succumbed to the attractions of inflationary finance, though in defence of some governments it should be borne in mind that with the Russian Revolution as the backdrop there was a widespread desire to take whatever action was needed to avert social unrest. Obviously a measure of weakness would be difficult to construct, and it is doubtful if anything could be arrived at that would be an improvement on the qualitative judgement. It is ironical, though, that Lenin is said to have looked to the destruction of a country's currency as the quickest road to the overthrow of capitalism. Keynes was happy to use the quote from Lenin to make a point. He wrote, 'Lenin is said to have declared that the best way to destroy the capitalist system was to debauch the currency. By a continuing process of inflation, governments can confiscate, secretly and unobserved, an important part of the wealth of their citizens. . .Lenin was certainly right' (Keynes 1920, 220). And while Frank W. Fetter (1977) disputed this, the general point still holds. Certainly, it was the printing of money that gave governments the real resources they sought, but the effectiveness of the method declined over time as ever larger issues were involved.

If there is one thing common to all these countries, it is the weakness of government. In and outside Austria there were general doubts about the viability of that new state. In Germany the new and inexperienced socialist government was thwarted in its attempts to pass tax reforms (Balderston 1993). In addition, in Germany the suggestion has often been made, and with some justification, that there was an element that looked to inflation to defeat the reparation burden. One reason this argument is not without foundation is that the Reichsbank could have supported the exchange rate in January 1923 and prevented the collapse of the currency, for its gold reserve was five times the total circulation at existing rates (Sommariva and Tullio 1985). Poland saw its own experienced officials leave the country and the new state was left without proper civil administration; and added to this was the Polish population's greater-than-average distaste for the tax collector. In the Soviet Union's case the new regime had a clear desire for rapid inflation to wipe out the middle classes and speed the revolutionary cause.

In all five countries in the 1920s the episodes occurred either in new states or new regimes where one problem was of coping with the needs/desires of the mass of the people for some restoration of their living standards. This was of such a nature that civil war was a distinct possibility or reality. Yet there were at least two countries that faced similar problems that escaped hyperinflation. One was Latvia and the other, Czechoslovakia. In these countries rigorous fiscal programmes enforced from the beginning of the new republic checked incipient hyperinflation by 1921.

THE EXPERIENCE OF THE 1940s

In the 1940s there were three extreme cases of hyperinflation: Hungary, Greece and China. These three cases are enlightening in certain ways, especially in relation to what has just been said about the 1920s. Hungary is an interesting case. This was a country that had experienced hyper-inflation in the 1920s and yet in the 1940s went through the most rapid inflation on record at any time anywhere. In the 13 months between July 1945 and August 1946, prices rose by 3 [1025]. The reason this episode is of particular interest is that there are distinct similarities between the 1940s and 1920s in Hungary in the conditions surrounding the hyperinflation. In particular there were reparation payments and military expenditures that far outran the possibilities for raising revenue. But on this second occasion there was a popular government in power and a central bank that clearly understood the dangers of inflation and warned against them. The interest lies in the role that the Allied Commission played in this, and within the Commission the part played by the Soviet Union. When the central bank objected to the huge volume of Treasury Bills issued to finance the inflation, the Soviets turned a deaf ear. Again the suggestion is that the Soviets were happy to see inflation proceed and destroy the middle class (Bomberger and Makinen 1983).

Between 1937 and 1949, China was either at war with Japan or all but cut off from the world and experiencing its own revolution. The Japanese invaded North China and Shanghai in 1937 and by 1949 the communists under Mao Tse Tung had control of mainland China. When the Japanese attacked, the leader of the Nationalist government pledged total war without regard to cost, and in the next few years no attempt was made to match increased expenditure with increased revenues. The data are very fragile in a case such as this, but the indices of wholesale prices for the whole country together with the cost of living index for Shanghai provide the basic picture (Chou 1963).

There was clearly a long and accelerating inflation through these years with prices rising first by 27 per cent then 68 per cent, then more than doubling and so on until in 1947 monthly rates in excess of 50 per cent were reached (Huang 1948, 255; Campbell and Tullock 1954). A budget deficit had opened up consequent to the war with Japan, and industrial and agricultural output had fallen drastically as resources were devoted to the war effort. No sooner was VJ Day past than the communists and nationalists began fighting for former Japanese-controlled territory. Civil war had broken out and the already substantial budget deficit began to soar. In the budget of 1946 there was a huge increase in the military outlay and the budget deficit moved from CN$266 billion to CN$276 billion in 1946. There was a corresponding expansion in the money supply; it grew by almost 700 per cent between 1946 and 1947. Price and wage controls introduced in 1947 were largely ineffective. By 1948 the war initiative was passing to the communists and they entered Peking in 1949. On 1 October of that year the People's Republic was founded.

Over the whole period of war, the money supply grew by about 15 000 per cent, wholesale prices rose by over 100 000 per cent, and the difference is made up by the change in velocity – the manifestation of a flight to goods. The vastly increased note issue of the Central Bank of China lay behind the huge expansion in the money supply.

The third case in the 1940s is that of Greece. The Greek economy was just one that was devastated by war. German occupation lasted from 1940 to 1944, and the government installed by the Germans provided the requirements of the occupation forces. The Germans extracted various payments from the government and progressively these were met by turning to the printing press. Circulation rose from a base of 100 in 1940 to 13 769 and 49 854 000 000 in 1944. The respective cost-of-living figures are 100 in 1940, 34 846 in 1943, and 163 910 000 000 in 1944. The fiscal system broke down, for there was, in effect, no recognized government for a large section of the community. By October 1944 when the Germans withdrew, 99 per cent of all expenditures were being covered by note issue. When the British liberated Athens from the Germans in 1944 much of the groundwork had been done by two resistance groups. One group, the monarchists and the other, the communists, began fighting each other after the German defeat. The events leading up to the Civil War are obviously much more complicated than this suggests, but for our purposes the point that matters is that monetary anarchy continued and the worst hyperinflation came in the period 1944–46. British troops were still in Greece and they supported the anti-communists. Stalin kept to commitments made to Churchill and did not intervene. The result was that although there was renewed fighting in 1947–49, the outcome was not really in doubt and the pro-Western group won in 1949.

THE CONDITIONS FOR INFLATION

A principal point of this brief survey of experience is to consider some common elements in the conditions that allowed such rapid inflation to occur and to hold these in view in considering the second half of the twentieth century. What were the conditions in which inflation appeared and rapidly accelerated? In most of the qualitative accounts of the episodes there emerge certain variables that are clear contenders for inclusion in the list of 'proximate conditions'. Obviously, increasing money supply is the first of these. Also, budget deficits are invariably found in parallel with or preceding the rapid inflation. Not surprisingly growth in public debt is generally found to accompany the growing deficit. Trade deficits, too, sometimes appear since as we have seen, the conditions were generally ones in which imports rose and exports fell as the domestic economy was unable to meet the demands being placed upon it. This was true in spite of floating exchange rates; in some instances where there were flexible rates the depreciating currency has been regarded as a further source, or at least accelerator, of inflationary pressure.

The relatively scarce data available allow only limited comment to be made. The variables were: the rate of inflation, budget deficit, balance of payments, public debt, the exchange rate and the money supply. There are frequently no aggregate output data against which to set whatever other data are available. (One obvious problem in measuring output is the unreliability of the price data. It does not matter greatly for our case if we cannot distinguish between some hundreds of per cent per annum in prices but such differences matter for computing output movements.) In seeking evidence on the conditions in which hyperinflation occurred, the emphasis has been placed on the period immediately before the worst phase of the inflation.

The first and striking feature common to all the episodes is that of an unbacked paper currency. In all cases the growth in the money supply was enormous. Such a growth was impossible without a paper currency. Kent (1920, 47) claimed that copper-coin debasement at the end of the third century AD in Rome was the main cause of the inflation in the Roman Empire:

> Copper coins could very easily be manufactured; numismatists testify that the coins of the fourth century often bear signs of hasty and careless minting; they were thrust out into circulation in many cases without having been properly trimmed or made tolerably respectable. This hasty manipulation of the mints was just as effective as our modern printing presses, with their floods of worthless or nearly worthless money.

But as we have seen, the rate of price increase was not on a par with what we have in the cases we consider, and it is not believable that sufficient coins could either be minted or carried around to produce the inflation of modern times. It is worth noting that the date of Kent's publication was 1920, that is, before all the really serious inflations in the world.

The fact that paper currency was rare before the twentieth century undoubtedly explains why very rapid inflation was rare. Without a paper currency, the technology available would not allow a sufficient expansion of the money supply or a rise in velocity sufficient to produce the rapid rise in prices. All experiences with unbacked paper money resulted in inflation, though they did not always degenerate into very rapid inflation. For example, in Spain, in the period 1779–88 when paper money was issued, prices rose quite steeply. And of course in Britain during the period of inconvertibility, during the Napoleonic Wars, the same was true. But vast increases in unbacked paper characterize all very rapid inflations. The Americans had the 'Continental' and the French the Assignat. In France the experience of John Law in the 1710s had been well remembered so that even in the 1780s the French were still vehemently opposed to the issue of paper money. On a king's edict proclaiming new money in 1788 one parish priest argued, 'Above all, we will not countenance the introduction of paper money or a national bank, either of which can only produce a great evil' (Harris 1930, 8). But the revolution came, and the attitude towards paper money changed (Harlow 1929). The people's revolution was impossible without it. The same was true of the Confederacy in the 1860s and of all the episodes of the twentieth century.

A vast expansion in paper currency preceded all these rapid inflations. This brings us to the second feature, for what comes out of most of the qualitative accounts is that the monetary growth derived from fiscal deficits. The view that deficits ultimately require monetizing and inexorably lead to inflation is quite widespread. It is implicit in much of the literature and explicit in some. In previous periods the view was not a controversial one. The monetary historian with a rough and ready acquaintance with periods of rapid price rises thinks first of all of heavy and usually war-induced government expenditure that could not be covered by revenue. For example, as far as the post-First World War inflations are concerned, the bulk of informed opinion at the time (represented, for instance, at the Brussels Financial Conference in 1920) was that governments could prevent inflation developing if they balanced their budgets. The 'Brussels doctrine was emphatic in pointing to budget deficits as the cause of inflation' (League of Nations, 1946). When government was unable to cover the gap by borrowing it resorted to the printing press. Where there was little prospect of revenue meeting expenditure, the whole debt had to be monetized. It is true that for a few years in the mid-1920s the opposite view took hold – that budget deficits were a consequence rather than a cause of inflation. The argument was that inflation reduced the real tax revenue and that the general rise in prices affected the goods and services that were the object of state expenditure and so raised state expenditure. This is rather an explanation for continuing inflation rather than an explanation of its origins. The view that was to dominate was that deficits were warning lights of inflation to follow.

In the few examples of very rapid inflation before the twentieth century, there is little doubt that when deficits and debt soar monetary growth followed quickly thereafter. The data again do not allow rigorous testing of even an examination of the precise timing in the relationship, but the accounts of these cases all suggest that sequence in the variables and that this preceded the price explosion. Fiscal needs led to monetary growth and to inflation. The American Revolution, the French Revolution and the Confederacy in the American Civil War are all examples.

In the 1920s the evidence is very similar. Austria, Germany, Hungary and Poland all had substantial and growing deficits built up before or coincidental with the inflation. There is little doubt that this was also the case with Russia. Obviously both views could have validity. If spending increased and led to the deficit, then inflation follows the deficit. However, if spending were stable but tax revenues fell as a result of inflation, then of course inflation caused the deficit. There are insufficient data to test for the timing of the relationship. In Russia, as noted earlier, there the intention was to float the revolution on a tide of paper that not only paid for the required resources but in the process destroyed the currency and wiped out the bourgeoisie.

There are fewer examples in the 1940s but a striking one is that of China and the case of Greece provides further support, and we also now know in greater detail the experience of Hungary at the end of the Second World War (Bomberger and Makinen, 1983). All these cases confirm the story of deficits leading to very rapid inflation.

Given that very rapid inflation has always appeared in a period of monetary expansion following or contemporaneous with growing budget deficits, the question arises: what circumstances produced the latter? A second question would be: did such deficits and monetary growth lead inexorably to high inflation?

As to what produces the deficit, one suggestion is that it is war:

The association of wars. . .with hyperinflation is easy to rationalize. The needs of war demand a major proportion of the nation's resources to be devoted to production that does not satisfy consumption goods. Thus shortages develop relative to the normal standard of living that exercises a major influence on price expectations (Ball 1964, 262).

But such an answer is clearly less than the whole one. After all it is obvious that the history of the world is essentially a chronicle of conflict, frequently on a huge and prolonged scale; and in two world wars in the twentieth century, when scores of countries were involved, there are still only a few cases of very rapid inflation. In the seventeenth and eighteenth centuries there were many wars and they often lasted longer than in the nineteenth and twentieth centuries, but the cases of very rapid inflation were fewer.

On some occasions prices actually fell during wars. According to Hamilton (1977) the first war that exerted an upward pressure on prices was the war of the Spanish Succession (1702–13). But even there and in spite of Madrid being a battlefield for more than a decade, prices rose by only 6 per cent over the whole war. Sometimes inflationary pressures did emerge, as in the War of Austrian Succession (1740–48), and again in the Seven Years War (1756–63) (Wicker 1985). But in none of these major wars nor in a whole string of others did any danger of very rapid inflation appear. War of itself is certainly not sufficient. It is perhaps worth recalling here that Germany's deficits in the First World War grew rapidly from 1914 onwards and were accompanied by a substantial growth in the money supply, but the very rapid inflation did not develop until 1923, and the First World War cannot really be seen as the prime source of that inflation (Graham 1930; Laursen and Pederson 1964). Indeed it has been argued that it was the weak federal structure of the new country after its foundation in 1871 that lay behind the serious fiscal problems that in turn produced the hyperinflation. A weak centre with relatively strong states resulted in high spending being unmatched by correspondingly controlled revenue collection (Hefeker 2001). This is another way of talking about weak government. In the 1990s Argentina may be another example of just such a structure.

On some occasions in wartime, price controls were introduced as a tool to combat inflation, and in some cases have been judged effective, at least temporarily, in holding down prices. They undoubtedly distorted the market, but the costs here have been reckoned to have been offset by the benefits of dampening inflation (Rockoff 1984). This does not prove that controls work but rather that they probably have a role to play in time of war and worked most effectively when supported by a system of rationing (Capie and Wood 2002). It is war that provides the common purpose and induces a toleration of the loss of economic freedom. Price controls backed with severe penalties were features of most periods of inflation, but outside of wartime they have been easily evaded.

A closer look at the episodes we have gathered together reveals that it was not simply war but rather civil war or revolution or at minimum serious social unrest that was present in almost all the cases: the American Revolution, the French Revolution, the American Civil War, Russia after 1917, Hungary in 1919 and Poland in the early 1920s. In Germany, too, there were attempted communist coups. In 1922 and 1923 there were armed uprisings and major breakdowns in public order. (There was a communist government in Bavaria.) In Austria the situation was similar. Some indications of the lesser known unrest there are given in Teichova (1983).

China and Greece in the years immediately after the Second World War suffered civil war – that is, in ten of the 11 cases. The recent view (Bomberger and Makinen 1983) expressed on Hungary in the 1940s is that Soviet influence in the Allied Commission prompted that case. Again the problem of measurement arises in what constitutes serious social unrest. Whether or not an indicator of social unrest could be constructed is an interesting question and perhaps some researcher will take it up.

Governments have always been keen to get hold of resources, and in times of great difficulty the temptation has been in the extreme to confiscate the resources. The easiest way of achieving this is to generate inflation and benefit from the inflation tax. The authorities maximize their revenue when inflation is in excess of a rate of 100 per cent per annum, but at these rates the government must be in serious danger of losing power. In other words while the inflation tax may look to be a tempting short-run policy, it is clearly potentially calamitous in anything except the shortest term. The production of very rapid inflation may be profitable for the authorities but the political consequences are potentially dire. Why then, or in what circumstances, would it be worth taking such a risk? The answer must be: when the state is seriously threatened from within.

The reason that an external threat is not critical is, of course, that that usually stimulates patriotism and tax revenue can be raised more easily and borrowing, too, is easier. When the threat is internal there is an immediate loss of tax revenue. If then there were a threat of overthrow from within, the government may calculate that the risk attached to very rapid inflation is worth running and the cost worth bearing. It could be argued that, in many cases, such a view was rational and in the end correct. After all, how many Americans would sooner have lost in the 1780s just to avoid the inflation?

Civil war is obviously a prime reason behind deficits. Expenditure rises sharply as the established authority fights to resist rebellion, but the revenue falls as tax revenue from the rebellious section is one of the first things to disappear. A deficit has opened up and resort to the printing press is immediate. But, of course, there have been many more revolutions and civil wars than there have been very rapid inflations, so why do some wars allow rapid inflation to develop and others do not?

The prevailing and the anticipated fiscal position has to be considered in conjunction with monetary policy. The argument is that in a fiat money regime, an appropriate fiscal policy can implicitly back the money stock. The view has been expressed as follows: the value of government liabilities is determined in the same way as the value of the firm's liabilities. An issue of additional shares in the absence of prospective improvement in the future stream of income leads to a fall in the price of the shares. In the case of government, an increase in its liabilities (notes) without an increase in prospective tax receipts provokes an expectation of a fall in the value of the liabilities – that is, an expectation of inflation (Smith 1984). Smith took this explanation back to an examination of Massachusetts in the first half of the eighteenth century and found support for it. However, it should be said that he was dealing with a highly specific set of circumstances. Deficits did not lead to inflation, not simply because there was a strong expectation that the deficit would not be monetized but rather because there was more or less a guarantee that they would not. The circumstances were that when a deficit opened up money was issued to cover it, but as soon as tax receipts came in the money was retired.

It is interesting to look at this argument in relation to certain examples in this chapter and elsewhere. Take, for example, the case of Britain in and immediately after the First World War. Britain, too, developed huge budget deficits and ran down its foreign assets on a huge scale. The national debt rose from £650 million in 1913 to £8000 million in 1920, equal in value to about 2.5 times national income. Yet by the standards of the time the rate of inflation, while gathering pace in the course of the period 1914–20, was not high, never higher than 20 per cent per annum. Why did higher rates of inflation not develop? What prevented Britain from suffering very rapid inflation? An explanation from the above would be that it must have been widely believed at some point in the course of the war – perhaps when victory seemed assured – that fiscal rectitude would follow and that surpluses would result in some debt being retired, money supply falling and prices falling. Certainly deficits were enormous in 1916–19 – of the order of £1800 million or 70 per cent of GNP. But the deficit fell to £326 million in 1919–20 and moved sharply into a surplus of £230 million in 1920–21. Of course, whether it was the belief that this would happen because of Britain's traditional adherence to Gladstonian finance or because of the actual reversal of the deficit requires closer examination. There are many other such examples that could be cited. England immediately after the French experience with the Assignat had an unbacked paper currency is just one.

For this thesis to be supported, detailed studies of the state of belief in these and other instances would have to be carried out. Sargent (1982) suggests it was the case for the 1920s, and Makinen (1984) and Bomberger and Makinen (1983) point to a similar conclusion for Greece and Hungary in the 1940s. There would seem to be a prima facie case for investigation in the case of the North in the United States Civil War (Hammond 1961). The danger, however, (perhaps particularly in trying to explain the origins of rapid inflation) would seem to be that of explaining the state of belief by the outcome. In other words, is it really testable?

In a civil war or revolution or even in a period of some social unrest, the course of events is uncertain in varying degrees. The future stream of income from taxation is likewise uncertain. In the absence of any commitment to the future, there can be little 'backing' for the note issue in a fiat money regime. But this explanation might prove useful in directing attention to some critical point that might constitute the necessary shock to the system that carries it over a critical threshold on the inflationary path.

INFLATION IN THE RECENT PAST

Set against the background described above it can readily be seen that the experience of inflation in the recent past – largely the period 1960 to the 1990s, and particularly in Latin America – in general has not been of the extremely severe kind and indeed seldom qualifies as hyperinflation. However, the inflation did persist over many years and using the very rapid inflation definition of 100 per cent per annum as the qualifying rate there are a large number of examples. Given the greater data availability in this period, it becomes possible to use monthly data for the 18 months that surround some of the worst experiences. These show the accelerating rate and the declining rate as a peak was passed. The monthly data were limited to money, prices and exchange rates except in the case of Argentina where there were some further data on government finance. Again the data must be treated with caution. Even with these relatively recent data it is not always possible to reconcile two different sources. But the annual data allow some comment even if several series are of limited value. The fact that *International financial statistics* showed a balanced budget for Brazil in the middle years of the 1980s will alert readers to the kind of caution required.

The experience of rapid inflation in the modern world has not been limited geographically but the dominance of Latin America is obvious. The other possible generalization is that almost all the countries are primary producers, though there are many different levels or stages of economic development. Before the mid-1980s there were nine cases involving eight countries – Argentina being the main culprit with two experiences. Six were in Latin America, one in Africa, one in the Middle East and Indonesia in the Far East. Argentina experienced a rapid inflation in the mid-1970s when an annual rate of 443 per cent was recorded. This fell steadily to about 100 per cent in 1980 and rose again to 364 per cent in 1983 and still higher in the late 1980s and early 1990s. Chile, too, had its worst experience in the mid-1970s with a rate of over 500 per cent in 1974. Uruguay had its worst experience in the late 1960s. The other countries who qualify on the basis described (Ghana, Israel, Brazil and Peru) were all in the grip of their worst experience in the mid-to late 1980s. Bolivia then followed a similar path.

Part of the information is of limited value and can be disposed of quickly. First, the exchange rates. These all move in the direction expected, though on occasion not quite on the scale expected. This is interesting only up to a point for the chief deficiency in the data is that they do not represent a market rate. The figures on debt are less reliable, but insofar as the trend goes it is an unsurprising parallel rise. The other data that yield little that is consistent are those on the balance of payments. There were several large deficits but the interesting point here is that these were almost never overwhelming. They were not large as a share of income – not out of line with many other countries at other times who experienced no rapid inflation. If the figures are to be believed, in the first Argentinian case there was no connection at all. In Ghana there were alternating surpluses and deficits, and in the years of the worst inflation the balance of payments was in surplus. Peru was similar as were Chile and Brazil.

The data about which there is little ambiguity are in money supply and budget deficits. Money supply soared in all the countries on which there is information, and the best guide to budget deficits suggests that they grew too and were strongly negative at the worst point of the inflation. To pursue the explanation found above may not be wise, but the first thing that stands out is that there are several cases of civil war or serious social unrest. Argentina and Chile (and to varying degrees other Latin American countries) and Indonesia at the time of the overthrow of Sukarno are all examples. Others such as Israel do not fit the mould so neatly, though some would argue that Israel has certainly had weak government and has tried, in much the way described above, to buy off social unrest so that there is now a large division in its society. (One way of expressing this might be to say that Israel had 'externalized' its civil war.) However, no pretence is intended here that the complexities of modern politics (especially Latin American) have begun to be disentangled. Simply put, there are hints that some similarities exist.

When the years after 1960 are examined it is clear that the scale and extent of inflation increased hugely. Staying with the definition of very rapid inflation where the cut out point is over 100 per cent, a recent paper by Fischer, Sahay and Vegh (2002) outlines this picture. In a sample of 133 market economies up to the 1990s more than two-thirds experienced an inflationary episode of more than 25 per cent. Over half of these countries (49) suffered an episode greater than 50 per cent, and 25 countries experienced inflation of more than 100 per cent. Even more remarkable, 11 of these countries had inflation in excess of 400 per cent at some point. These episodes lasted for longer than might have been expected with the average duration being three to four years.

In transition economies, of which 28 were examined, the experience was worse. All of these countries had inflation of more than 25 per cent. And most of them had episodes where it was greater than 400 per cent. In market economies there were 45 episodes in 25 countries of inflation over 100 per cent. Twelve of the countries and 18 of the episodes were in Latin America or the Caribbean, nine countries and 19 episodes were in Africa. The remainder were in the Middle East.

THE CONSEQUENCES OF INFLATION

Frederic Bastiat, the nineteenth-century French philosopher, wrote that the function and the duty of government was to provide a framework of law that allowed the defence of persons, liberty and property – the three basic requirements of life. In the middle of the nineteenth century – at a time of stable prices – Bastiat (1850) found fault with the United States in two respects: slavery and tariffs. 'Slavery is a violation, by law, of liberty. The protective tariff is a violation, by law, of property', he wrote. Had he been writing in the middle of the twentieth century he would have found governments everywhere guilty of another crime – plundering their peoples by committing the crime of theft of property through inflation.

One of the extreme experiences of the twentieth century, that of Germany in 1923, is frequently cited as an illustration of the destruction of the middle classes by wiping out their savings (Holtferich 1984). These were certainly the immediate consequences. The medium-term consequences were the preparation of the ground for the rise of fascism. The longer-term consequences might be viewed more positively. Long after the experience was over it was so deeply ingrained that the people would never tolerate inflation of that kind again. And in the world after the post-1945 adjustment period Germany had one of the best inflationary records in the second half of the twentieth century.

The short- and medium-term consequences of inflation are, however, almost invariably deleterious. The immediate consequences of high inflation damage the economy in several ways. When inflation begins to rise it also becomes more volatile and uncertainty increases. When it reaches the heights described in this chapter in the 1920s and 1940s it severely damages economic activity. Price stability is a necessary condition for successful market activity. Prices are the key signal that allow optimal decisions to be taken. When they are distorted the world becomes blurred and the future more uncertain. Investment and saving are inevitably curtailed. Capital flight is likely to follow. Output slumps. Whether or not Lenin ever wrote, or even said, that the way to destroy capitalism was to debauch the currency, a great deal of truth nevertheless lies in that idea.

By the means we have already suggested inflation damages economic performance – slows economic growth. Khan and Senhadji (2001) showed that the threshold level above which inflation slows growth is 1–3 per cent for industrial countries and 7–11 per cent for developing economies. Above these rates inflation and growth are negatively correlated.

Fischer et al. (2002) provide further evidence of the damaging consequences. These are not surprising. Real GDP per head fell during high inflation years and rose during low inflation years. Investment growth was damaged by inflation, falling in high inflation years and rising in low inflation years. Inflation led to a contraction of investment, consumption and GDP.

Disenchantment with inflation began to spread in the late twentieth century as it became more and more appreciated that it damaged economic performance as we have noted. What was needed was either greater fiscal and monetary discipline that was self-imposed, or a country should find some other means of achieving the results that such discipline would provide. Many approaches have been tried. For example, in some of the OECD countries measures such as index-linked bonds were introduced. Such bonds enabled governments to go on borrowing since the bond's return was not damaged by government behaviour.

More drastically, the lesson was learned that governments had the power to inflate whenever they chose and it was better to remove the power from them and give it to an independent central bank. Central bank independence began to flourish in the last decade of the century as people were dissatisfied with price performance and governments accepted that stable prices were desirable and that governments could no longer be relied upon to deliver them.

Some countries opted for a different route to stable prices for a variety of reasons. One, which had proved successful in the nineteenth century, was currency boards. Some of the Baltic states took this route, as did Argentina, and there were serious proposals for Russia. A country would attach its currency to a foreign stable currency – usually a country it carried on a lot of trade with. It would use that currency to back its own currency 100 per cent. In fact it would sometimes hold the foreign exchange reserves in excess of 100 per cent. After that its money supply would then be determined through its external accounts. A surplus on the current account would result in an inflow of reserves and allow an expansion of the domestic money supply. This then imposes the necessary discipline and control of the money stock.

A more extreme version of this is to adopt a foreign currency in place of the domestic version. This is currently called 'dollarization' since the dollar has been the most used currency. Ecuador is one example and Argentina has been considering it. This is similar in kind to the currency board. But it abandons the domestic currency and substitutes the foreign currency. Belief is generally restored and stable prices return. However, if a government persists in overspending, such a system – like the currency board – will inevitably break down. Argentina could be one such example.

Another possibility is to seek shelter in an irrevocably fixed exchange-rate regime. The exchange-rate mechanism in Europe in the late 1980s and early 1990s was one such attempt and Britain joined that for these reasons.

The strongest version of this is a monetary union and the European case is an illustration of this. There are, of course, powerful political motives for the union. But for many of the participants it was a way of importing the required discipline for stable prices that they were unable to deliver on their own. Italians readily accept that their politicians and institutions were failing them and they required outside pressure from an independent central bank to make them comply. Monetary union means adoption of a common currency, the giving up of monetary policy, and in this particular case the acceptance of a heavily constrained fiscal policy.

CONCLUSION

In summary, before the experience of high inflation in the second half of the twentieth century all historical episodes of very rapid inflation took place when there was an unbacked paper currency that was issued at a time of civil disorder, which in turn had produced a budget deficit. It is clear that there have been cases of serious disorder and even revolution where there was no rapid inflation. The question that raises is: was that because the resolution was imminent and widely desired and anticipated? Or could it be that the conditions for raising taxes provide part of the explanation? A system based on indirect taxation would be less elastic than a direct system. The tax base in the former could not be rapidly expanded when required. Thus a country (and perhaps Britain is an example) with a direct tax system would be less likely to run into budget difficulties. In the circumstances we have been discussing, a wide variety of alternative policies to choose from is unlikely, and the inflation can hardly be regarded as a consequence of the wrong choice of policy other than abandonment of a backed currency.

Another point to be made in summing up is that this thesis goes some way towards identifying the direction of causation involved in social unrest and rapid inflation. Many have argued that inflation leads to social upheaval. Keynes (1920, 220) wrote:

> There is no subtler, no surer means of overturning the existing basis of society than to debauch the currency, the process engages all the hidden forces of economic law on the side of destruction and does it in a manner which not one man in a million can diagnose.

However, in the examples of very rapid inflation where the events are quite dramatic, the sequence is rather the opposite, with unrest leading to government difficulties and deficits and on to rapid inflation. Then the inflation produced further social disorder and the causality can be seen to run both ways. In seeking the origins of these extreme examples it runs from social disorder to inflation. Thereafter the consequences are diverse but extremely serious.

REFERENCES

Aldcroft, D.H. (1977), *From Versailles to Wall Street 1919–1929*, London: Allen Lane.
Balderston, T. (1993), *The origins and course of the German economic crisis, 1923–1932*, Berlin: Haude & Spencer.
Ball, R.J. (1964), *Inflation and the theory of money*, London: George Allen & Unwin.
Bastiat, F. (1850), *The law* (reprinted IEA, London 2001).
Bomberger, W.A. and Makinen, G.E. (1983), 'The Hungarian hyperinflation and stabilisation of 1945/1946', *Journal of Political Economy*, 91.
Cagan, P. (1956), 'The monetary dynamics of hyperinflation', in M. Friedman (ed.), *Studies in the quantity theory of money*, Chicago: University of Chicago Press.
Cagan, P. (1972), *The channels of monetary effects on interest rates*, New York: Columbia University Press.
Campbell, C. and Tullock, G. (1954), 'Hyperinflation in China 1937–1949', *Journal of Political Economy*, 62.
Capie, F. and Wood, G.E. (2002), 'Price controls in war and peace: a Marshallian conclusion', *Scottish Journal of Political Economy*, 49.
Chou, S.H. (1963), *The Chinese inflation, 1937–1949*, Columbia: New York.
Fetter, F. (1977), '*Lenin, Keynes and inflation*', *Economica*, 44.
Fischer, S., Sahay, R. and Vegh, C. (2002), 'Modern hyper and high inflations', *Journal of Economic Literature*, 40.
Graham, F.D. (1930), *Exchange, prices and production in hyperinflation, Germany 1920–1923*, Princeton: Princeton University Press.
Hamilton, J. (1977), 'The role of war in modern inflation', *Journal of Economic History*, 37.
Hammond, B. (1961), 'The North's empty purse, 1861–1862', *American Historical Review*, 67.
Harris, S.E. (1930), *The Assignats*, Cambridge, MA: Harvard University Press.
Harlow, R.V. (1929), 'Aspects of revolutionary finance 1775–1783', *American Historical Review*, 35.
Hefeker, C. (2001), 'The agony of central power: fiscal federalism in the German Reich', *European Review of Economic History*, 5.
Holtferich, C.L. (1984), 'The road to hyperinflation: fiscal problems and policies in Germany 1914–1923', mimeograph, Freie Universität Berlin.
Huang, A.C. (1948), 'The inflation in China', *Quarterly Journal of Economics*, 62.
Khan, M.S. and Senhadji, A. S. (2001), 'Threshold effects in the relationship between inflation and growth', *IMF Staff Papers*, 48.
Kent, R. (1920), 'The Edict of Diocletian fixing maximum prices', *The University of Pennsylvania Law Review*, 23.
Keynes, J.M. (1920), *The economic consequences of the peace*, London: Macmillan.
Keynes, J.M. (1923), *A Tract on Monetary Reform*, reprinted in *The collected writings of John Maynard Keynes vol. IV*, Basingstoke: Macmillan.
Laursen, K. and Pederson, J. (1964), *The German inflation, 1918–1923*, Amsterdam: North Holland.

League of Nations (1946), *Monthly bulletin of statistics.*

Lerner, M. (1954), 'The monetary and fiscal programs of the Confederate Government 1861–1865', *Journal of Political Economy*, 62.

Lerner, M. (1955), 'Money, prices and wages in the Confederacy 1961–1865', *Journal of Political Economy*, 63.

Makinen, G.E. (1984), 'The Greek stabilization of 1944–1946', *American Economic Review*, 74.

Mitchell, H. (1947), 'The Edict of Diocletian: a study of price fixing in the Roman Empire', *The Canadian Journal of Economic and Political Science*, 13.

Notel, R. (1984), 'Money, banking and industry in interwar Austria and Hungary', *Journal of European Economic History*, 13.

Pearce, D.W. (1981), *The dictionary of modern economics*, London: Macmillan.

Rockoff, H. (1984), *Drastic measures, a history of wage and price controls in the United States*, Cambridge: Cambridge University Press.

Sargent, T.J. (1982), 'The ends of four big inflations' in R.H. Hall (ed.), *Inflation: causes and effects*, Chicago, IL: Chicago University Press.

Smith, B.D. (1984), 'Money and inflation in colonial Massachusetts', *Federal Reserve Bank of Minneapolis Quarterly Review*, 8.

Sommariva, A. and Tullio, G. (1985), 'Inflation and currency depreciation in Germany 1919–1923: a disequilibrium model of prices and the exchange rate', mimeograph, Washington.

Teichova, A. (1983), 'A comparative view of the inflation of the 1920s in Austria and Czechoslovakia', in M.E. Schmukler (ed.), *Inflation through the ages*, New York: Columbia University Press.

Wicker, E. (1985), 'Colonial monetary standards contrasted: evidence from the Seven Years War', mimeographed, Indiana University.

6. Financial crises[1]

Michael J. Oliver

For those who have studied the history of money over the very long run it is unsurprising that there have been recurrent financial crises during the twentieth century. As Chancellor (1999) has recently reminded us in his book on financial speculation, financial crises have stretched back at least as far as Ancient Rome during the second century BC. In the fourth edition of his classic book, *Manias, panics and crashes*, Charles Kindleberger (2000) has shown that since 1618, there have been around 50 world-class manias and panics. The distinguishing feature of the financial crises of the twentieth century, however, is that they continued to occur despite vigorous attempts to strengthen the international financial architecture and when our understanding about nominal variables, financial markets and banking structures has made enormous strides.

For the less specialized reader, this might come as a surprise as it is well known that the Bretton Woods institutions that were set up in the wake of the crisis-ridden interwar years were designed to bolster the international monetary system and prevent a repetition of such crises. However, even in the heyday of Bretton Woods, when the supranational institutions were at the zenith of their power and international capital markets were relatively subdued, the frequency of currency crises was greater than in the interwar years although there was an absence of banking crises. Over the last 25 years, there has been an increased tendency for banking crises to spill over into the currency markets, creating what has become known as the 'twin crisis' problem (Kaminsky and Reinhart 1999). Before we turn first to examine the causes and consequences of financial crises, we need to be more precise about what it is we are discussing and distinguish between a 'financial crisis', 'banking crisis' and 'currency crisis'.

DEFINITIONS OF A FINANCIAL CRISIS

Anna Schwartz (1986) has argued that the term 'financial crisis' is an overused description for events that are in essence only 'pseudo-financial crises'. Her description of a real financial crisis is one in which the private sector fears convertibility between bank deposits and high-powered money, which leads to a scramble for high-powered money. To restore reserves, banks call in existing loans and resort to selling assets; banks fail because the level of bad debts has wiped out their capital. The failures destroy deposits and the contraction in the money supply results in a fall in real economic activity and the price level. Crucially for Schwartz, a real financial crisis occurs when the central bank fails to act as lender-of-last-resort, which last occurred in the United Kingdom in 1866 and in the United States in 1933 (see also Kindleberger 2000, 211–13). In short, 'all the phenomena of recent years that have been characterised as financial crisis – a decline in asset prices of equity stocks, real estate, commodities, depreciation of the exchange value of a national currency; financial distress of a large non-financial firm, a large municipality, a financial industry, or sovereign debtors – are pseudo-financial crises' (Schwartz 1986, 12).

Schwartz's strictures of a financial crisis are in the tradition of Thornton and Bagehot who restrict the term to problems in the banking sector (Wood 1999) and are connected to her work with Milton Friedman, which identified financial crises with banking panics (Friedman and Schwartz 1963; Cagan 1965). However, for some this is too restrictive a definition (Moggeridge 1986) and definitions by other economists and economic historians have been more flexible. For example, Bordo et al. (2001, 4) define financial crises as 'episodes of financial-market volatility marked by significant problems of illiquidity and insolvency among financial-market participants and/or by official intervention to contain such consequences'. To be more specific, a financial crisis can be comprised of a banking crisis and currency crisis or a combination of the two (a 'twin' crisis).[2]

The accepted definition of a banking crisis is when actual or potential bank runs or failures provoke banks to suspend the internal convertibility of their liabilities or which forces a government to intervene and prop up the banking system by extending financial assistance (Bordo 1985; Caprio and Klingebiel 1997; Eichengreen and Rose 2001). One statistical indicator of a banking crisis, which is a measure of the confidence of the public in the banking system and emphasized by Friedman and Schwartz (1963) in their classic study, is the deposit-currency ratio. Nearly all of the major banking crises in the interwar years were associated with sharp declines in the ratio, although there were some instances when the fall in the deposit-currency ratio was not associated with panics but with restructuring of the banking system or with exchange rate difficulties (Bernanke and James 1991, 50).

If governments fail to strengthen the banking system, the result could be a systemic crisis. In a recent study examining banking sector distress between 1980 and 1994, Demirgüç-Kunt and Detragiache (1998), suggest that for a banking crisis to become systemic it would have to meet one of four criteria: (1) the ratio of non-performing assets to total assets in the banking system would be above 10 per cent; (2) the cost of the rescue operation would be at least 2 per cent of GDP; (3) the crisis would lead to large-scale nationalization of banks; and (4) extensive bank runs take place or emergency measures such as deposit freezes or prolonged bank holidays are adopted in response to the crisis. In a series of papers, McKinnon and Pill (1996, 1997, 1998) have modelled how financial liberalization and distortions to the banking system can fuel a lending boom, which leads to the collapse of the banking system. Demirgüç-Kunt and Detragiache's (1998) empirical study of 53 countries during the period 1980–95 found that poorly designed financial liberalization increased the probability of a banking crisis. One of the case studies examined in this chapter, that of the three Nordic countries in the early-1990s, provides a classic example. A delayed policy response coupled to inadequate internal risk management controls led to a meltdown in the banking sector.

Bordo and Schwartz (1996, 438) have defined a currency crisis as a 'market-based attack on the exchange value of a currency. It involves a break with earlier market judgment about the exchange value of a currency. If a devaluation, which also involves a change in the peg, does not occur because of market pressure, it does not qualify as a currency crisis'. A similar definition has been employed by Bordo et al. (2001, 55) who identify a crisis by a forced changed in parity, abandonment of a pegged exchange rate or an international bailout. In their pioneering study of 100 developing countries from 1971 to 1992, Frankel and Rose (1996, 352) identify a currency crisis as a nominal depreciation of at least 25 per cent combined with at least a 10 per cent increase in the rate of depreciation.

How banking and currency crisis can feed on each other and how they spread from one country to another has been a source of considerable interest to economists, particularly after the experiences of the last two decades (Kaminsky and Reinhart 1999). As Diaz-Alejandro (1985) and Velasco (1987) have shown, there is evidence that a problem in the financial sector can lead to a balance-of-payments crisis. For example, as the central bank finances the bailout of troubled institutions, its ability to maintain the exchange rate commitment is threatened. If the central bank resorts to creating printing press money, markets expect future debt monetization and the crisis becomes self-fulfilling. Defending the currency by raising interest rates may then be impossible, which further undermines the central bank's ability to defend the parity.

Other models have stressed that currency crises and banking crises are caused by common factors or events. Examples include the exchange-rate-based inflation stabilization of Mexico in 1987 and the Southern Cone in the late-1970s. Reinhart and Végh have shown how these plans have well-defined dynamics. During the early stage of the plan there is a boom in consumption, financed by expansive bank lending accompanied by capital inflows. As inflation only converges gradually to international levels, there is a real exchange rate appreciation. The appreciation can lead to a squeeze in profits that leads to a rise in bankruptcies. There comes a point when the financial markets think the current account deficit is unsustainable, which then prompts a speculative attack on the currency. Following the outflow of capital and the bursting of the asset price bubble, the banking system is threatened (Kaminsky and Reinhart 1999).

Since the late-1970s, three generational models have shaped the theoretical literature on speculative attacks, or balance-of-payments crises. The first-generation model was developed by Salant and Henderson (1978) who built a model to study attacks on government-controlled price of gold (Flood and Marion 1999). A year later, Paul Krugman (1979) applied Salant and Henderson's work to fixed exchange rates and, although it was amended in later years (e.g., Flood, Garber and Kramer 1996), the first-generation model had become established. In essence, the early first-generation model showed that if the authorities are following economic policies inconsistent with a fixed exchange rate regime there comes a point at which the peg is abandoned. The dissolution of the parity does not necessarily have to be at the point where the reserves are exhausted; speculators sell the currency short in lieu of the inevitable depreciation (a speculative attack occurs when the shadow exchange rate just equals the fixed rate). These models were developed to explain the devaluation of the Mexican peso in 1976 and 1982 (Blanco and Garber 1986) and have also been used to account for currency crises in the Bretton Woods system, for example, the 1967 devaluation of sterling (Eichengreen 2003a).

The failure of the first-generation model to explain why currency crises spread to other countries and how crises can occur in the absence of deterioration in the macroeconomic fundamentals, led to the development of second-generation models (Obstfeld 1994; Eichengreen, Rose and Wyplosz 1996). These models gained popularity after the inadequacy of the first-generation models to account for the speculative attacks in Europe and Mexico in the 1990s (Eichengreen and Jeanne 2000 have also applied a second-generation model to account for sterling's exit from the gold standard in 1931). In this new framework, speculative attacks occur without deterioration in the macroeconomic fundamentals. Speculators assess whether current policy is credible and can be sustained against the long-run economic fundamentals. When governments are viewed as optimizing agents, the growth of domestic credit can be endogenous and there can be multiple equilibria and self-fulfilling speculative attacks (Obstfeld 1994). The currency crisis can spill over into neighbouring countries through an exogenous shock such as war or it can be transmitted through trade link-ages. The probability of devaluation will be increased in other countries that share a similar macroeconomic framework or economic conditions.

The Asian crisis of the late-1990s inspired a new generation of models to link banking and currency crises (Aghion, Bacchetta, Banerjee 1999, 2001, 2004; Krugman 1999; Chang and Valesco 2000a, b). The third-generation literature has shown how the combination of increasing debt, low foreign exchange reserves, declining government revenue and rising expectations of devaluation causes a currency crisis. The collapse of the currency is only part of a wider problem with the financial system, which can include 'crony capitalism' and moral hazard. Hence in Asia, the macroeconomic funda-mentals were strong but the banking sector was characterized by bad loans and unhedged short-term borrowing from foreign banks.

There has been considerable interest in the recent literature on the inci-dence of contagion and spillovers of financial shocks. In a series of papers, Kaminksy and Reinhart have studied how these disturbances are channelled and why some financial contagion occurs in some instances and not in others (Calvo and Reinhart 1996; Kaminsky and Reinhart 2000; Kaminsky, Reinhart and Végh 2003). They define contagion as significant immediate effects in a number of countries following an event (i.e., 'fast and furious' repercussions evolving over hours or days). The crises of the 1990s were characterized by a 'sudden stop' problem in emerging markets (and in the case of the developed countries, the clustering of the crises in the European Monetary System [EMS] reflects contagion), in which the immediate cessa-tion of capital inflows forced countries to liquidate their international reserves and reduce their current account deficit. As aggregate demand was cut back it resulted in sharp falls in output and employment, which damaged the financial system (Calvo 1998, 2001). The more protracted and gradual effects, perhaps as a result of common external shocks, are dubbed spillovers. However, the literature on financial contagion has not reached a consensus on what constitutes financial contagion. For example, Bordo, Mizrach and Schwartz (1998) discriminate between 'pure contagion' and shock propagation through fundamentals, which they label 'transmission'.

Empirical studies have examined various explanations for cross-border shocks, including the role of hedging, financial linkages and bilateral and third party trade linkages. Eichengreen et al. (1996) uncovered evidence that trade links explain the pattern of contagion in 20 industrial countries during the period 1969–93 and such results have been confirmed by other authors (e.g., Glick and Rose 1999). To account for the spread of the financial crises during the 1990s (particularly the Mexican, Thai and Russian currency crises), a number of studies have focused on financial channels of transmis-sion. These have shown how US-based mutual funds have spread shocks through Latin America, for example, Mexico in 1994 (Kaminsky, Lyons and Schmukler 2004), and on the role of commercial banks in spreading shocks and 'sudden stops', such as Asia in 1997 (Van Rijckeghem and Weder 2001, 2003; Tai 2004). Caramazza, Ricci and Salgado (2004), who conducted panel probit regressions for 41 emerging market economies between 1990–98, conclude that financial linkages played a significant role in the spread of the Mexican, Asian and Russian crises.

Kaminsky et al. (2003) argue that it is the 'unholy trinity' of capital inflows, surprises and common creditors that explains why contagion occurs in some instances and not in others. Although they acknowledge that history matters, their analysis is largely drawn from the last ten years of the twentieth century when sudden stops and 'fast and furious' episodes were legion. Bordo et al. (2001, 68–9) have noted that pre-1972 sudden stops were far less common. Before 1913, this can be attributed to the ability of countries to run constant current account deficits, financed by private-to-private flows and adherence to monetary and fiscal stability required by the gold standard (Feis 1930; Fishlow 1985).

It is worth emphasizing that the turbulent decade of the 1990s had a precursor over a 100 years ago when financial crises threatened to become systemic. The difference was that at the end of the nineteenth century, it was the London Stock Exchange that helped to boost international liquidity, whereas in the 1990s it was capital markets in the United States (Neal and Weidenmier 2003). Then the international monetary regime was the gold standard, whereas in the 1990s the regime was managed flexibility. Finally, contagion was prominent in the earlier episodes, and moved from the periphery to the core, whereas today the advanced countries are more likely to be protected from peripheral shocks (Bordo and Eichengreen 1999, 21).

The comparisons and contrasts of financial crises over the long run have begun to attract the attention of economists and economic historians, and it is to this that we now turn.

FREQUENCY, DEPTH AND RECOVERY TIME

Bordo et al. (2001) have provided us with the best long-run data set on financial crises. Distinguishing between banking crises, currency crises and twin crises, they have provided data for a 21-country sample for the 1880–1997 period and 56 countries starting in 1973, allowing a comparison to be made across time of the frequency, depth and duration of crises. Figure 6.1 summarizes the crisis frequency between 1880 and 1997 (that is the number of crises divided by the number of country-year observations by period).

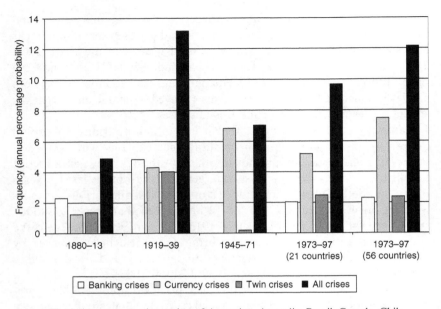

Note: The 21-country sample consists of Argentina, Australia, Brazil, Canada, Chile, Denmark, Finland, Greece, Italy, Japan, Norway, Portugal, Spain, Sweden and United States (defined as 'Emerging Markets' in the pre-1914 period), Belgium, France, Germany, the Netherlands, Switzerland and Great Britain (the pre-1914 'Industrial Economies'). Australia, Canada, Denmark, Finland, Italy, Japan, Norway, Sweden and the United States are reclassified as Industrial in 1919. The 56-country sample includes the additional countries: Austria, Bangladesh, Brazil, China, Columbia, Costa Rica, Ecuador, Egypt, Ghana and Côte d'Ivoire, Hong Kong, Iceland, India, Indonesia, Ireland, Israel, Jamaica, Korea, Malaysia, Mexico, New Zealand, Nigeria, Pakistan, Paraguay, Peru, Philippines, Senegal, Singapore, South Africa, Sri Lanka, Taiwan, Thailand, Turkey, Uruguay, Venezuela, Zimbabwe. A full discussion of the data and methods used can be found in a web appendix (http://www.economic-policy.org/).

Source: Bordo et al. (2001, 56).

Figure 6.1   Crisis frequency, 1880–1997

Several things stand out. First, the frequency of banking crises was roughly the same pre-1914 and post-1972, but currency crises were more frequent post-1972 (on the basis of the 56-country sample). Second, the interwar and Bretton Woods periods are very different, with frequent banking crises during the former (primarily during the 1930s) and no banking crises during the latter. Third, for the 21 countries, there was a greater chance of a currency crisis during the Bretton Woods period than in any other period. Fourth, the occurrence of twin crises has been more prominent during the last quarter of the twentieth century but does not come close to matching the incidence of the interwar years.

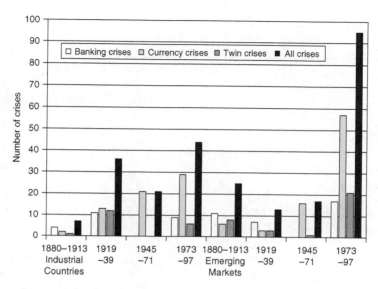

Source: Bordo et al. (2001).

Figure 6.2 Number of financial crises, 1880–1997

Categorizing the distribution of crises according to 'industrial countries' or 'emerging markets' (Figure 6.2), shows that three-quarters of all pre-1914 crises were confined to the gold standard periphery, while during the interwar years, three-quarters of the observed crises are to be found among the gold standard core countries.

As Eichengreen and Bordo (2003, 71) have argued, banking crises pre-1914 did not undermine the confidence in the currency in the countries that were at the core of the gold standard. Banks would suspend the convertibility of deposits into currency, currency would go to a premium and foreign capital flowed in to arbitrage the difference, provided the country remained on the gold standard. It is instructive to note, however, that during the interwar years when twin crises were also common, the unstable macroeconomic environment precluded the smooth operation of the international monetary system. As successive countries faced banking crises and a collapse of production and trade, currencies were frequently forced to depreciate.

To consider further the differences across time it is instructive to compare the duration and depth of crises (Tables 6.1 and 6.2).

McKinnon (1997) and Goodhart and Delargy (1998) have argued that recovery from financial crises was relatively rapid before 1913 because of the resumption or restoration rule. The findings of Bordo et al. (2001), however, do not support the contention that currency crises were shorter

Table 6.1   *Recovery time from financial crises, 1880–1997 (average
               number of years)*

	1880–1913 (21 countries)	1919–39 (21 countries)	1945–71 (21 countries)	1973–97 (21 countries)	1973–97 (56 countries)
Banking crises					
All countries	2.27	2.39	–	3.11	1.62
Industrial countries	3.00	2.55	–	3.38	3.11
Emerging markets	2.00	2.14	–	1.00	2.35
Currency crises					
All countries	2.63	1.94	1.84	1.87	2.07
Industrial countries	3.00	1.92	1.67	1.84	2.04
Emerging markets	2.50	2.00	2.06	2.00	2.09
Twin crises					
All countries	2.22	2.73	1.00	3.73	3.78
Industrial countries	1.00	2.33	–	5.40	5.00
Emerging markets	2.38	4.33	1.00	2.33	3.43
All crises					
All countries	2.35	2.35	1.78	2.63	2.53
Industrial countries	2.71	2.26	1.60	2.84	2.71
Emerging markets	2.25	2.62	2.00	2.09	2.45

Source: Eichengreen and Bordo (2003).

before 1913 for either the emerging markets or industrial countries. In fact, the opposite was the case. In all periods other than pre-1913, growth resumed at a faster pace in both groups of countries and the rapid resumption of the old parity 'was actually the exception, not the rule' (Eichengreen and Bordo 2003, 71). Recovery from banking crises and twin crises does appear to be faster pre-1914, although as Eichengreen and Bordo (2003) admit, this result is heavily influenced by the single industrial case of France in 1888–89. If this is removed from the dataset, then there is no evidence of faster recovery from banking and twin crises before 1914. Moreover, the depths of crises appear more intense between 1880 and 1913 than after 1973 (Table 6.2). The output loss from currency crises in recent times is only one half to two-thirds what it was before 1913 and for banking crises it is between 75 per cent to 80 per cent. Twin crises have grown more severe post-1973, although the output losses are not on the scale of the interwar years, particularly for the emerging markets. In all periods, the output losses were greater in emerging markets than industrial countries. The average drop in output following a crisis in a sample of ten emerging

Table 6.2   Output loss from financial crises, 1880–1997 (percentage of GDP loss)

	1880–1913 (21 countries)	1919–39 (21 countries)	1945–71 (21 countries)	1973–97 (21 countries)	1973–97 (56 countries)
Banking crises					
All countries	8.35	10.49	–	7.04	6.21
Industrial countries	11.58	11.51	–	7.92	7.04
Emerging markets	7.18	8.89	–	0.00	5.78
Currency crises					
All countries	8.31	14.21	5.25	3.81	5.91
Industrial countries	3.73	11.36	2.36	2.86	3.66
Emerging markets	9.84	26.53	9.03	8.54	7.00
Twin crises					
All countries	14.50	15.84	1.65	15.67	18.61
Industrial countries	0.00	13.79	–	17.54	15.64
Emerging markets	16.31	24.03	1.65	14.10	19.46
All crises					
All countries	9.76	13.42	5.24	7.77	8.29
Industrial countries	7.68	12.29	2.39	6.69	6.25
Emerging markets	10.37	16.46	8.60	10.80	9.21

Note: The output loss is calculated as the sum of the differences between actual GDP growth and the five-year average preceding the crisis until growth returns to trend.

Source: Eichengreen and Bordo (2003).

markets, however, is greater in the post-Bretton Woods period than the average drop in output following a crisis in any other period in the twentieth century.

Work by other economists on the output losses in emerging markets has painted a similar picture. Hutchinson (2003) identified 160 currency crises over the 1975–97 period covering 67 developing and emerging-market economies. After controlling for macroeconomic developments, political and regional factors, he found that currency crises reduce output growth for one to two years by about two percentage points.

Research by the IMF (1998), based on identifying banking and currency crises for 50 countries post-1975 and that was influential on the work of Bordo et al. (2001), produces dissimilar results because it is based on a slightly different methodology. In estimating the length and depth of crises, Bordo et al. (2001) considered growth relative to a five-year pre-crisis trend while the IMF used a three-year pre-crisis trend. The classification of banking and currency crises also differs. Bordo et al. (2001) include twin crises in which currency and banking crises occurred in the same or adjoining years but then do not include them in their 'banking crisis' and 'currency crisis' headings. They also identify fewer crises post-1972 than the IMF because additional crises occurring before recovery from an initial crisis was complete (including crises occurring in consecutive years) are counted as a single event. The IMF results are reported in Table 6.3.

For approximately 40 per cent of the currency crises and 20 per cent of the banking crises, the IMF (1998, 78–9) calculated there were no significant output losses. They found that for the currency crises, output growth on average, returned to trend in a little over 2.5 years, and the cumulative loss in output growth per crisis was 4.25 percentage points (relative to trend). This compares with a recovery time of 2.25 years and a cumulative loss of output growth of 8.25 years for a 'severe' currency crisis. Banking crises were more protracted and costly than currency crises, with an average recovery time of three years and a cumulative loss in output of 11.5 percentage points. When banking crises occurred within a year of currency crises, the losses amounted to 14.5 percentage points, on average. The IMF found that that the average recovery time in industrial countries was longer than that in the emerging markets, although the cumulative output loss was on average smaller. Over the longer period, examined by Bordo et al. (2001), the recovery time from a currency crisis was longer in the emerging market countries for all periods except the pre-1913 period.

Financial crises also have high costs in emerging markets, both in terms of the fiscal and quasi-fiscal costs of restructuring and because they disrupt the ability of financial markets to function effectively (IMF 1998). Table 6.4 shows how the resolution costs for banking crises have in some cases reached over 40 per cent of GDP (for example, in Chile and Argentina in the early 1980s), while non-performing loans have exceeded 30 per cent of total loans (for example, in Malaysia during 1988 and for state banks in Sri Lanka during the early 1990s).

Clearly, the history of the international financial system in the twentieth century is punctuated by a series of financial crises, although as Eichengreen and Rose (1999, 1) note, they are 'potholes on the road to financial liberalization. It is relatively rare for them to cause the vehicle to break an axle – to bring the process of growth and liberalization to an utter and extended halt. But the flats they cause can result in significant losses of time and output and set back the process of policy reform'. It is not possible to cover every 'pothole' in the space available here and a certain amount of cherry picking is involved. This chapter examines a number of

Table 6.3   Costs of crises in lost output relative to trend

	Number of crises	Average recovery time (in years)[a]	Cumulative loss of output per crisis (in percentage points)[b]	Crises with output losses (in per cent)[c]	Cumulative loss of output per crisis with output loss (in percentage points)[d]
Currency crises	158	1.6	4.3	61	7.1
Industrial countries	42	1.9	3.1	55	5.6
Emerging market	116	1.5	4.8	64	7.6
Currency crashes[e]	55	2.0	7.1	71	10.1
Industrial countries	13	2.1	5.0	62	8.0
Emerging market	42	1.9	7.9	74	10.7
Banking crises	54	3.1	11.6	82	14.2
Industrial countries	12	4.1	10.2	67	15.2
Emerging market	42	2.8	12.1	86	14.0
Currency and banking crises[f]	32	3.2	14.4	78	18.5
Industrial countries	6	5.8	17.6	100	17.6
Emerging market	26	2.6	13.6	73	18.8

Notes:
a   Average amount of time until GDP growth returned to trend. Because GDP growth data are available for all countries only on an annual basis, by construction the minimum recovery time was one year.
b   Calculated by summing the differences between trend growth and output growth after the crisis began until the time when annual output growth returned to its trend and by averaging over all crises.
c   Percentage of crises in which output was lower than trend after the crisis began.
d   Calculated by summing the differences between trend growth and output growth after the crisis began until the time when annual output growth returned to its trend and by averaging over all crises that had output losses.
e   Currency 'crashes' are identified by crises where the currency component of the exchange market pressure index accounts for 75 per cent or more of the index when the index signals a crisis.
f   Identified when a banking crisis occurred within a year of a currency crisis.

Source: IMF (1998, 79).

Table 6.4   Selected crises: costs of restructuring financial sectors and non-performing loans

Country	Years	Fiscal and quasi-fiscal costs[a]	Non-performing loans[b]
Argentina	1980–82	13–55	9
	1985	. . .	30
Brazil	1994–96	4–10	9
Chile	1981–85	19–41	16
Colombia	1982–87	5–6	25
Finland	1991–93	8–10	9
Indonesia	1994	2	. . .
Japan[c]	1990s	3	10
Malaysia	1985–88	5	33
Mexico	1994–95	12–15	11
Norway	1988–92	4	9
Philippines	1981–87	3–4	. . .
Spain	1977–85	15–17	. . .
Sri Lanka	1989–93	9	35
Sweden	1991–93	4–5	11
Thailand	1983–87	1	15
Turkey	1982–85	3	. . .
US	1984–91	5–7	4
Uruguay	1981–84	31	. . .
Venezuela	1980–83	. . .	15
	1994–95	17	. . .

Notes:

a   Estimated in percentage of annual GDP during the restructuring period. Where a range is shown, the lower estimate includes only costs of funds, credit and bonds injected directly into the banking system, while the higher estimate includes other fiscal costs, such as exchange rate subsidies.

b   Estimated at peak of non-performing loans in percentage of total loans. Measure is dependent on country definition of non-performing loans.

c   Cost estimates through 1995 only. Official estimates of the costs, which take into account the costs of settling housing loan corporations ('Jusen'), and of non-performing loans are 0.14 per cent and 3 per cent, respectively.

Source: IMF (1998, 78).

crises from the post-1914 period. We consider the financial crises in the interwar years, currency crises in Bretton Woods, the crisis in the EMS between 1991 and 1993 and the emerging market crises of the 1990s (Mexico, Asia and Russia).

FINANCIAL CRISES IN THE INTERWAR YEARS

As Barry Eichengreen (2003b, 35) has remarked, the list of countries that experienced banking and currency crises by the end of the interwar years reads like an atlas of the world. Figure 6.1 illustrates the frequency of some of the crises between 1919 and 1939 and Table 6.2 shows the output losses associated with the interwar years, but this does not provide a sense of the geography of the crises to which Eichengreen alludes, nor does it give us any sense of the affects of the crises at a country level. Some of this is addressed in Tables 6.5 and 6.6.

Table 6.5 provides a chronology of the banking crises between 1921 and 1936. It is noteworthy that in the 1920s, three of the four Nordic countries had experienced banking panics even before the post-1931 fallout. These are discussed below. Table 6.6 shows the extent of the currency deprecia- tion by the mid-1930s. The devaluations fell within the range of 40–50 per cent and were the outcome of a period of severe currency turmoil (Aldcroft and Oliver 1998, 63–4). The most intense phase of currency depreciation occurred between the latter half of 1931 and the end of 1933, the period when the majority of countries broke the link with gold and when, for the most part, currencies were allowed to fluctuate fairly freely.

The attention of economists and economic historians has long been focused on this period to establish the common causes of the financial crises that pervaded the interwar years. As several authors have argued, the financial crises of the interwar years are linked through adherence to the gold standard. Although the banking crises of the early 1930s were exac- erbated by deflation and the collapse of incomes, the monetary regime also imposed constraints on central bank policy. The volatility of short-term capital movements between countries, which undoubtedly contributed to the crisis of 1931, was made worse by the growing doubts as to the contin- ued commitment to the existing monetary system (Hamilton 1988, 87). Moreover, the gold standard was an important factor in the transmission of deflationary forces internationally (Friedman and Schwartz 1963; Meltzer 1976; Huffman and Lothian 1984, 456) and constrained domestic policy action in promoting recovery (Eichengreen 1992). This section will not consider the international monetary regime at length as Garside earlier in this volume (Chapter 2) has focused on the exchange rate problems of this period. Instead it will concentrate on the banking crises of the period.

Bernanke and James (1991, 54–7) have identified three factors that help to explain which countries were the ones to suffer banking panics. First, those countries that emerged from the 1920s with weakened economies were more likely to suffer panics in the 1930s. For example, in Austria, Germany, Hungary and Poland, the hyperinflation of the early 1920s left a legacy of

Table 6.5 A chronology of interwar banking crises, 1921–36

Date	Country	Crises
June 1921	Sweden	Beginning of deposit contraction of 1921–22, leading to bank restructurings. Government assistance administered through Credit Bank of 1922
1921–22	Netherlands	Bank failures (notably Marx and Co.) and amalgamations
1922	Denmark	Heavy losses of one of the largest banks, Danske Landmandsbank, and liquidation of smaller banks. Landmandsbank continues to operate until a restructuring in April 1928 under a government gurantee
April 1923	Norway	Failure of Centralbanken for Norge
May 1923	Austria	Difficulties of a major bank, Allgemeine Depositenbank; liquidation in July
September 1923	Japan	In wake of the Tokyo earthquake, bad debts threaten Bank of Taiwan and Bank of Chosen, which are restructured with government help
September 1925	Spain	Failure of Banco de la Unión Meniera and Banco Vasca
July–September 1926	Poland	Bank runs cause three large banks to stop payments. The shakeout of banks continues through 1927
1927	Norway, Italy	Numerous smaller banks in difficulties, but no major failures
April 1927	Japan	Thirty-two banks unable to make payments. Restructuring of 15th Bank and Bank of Taiwan
August 1929	Germany	Collapse of Frankfurter Allgemeine Versicherungs AG, followed by failures of smaller banks, and runs on Berlin and Frankfurt savings banks
November 1929	Austria	Bodencreditanstalt, second largest bank, fails and is merged with Creditanstalt.
November 1930	France	Failure of Banque Adam, Boulogne-sur-Mer, and Oustric Group. Runs on provincial banks
	Estonia	Failure of two medium-sized banks, Estonia Government Bank Tallin and Reval Credit Bank; crisis lasts until January
December 1930	US	Failure of Bank of the United States
	Italy	Withdrawals from three largest banks begin. A panic ensues in April 1931, followed by a government reorganization and takeover of frozen industrial assets

196

Date	Country	Event
April 1931	Argentina	Government deals with banking panic by allowing Banco de Nación to discount commercial paper from other banks at government-owned Caja de Conversión
May 1931	Austria	Failure of Creditanstalt and run of foreign depositors
	Belgium	Rumours about imminent failure of Banque de Bruxelles, the country's second largest bank, induce withdrawals from all banks. Later in the year, expectations of devaluation lead to withdrawal of foreign deposits
June 1931	Poland	Run on banks, especially on Warsaw Discount Bank, associated with Creditanstalt; a spread of the Austrian crisis
April–July 1931	Germany	Bank runs, extending difficulties plaguing the banking system since the summer of 1930. After large loss of deposits in June and increasing strain on foreign exchanges, many banks are unable to make payments and Darmstader Bank closes. Bank holiday
July 1931	Hungary	Run on Budapest banks (especially General Credit Bank). Foreign withdrawals followed by a foreign creditors' standstill agreement. Bank holiday
	Latvia	Run on banks with German connections. Bank of Libau and International Bank of Riga particularly hard hit
	Austria	Failure of Vienna Mercur-Bank
	Czechoslovakia	Withdrawal of foreign deposits sparks domestic withdrawals but no general banking panic
	Turkey	Run on branches of Deutsche Bank and collapse of Banque Turque pour le Commerce et l'Industrie, in wake of German crisis
	Egypt	Run on Cairo and Alexandria branches of Deutsche Orientbank
	Switzerland	Union Financière de Genève rescued by takeover by Comptoir d'Escompte de Genève
	Romania	Collapse of German-controlled Banca Generala a Tarii Romanesti. Run on Banca de Credit Roman and Banca Romaneasca
	Mexico	Suspension of payments after run on Crédito Español de México. Run on Banco Nacional de México
August 1931	US	Series of banking panics, with October 1931 the worst month. Between August 1931 and January 1932, 1860 banks fail
September 1931	UK	External drain, combined with rumours of threat to London merchant banks with heavy European (particularly Hungarian and German) involvements
	Estonia	General bank run following sterling crisis; second wave of runs in November

Table 6.5 (continued)

Date	Country	Crises
October 1931	Romania	Failure of Banca Marmerosch, Blank & Co. Heavy bank runs
	France	Collapse of major deposit bank Banque Nationale de Crédit (restructured as Banque Nationale pour le Commerce et l'Industrie). Other bank failures and bank runs
March 1932	Sweden	Weakness of one large bank (Skandinaviska Kreditaktiebolaget) as result of collapse of Kreuger industrial and financial empire, but no general panic
May 1932	France	Losses of large investment bank Banque de l'Union Parisienne forces merger with Crédit Mobilier Français
June 1932	US	Series of bank failures in Chicago
October 1932	US	New wave of bank failures, especially in the Midwest and Far West
February 1933	US	General banking panic, leading to state holidays and a nationwide bank holiday in March
November 1933	Switzerland	Restructuring of large bank (Banque Populaire Suisse) after heavy losses
March 1934	Belgium	Failure of Banque Belge de Travail develops into general banking and exchange crisis
September 1934	Argentina	Bank problems throughout the fall induce government-sponsored merger of four weak banks (Banco Español Río de la Plata, Banco el Hogar Argentina, Banco Argentina-Uruguayo, Ernesto Tornquist & Co.)
October 1935	Italy	Deposits fall after Italian invasion of Abyssinia
January 1936	Norway	After years of deposit stability, legislation introducing a tax on bank deposits leads to withdrawals (until fall)
October 1936	Czechoslovakia	Anticipation of second devaluation of the crown leads to deposit withdrawals

Source: Bernanke and James (1991, 51–3).

198

Table 6.6   Exchange rates and exchange control in the 1930s

Country	Official suspension of gold standard	Introduction of exchange control	Depreciation or devaluation in relation to gold	Extent of depreciation by early 1935 (%)	Introduction of new gold parity
Albania	–	–	–	–	–
Argentine	17-12-29	13-10-31	11–29	54	–
Australia	17-12-29	–	3–30	52	–
Austria	5-4-33	9-10-31	12–31; 4–34	22	*30-4-34
Belgium	30-3-35	18-3-35	3–35	28	*31-3-36
Bolivia	25-9-31	3-10-31	3–30	59	–
Brazil	–	18-5-31	12–29	59	–
Bulgaria	–	1918	–	–	–
Canada	19-10-31	–	12–31	40	–
Chile	20-4-32	30-7-31	4–32	75	–
China	–	9-9-34	–	50	–
Columbia	25-9-31	25-9-31	1–32	61	–
Costa Rica	–	16-1-32	1–32	44	–
Cuba	21-11-33	2-6-34	4–33	–	*22-5-34
Czechoslovkia	–	2-10-31	2–34; 10–36	16	17-2-34; *9-10-36
Danzig	–	12-6-35	5–35	0	2-5-35
Denmark	29-9-31	18-11-31	9–31	52	–
Ecuador	8-2-32	2-5-32	6–32	73	*19-12-35
Egypt	21-9-31	–	9–31	–	–
Estonia	28-6-33	18-11-31	6–33	42	–
Finland	12-10-31	–	10–31	50	–
France	–	–	9–36	0	*1-10-36
Germany	–	13-7-31	–	–	–
Greece	26–4–32	28-9-31	4–32	57	–
Guatemala	–	–	4–33	–	–
Honduras	–	27-3-34	4–33	–	–
Hong Kong	–	9-11-35	–	–	–
Hungary	–	17-7-31	–	–	–
India	21-9-31	–	9–31	40	–
Iran	–	25-2-30	–	57	–
Irish Free State	26-9-31	–	9–31	41	–
Italy	–	26-5-34	3–34; 10–36	4	*8-10-36
Japan	13-12-31	1-7-32	12–31	66	–
Latvia	28-9-36	8-10-31	9–36	–	–
Lithuania	–	1-10-35	–	–	–
Luxembourg	–	18-3-35	3–35	0	1-4-35
Malaya	21-9-31	–	9–31	40	–

Table 6.6 (continued)

Country	Official suspension of gold standard	Introduction of exchange control	Depreciation or devaluation in relation to gold	Extent of depreciation by early 1935 (%)	Introduction of new gold parity
Mexico	25-7-31	–	8–31	67	–
Netherlands	27-9-36	–	0–36	0	–
New Zealand	21-9-31	–	4–30	52	–
Nicaragua	13-11-31	13-11-31	1–32	46	–
Norway	28-9-31	–	9–31	46	–
Palestine	21-9-31	–	9–31	–	–
Panama	–	–	4–33	–	–
Paraguay	–	20-8-32	11–29	–	–
Peru	14-5-32	–	5–32	63	–
Philippines	–	–	4–33	–	–
Poland	–	26-4-36	–	–	–
Portugal	31-12-31	21-10-22	10–31	42	–
Romania	–	18-5-32	7–35	0	–
Salvador, El	9-10-31	20-8-33	10–31	52	–
Siam	11-5-32	–	6–32	40	–
South Africa	28-12-32	–	1–33	41	–
Spain	–	18–5–31	1920	45	–
Sweden	29-9-31	–	9–31	44	–
Switzerland	–	–	9–36	0	*27-9-36
Turkey	–	26-2-30	1915	–	–
UK	21-9-31	–	9–31	41	–
USA	20-4-33	6-3-33	4–33	41	*31-1-34
Uruguay	20-12-29	7-9-31	4–29	54	–
USSR	–	–	4–36	–	*1-4-36
Venezuela	–	12-12-36	9–30	19	–
Yugoslavia	–	7-10-31	7–32	23	–

Note: * Provisional parity.

Sources: Bank for International Settlements (1935, 9); League of Nations (1937, 111–13)

structural and financial weakness and these countries were forced to introduce new currencies (Aldcroft 1997, 65, 67; Aldcroft and Oliver 1998, 15–19).

Second, the structure of the banking system in many countries was a contributory factor. Countries with universal or mixed banking, such as Belgium, were more vulnerable to deflation failure than those with branch banking (Vanthemsche 1991). When the Depression struck, countries with unit banking such as the United States were more vulnerable to failure than those with branch banking such as Canada or the United Kingdom

(Drummond 1991; Capie 1995). In the United States, the vast majority of the 30 000 new banks that had been established between 1900 and 1920 were required by national and state charters to be unit banks. Bank failures averaged about 66 per annum between 1910 and 1919, but this figure increased almost ten-fold during the agricultural depression of the 1920s (Wicker 1996, 5). Although there were no banking panics of national significance or disturbances in the New York money market, the banking system, especially in rural America, entered the Great Depression in a fragile state. Wicker argues that the banking panics of 1930–33 were strictly local and that there was no nationwide contagion, but Bordo, Mizrach and Schwartz (1998) point out that the deposit-currency ratio declined nation-wide, which was a sure sign of contagion. The contraction turned severe following a contagious banking panic in October 1930. Depositors scrambled to convert deposits to cash and the Federal Reserve did not undertake an expansionary monetary policy. The money supply declined, further contracting output, commodity prices and asset prices.

Third, the reliance of banks on short-term foreign liabilities ('hot money') destabilized bank balance sheets. The classic example is Germany. Between 1924 and 1930, the flow of capital from creditor nations into Europe amounted to $9 billion, of which one-third was invested in Germany, with short-term flows accounting for over 50 per cent of the total inflow (Feinstein and Watson 1995, 100–101, 115; Hardach 1995, 278). Crucially for the banking system, short-term liabilities made up 35 per cent of total liabilities (900 billion reichsmarks) in 1930 compared with 15 per cent in 1913, when short-term deposits were supplemented with long-term bond flotations (Adalet 2004, 10). The inflow of foreign capital disguised the weak fundamentals of the German banks, which included the acceptance of more risky business during the 1920s (Born 1967; Balderston 1993, 1994). As the real economy contracted between 1928 and 1929, capital flight gathered pace (James 1986).

The experiences of Sweden, Norway and Denmark are worth considering in a little more detail because they had their banking crises in the 1920s and, unlike many other European nations, were left relatively unscathed by the financial crisis of 1931. In all three Scandinavian economies, the crises of the 1920s were caused by the lending practices during the First World War. For example, Norway and Sweden increased their lending to industrial companies and private individuals against shares as collateral (Larsson 1991, 85). Both the direct and indirect affects of this were potentially dangerous because without continuous inflation there would inevitably be problems in repaying the advances by the banks. When the deflation began in the early 1920s, amortization was impossible and the banks had to take the shares as collateral.

In Denmark, banks had become saturated with deposits during the First World War due to the increase in liquidity caused by favourable developments in the balance of payments (Hansen 1991, 28). The banks dramatically increased their lending to companies during the war and many new banks were established, but concerns were later expressed that overbanking contributed to financial instability (Hansen 2001, 60). Hansen (1991, 20) argues that the banking crises of the 1920s could have been avoided if bank regulations had been brought in earlier. The 1919 Commercial Bank Act was too late to save the country's banking system from collapse. Between 1921 and 1933, 39 banks out of a total of 208 were liquidated, 21 merged with other banks and 34 had to be reconstructed with new capital (Hansen 1995). Scandinavia's largest bank, Landmandsbanken, failed in 1922 but was propped up by the Nationalbanken. After 1924, the Nationalbanken changed its policy of lender-of-last-resort and allowed two large Copenhagen banks to fail in 1924 and 1925. From 1924, the Nationalbanken undertook deflationary policies (Hansen 1991, 39).

Attempts were made to introduce new banking legislation in Denmark every year between 1923 and 1928 but it was not until 1930 that new legislation was passed. After reflecting on the experiences between 1914–20, the authorities concluded that lending to a single borrower should be restricted to a maximum of 35 per cent of the bank's liquidity and 50 per cent with the unanimous approval of the board of directors. Liquidity and solvency provisions were more far reaching than the 1919 Act and bankers were prohibited from having seats on the board of industrial companies. The consequences of the 1930 Act were far reaching; it marked the end of German-style universal banking and made Danish banks more risk-averse in the following decades (Hansen 2001, 62).

Norway, like Denmark, later suffered from the bank-lending boom during the First World War through increased financial fragility and systematic risk. When the international downswing and price fall occurred in the early-1920s the commercial banks encountered a huge non-performing loans problem. There were signs of an evolving bank crisis as early as the summer and fall of 1920 when several provincial banks failed. In 1921, 38 commercial banks and ten savings banks turned to the central bank for support while several commercial and savings failed (Nordvik 1995; Knutsen 2001). The situation worsened between 1922 and the spring of 1923 with renewed problems in some of the banks that had received support and new problems in others. The failure of efforts to reconstruct the banks led to a widespread banking crisis that resulted in commercial bank failures and depositor runs. Centralbanken and Foreningsbanken were placed under public administration and in May 1923, another major bank, Norwegian Handelsbank, managed to secure 25 billion Norwegian kroner from the conservative government. This secret deal resulted in the impeachment of the Prime Minister, Abraham Berge, in 1926. In total, 20 commercial banks and five savings banks were taken under public administration during 1923. Table 6.5 does not do justice to the precarious situation in Norway between 1922 and 1928: 129 banks failed and the commercial bank losses totalled at least 1500 million kroner (Knutsen 1991, 55–6; Nordvik 1995, 448). Although Norway's worst banking difficulties had occurred in the 1920s, two of the three largest commercial banks (Den norske Creditbank and Bergens Privatbank) continued to suffer into the early 1930s as non-performing loans and loan losses increased.

The other contributing factor to the banking problems of the three Nordic countries was the preparation to return to the gold standard. In September 1920, the Swedish Minister of Finance made a commitment to re-establish the krona's gold parity, but did not specify a date for when this was to occur (Jonung and Fregert 2004). A severe tightening of monetary policy resulted in the largest deflation on record and by 1922, the price level had almost halved and Sweden was the first country to return to a de facto gold standard in that year (it became de jure in 1924). However, the contraction of GDP by almost 6 per cent led to bankruptcies, a collapse in demand and a rise in the real value of debts. A severe banking crisis occurred in 1922, despite the recovery of the real economy. In the Swedish case, the deposit-cash ratio did not fall. The state was forced to act as lender-of-last-resort and established a fund, AB Kreditkassan, to help banks rid themselves of bad loans. No losses to depositors occurred, but the public cost for rescuing the financial system was estimated at 70 million Swedish kronor.

Nordvik (1992, 1995) has suggested that after the slump in the international economy in 1920, Norwegian export industries suffered a large drop in earnings; concomitantly, the Bank of Norway introduced a contractionary policy as the authorities wished to return to the gold standard and this 'par policy' was a major cause of the banking crises that followed. Knutsen (2001) challenges this interpretation of events by disputing the evidence that the central bank slavishly followed a 'par policy' like the Swedish Riksbank, noting that the upsurge of the value of the krone took place during 1925 and 1926. The sharp monetary squeeze in Norway after 1925 echoed that in Denmark, and Norway was probably more severely affected than in the Depression of 1929–32 (Heckscher 1930, 246–9). Moreover, once the decision to return to parity was made known, speculators moved in and drove the currencies close to their pre-war levels, which virtually forced governments to honour their commitments (Aliber 1962, 241).

The difficulties Sweden, Denmark and Norway experienced in the 1920s were not replicated in the 1930s. Sweden had managed to restructure its banking system so that even with the collapse of the Kreuger financial empire, which inflicted heavy losses on Skandinaviska Kreditaktiebolaget, the banking system weathered the storm (Larsson 1991).

The 'bunching' of the banking crises of the early 1930s, which began with the Austrian financial collapse in the spring of 1931, has yet to be fully explained by economic historians, in particular, whether events in Austria caused the German crisis. The decision by the Credit-Anstalt to merge with the Boden-Credit-Anstalt in 1931, admittedly under government pressure, was not a propitious move for the rescuing bank (Weber 1995, 352). The Credit-Anstalt was in a weak position, operating in the 1920s 'as if the Habsburg Empire had not been broken up' (Feinstein, Temin and Toniolo 1997, 108). The proximate cause of the bank's failure was bad debts and the fall of its security portfolio but it was the wider implications of the bank's collapse that led to the crisis of confidence (James 1992, 599). The bank's losses (calculated at 140 million Austrian schillings in May 1931, 500 million in June and at the year's end, 923 million) were to be covered by purchases of Credit-Anstalt paper by the National Bank with a government guarantee. The promise of a transfer of liabilities from the private to the public sector (the 'socialization of debt') on this scale panicked the markets who feared massive debt monetization as an alternative to default on domestic and foreign debt. Creditors were thus alerted to the implications that this might have for currency convertibility, not just in Austria but elsewhere in Central Europe, which had experienced serious inflation in the previous decade (Eichengreen and Portes 1987, 25–7). It led to severe pressure on many continental banks, resulting in large-scale withdrawals of short-term funds, both by nationals and foreigners, and the loss of reserves from Germany and Eastern Europe through the summer of 1931 until brought to a halt by the imposition of exchange control. Some 30 per cent of the foreign short-term assets located in Germany, for example, were withdrawn in the months through to the introduction of exchange control in the middle of July 1931. The gold and foreign exchange reserves of 18 European debtor countries fell by nearly one half between 1928 and 1931, with most of the losses taking place in 1930–31 (Aldcroft and Oliver 1998).

It is clear that the failure of the Credit-Anstalt shook the whole economic and financial structure in Europe and had severe repercussions on the banking systems of Germany and Eastern Europe. Even if there were no direct deposit links between Austria and Germany, economic historians have argued that the loss of confidence created by the Austrian crisis was deleterious to the financial infrastructure (Eichengreen 1992, 271–2). The episode is a classic example of international systemic risk (Bordo et al. 1998) and firm-specific contagion (Kaufman 1994).

Recent research has also tended to attribute greater causal connection between exchange rate instability and debt default as propagating mechanisms (Eichengreen and Portes 1987; Temin 1989; Eichengreen 1992). The gold standard 'set the stage for the Depression of the 1930s by heightening the fragility of the international monetary system' and contributed to the banking failures of 1931 because it was 'the binding constraint preventing policymakers from averting the failure of banks and containing the spread of financial panic' (Eichengreen 1992, xi). The 'Midas touch' of the gold standard thus affected the mindset of central bankers and prevented international monetary cooperation in 1931, standing in marked contrast to previous episodes of financial crisis, for example, the Baring crisis of 1890. Moreover, when the Reichsbank attempted to borrow on the international credit market in July 1931, the French who were 'still fighting the First World War' (Feinstein, Temin and Toniolo 1995, 39) refused help, while the Americans did not believe that the consequences of the German banking crisis were anything other than short-term in nature (Bennett 1962).

As Table 6.5 shows, the peak of the banking crises occurred in 1931 and thereafter there were only isolated failures. Eichengreen (1992) has argued that it was only possible for a country to resolve a banking crisis by aborting the gold standard. Those countries that moved to floating rates did gain monetary and fiscal independence, while the general departure from gold has been seen as important to recovery in the 1930s (Aldcroft and Oliver 1998). However, even if we were to go as far as Feinstein et al. (1997, 191) and accept that the rigidity of the interwar monetary regime was the prime cause of the Great Depression, not everything that went wrong in the interwar years can be pinned on the gold standard.

CURRENCY CRISES IN BRETTON WOODS

One of the noteworthy features between 1940–71 is the absence of banking crises. An explanation for this is that banking regulations were restrictive and capital flows were low for most of the period, hence there were no banking crises driven by capital flight. However, there were more currency crises than in any other period on the basis of the 21-country sample shown in Figure 6.1. As capital restrictions were relaxed from the 1950s and outstanding dollar liabilities increased relative to US gold reserves, so the Bretton Woods system was threatened by systemic risk (Bordo and Schwartz 1996, 1999). On reflecting on the exchange rate changes under Bretton Woods between 1949 and 1969, however, Bordo et al. (1998, 45–6) suggest that there is no evidence of international transmission and systematic risk. The disturbances in the currency markets would appear to come under their definition of financial distress, although towards the end of the 1960s the shocks to the international monetary system were connected, eventually leading to the dissolution of the system. While we have already remarked on the value of the dataset provided by Bordo et al. (2001), this is one occasion in which we cannot get a sense of the build-up in pressure in the international monetary system over the period from the data alone. The data for 1940–71 show two things that are worthy of further exploration. First, the United Kingdom experienced more crises in this period than any other country and, second, the bulk of the crises were clustered in 1971.

In the Bretton Woods system, the United States was at the core of the system and Europe was at the periphery. The role of the United Kingdom became slightly more complicated as the system evolved. Technically, the pound was the second reserve currency to the dollar and this allowed sterling to be used in lieu of gold to settle international transactions. The credibility of sterling to fulfil its reserve currency role was tested twice in the 1940s: first by the convertibility crisis of July 1947 and then in September 1949 when the pound was devalued by 30 per cent. At the beginning of the period however, sterling was the dominant currency in world reserves but it was eclipsed by the dollar at the end of the 1950s and the dollar then took over the function of gold as a major international reserve asset following current account convertibility across Europe in 1958.

The problems for the United Kingdom, which intensified post-1964, were four-fold (Middleton 2002). First, that in terms of foreign trade Britain seemed, since the end of the Second World War, to be in constant balance of payments deficit. Second, in its role as banker to the sterling area the United Kingdom held on deposit in London sterling liabilities that far outstripped the reserves available to back those claims. The ratio of assets to liabilities was thought to be somewhere in the region of 1:4 and should the sterling holders have decided en masse to cash in their holdings, the sterling ship would have been sunk. Third, the foreign exchange reserves held by the United Kingdom to prop up the pound were woefully inadequate. Finally, these three weaknesses undermined confidence in the pound, to such a degree that speculation against it was rife.

As Eichengreen and Rose (2003) have shown, the failure to defend an exchange rate peg can lead to domestic and international macroeconomic credibility being called into question, increased exchange rate volatility and higher inflation, whilst decreasing domestic consumption and investment. We might add that within the context of Bretton Woods, devaluation could call into serious question the legitimacy of the pound's role to act as a reserve currency and also threatened the stability of the international monetary system. This was recognized by HM Treasury in 1964, who feared that a devaluation would severely strain Britain's relations with other countries, particularly the sterling area, where the main holders of sterling would begin to withdraw their balances from London; threatening the stability of the international monetary system by throwing into question the practice of reserve currencies; and finally, provoking retaliatory measures in Western Europe and a 'scramble for gold' as the future of the dollar would be put into question (HM Treasury 1964).

It was for these reasons – a combination of economic, political and moral – that the incoming Labour government were committed to maintain the value of the pound; it therefore performed a precarious balancing act for three years defending sterling's parity. During this time it endured four currency crises and spent an enormous amount of intellectual and financial capital in trying to avoid devaluation. However, as Eichengreen (2003a, 1092) has remarked in a stringent criticism of economic policy between 1964–67, the 'wishful thinking' of the Labour government was that it believed it could achieve faster rates of economic growth and not devalue the currency. Expansionary monetary and fiscal policies were inconsistent with the external constraint but because the government did not wish to sacrifice its goal of full employment and it was impossible to sustain foreign assistance indefinitely to prop up the pound, it was caught trying to steer the British economy between Scylla and Charybdis. The end result was the 1967 devaluation, which was a classic example of a first-generation currency crisis.

Although the devaluation had long been expected, it shook the Bretton Woods regime to its foundations and was the first phase in its disintegration (Oliver and Hamilton 2007). The devaluation was followed by a huge increase in the speculative demand for gold in November and December 1967 and members of the London gold pool extended their commitments by over two billion dollars. The French did not extend any more resources, having withdrawn from the pool six months earlier, and caused mischief in the market by suggesting publicly that the dollar price of gold was to be raised. The rush into gold slowed during January and much of February 1968, but pressure had resumed by March. Much of this was precipitated by the release of the US balance of payments figures for 1967, which revealed a glaring deficit of $3.6 billion. This, coupled with the fact that yet more troops were to be sent to Vietnam, triggered off a new bout of speculation in the gold market. Indeed, the orthodoxy at the time was that the balance of payments deficit was largely the result of the Vietnam conflict and more troops could only mean a worsening in the balance of payments throughout 1968. After heavy pressure against the dollar and sterling and a rush into gold, on 17 March 1968, the London gold pool was replaced by a dual price system. Transactions between monetary authorities would continue to operate as before (at the official price of $35 an ounce) but non-official transactions would be conducted at a free market price, determined by supply and demand. The wider impact of the two-tier grouping was far reaching as the link between the supply of dollars and a fixed market price of gold was severed and marked the second stage in the death of Bretton Woods.

The currency crises of May 1971 ushered in the final stages of the demise of Bretton Woods. The underlying cause was the US deficit and the weakness of the dollar in the foreign exchange markets. There was a large conversion of dollar reserves into gold by several European countries in March, which reduced the US gold stock to its lowest level since 1936 (Bordo and Schwartz 1996, 454). The outflow of dollars into strong European currencies – particularly the deutschmark – was enormous between March and April. There was speculation that the deutschmark would be either revalued or would float. On 5 May, $2 billion was taken in within the first 40 minutes of dealing and to prevent the deutschmark going through its ceiling, the Bundesbank responded by withdrawing and then closing the market in Frankfurt. Other markets swiftly followed suit and remained closed for five days. Both the deutschmark and the Dutch guilder floated after the reopening of the markets and the Swiss franc and Austrian schilling were revalued. There was heavy selling of dollars again during the first 14 days of August, which prompted the United States to suspend the convertibility of the dollar into gold or other reserve assets on 15 August 1971. Although exchange rates were adjusted at the Smithsonian Agreement in December 1971, the suspension of convertibility was not lifted and within 15 months most countries had moved to floating exchange rates.

THE EMS CRISES, 1992–93

European countries were not affected by financial crises on the scale of the 1971 disruption until the early 1990s. The banking crisis that struck Finland, Norway and Sweden and the currency crisis that hit several members of the European Monetary System (EMS) were the most disruptive financial events since the Second World War for the European continent. For the three Nordic countries, the banking crisis was the worst since the 1920s and the first for the industrial countries since 1945 to take place in an environment of free capital mobility, which increased the scope for reserve losses and financial dislocation (Eichengreen 2003b, 244).

We can get a sense of the disruption from Tables 6.7 and 6.8. Table 6.7 shows that typically GDP growth falls by three percentage points between the years preceding and following a crisis in an emerging market country

Table 6.7   GDP growth before and after currency crises, 1970–98

Country group	t−1	t (crisis year)	t+1	Change from t−1 to t+1
LDC crises except Mexico 1995 crisis	3.95	2.06	0.61	−3.34
Mexico 1995 crisis	4.41	−6.17	5.15	0.74
OECD crises except EMS 1991–92 crises	3.16	2.91	3.16	0.00
EMS 1991–92 crises	0.44	−0.88	−1.19	−1.63

Note: Values are country-group averages (except for Mexico 1995, which shows actual value). First row includes 45 emerging market crises (excluding Mexico 1995). Third row includes 22 industrial-country crises (other than the 1991–92 EMS crises). Fourth row includes the following crises: Finland 1991, Italy 1992, Portugal 1992, Spain 1992, Sweden 1992 and United Kingdom 1992.

Source: Eichengreen (2003b, 241).

Table 6.8   Cumulative percentage increase in GDP over three years following currency crises, 1970–98

Country group	t (crisis year)	t+1	t+2	t+3	Sum from t to t+3
LDC crises except Mexico 1995 crisis	1.93	1.91	3.12	4.38	11.34
Mexico 1995 crisis	−6.17	5.15	6.76	4.80	10.54
OECD crisis except EMS 1991–92 crises	2.91	3.16	3.44	2.08	11.59
EMS 1991–92 crises	−0.88	−1.19	2.19	3.29	3.41

Note: Values are country-group averages (except for Mexico 1995, which shows actual value). First row includes 38 emerging market crises (excluding Mexico 1995). Third row includes 22 industrial-country crises (other than the 1991–92 EMS crises). Fourth row includes the following crises: Finland 1991, Italy 1992, Portugal 1992, Spain 1992, Sweden 1992 and United Kingdom 1992.

Source: Eichengreen (2003b, 241).

but does not change in a typical OECD country. In the six European countries affected by the early-1990s crisis, GDP fell by 1.6 percentage points, midway between the emerging markets and developed countries. The recovery from the EMS crisis, where the cumulative percentage increase in output was 3.4 per cent, is far below Mexico's figure of 10.5 per cent and one-third below that of OECD countries. Mexico's experience is not atypical of post-1970 emerging markets but the 1991–92 EMS case is atypical of OECD countries.

From 1979 until the late-1980s, the exchange rate mechanism (ERM) of the EMS worked well. Periods of exchange rate stability provided many of the benefits of fixed exchange rates and the realignments (of which there were 11 between 1979 and 1987) readdressed serious competitiveness problems. This stability was only possible, however, because capital controls protected central banks' reserves against speculative attacks driven by anticipations of realignment (Eichengreen 1993). By July 1990, most members of the EMS had removed exchange and capital controls (the exceptions were Ireland, Spain, Portugal and Greece). Ironically, it was the removal of capital controls as part of the requirement of fulfilling the 1986 Single European Act that fatally undermined the viability of the 'old' (flexible) ERM. The 'new' (rigid) ERM was described by some economists as 'half-baked' (Walters 1988) and Padoa-Schioppa (1988) pointed out that there was now an 'inconsistent quartet' of policy objectives: free trade, capital mobility, fixed (managed) exchange rates and independent monetary policies. With the absence of capital controls, markets were now in a stronger position to launch pre-emptive strikes if it appeared that a country was going to change its parity. Discussions of realignments became non dit and while the 'new' ERM appeared more stable it was actually unsound. This instability was not merely confined to the ERM: the global environment had become more volatile, with further deregulation of financial markets, the growth of international financial transactions following the Brady Plan for LDC debt crisis, the collapse of the Soviet Union and German reunification (Eichengreen 2003b, 216).

Against this backdrop, Finland and Sweden experienced their most severe banking crises since the 1920s and entered the deepest recession since the early 1930s. At the peak of the banking crisis, non-performing loans in Sweden accounted for 18 per cent of loans outstanding for the entire banking industry, 13 per cent in Finland and 6 per cent in Norway (Hutchinson 2002, 383–5). While these figures are high for industrial countries, Indonesia and Thailand were more severely affected at the height of the Asian crisis, with figures of 70 per cent and 33 per cent, respectively (Kane and Klingebiel 2002). In Sweden, the contraction of GDP between 1990 and 1993 was almost 6 per cent and lasted longer than the decline in the 1920s and 1930s (Jonung and Stymne 1997, 48–9). The unemployment rate rose from just under 1 per cent in June 1990, to 9 per cent three years later. In Finland, the unemployment rate soared from just under 4 per cent in 1990 to 17 per cent in 1993 (OECD 1995) and GDP fell by about 12 per cent between 1990 and 1993 (Kokko and Suzuki 2005). There was a rapid deterioration in government finances in both countries: by 1994, Sweden's budget deficit was almost 12 per cent of GDP and in Finland the central government debt grew from 10 per cent of GDP in 1990 to 60 per cent in 1994 (Kokko and Suzuki 2005). In the case of Sweden and Finland, the story is clearly of a credit boom gone wrong while the situation in Norway is slightly different (Jonung, Kiander and Vartia 2005).

In Sweden, the deregulation of the financial market in 1985 led to a substantial increase in the supply of credit. Banks were allowed to compete with finance companies and their traditional strategy of minimizing risk and maximizing profitability on a fairly constant volume of loans was replaced by a new strategy of chasing volume and market share (Jonung and Stymne 1997, 24–5; Kokko and Suzuki 2005). Following the deregulation of the Swedish capital market, an increasing share of banking lending was financed on the international interbank market, which introduced an important element of currency risk into the economy. The demand for credit was initiated by two devaluations in 1981 and 1982. Excess liquidity from companies was invested in shares and the money markets and the corporate demand for commercial property and financial investments led to rising asset prices. Between 1985 and 1990, the indebtedness of the private sector increased from 100 per cent to 150 per cent of GDP. An expansionary monetary and fiscal policy during the 1980s kept private indebtedness aloft and demand was further bolstered by a tax cut in 1988.

The Swedish bubble burst at the end of September 1990 when a leading finance company, Nycklen, announced credit losses of 250 million Swedish kronor. The banks refused to roll over the maturing securities of Nycklen and other finance companies, forcing them into an acute liquidity crisis. Two hundred of the 300 finance companies went into liquidation and over the next two years three major banks – Nordbanken, Första Sparbanken and Gota Bank – were declared insolvent (Englund and Vihriälä 2005). By September 1992, the government was concerned about systemic crisis and announced it would extend the deposit insurance of the banks' liabilities that it had already offered Första Sparbanken and Gota Bank to all the other banks. Total credit losses between 1990 and 1993 are estimated at almost 200 billion, or nearly 10 per cent of GDP (Lybeck 1994, 23). By the end of 1994, the government commitments to bank support totalled 88 billion kronor and total disbursements were just over 65 billion kronor (Jonung and Stymne 1997, 43).

In Norway, the banking crisis was a commercial banking crisis caused by low profitability and inadequate capitalization (Steigum 2005). Unlike Sweden and Finland, financial deregulation in the 1980s did not improve the profitability of the commercial banking sector in Norway. In Norway, lending increased by 40 per cent in 1985 and 1986 (Heiskanen 1993) and led to a rapid rise in asset prices. The profitability of Norwegian savings banks deteriorated between 1987 and 1990 but economists did not predict the systematic crisis that broke out in 1991 involving all the commercial banks. In two of the biggest commercial banks, Den norske Creditbank and Christiania Bank, inexperienced and newly recruited staff had pursued aggressive new policies in order to attract new loans (Knutsen, Lange and Nordvik 1998). Inadequate accounting systems gave the management wrong signals about profitability and many loans soon turned sour. There is evidence that several banks copied the aggressive lending behaviour of the two leading commercial banks and that this stimulated rational herd behaviour, even among those managers who realized that this would be a counter-productive policy (Scharfstein and Stein 1990; Banerjee 1992; Johnsen et al. 1992). Although Christiania Bank, Den norske Creditbank and another large commercial bank, Fokus Bank, were supported by injections of government share capital in 1991, new losses in 1992 ended with the nationalization of all three banks.

Finland's financial crisis had its origins in the domestic financial liberalization, that began in 1983 and was completed by the beginning of 1988. The liberalization of capital movements took a further two years (Englund and Vihriälä 2005). Once the lending guidelines that had governed the Finnish banking system were abolished, banks began to compete more aggressively for borrowers, as in Sweden and Norway (Drees and Pazarbasioglu 1998). The savings banks and Skopbank were the most aggressive lenders between 1986 and 1990 with combined lending totalling over 140 per cent, compared with over 90 per cent for the cooperative banking group and less than 80 per cent for commercial banks (Englund and Vihriälä 2005). The commercial banks had a capital requirement of 4 per cent and the savings and cooperative banks had a 2 per cent requirement, while local banks had less than 2 per cent. Unlike the other banks, the savings and cooperative banks could not augment their capital via equity issues and had to rely on retained earnings, which were low (Vihriälä 1997). The savings and cooperative banks successfully resisted a tightening of capital requirements and managed to prosper in an environment where financial supervision was passive (Halme 1999). The way in which Finland's banking system was liberalized was thus a classic case of how poorly designed financial liberalization can increase the probability of a banking crisis (Drees and Pazarbasioglu 1998, 36).

The monetary authorities attempted to slow down the growth of credit expansion by tightening monetary policy in 1988, but interest rates could only be raised slightly as long as confidence in the currency peg led to large short-term capital inflows (Englund and Vihriälä 2005). The capital flows prevented a change in the exchange rate and also financed an increasing share of bank lending denominated in foreign currency. Fiscal policy continued to be expansionary and it was only in 1989 that the monetary authorities attempted to restrain credit growth by widening the exchange rate band and revaluing the markka by 4 per cent and subjecting banks to special cash reserve requirements (Vihriälä 1997, 35). The savings banks chose to pay the penalty rates and disregarded the central bank's recommendation that credit growth should be slowed; indeed, the savings banks used the slowdown in commercial bank lending as an opportunity to capture market shares (Englund and Vihriälä 2005). However, on 19 September 1991, the central bank of the savings bank, Skopbank, was unable to obtain overnight funding. The Bank of Finland prevented it from bankruptcy by injecting FIM 2 billion in share capital and investment and split the bank into three holding companies.

The near failure of Skopbank added to the crisis of confidence that had followed the collapse of exports to the Soviet Union, a decline in the terms of trade and a weakening of domestic demand (Honkapohja and Koskela 1999, 405). Although Finland was not part of the EMS, during the 1980s it had pegged its currency to the system and gradually adopted a hard currency stance. In June 1991, the authorities strengthened their commitment to the currency peg by tying the markka to the European Currency Unit. This was not a propitious move however, and although the interest rate spread relative to Germany initially declined, rates began to rise and further contracted the domestic economy whilst increasing the debt burden (Dornbusch, Goldfajn and Valdes 1995, 234). In November 1991, the markka came under repeated speculative attacks and was devalued by 13 per cent and short-term interest rates were brought down by four percentage points although long-term rates remained unaffected.

The banking system suffered a further collapse and, in early 1992, the government offered an aggregate capital injection of FIM 8 billion to the deposit banks and established a Government Guarantee Fund (GGF) to safeguard the deposit banks and the claims of the depositors, but, by the summer, many of the savings banks were on the brink of collapse. In June, GGF committed FIM 7.2 billion to support 40 savings banks that had merged to form the Savings Bank of Finland (SBF), but within three months the capital had been written off and by the end of the year another FIM 5.3 billion had been allocated to SBF (Englund and Vihriälä 2005). In September, pressure on the markka began again and the Bank of Finland was forced to abandon the peg on 8 September, whereupon the markka depreciated by 12 per cent. The banking system continued to suffer from jitters and in November 1992, a former savings bank, STS, which had been converted to a commercial bank in 1990, was also taken over by the government. The total funds used in the rescue of the Finnish banking system between 1991 and 1992, that is, by the Bank of Finland, the Council of

State and the GGF, have been calculated at FIM 35.3 billion (Drees and Pazarbasioglu 1998, 32).

As Dornbusch et al. (1995) note, Finland was not alone in its determination to buy credibility with a 'hard currency posture'. The United Kingdom, Spain and Italy also tried to buy credibility by fixing the exchange rate, and their currencies came under pressure in the foreign exchange markets in 1992, along with the French franc and the Danish krone. Italy raised its interest rate on 5 June, and in the succeeding weeks the lira was allowed to depreciate against the deutschmark within the narrow band, while the Italian authorities intervened heavily in the foreign exchange market. Despite these measures, speculation in the Italian currency continued to intensify. While the initial EMS agreement did commit central banks to unlimited intervention when currencies reached their fluctuation margins (which was further strengthened by the Basle-Nyborg Agreement), there had not been a case when this commitment was tested.

An emergency meeting of the Bundesbank Council on 11 September proposed a package of measures with the Italian government in which the lira would be devalued by 3 per cent and the deutschmark revalued by 3 per cent against the other EMS currencies. As this was a de facto devaluation of all currencies relative to the deutschmark, France (who had a crucial referendum pending on the Maastricht Treaty) and the United Kingdom (who had argued that sterling's parity was correctly valued), rejected these measures. Italy was forced to go it alone and devalued by 7 per cent on 13 September and was forced out of the ERM on 17 September.

UK entry into the ERM also coincided with the start of a major recession. Interest rates were gradually reduced, but it was only a matter of time before Britain's commitment to the ERM would be severely challenged. During the summer of 1992, when the Bundesbank raised interest rates to curb post-unification inflation in Germany, the UK authorities simply tried to wait until the tensions in the mechanism had eased. The authorities repeatedly ruled out devaluation and refused to raise interest rates, which gave confusing signals to the financial markets. By the end of August 1992, it was estimated that the Bank of England had used at least $1.3 billion of reserves to prevent sterling falling through the floor of its wide band, while during the first week in September, it borrowed $14.5 billion to finance further intervention. On 16 September, the Bank of England extended its support for sterling, by reportedly using half its total foreign exchange reserves. The discount rate was raised from 10 to 15 per cent but these measures were not sufficient to stem the orgy of speculation, which was only quelled when sterling withdrew from the ERM on the same day.

Can the cause of the European currency crises be explained in terms of first- or second-generation models? Despite Eichengreen's (2003b, 222–34) retrospective on the EMS crisis where he tried to identify a synthesis between the two models, he is forced to admit, even ten years after the event, that there is little consensus between the first- and second-generation models.

The evidence in support of the first-generation model does not seem that compelling (cf. Bordo and Schwartz 1996). Unit labour costs and producer prices show no clear deterioration except in Italy among the 'old' (pre-1987) members of the EMS between 1987 and 1992. Among the 'new' (post-1989) EMS countries, the deterioration in competitiveness is less clear-cut in Spain and Portugal, while the United Kingdom's increase in relative unit labour costs predated the October 1990 entry into the ERM by four years (Eichengreen 1996, 177). Some authors have suggested that the reunification of Germany forced the other ERM countries to deflate with deleterious effects (Branson 1994). Eichengreen and Wyplosz (1993) have presented evidence suggesting that apart from Italy, the other ERM members had already moved a long way towards adjusting to the unification shock by September 1992; moreover, a time span of two years had elapsed between Germany's unification and the events of September 1992 and this cannot be considered an adequate explanation of the upheaval in 1992 of the intra-European exchange rates.

The alternative explanation for the turmoil on the foreign exchanges between June 1992 and early August 1993 is self-fulfilling speculative attacks. As numerous authors have argued (Eichengreen and Wyplosz 1993; Rose and Svennsson 1994; Obstfeld 1996), the Maastricht Treaty provided an environment conducive to self-fulfilling speculative attacks. To qualify for monetary union, the Treaty required currencies to be within the ERM's narrow band without severe tension for at least two years (the Treaty suggested that the third and final stage towards monetary union should begin any time after 1 January 1994). The Danish referendum on 2 June 1992 was the trigger because the 'no' vote raised serious questions about whether the Maastricht Treaty would come into effect. If the Treaty was abandoned, the incentive for countries to hold their currencies within their ERM bands in order to qualify for monetary union would be weakened and high-debt countries like Italy would have less reason to cut their deficits and follow expansionary policies. After the devaluation of the lira on 13 September 1992, the markets realized that changes in EMS exchange rates were still possible. Pressure mounted on Britain, Spain, Portugal and Italy until either a currency left the ERM (Italy and Britain) or until capital controls were tightened (Ireland, Spain and Portugal).

Stability returned to the foreign exchanges following the endorsement of the Maastricht Treaty by the Danish electorate in May 1993. The French franc and the other weak ERM currencies strengthened following the

Bundesbank's decision to lower its discount and Lombard rates. As inflation in France was running below that of Germany, French officials suggested that the franc had assumed the role of anchor currency in the ERM and persuaded the Bank of France to reduce interest rates to alleviate high unemployment. The Bundesbank did not follow suit and when it finally cut its rate the reduction was very small. A scheduled Franco-German meeting to coordinate interest rate reductions was cancelled by German officials and the foreign exchange markets became jittery. Speculative pressures on the ERM, particularly against the franc, developed during July 1993. On Friday 23 July, the Bank of France was forced to raise its interest rates sharply to prevent the franc falling through its ERM lower band. A coordinated statement by the German and French authorities could not contain the speculative pressure on the franc and the pressures peaked at the end of July 1993 with massive sales of French francs and also the Belgian franc, the Danish krone, the Spanish peseta and the Portuguese escudo. This forced EC monetary officials to decide on 2 August against realigning exchange rates and instead they widened the permitted band of fluctuation from 2.25 per cent to 15 per cent.

We have already suggested that the crisis in the EMS during the early 1990s was similar in many ways to emerging markets and in the three Nordic countries this was particularly so. We now turn to account for the sickness in the emerging markets of Russia, Mexico and Asia during the 1990s.

EMERGING SICKNESS: THE TEQUILA CRISIS, THE ASIAN FLU AND THE RUSSIAN VIRUS

As Figures 6.1 and 6.2 have shown, there was an explosion of financial crises during the 1990s. Aside from the European countries, the biggest victims were the so-called 'emerging markets' of Asia, Russia and South America. Although Kamin (1999, 514) has suggested that the uniqueness of the currency crises in the emerging markets during the 1990s should not be exaggerated, there are some important differences with preceding crises. The crisis of the 1990s have been accorded the label 'twenty-first-century-type', although as Eichengreen (2003b, 187) piquantly notes, the Mexican crisis of 1994–95 might be better described as the last financial crisis of the nineteenth century with its similarities to the 1890 Baring crisis. In essence, each of the crises we consider below was a product of globalization and they were more intense and led to a different type of large-scale international lending than had existed pre-1914. Each episode was marked by a reversal of financial flows and to some extent unanticipated by agents, generating deep economic contractions in the debtor countries and losses to foreign investors (Radelet and Sachs 1998, 5).

Mexico

The Mexican crisis began on 21 December 1994 when the monetary authorities devalued the peso by 15 per cent. Short-term capital inflows, which had made Mexico the second-biggest importer of capital after China during the early 1990s, reversed direction. The size of the outflow forced the authorities to move to a floating rate on 22 December and over the following week, the peso fell by 50 per cent. At the end of January 1995, President Clinton announced a package of loans to Mexico, including $20 billion from the US Treasury's Exchange Stabilization Fund. The IMF agreed to a standby loan of 12.7 billion SDR (Special Drawing Rights) in February 1995. Although the Mexican bailout appeared successful and capital inflows returned to Latin America by the third quarter of 1995 (Kaminsky et al. 2004, 17), the federal debt continued to rise and per capita real GDP in 1997 was barely equal to its 1994 level (Bordo and Schwartz 1999, 703). The crisis was also contagious and spread to the liquid markets of Argentina and Brazil. Although Argentina had negligible bilateral or third-party trade links with Mexico, the country was badly hit by the crisis and lost 20 per cent of its foreign reserves in the weeks after the peso devaluation and was forced to adopt an austerity programme and the currency board was maintained with a $7 billion international loan (Kaminsky and Reinhart 2000, 150).

For some observers, the Mexican crisis was 'death foretold': a combination of shocks and inadequate policies, which between 1989–94 set the economy on an unstable course and made a crisis inevitable. There are two variants on this view. First, the Mexican experience can be explained by the real disequilibria hypothesis, namely, an overvalued exchange rate and an unsustainable current account deficit (Dornbusch and Werner 1994). Concomitantly, a second variant on the death foretold theme is self-fulfilling expectations: the balance of payments crisis did not stem from a fiscal deficit à la Krugman (1979), but in the anticipation of a banking-system bailout, which led to an attack on foreign reserves (Calvo and Mendoza 1996). An alternative explanation to the death foretold scenario is advanced by Sachs, Tornell and Velasco (1996), who suggest that Mexico underwent 'sudden death'. Real disequilibria set the stage for what was to come but Mexico did not appear to be on an unsustainable course and agents did not expect the crisis.

Sachs has discussed Mexico's problems in the 1980s in detail in this volume and the salient point for this chapter is that in December 1987, the peso was pegged to the dollar and from January 1989, the authorities adopted a 'crawling peg' based on a pre-announced rate of devaluation (the actual devaluation was set below the inflation rate). In November 1991, adjustable bands were introduced. The upper edge rose slowly over time (at a rate of 0.0004 pesos per day) and the floor of the band remained constant (fixed at 3.05 pesos per dollar). Mexico lowered import barriers, privatized state-owned enterprises and reduced the public sector's budget deficit and national debt. Its financial sector underwent a substantial liberalization (Dornbusch and Werner 1994). The effects of the reforms were dramatic. Between 1988 and 1994, GDP and private consumption rose by 30 per cent and investment grew by more than 70 per cent. Inflation had fallen but because the peso was pegged to the dollar, inflation was substantially higher than it was in the United States. The peso's real exchange rate rose markedly, particularly in 1988 and between 1991–93, and the trade deficit worsened. The burgeoning deficit was regarded as a temporary occurrence caused by the capital inflows attracted by the excellent growth prospects in Mexico. However, imports had grown by more than 300 per cent relative to their December 1987 levels and, by late 1994, the trade balance showed a deficit exceeding US$1.5 billion a month (Calvo and Mendoza 1996, 238). The problem was that Mexico had become too dependent on portfolio investment that could easily reverse direction. In Latin America in 1993, portfolio capital peaked at $62 billion compared with $21 billion in direct investment; Mexico received $28 billion of portfolio investment and only $7 billion of direct investment (Maskooki 2002, 164).

The method of financial liberalization in Mexico, as in the Nordic countries in the early 1990s, was a cause for concern, as weak supervision underpinned a substantial growth in the credit. From December 1988 to November 1994, credit from local commercial banks to the private sector rose in real terms by 277 per cent, or 25 per cent per year (Gil-Diaz 1998). There were some commentators who were sceptical about the sustainability of an economic policy that relied on a pegged exchange rate to control inflation and that ignored the enormous monetary growth. Meigs (1997, 1998) reports how Milton Friedman argued in public in 1992 that the Mexican monetary authorities had to choose between freeing the peso and reducing monetary growth. They did neither and before the crisis, the stock of highly liquid M2 in dollars reached US$110 billion, which far exceeded the maximum reserves (Calvo and Mendoza 1996, 243). Although the ratio of M2 to reserves can be very large for some countries without provoking difficulties for the banking sector, it is usually because the ratio is very stable. This was not so in Mexico. The large expansion of M2 was caused by the financial liberalization and its associated precarious growth of credit, coupled to the capital inflows (part of which took the form of bank deposits) and the recovery in economic activity.

When interest rates began to rise in the United States in February 1994 for the first time since 1989, capital inflows to developing countries began to reverse. The assassination of presidential candidate Luis Donaldo Colosio in March and the political uncertainty that followed also contributed to a slowing of these inward flows. The exchange rate was allowed to depreciate to the top of the band, fiscal policy was eased and the foreign reserves fell from $29 billion in February 1994 to around $6 billion in December 1994 (Sachs et al. 1996, 267–8). By 1994, it was difficult to issue *cetes* (peso-denominated Treasury bills of less than one year maturity) and the government switched to *tesobonos* (short-term dollar-denominated bonds) that paid a lower interest rate. Although the government increased its issuance of *tesobonos* to service its short-term debt costs and to demonstrate its commitment to the dollar peg, it did expose the government to interest rate and exchange rate risks (Bordo and Schwartz 1996, 461). By December 1994, the outstanding stock of *tesobonos* had risen to $18 billion (Eichengreen 2003b, 198).

Given the developments in Mexico between 1989–94, it is perhaps understandable that the crisis has been described as 'death foretold' rather than 'sudden death'. However, Sachs et al. (1996) draw attention to two pieces of evidence that suggest that the December crisis does not fit the speculative attack literature. First, they highlight the interest rate differential between *cetes* and *tesobonos* and the US T-bill, which is a proxy for Mexico's risk premium. Both spreads rose after the Colosio assassination in March 1994, then fell after Ernesto Zedillo's election victory in August and remained constant until November. The jump in spreads only took place after the December devaluation, while according to the speculative attack model, the rate differential should have increased as the reserves fell and the prospect of devaluation grew (as in the run-up to the EMS crisis in 1992). Following an attack the real differential should fall while the nominal differential may increase, but in Mexico both the nominal and real interest rate differential increased substantially. Second, they draw on international press coverage that did not suggest that agents expected the peso to collapse in December nor that there was a possibility Mexico might default. Per contra, articles written on Mexico during 1994 were ebullient about the country's future growth prospects. Thus while the erosion of reserves set the stage for a crisis, 'the timing and, especially, the magnitude of the attacked were not pinned down . . . the shift to the "bad" equilibrium was largely unanticipated by agents' (Sachs et al. 1996, 268).

East Asia

Even if the debate is unresolved over whether or not the financial crisis in Mexico was anticipated, there is greater consensus that virtually all agents did not predict the onset of the East Asian financial crisis in 1997. The notable exception to this is Park (1996) and even the normally perceptive Paul Krugman only predicted a slowdown in growth and not a collapse (Krugman 1994).

The explanations for the Asian crisis have fallen into two categories: fundamental macroeconomic imbalances and financial sector weaknesses (Berg 1999; Cerra and Saxena 2002). The region's growth was sustained partly by capital inflows and concomitant growing current account deficits. The capital inflows to Thailand and Malaysia were very large, averaging over 10 per cent of GDP between 1990 and 1996 (Radelet and Sachs 1998, 24). The crisis is the locus classicus of the 'sudden stop' syndrome: there was a massive reversal of capital inflows in the second half of 1997 that amounted to 11 per cent of the pre-crisis dollar GDP of Indonesia, Korea, Malaysia, the Philippines and Thailand (Radelet and Sachs 1998, 2). Several authors have argued that the quasi-dollar peg was a major contributory factor in the crisis, causing the overvaluation of the currencies and excessive unhedged foreign currency borrowing against the guarantee of exchange rate stability (Ito, Ogawa and Sasaki 1998; Edwards 1999; Eichengreen 1999; Eichengreen and Hausmann 1999).

Several of the Asian economies had enjoyed spectacular rates of economic growth for many years before the crisis struck and during the early 1990s they had been singled out for praise by the World Bank (1993) for their economic performance, which, it was argued, stemmed from market-orientated policies. Indonesia and Malaysia in particular had enjoyed strong macroeconomic fundamentals and there appeared to be little signs of weakness. For example, Standard and Poor had given Indonesian debt an investment-grade rating of BBB because of its sound and prudent fiscal policies, the high rate of savings and investment and a well balanced trade structure. It is true that some critics had identified problems in the East Asian banking sector before the crisis, which included low capital-adequacy ratios of banks, ineffective auditing and accounting procedures and excessive exposure of banks to single borrowers (White 1995). The IMF Executive Board also expressed concern about the Asian economies, following its Article IV consultations in 1996, and had recommended more flexible exchange rates, improved banking sector supervision, a tightening of fiscal policy and increased openness to capital flows. However, the IMF was generally sanguine about future growth prospects (Radelet and Sachs 2000, 151–2). In short, with the exception of Thailand, which had a growing current account deficit between 1995 and 1996, there was no inkling that various economies in the region were about to undergo a period of severe currency turbulence and their deepest recession since 1945 (Berg 1999; Woo, Carleton and Rosario 2000, 120).

Table 6.9 summarizes the movements of the currencies of the Asian-5 against the US dollar between 1990 and 1998. Both the Thai baht and the Malaysian ringitt were closely pegged to the dollar between 1990 and 1996 and the Indonesian rupiah was on a sliding peg against the dollar. Until 1995, Thailand's current account deficit was offset by capital inflows and the country's foreign exchange reserves grew. As the dollar strengthened, however, the Thai authorities allowed their trade-weighted real exchange rate to appreciate and the current account deficit widened, reaching 8 per cent of GDP in 1995 and 1996. By the end of 1996, short-term borrowings from foreign banks in Thailand exceeded the foreign exchange reserves. Concerns grew about the sustainability of the currency peg with a rising short-term debt and a sluggish export performance. The authorities responded by raising short-term interest rates in May 1997 and conducting an aggressive defence of the baht against the large-scale selling by hedge funds. Yet by intervening in the forward market rather than correcting the fundamentals, there was a huge short position in dollar futures (Eichengreen 2003b, 258). The monetary authorities were forced to abandon the dollar peg on 2 July 1997, which ushered in a period of currency and monetary crises in the Asian economies.

The spread of the Asian flu following the baht's managed float was dramatic.[3] Within six months, the Thai baht and Indonesian rupiah had depreciated by about 50 per cent and the Malaysian ringitt and the Philippine peso had lost 30 per cent from before the start of the crisis (both the peso and ringitt had floated following the devaluation of the baht). The Taiwan dollar was forced to devalue, which prompted a speculative attack on the Hong Kong dollar and the spread of the crisis to South Korea. Alongside Thailand, the economies of both Indonesia and South Korea were badly affected in 1997 and into 1998. The governments in both countries sought to soften the liquidity crunch but were forced to turn to the IMF, World Bank and other international banks for support. In both cases the rescue packages did little to stabilize the financial markets. In South Korea, a $57 billion package announced in December 1997 failed to restore investor confidence into 1998, largely because the corporate sector was too highly leveraged and the government was reluctant to close troubled banks. Indonesia signed a $23 billion package with the IMF in October and promised to reform its financial system and closed 16 banks. This prompted a run on the commercial banks and depositors transferred their money to state and foreign banks or out of the system entirely (Berg 1999, 55).

Table 6.9   Exchange rate movements of the Asian-5 crisis (vis-à-vis the US$ in percentages)

	Indonesia	Malaysia	Philippines	South Korea	Thailand
Part A: Movement of currency against the US$ (nominal exchange rate)					
avg 1970–79	7.67	23.15	7.84	5.02	−0.24
avg 1980–89	12.17	2.20	12.93	4.17	2.51
1990	5.79	−0.07	24.78	5.41	−1.56
1991	4.79	0.83	−4.82	6.20	−0.04
1992	3.51	−4.11	−5.83	3.63	0.95
1993	2.33	3.43	10.37	2.50	0.08
1994	4.27	−5.24	−11.85	−2.40	−1.76
1995	4.91	−0.70	7.36	−1.78	0.40
1996	3.25	−0.51	0.28	8.97	1.67
1997	95.13	53.89	52.07	100.78	84.49
1998	72.58	−2.36	−2.29	−28.97	−22.34
Part B: Movement of currency against the US$ after adjustment for changes in consumer price index (CPI) vis- à-vis US CPI (real exchange rate)					
1990	3.37	2.71	16.97	2.23	−2.14
1991	−0.39	0.71	−19.08	1.13	−1.54
1992	−0.98	−5.85	−11.39	0.42	−0.09
1993	−4.40	2.84	6.44	0.69	−0.33
1994	−1.65	−6.36	−17.60	−6.01	−4.20
1995	−1.72	−3.20	2.13	−3.47	−2.59
1996	−1.79	−1.07	−5.80	6.98	−1.22
1997	90.74	53.57	48.46	98.68	81.22
1998	16.48	−6.08	−10.45	−34.93	−28.86
Part C: Current account balance as percentage of GDP					
1990	−4.07	−2.27	−6.31	−1.26	−8.78
1991	−3.96	−8.87	−2.47	−3.11	−8.01
1992	−2.07	−4.01	−3.18	−1.62	−6.23
1993	−0.82	−.511	−6.70	−0.09	−5.67
1994	−1.54	−6.59	−3.74	−1.32	−6.37
1995	−4.27	−8.75	−5.06	−1.75	−8.21
1996	−3.30	−3.27	−4.67	−4.44	−8.21
1997	−3.20	−4.29	−6.08	−1.55	0.02
1998	0.67	N/A	0.50	11.50	N/A

Note: + = depreciation, − = appreciation.

Source: Woo et al. (2000, 124).

Further financial support from the IMF did not quell Indonesia's financial woes. The authorities had enormous trouble implementing economic reform and the country underwent widespread political turmoil.

What was the lasting impact of the Asian crisis? Athukorala (2003, 206–7) has shown that despite the sharp reversal in foreign portfolio investment and bank credit during the crisis, there was not a major discontinuity in foreign direct investment in all of the countries. In Korea, for example, the crisis-driven slowdown in FDI lasted two quarters and in Thailand it picked up from the second quarter of 1998. Yet despite the rapid recovery in positive growth rates, Cerra and Saxena (2003) warn that the crisis has resulted in a permanent output loss in all countries.

Russia

As investors undertook 'portfolio shuffling' and reassessed risk across emerging markets, it was only a matter of time before Central and Eastern Europe (CEE) and the Confederation of Independent States (CIS) were affected by the Asian crisis. Fries, Raiser and Stern (1999, 540) suggest that the impact of the contagion on the transition economies of CEE and the CIS was between 20 October 1997 (when the Hong Kong stock exchange collapsed) and the end of January 1998. In October 1997 the Moscow stock exchange index dropped by 34 per cent and then fell another 11 per cent by the end of December and continued to fall in January 1998 (Chapman and Mulino 2001, 16). The rouble came under attack in November 1997 but the Central Bank of Russia (TsBR) promptly raised the refinance rate by seven percentage points. Foreign exchange reserves fell in Russia until the end of 1997 but this was probably due to Russian residents purchasing foreign currency because of confiscation fears (the rouble was going to be redenominated in January 1998), rather than foreign investors withdrawing from the three-month Treasury bills (Buchs 1999, 690). Early in 1998, Bulgaria, Romania and the Czech Republic experienced financial instability (United Nations Economic Commission of Europe 1998, 50–58) and foreign capital began to retreat from the Russian financial markets and the rouble came under more pressure.

Since 1995, Russia had pegged the exchange rate to lower inflation. The rouble was allowed to fluctuate against the US dollar between 4300 and 4900 RUR/US$. This proved successful at stabilizing the economy and received strong support from the IMF (IMF 1996). In July 1996, the monetary authorities adopted a crawling peg and fixed the limits in advance for six months and later for a whole year. The exchange rate target was taken very seriously by the monetary authorities and as the rouble fell in 1998, they supported the exchange rate by buying roubles and then raised the refinancing rate a further 14 percentage points in early February 1998, before it fell back later in the month. The TsBR set a target guide for 1998 to 2000 of 6.2 redenominated roubles to the dollar and the exchange rate was allowed to fluctuate up to 15 per cent around this target. Nearly 45 per cent of Russia's foreign reserves were lost between October 1997 and February 1998 but the exchange rate was stabilized (Chapman and Mulino 2001, 17). The European continental banks continued to provide long-term credit to Russia despite several warning signs that the Russian peg was unstable because of structural problems in the economy.

The structural problems with the Russian economy post-1995 are those typically associated with a transitional economy and include budget difficulties, inadequate regulation of financial markets, a poorly monetized economy, weak corporate governance, poorly defined property rights and inadequate restructuring of production. Perotti (2002, 366) argues that Russia's institutional problems were different from those in other transitional or emerging markets because the reforms were carried out without any real enforcement. The international financial community and the IMF endorsed Russia's 'soft legal constraints' by providing loans, which sent strong incentive signals to other investors. Moreover, the IMF stabilization and liberalization policies were ill-suited to Russia, even if the authorities intended to tie themselves to the mast of a pegged exchange rate. The federal debt/GDP ratio climbed to more than 50 per cent during the first few months of 1998 and the authorities were forced to keep real interest rates on the growing issues of GKOs (less than one year rouble-denominated Treasury bills) at very high levels (Westin 1999, Chapman and Mulino 2001, 20).

From February 1998, the total amount of GKOs (short-term state bonds) and OFZs (longer maturity bonds) held by non-residents began to exceed the value of the foreign exchange reserves. By May 1998, investors began to question whether the government could honour its debts and maintain currency stability. The refinancing rate was raised to 150 per cent but the take-up of GKOs was slackening and the pressure on the reserves grew.

On 20 July, the IMF provided the first tranche of its $20 billion loan, all of which was dissipated by the TsBR on defending the currency. The loans did not stabilize market confidence and doubts continued to grow about the government's ability to continue to roll over its short-term domestic debt. By the middle of August, the TsBR was spending between $0.8 and $1 billion a week defending the exchange rate and by 17 August the government announced that it would devalue, default on its debt and introduce capital controls (Hanson 1999, 1152). The government froze trading in GKOs, which, combined with the devaluation, made most Russian banks illiquid. On 26 August, the TsBR announced it would no longer support the rouble and within four weeks, the currency had collapsed from 6.2 roubles to the dollar to over 20. This enormous uncertainty about the exchange rate led to the cessation of import deals and Russians who sought to convert roubles into dollars faced very large spreads and a refusal by the banks to sell dollars (Hanson 1999, 1152). As settlements through the Russian banking system were blocked, economic activity fell and there was a rapid rise in prices.

As several authors have shown, the resulting crisis in the summer of 1998 can be explained by a mixture of the first-generation and twin crises framework. Unlike the traditional first-generation models, the policy inconsistencies in Russia did not stem from a fixed peg and monetization of the public deficit but from holding the exchange rate fixed and a debt-financed fiscal deficit (Hanson 1999, 1155; Montes and Popov 1999; Chapman and Mulino 2001, 23; Basdevant and Hall 2002, 152). Due to the fact that the crisis spread from the currency to the banking sector, it was also a twin crisis and suggests 'that existing banking problems were aggravated or new ones created by the high interest rate required to defend the exchange-rate peg or the foreign exchange exposure of banks' (Kaminsky and Reinhart 1999, 472). Surprisingly, the Russian virus appears to have been a shortlived affair. The rapid pace of economic growth, averaging over 6 per cent per year in the five years following the devaluation, accompanied by a prudent fiscal and monetary policy has led some commentators to be more sanguine about Russia's prospects (Hanson 2003). However, a recent IMF Economic Forum sounded a more cautious note and warned that despite the recent good performance, there had not been a fundamental change in policy-making to sustain the process of economic recovery (IMF 2003).

CONCLUSIONS

One of the common themes to emerge from our survey of financial crises in the twentieth century is 'this time it's different'. As Kaminsky et al. (2003, 71) have remarked, these are perhaps the four most expensive words in financial history.

In a comment on the Bordo et al. (2001) paper, Rose (2001) has suggested that there is not much to be learnt from past crises: current data says little about the causes of financial crises and therefore little about prediction and prevention. It is a depressing thought, but the heterogeneity of financial crises might preclude us from predicting them. To be sure there has been work done on 'early warning systems' and leading indicators of currency crises, but although there have been some successes, there are also many false positives (Furman and Stiglitz 1998, 40–46; Kaminsky, Lizondo and

Reinhart 1998; Berg and Pattillo 1999, 2000). In truth, the economics pro-
fession has been struggling to provide a theoretical framework with which
to analyse crises. As one economist has lamented, it is a 'sad commentary
on our understanding of what drives capital flows . . . every crisis spawns a
new generation of economic models. When a new crisis hits, the previous
generation of models is judged to have been inadequate' (Rodrik 1998, 58).
Indeed, Frankel and Wei's (2004) data set shows it is probably not possible
to separate crises into such neat divisions as first, second or third generation as there are elements of all three in each crisis.

Although we would do well to pay heed to Mishkin's (2003) litany of
measures designed to prevent a financial crisis for emerging market
economies, we also need to recall that globalization is not a new phenomenon and that financial crises at a time of globalization are nothing new,
hence the emerging market sickness of the last quarter of the twentieth
century should not be a cause for surprise nor perhaps a cause for concern.
Delong (1999) is sanguine on the pervasiveness of financial crises in his
long-run comparison between the 1890s and the 1990s. He notes that the
data set that later resulted in the Bordo et al. (2001) paper shows that economic growth was far lower in the year that followed the two most severe
crises of the pre-1914 period, Argentina in 1890 and the United States in
1893, than it was in the wake of the 1990s' Mexican and Asian crisis. He
remarks that:

> history gives no strong reason to think that the Mexican or the Asian crisis was
> outside the bounds of what the 'normal' workings of a market economy with
> large international capital flows might generate. If the Mexican and Asian crises
> had no counterparts as large or larger in relative terms back before World War
> I, it would be good reason to think that the current international monetary
> systems – of which IMF-led rescues packages are a significant part – is a less
> effective social mechanism for handling crises than the pre-1914 classical gold
> standard was. (Delong 1999, 274)

Consider how the perception of financial crises has changed over the last
100 years. In the late nineteenth century, capital markets were viewed
as benign, despite the severity of the banking and currency crises
(Eichengreen and James 2003). Until the serious economic dislocation of
the interwar years, there was little interest amongst policy-makers in
strengthening the international financial architecture. The outcome of the
Bretton Woods discussions in July 1944 changed all this and the next
quarter of a century was marked by surveillance by the IMF on an enormous scale, although it was not until 1982, in the wake of the international
debt crises, that the institution had a central role as the manager of international financial crises (Boughton 2001, 42; Oliver 2006). Yet the IMF has

also been cited as a source of financial instability by creating moral hazard. A study by Bordo and Schwartz (2000, 155) has examined crisis countries between 1973 and 1999 and compared those that received IMF assistance with those that did not. The authors' conclusions were that 'turning to the IMF may be harmful for a country's economic performance' and that this effect has grown since the Mexican crisis. It would be unwise, however, to conclude from this evidence that should the IMF be reformed or even abolished, financial crises would disappear. The experience of Argentina and the United States during the last 30 years of the nineteenth century, without IMF, suggests otherwise.

In the final analysis, it is probably a sobering thought to conclude that whatever reforms are made to the international financial architecture and however robust domestic financial systems are made, economists and policy-makers will still be dealing with financial crises 100 years hence.

NOTES

1. The author wishes to thank Lars Jonung, Mike Bordo and Barry Eichengreen for their help when writing this chapter. Chi Nguyen and Oi Yen Lam provided excellent research assistance.
2. Debt crises are also associated with financial crises but are not considered explicitly in this chapter.
3. A full chronology of the Asian crisis can be obtained from Nouriel Roubini's website http://www.rgemonitor.com/.

REFERENCES

Adalet, M. (2004), 'Fundamentals, capital flows and capital flight: the German banking crisis of 1931', unpub. PhD thesis, University of California, Berkeley.

Aghion, P., Bacchetta, P. and Banerjee, A.V. (1999), 'Capital markets and the instability of open economies', in P.R. Agénor, M. Miller, D. Vines and A. Weber (eds), *The Asian financial crisis: causes, contagion and consequences*, Cambridge: CUP.

Aghion, P., Bacchetta, P. and Banerjee, A.V. (2001), 'Currency crises and monetary policy in an economy with credit constraints', *European Economic Review*, 45.

Aghion, P., Bacchetta, P. and Banerjee, A.V. (2004), 'A corporate balance-sheet approach to currency crises', *Journal of Economic Theory*, 118.

Aldcroft, D.H. (1997), *Studies in the interwar European economy*, Aldershot: Ashgate.

Aldcroft, D.H. and Oliver, M.J. (1998), *Exchange rate regimes in the twentieth century*, Cheltenham, UK and Lyme, USA: Edward Elgar.

Aliber, R.Z. (1962), 'Speculation in the foreign exchanges: the European experience, 1919–1926', *Yale Economic Essays*, 2.

Athukorala, P.-C. (2003), 'Foreign direct investment in crisis and recovery: lessons from the 1997–1998 Asian crisis', *Australian Economic History Review*, 43.

Balderston, T. (1993), *The origins and course of the German economic crisis, 1923–1932*, Berlin: Haude and Spener.

Balderston, T. (1994), 'The banks and the gold standard in the German financial crisis of 1931', *Financial History Review*, 1.

Banerjee, A.V. (1992), 'A simple model of herd behavior', *Quarterly Journal of Economics*, 107, 797–817.

Bank for International Settlements (1935), *Fifth annual report, 1 April–31 March 1935*, Basle: Bank for International Settlements.

Basdevant, O. and Hall, S.G. (2002), 'The 1998 Russian crisis; could the exchange rate volatility have predicted it?', *Journal of Policy Modeling*, 24.

Bennett, E.W. (1962), *Germany and the diplomacy of the financial crisis*, Cambridge, MA: Harvard University Press.

Berg, A. (1999), 'The Asia crisis: causes, policy responses and outcomes', *IMF Working Paper*, WP/99/138.

Berg, A. and Pattillo, C. (1999), 'Predicting currency crises: the indicators approach and an alternative', *Journal of International Money and Finance*, 18.

Berg, A. and Pattillo, C. (2000), 'The challenges of predicting economic crises', *Economic Issues*, 22, IMF.

Bernanke, B. and James, H. (1991), 'The gold standard, deflation and financial crises in the Great Depression: an international comparison', in R. Glenn Hubbard (ed.), *Financial markets and financial crises*, Chicago, IL: University of Chicago Press.

Blanco, H. and Garber, P. (1986), 'Recurrent devaluation and speculative attacks on the Mexican peso', *Journal of Political Economy*, 94.

Bordo, M. (1985), 'Financial crises, banking crises, stock market crashes, and the money supply: some international evidence, 1870–1933', in F. Capie and G.E. Wood (eds), *Financial crises and the world banking system*, London: Macmillan.

Bordo, M. and Eichengreen, B. (1999), 'Is our current international economic environment unusually crisis prone?', in D. Gruen and L. Gower (eds), *Capital flows and the international financial system*, Sydney: Reserve Bank of Australia.

Bordo, M. and Schwartz, A. (1996), 'Why clashes between internal and external goals end in currency crisis, 1797–1994', *Open Economies Review*, 7.

Bordo, M. and Schwartz, A. (1999), 'Under what circumstances, past and present, have international rescues of countries in financial distress been successful?', *Journal of International Money and Finance*, 18.

Bordo, M. and Schwartz, A. (2000), 'Measuring real economic effects of bailouts: historical perspectives on how countries in financial distress have fared with and without bailouts', *Carnegie-Rochester Conference Series on Public Policy*, 53.

Bordo, M., Mizrach, B. and Schwartz, A.J. (1998), 'Real versus pseudo-international systemic risk: some lessons from history', *Review of Pacific Basin Financial Markets and Policies*, 1.

Bordo, M., Eichengreen, B., Klingebiel, D. and Martinez-Peri, M.S. (2001), 'Is the crisis problem growing more severe?', *Economic Policy*, 16.

Born, K.E. (1967), *Die deutsche Bankenkrise 1931: Finanzen und Politik*, Munich: Piper.

Boughton, J.M. (2001), *Silent revolution: the International Monetary Fund, 1979–1989*, Washington, DC: International Monetary Fund.

Branson, G. (1994), 'German reunification, the breakdown of the EMS, and the path to stage three', in D. Cobham (ed.), *European monetary upheavals*, Manchester: Manchester University Press.

Buchs, T. (1999), 'Financial crisis in the Russian Federation: are the Russians learning to tango?', *Economics of Transition*, 7.

Cagan, P. (1965), *Determinants and effects of changes in the stock of money, 1875–1960*, New York: Columbia University Press.

Calvo, G.A. (1998), 'Capital flows and capital-market crises: the simple economics of sudden stops', *Journal of Applied Economics*, 1.

Calvo, G.A. (2001), 'Capital markets and the exchange rate: with special reference to the dollarization debate in Latin America', *Journal of Money, Credit and Banking*, 33.

Calvo, G.A. and Mendoza, E.G. (1996), 'Mexico's balance-of-payments crisis: a chronicle of a death foretold', *Journal of International Economics*, 41.

Calvo, S. and Reinhart, C.M. (1996), 'Capital flows to Latin America: is there evidence of contagion effects?', in G.A. Calvo, M. Goldstein and E. Hochreitter (eds), *Private capital flows to emerging markets*, Washington, DC: Institute for International Economics.

Capie, F. (1995), 'Commercial banking in Britain between the wars', in C.H. Feinstein (ed.), *Banking, currency, and finance in Europe between the wars*, Oxford: Oxford University Press.

Caprio, G. and Klingebiel, D. (1997), 'Banking insolvency: bad luck, bad policy, or bad banking', in World Bank, *Annual World Bank conference on development economics 1996*, Washington, DC.

Caramazza, F., Ricci, L.A. and Salgado, R. (2004), 'International financial contagion in currency crises', *Journal of International Money and Finance*, 23.

Cerra, V. and Saxena, S.C. (2002), 'Contagion, monsoons and domestic turmoil in Indonesia's currency crisis', *Review of International Economics*, 10.

Cerra, V. and Saxena, S.C. (2003), 'Did output recover from the Asian crisis?', IMF Working Paper No. 03/48.

Chancellor, E. (1999), *Devil take the hindmost: a history of financial speculation*, London: Macmillan.

Chang, R. and Valesco, R. (2000a), 'Financial fragility and the exchange rate regime', *Journal of Economic Theory*, 92.

Chang, R. and Valesco, R. (2000b), 'Banks, debt maturity and financial crises', *Journal of International Economics*, 51.

Chapman, S.A. and Mulino, M. (2001), 'Explaining Russia's currency and financial crisis', *Economic Policy in Transitional Economies, MOCT-MOST*, 11.

Delong, J.B. (1999), 'Financial crises in the 1890s and the 1990s: must history repeat?', *Brookings Papers on Economic Activity*, 2.

Demirgüç-Kunt, A. and Detragiache, E. (1998), 'The determinants of banking crises in developing and developed countries', *IMF Staff Papers*, 45.

Diaz-Alejandro, C. (1985), 'Goodbye financial repression, hello financial crash', *Journal of Development Economics*, 19.

Dornbusch, R. and Werner, A. (1994), 'Mexico: stabilization, reform and no growth', *Brookings Papers on Economic Activity*, 1.

Dornbusch, R., Goldfajn, I. and Valdes, R.O. (1995), 'Currency crises and collapses', *Brookings Papers on Economic Activity*, 2.

Drees, B. and Pazarbasioglu, C. (1998), 'The Nordic banking crises: pitfalls in financial liberalization?', IMF *Occasional Paper*, No. 161.

Drummond, I. (1991), 'Why Canadian banks did not collapse in the 1930s', in H. James, H. Lindgren and A. Teichova (eds), *The role of banks in the interwar economy*, Cambridge: Cambridge University Press.

Edwards, S. (1999), 'On crisis prevention: lessons from Mexico and East Asia', in A. Harwood, and R.E. Litan and M. Pomerleano (eds), *Financial markets and development: the crisis in emerging markets*, Washington, DC: Brookings Institution Press.

Eichengreen, B. (1992), *Golden fetters: the gold standard and the Great Depression, 1919–1939*, Oxford: Oxford University Press.

Eichengreen, B. (1993), 'European monetary unification', *Journal of Economic Literature*, 31.

Eichengreen, B. (1996), *Globalizing capital: a history of the international monetary system*, Princeton, NJ: Princeton University Press.

Eichengreen, B. (1999), *Toward a new international financial architecture: a practical post-Asia agenda*, Washington, DC: Institute for International Economics.

Eichengreen, B. (2003a), 'Three generations of crises, three generations of crisis models', *Journal of International Money and Finance*, 22.

Eichengreen, B. (2003b), *Capital flows and crises*, Cambridge, MA: The MIT Press.

Eichengreen, B. and Bordo, M. (2003), 'Crises now and then: what lessons from the last era of financial globalization?', in P. Mizen (ed.), *Monetary history, exchange rates and financial markets, essays in honour of Charles Goodhart, volume two*, Cheltenham, UK and Northampton, MA, USA: Edward Elgar.

Eichengreen, B. and Hausmann, R. (1999), 'Exchange rates and financial fragility', in Federal Reserve Bank of Kansas City (ed.), *New challenges for monetary policy: a symposium*, Kansas City, MO: Federal Reserve Bank of Kansas City, available at http://www.kc.frb.org/publicat/sympos/1999/sym99prg.htm.

Eichengreen, B. and James, H. (2003), 'Monetary and financial reform in two eras of globalization', in M. Bordo, A. Taylor and J.G. Williamson (eds), *Globalization in historical perspective*, Chicago, IL: University of Chicago Press.

Eichengreen, B. and Jeanne, O. (2000), 'Currency crises and unemployment: sterling in 1931', in Paul Krugman (ed.), *Currency crises*, Chicago, IL: University of Chicago Press.

Eichengreen, B. and Portes, R. (1987), 'The anatomy of financial crises', in R. Portes and A.K. Swoboda (eds), *Threats to international financial stability*, Cambridge: Cambridge University Press.

Eichengreen, B. and Rose, A.K. (1999), 'Research summary', NBER website, 14 June 2006, available at http://www.nber.org/reporter/winter 99/eichengreen.html.

Eichengreen, B. and Rose, A.K. (2001), 'Staying afloat when the wind shifts: external factors and emerging-market banking crises', in G. Calvo, M. Obstfeld and R. Dornbusch (eds), *Money, capital mobility, and trade: essays in honor of Robert Mundell*, Cambridge, MA: MIT Press.

Eichengreen, B. and Rose, A.K. (2003), 'Does it pay to defend against a speculative attack?', in Michael P. Dooley and Jeffrey A. Frankel (eds), *Managing currency crises in emerging markets*, Chicago, IL: The University of Chicago Press.

Eichengreen, B. and Wyplosz, C. (1993), 'The unstable EMS', *Brookings Papers on Economic Activity*, 1.

Eichengreen, B., Rose, A.K. and Wyplosz, C. (1996), 'Contagious currency crises: first tests', *Scandinavian Journal of Economics*, 98.

Englund, P. and Vihriälä, V. (2005), 'Financial crises in developed economies: the cases of Sweden and Finland', in Lars Jonung and Pentti Vartia (eds), *Crises, macroeconomic performance and economic policies in Finland and Sweden in the 1990s: a comparative approach*, Cambridge: Cambridge University Press.

Feinstein, C. and Watson, K. (1995), 'Private international flows in Europe in the interwar period', in C.H. Feinstein (ed.), *Banking, currency, and finance in Europe between the wars*, Oxford: Oxford University Press.

Feinstein, C.H., Temin, P. and Toniolo, G. (1995), 'International economic organization: banking, finance and trade in Europe between the wars', in C.H. Feinstein (ed.), *Banking, currency, and finance in Europe between the wars*, Oxford: Oxford University Press.

Feinstein, C.H., Temin, P. and Toniolo, G. (1997), *The European economy between the Wars*, Oxford: Oxford University Press.

Feis, H. (1930), *Europe, the world's banker*, New Haven, CT: Yale University Press.

Fishlow, A. (1985), 'Lessons from the past: capital markets during the 19th century and the interwar period', *International Organization*, 39.

Flood, R. and Marion, N. (1999), 'Perspectives on the recent currency crisis literature', *International Journal of Finance and Economics*, 4.

Flood, R., Garber, P. and Kramer, C. (1996), 'Collapsing exchange rate regimes: another linear example', *Journal of International Economics*, 41.

Frankel, J. and Rose, A.K. (1996), 'Currency crashes in emerging markets: an empirical treatment', *Journal of International Economics*, 41.

Frankel, J. and Wei, S.-J. (2004), 'Managing macroeconomic crises: policy lessons', in J. Aizenman and B. Pinto (eds), *Economic volatility and crises: a policy-oriented guide*, Washington, DC: World Bank.

Friedman, M. and Schwartz, A. (1963), *Monetary trends in the United States 1867–1960*, New York: NBER.

Fries, S., Raiser, M. and Stern, N. (1999), 'Stress test for reforms: transition and East Asian "contagion"', *The Economics of Transition*, 7.

Furman, J. and Stiglitz, J.E. (1998), 'Economic crises: evidence and insights from East Asia', *Brookings Papers on Economic Activity*, 2.

Gil-Diaz, F. (1998), 'The origin of Mexico's 1994 financial crisis', *Cato Journal*, 17.

Glick, R. and Rose, A.K. (1999), 'Contagion and trade: why are currency crises regional?', *Journal of International Money and Finance*, 18.

Goodhart, C. and Delargy, P.J.R. (1998), 'Financial crises: plus ça change, plus c'est la même chose', *International Finance*, 1.

Halme, L. (1999), 'Banking regulation and supervision: a legal policy study of risk taking by savings banks', *Bank of Finland Studies*, E:15, Helsinki.

Hamilton, J.D. (1988), 'The role of the international gold standard in propagating the Great Depression', *Contemporary Policy Issues*, 6.

Hansen, P.H. (1991), 'From growth to crisis. the Danish banking system from 1850 to the interwar years', *Scandinavian Economic History Review*, 39.

Hansen, P. H. (1995), 'Banking crises and lenders of last resort: Denmark in the 1920s and the 1990s', in Y. Cassis, G. Feldman and U. Olsson (eds), *The evolution of financial institutions and market in twentieth-century Europe*, Aldershot: Ashgate.

Hansen, P.H. (2001), 'Bank regulation in Denmark from 1880 to World War Two: public interests and private interests', *Business History*, 43.

Hanson, P. (1999), 'The Russian economic crisis and the future of Russian economic reform', *Europe-Asia Studies*, 51.

Hanson, P. (2003), 'The Russian economic recovery: do four years of growth tell us that the fundamentals have changed?', *Europe-Asia Studies*, 55.

Hardach, G. (1995), 'Banking in Germany, 1918–1939', in C.H. Feinstein (ed.), *Banking, currency, and finance in Europe between the wars*, Oxford: Oxford University Press.

Heckscher, E.F. (1930), *Sweden, Norway, Denmark and Iceland in the World War*, New York: Oxford University Press.

Heiskanen, R. (1993), 'The banking crisis in the Nordic countries', *Kansallis Economic Review*, 2.

HM Treasury (1964), 'Devaluation', 15 October, Kew, UK: The National Archive, T171/758.

Honkapohja, S. and Koskela. E. (1999), 'The economic crisis of the 1990s in Finland', *Economic Policy*, 14.

Huffman, W.E. and Lothian, J.R. (1984), 'The gold standard and the transmission of business cycles', in M.D. Bordo and A.J. Schwartz (eds), *A retrospective on the classical gold standard, 1821–1931,* Chicago, IL: University of Chicago Press.

Hutchinson, M.M. (2002), 'European banking distress and EMU: institutional and macroeconomic risks', *Scandinavian Journal of Economics*, 104.

Hutchinson, M.M. (2003), 'A cure worse than the disease? Currency crises and the output costs of IMF-supported stabilization programs', in Michael P. Dooley and Jeffrey A. Frankel (eds), *Managing currency crises in emerging markets*, Chicago: University of Chicago Press.

IMF (1996), 'IMF approves three-year EFF credit for the Russian Federation', Press Release Number 96/13, http://www.imf.org/external/np/sec/pr/1996/PR9613.htm, accessed 10 February 2004.

IMF (1998), *World economic outlook*, May, Washington, DC: IMF.

IMF (2003), 'Russia rebounds', IMF Economic Forum, 11 December, http://www.imf.org/external/np/tr/2003/tr 031211.htm, accessed 10 February 2004.

Ito, T., Ogawa, E. and Sasaki, Y.N. (1998), 'How did the dollar peg fail in Asia?', *Journal of Japanese and International Economics*, 12.

James, H. (1986), *The German slump: politics and economics, 1924–1936*, Oxford: Oxford University Press.

James, H. (1992), 'Financial flows across frontiers during the interwar depression', *Economic History Review*, 45.

Johnsen, T., Reve T., Steigum, E., Sættem, F., Meyer, C. and Høyland, E. (1992), *Bankkrisen i Norge*, SNF-rapport 29/92, Centre for Research in Economics and Business Administration (SNF), Bergen.

Jonung, L. and Fregert, K. (2004), 'Deflation dynamics in Sweden: perceptions, expectations and adjustment during the deflations of 1921–23 and 1931–1933' in R.C.K. Burdekin and P.L. Siklos (eds), *Deflation: current and historical perspectives*, Cambridge: Cambridge University Press.

Jonung, L. and Stymne, J. (1997), 'The great regime shift: asset markets and economic activity in Sweden, 1985–93', in F. Capie and G. Wood (eds), *Asset prices and the real economy*, London: Macmillan.

Jonung, L., Kiander, J. and Vartia, P. (2005), 'The great crisis in Finland and Sweden: the macrodynamics of boom, bust and recovery 1985–2000', in Lars Jonung and Pentti Vartia (eds), *Crises, macroeconomic performance and economic policies in Finland and Sweden in the 1990s: a comparative approach*, Cambridge: Cambridge University Press.

Kamin, S.B. (1999), 'The current international financial crisis: how much is new?', *Journal of International Money and Finance*, 18.

Kaminsky, G.L. and Reinhart, C.M. (1999), 'The twin crises: the causes of banking and balance-of-payments problems', *American Economic Review*, 89.

Kaminsky, G.L. and Reinhart, C.M. (2000), 'On crises, contagion, and confusion, *Journal of International Economics*, 51.

Kaminsky, G.L., Lizondo, S. and Reinhart, C. (1998), 'Leading indicators of currency crises', *IMF Staff Papers*, 45.

Kaminsky, G.L., Lyons, R.K. and Schmukler, S.L. (2004), 'Managers, investors, and crises: mutual fund strategies in emerging markets', *Journal of International Economics*, 64.

Kaminsky, G.L., Reinhart, C.M. and Végh, C.A. (2003), 'The unholy trinity of financial contagion', *Journal of Economic Perspectives*, 17.

Kane, E.J. and Klingebiel, D. (2002), 'Alternatives to blanket guarantees for containing a systemic crisis', paper presented at WB/IMF/FRB seminar on *Policy Challenges for the Financial Sector in the Context of Globalization*, 5–7 June 2002, Washington, DC. Available at http://www2.bc.edu/%7Ekaneeb/BLANKET%20GUARANTEE%20PAPER.doc, accessed 10 April 2004.

Kaufmann, G. (1994), 'Bank contagion: a review of the theory and evidence', *Journal of Financial Services Research*, 8.

Kindleberger, C.P. (2000), *Manias, panics and crashes – a history of financial crises*, 4th edn, Chichester: John Wiley.

Knutsen, S. (1991), 'From expansion to panic and crash, the Norwegian banking system and its customers, 1913–1924', *Scandinavian Economic History Review*, 39.

Knutsen, S. (2001), 'Financial fragility or information asymmetry? – the inter-war banking crisis in Norway', 5th EBHA Conference, Norway.

Knutsen, S., Lange, E. and Nordvik, H.W., (1998), *Mellom næringsliv og politikk. Kredittkassen i vekst og kriser 1918–1998*, Oslo: Universitetsforlaget.

Kokko, A. and Suzuki, K. (2005), 'The Nordic and Asian crises – common causes, different outcomes', in Lars Jonung and Pentti Vartia (eds), *Crises, macroeconomic performance and economic policies in Finland and Sweden in the 1990s: a comparative approach*, Cambridge: Cambridge University Press.

Krugman, P. (1979), 'A model of balance of payments crises', *Journal of Money, Credit and Banking*, 11.

Krugman, P. (1994), 'The myth of Asia's miracle', *Foreign Affairs*, 73, November/December.

Krugman, P. (1999), 'Balance sheets, the transfer problem, and financial crises', *International Tax and Public Finance*, 6.

Larsson, M. (1991), 'State, banks and industry in Sweden, with some reference to the Scandinavian countries', in H. James, H. Lindgren and A. Teichova (eds), *The role of banks in the interwar economy*, Cambridge: Cambridge University Press.

League of Nations (1937), *Money and banking 1936/37*, Geneva: League of Nations.

Lybeck, Johan A. (1994), *Facit av finanskrisen*, Stockholm: SNS Förlag.

Maskooki, K. (2002), 'Mexico's 1994 peso crisis and its aftermath', *European Business Review*, 14.

McKinnon, R. (1997), *The rules of the game*, Cambridge, MA: MIT Press.

McKinnon, R.I. and Pill, H. (1996), 'Credible liberalizations and international capital flows: the "overborrowing syndrome"' in T. Ito and A.O. Krueger (eds), *Financial deregulation and integration in East Asia*, Chicago, IL: University of Chicago Press.

McKinnon, R.I. and Pill, H. (1997), 'Credible economic liberalizations and overborrowing', *American Economic Review*, 87.

McKinnon, R.I. and Pill, H. (1998), 'The overborrowing syndrome: are East Asian economies different?', in R. Glick (ed.), *Exchange rates and capital flows in the Pacific Basin*, Cambridge, Cambridge University Press.

Meigs, A.J. (1997), 'Mexican monetary lessons', *Cato Journal*, 17.

Meigs, A.J. (1998), 'Lessons for Asia from Mexico', *Cato Journal*, 17.

Meltzer, A.H. (1976), 'Monetary and other explanations of the Great Depression', *Journal of Monetary Economics*, 2.

Middleton, R. (2002) 'Struggling with the impossible: sterling, the balance of payments and British economic policy, 1949–72', in A. Arnon and W.L. Young (eds), *The open economy macromodel: past, present and future*, Boston, MA: Kluwer Academic Press.

Mishkin, F.S. (2003), 'Financial policies and the prevention of financial crises in emerging market countries', in M. Feldstein (ed.), *Economic and Financial Crises in Emerging Market Countries*, Chicago, IL: University of Chicago Press.

Moggeridge, D.E. (1986), 'Comment on Anna Schwartz's chapter', in F. Capie and G.E. Wood (eds), *Financial crises and the world banking system*, London: Macmillan.

Montes, M.F. and Popov, V. (1999), *The Asian crisis turns global*, Singapore: Institute of Southeast Asian Studies.

Neal, L. and Weidenmier, M. (2003), 'Crises in the global economy from tulips to today: contagion and consequences', in M. Bordo, A. Taylor and J.G. Williamson (eds), *Globalization in historical perspective*, Chicago, IL: University of Chicago Press.

Nordvik, H.W. (1992), 'Bankkrise, bankstruktur og bankpolitikk i Norge I mellomkrigstiden', *Historisk tidsskrift*, 71.

Nordvik, H.W. (1995), 'Norwegian banking in the inter-war period: a Scandinavian perspective', in C.H. Feinstein (ed.), *Banking, currency, and finance in Europe between the wars*, Oxford: Oxford University Press.

Obstfeld, M. (1994), 'The logic of currency crises', *Cahiers Economiques et Monétaires*, Banque de France, 43.

Obstfeld, M. (1996), 'Models of currency crises with self-fulfilling features', *European Economic Review*, 40.

OECD (1995), *Economic outlook*, Paris: OECD.

Oliver, M.J. (2006), 'Civilising international monetary systems', in Brett Bowden and Leonard Seabrooke (eds), *Global standards of market civilization*, London: Routledge.

Oliver, M.J. and Hamilton, A. (2007), 'Downhill from devaluation: the battle for sterling, 1967–1972', *Economic History Review*, 60.

Padoa-Schioppa, T. (1988), 'The European Monetary System: a long-term view', in F. Giavazzi, S. Micossi and M. Miller (eds), *The European Monetary System*, Cambridge: Cambridge University Press.

Park, Y.C. (1996), 'East Asian liberalization, bubbles, and the challenges from China', *Brookings Papers on Economic Activity*, 2.

Perotti, E. (2001), 'Lessons from the Russian meltdown: the economics of soft legal constraints', *International Finance*, 5.

Radelet, S. and Sachs, J. (1998), 'The East Asian financial crisis: diagnosis, remedies, prospects', *Brookings Papers on Economic Activity*, 1.

Radelet, S. and Sachs, J. (2000), 'The onset of the East Asian financial crisis', in P. Krugman (ed.), *Currency crises*, Chicago: University of Chicago.

Rodrik, D. (1998). 'Who needs capital-account convertibility?', in *Should the IMF pursue capital account convertibility?*, Princeton Essays in International Finance 207, International Economics Section, Princeton University.

Rose, A.K. (2001), 'Discussion', *Economic Policy*, 16.

Rose, A.K. and Svensson, L.E.O. (1994), 'European exchange rate credibility before the fall', *European Economic Review*, 38.

Sachs, J., Tornell, A. and Velasco, A. (1996), 'The Mexican peso crisis; sudden death or death foretold?', *Journal of International Economics*, 41.

Salant, S. and Henderson, D. (1978), 'Market anticipations of government policies and the price of gold', *Journal of Political Economy*, 86.

Scharfstein, D. and Stein, J. (1990), 'Herd behavior and investment', *American Economic Review*, 80, 465–79.

Schwartz, A. (1986), 'Real and pseudo-financial crises', in F. Capie and G.E. Wood (eds), *Financial crises and the world banking system*, London: Macmillan.

Steigum, E. (2005), 'Financial deregulation with a fixed exchange rate: lessons from Norway's boom-bust cycle and banking crisis', in Lars Jonung and Pentti Vartia (eds), *Crises, macroeconomic performance and economic policies in Finland and Sweden in the 1990s: a comparative approach*, Cambridge: Cambridge University Press.

Tai, C.-S. (2004), 'Can banks be a source of contagion during the 1997 Asian crisis?', *Journal of Banking and Finance*, 28.

Temin, P. (1989), *Lessons from the Great Depression*, Cambridge, MA: MIT Press.

United Nations Economic Commission of Europe (1998), *Economic survey of Europe 1998*, Number 1 & Number 2, New York and Geneva.

Van Rijckeghem, C. and Weder, B. (2001), 'Sources of contagion: is it finance or trade?', *Journal of International Economics*, 54.

Van Rijckeghem, C. and Weder, B. (2003), 'Spillovers through banking centers: a panel data analysis of bank flows', *Journal of International Money and Finance*, 22 (4).

Vanthemsche, G. (1991), 'State, banks and industry in Belgium and the Netherlands, 1919–1939', in H. James, H. Lindgren and A. Teichova (eds), *The role of banks in the interwar economy*, Cambridge: Cambridge University Press.

Velasco, A. (1987), 'Financial crises and balance of payments crises: a simple model of the Southern Cone experience', *Journal of Development Economics*, 27.

Vihriälä, V. (1997), 'Banks and the Finnish credit cycle 1986–95', *Bank of Finland Studies*, E:7, Helsinki.

Walters, A.A. (1988), 'Money on a roller-coaster', *The Independent*, 14 July.

Weber, F. (1995), 'From imperial to regional banking: the Austrian banking system, 1918–1938', in C.H. Feinstein (ed.), *Banking, currency, and finance in Europe between the wars*, Oxford: Oxford University Press.

Westin, P. (1999), 'One year after the crisis: what went right?', *Russian Economic Trends*, 10 September.

White, L.J. (1995), 'Financial infrastructure and policy reform in developing Asia', in S.N. Zahid (ed.), *Financial sector development in Asia*, Hong Kong: Oxford University Press.

Wicker, E. (1996), *The banking panics of the Great Depression*, New York: Cambridge University Press.

Woo, W.T., Carleton, P.D. and Rosario, B.P. (2000), 'The unorthodox origins of the Asian currency crisis – evidence from logit estimation', *ASEAN Economic Bulletin*, 17.

Wood, G. (1999), 'Great crashes in history: have they lessons for today?', *Oxford Review of Economic Policy*, 15.

World Bank (1993), *The East Asian miracle*, New York: Oxford University Press.

7.   Stock market crashes
Geoffrey E. Wood[1]

There is, unsurprisingly, no formal, rigorous definition of what comprises a stock market crash, as opposed to a fall, decline, or, to borrow a broker's term, correction. The fall in stock prices in the United States in 1929 is regarded universally as a crash, but it owes this to the vividness of J.K. Galbraith's writing and to his choosing of book titles – his 1955 book was called the *The Great Crash*. Because that stock market fall was so large, and because of its dramatic economic aftermath, that episode will undoubtedly figure in this chapter. It will, indeed, be a core episode, as the period has been thoroughly studied, and thus provides a good basis to evaluate the connection between market crashes and the subsequent behaviour of the economy.

Of course there have been, as goes without saying so far as readers of the financial pages are concerned, other sharp market falls. Those examined here, in addition to 1929 in the United States, are London in 1914, the behaviour of the London market over the period 1929–31 and East Asia in 1999/2000. 1940 and 1974 in London are also touched on, but only briefly.

The aim, in other words, is not to be comprehensive – impossible in the absence of agreement about what comprises a 'crash' – but rather to focus on some major individual episodes that will help clarify the extent to which and way in which stock market crashes are 'economic disasters'.

The structure of the chapter is chronological, except where, as in 1929 for example, events were close to simultaneous. Then the choice is dictated by the nature of the interconnection between the episodes. The chapter will conclude with a summing up of what the episodes suggest about the economic significance of major stock market declines.

LONDON 1914

The financial problems in London in 1914 were associated with the outbreak of war. That does not mean that it is impossible to generalize from the events; rather, it means that if there seem to be any effects on the economy, one would have to consider how to disentangle them from those of the war. This section therefore starts by laying out and analysing the facts on the 1914 crisis in London.

Although the Balkan Wars had created much political unrest in Europe, international tension was not noticeably higher in June 1914 than it had been at any time since the Agadir crisis in 1911. There had been 40 years of growth since the Franco-Prussian War and nearly a century since any general European war. In Britain, the chief political concern centred on the civil unrest in Ireland. Then, on 29 June, tension increased dramatically with the assassination of the heir to the Austrian throne. The gravity of this event was not generally realized until a month later when Austria sent its ultimatum to Serbia on 24 July. From that moment, war between Austria and Serbia appeared inevitable. This, together with the fear that hostilities would spread throughout Europe, produced a major financial crisis.

The financial implications of war were first felt on the world's stock exchanges. Heavy selling in internationally traded securities caused prices to plummet. As political tension mounted, sales increased and this in turn began to produce erratic fluctuations in the foreign exchanges beyond the normal export/import gold points. Within a matter of days one bourse after another ceased trading, exchange rates became purely notional (no transactions were executed) and the whole system of international remittance, and hence international credit, was frozen.

In Britain the financial consequences of a pending European conflict placed the London Stock Exchange under great pressure during the last two weeks of July. Of even greater concern, however (owing to Britain's position as the great international short-term creditor) was the foreign exchange situation. It was becoming apparent that foreign borrowers would be unable to remit in due time to the London acceptance houses. With the declaration of war between Austria and Serbia on Tuesday, 28 July a rush for liquidity began. The banks started to call in loans from the Stock Exchange and the discount market, further weakening the former and forcing the latter to the Bank of England for assistance. The bank rate was raised from 3 per cent to 4 per cent on Thursday, 30 July. On the mobilization of German, Russian and French troops the financial situation deteriorated rapidly. On Friday, 31 July the London Stock Exchange followed the example of the foreign bourses and closed its doors. The bank rate was raised to 8 per cent and then to the crisis level of 10 per cent the following day. Also on the Friday and Saturday, the financial situation caused a panic among the general public, largely triggered by the banks, which, fearing an internal drain on their gold reserves, refused to pay out gold to their customers.

On Sunday, 2 August military action escalated with the formal declaration of war between Russia and Germany. For Britain the financial implications of this were postponed, because Monday, 2 August was a Bank

Holiday. Clearly, however, the crisis could not be left to run its course. To provide further room for manoeuvre the Bank Holiday was extended for three days, and to relieve the acceptance houses from their immediate difficulties a moratorium on bills of exchange was proclaimed. Britain declared war on Germany at midday on Wednesday, 5 August 1914.

By 6 August the main measures to deal with the crisis had been decided. A general moratorium was proclaimed, the 1844 Bank Act was suspended, and the bank rate was reduced. Treasury notes were to be issued. When the banks reopened on Friday, 7 August fears of an internal currency crisis proved unfounded, and the bank rate was further reduced to 5 per cent the following day. Problems in the bill market, however, remained and had to be dealt with by direct government assistance, plans for which were announced on 13 August and 5 September.

The 'crisis' itself had thus come and gone within a matter of days. Although the events of the crisis and the measures introduced to deal with them were not without their repercussions, the main focus of attention shifted to the central issue of how to finance the war.

Describing the financial crisis at the beginning of the First World War, Withers (1915) writes, 'it came upon us like a thunderbolt from a clear sky. . .no credit system could have stood up to the events', a statement that reflected the sentiments of most contemporary financiers and journalists.

The failure of remittance was the root cause of the crisis. The normal channels of remittance, namely the shipment of goods or gold, the sale of securities and the discounting of bills of exchange, were all rendered inoperative by the outbreak of war. The shipment of goods, besides being too slow to help out in a crisis, became prohibitively expensive because of rising insurance costs and also extremely hazardous due to enemy action. Gold shipments were further hampered by the announcement of gold export embargoes in a number of countries. Although the beginning of the crisis was marked by heavy security sales, the closure of all principal stock exchanges rendered further sales impossible, while the most common means of remittance, the granting of new bills of exchange, was frustrated by London's unwillingness to extend fresh credits. In addition to these factors, some foreign clients, under the protection of moratoria in their own countries, postponed repayment, while after 5 August sums owed by enemy debtors had to be written off indefinitely. In addition, the movement in foreign exchange rates, which, with the exception of France, all swung in Britain's favour, made it extremely expensive for foreign clients to remit. For one reason or another, therefore, even solvent foreign debtors were prevented from remitting what they owed, placing those sections of the London money market that financed or guaranteed such credit in danger of insolvency.

During July, as relations between Austria and Serbia deteriorated, so the probability of war increased. Once this outcome became more certain, so people could begin to calculate and thus prepare themselves for the financial risks involved. This they did by selling vast quantities of internationally traded securities. On Friday, 24 July Austria's ultimatum to Serbia produced something of a panic. A large number of investors was reported as giving orders to 'sell at any price' and this produced the largest fall in international quotations since 1895.

By Thursday, 30 July all the principal bourses with the exception of London, New York and the official Paris Parquet had been forced to close. Their closure brought a torrent of foreign sales on the London Stock Exchange where, of course, it still remained possible to obtain sterling through the sale of securities. The foreign exchanges moved in Britain's favour, suggesting that investors preferred to hold their sale proceeds in sterling rather than convert them into their own currencies. During the last week of July the volume of sales on the London Stock Exchange caused prices to plummet. Between 20 July and 30 July the value of 387 representative securities fell by a record £187 992 000 or some 5.6 per cent. A fall of 5.6 per cent in just ten days was very substantial when compared with the normal monthly movement in quotations (prices fell by just 0.67 per cent over the previous 30 days), and came at a time when the market was already depressed.

The London Stock Exchange began to show signs that it could not take the strain. Wednesday, 29 July was settlement day and by tacit agreement jobbers in every part of the exchange declined to deal and in some cases refused even to quote prices. The previous day had seen one failure and Wednesday witnessed seven more. On Thursday, 30 July the failure of an important firm, Messrs Derenburg & Co., (which was largely concerned with business in Germany), brought home to members of the Stock Exchange the gravity of the situation. The Stock Exchange Committee met on Thursday afternoon and again the following morning to discuss what measures should be taken to prevent further failures. They decided to take the unprecedented step of closing the Stock Exchange on Friday, 31 July. This marked the climax of the crisis in the stock market.

Never before had the Stock Exchange been closed since it was founded in 1773. Leading authorities, such as Withers (1915), Hawtrey (1933), Clapham (1944), Brown (1940) and Sayers (1976) have tended to attribute the closure of the London Stock Exchange solely to the flood of sales from abroad. However, as Keynes (1914b) observed, the most immediate difficulties arose because of the liabilities of foreigners to the London Stock Exchange arising from previous purchases. (He also blamed what he termed the 'disgraceful' action of the joint stock banks.) British stockbrokers were owed money by foreign clients on whose behalf they had purchased securities. These sums were expected to be paid at the end of a 19-day account, which fell due at the end of July. However, the closing of the foreign bourses, the imposition of complete or partial moratoria in other countries, and finally the news that the Paris settlement would be postponed on 31 July, made such debts from foreign clients irrecoverable for the time being. Thus Keynes saw the cause of the problems in the stock market as identical to those in the bill market, namely, the inability of foreign clients to remit.

The failure of remittance in the stock market placed many brokers in a difficult position since they themselves had borrowed funds in order to finance the purchase of securities for their clients, using those securities as collateral. The total amount of loans outstanding was reported to be £81 million, of which £40 million had been lent by the joint stock banks, a further £20 million from other British and foreign banks and the remainder from the non-banking sector. Most of this money had been advanced 'on margin', that is, collateral had been deposited and had to be maintained at approximately 10 per cent to 20 per cent above the market value of the loan. The rapid decline in security values during the last ten days of July eroded this margin, and hence the banks began either to call in loans or to ask for more margin. Brokers were forced to sell some of their less 'gilt-edged' securities. This depressed prices further, not only of the stocks sold but of all stocks and so the process went on. The banks therefore by calling in loans undoubtedly weakened the stock market further and it was for this reason that Keynes and other contemporaries, together with some subsequent researchers such as de Cecco (1974), criticized the banks for their behaviour.

In connection with their operations in the London money market the banks again came under attack, this time for calling in money lent to the discount market. To understand the position it is necessary to draw a distinction between the acceptance houses who guarantee bills of exchange but do not advance any capital, and the banks and discount houses who, on the basis of those guarantees, do actually advance the capital. To finance the discounting of bills the banks employ their depositors' funds, while the discount houses, in addition to their own funds, employ money borrowed from the banks at call or short notice.

At the end of July 1914 the value of outstanding bills in London was approximately £350 million, of which £3–4 million fell due each day. The failure of international remittance rendered a large proportion of this total irrecoverable from foreign clients. This immediately affected the acceptance houses who, having guaranteed bills of exchange, were ultimately liable to meet them on maturity. The banks, concerned about their liquidity position, began to call in loans from the bill brokers, who, in turn, followed the traditional course and sought assistance from the Bank of England.

The banks were chastized for forcing the market to the Bank of England. Keynes (1914a, 471) says they should have shown greater consideration for the bill brokers and had a greater regard for the country's reserve position. De Cecco (1974, 132) goes even further, arguing that 'the banks used the 1914 crisis as an occasion to ruin the Inner Circle of the international business'. De Cecco, however, cites no evidence to support his contention and indeed it hardly seems tenable given the facts, for if the acceptance houses had stopped payment the discount houses would have followed suit and the whole burden of the crisis would have fallen on the banks.

While the banks as a whole may, from a macroeconomic perspective, have aggravated the financial crisis in London, their behaviour can certainly be justified at the microeconomic level. As Withers (1915), Sayers (1976) and Morgan (1962) all separately point out, if their liquidity position is taken into account then the banks had good reason to call in loans from the stock and discount markets, withdraw gold held at the Bank of England and refuse gold to their depositors. That much of the criticism levied at the banks was unjustified was ultimately accepted by Keynes ([1921] 1971, 633). He then wrote, 'imperfect knowledge caused me to describe the action of the Clearing Banks, as distinguished from some other banks, with less than fairness'.

The banks' chief liabilities are, of course, their customer accounts, the meeting of which is essential for survival. To meet their immediate liabilities the banks hold a variety of more or less liquid assets. Next to cash in hand and at the Bank of England, the banks' most liquid resources are money at call or short notice, bills discounted and loans and advances. In 1914, this last item included some £40 million lent directly to the Stock Exchange by the joint stock banks and a further £250 million lent against stock exchange securities.

While the banks were expecting heavy withdrawals from their depositors, a large proportion of their assets had become illiquid or of doubtful value during the last week of July. The fall in security prices had reduced the value of collateral held against loans while stockbrokers, unable to obtain funds from foreign clients, were in no position to repay the banks what they owed. The subsequent closure of the Stock Exchange prevented the banks from selling any of their securities and effectively locked up most of their longer-term investments. The failure of international remittance rendered their most valued asset, the bill of exchange (some 9 per cent of total assets), illiquid. This, incidentally, hit the banks on both sides of their balance sheet since they had also accepted bills of exchange (some £69 million) and were therefore ultimately liable to meet them on maturity. Given this increase in immediate liabilities and reduction in liquid assets, it was not unreasonable of the banks to mobilize their remaining resources. Expecting the demand

for cash to increase, individual banks were following normal banking practice by withdrawing cash held at the Bank of England and calling in short-
term loans. In the aggregate, however, each bank pursuing such a policy
aggravated the overall financial difficulties in London.

Since the closure of the Stock Exchange, limited trading had been
conducted on the street markets. Prices gradually began to rise and by
December were approaching pre-crisis values. On this basis it was decided
to reopen the Stock Exchange on 4 January 1915, subject to certain trading
restrictions designed to close the market to the enemy. The reopening of the
Stock Exchange effectively marked the end of the financial crisis in
London.

The 1914 financial crisis was unique in the sense that it was a war-related
crisis but this does not prevent some general conclusions from being
reached. Perhaps the most significant legacy of the episode was the realization of how effective intervention could be in redressing a crisis of
confidence. The 1914 financial crisis differed from previous crises in that the
traditional methods of redress, namely raising the bank rate and suspend-
ing the 1844 Bank Act, had little effect in resolving the difficulties encountered in 1914. The growth and complexity of international finance
demanded new methods. The closure of the Stock Exchange, the imposition of a moratorium to prevent wide-scale bankruptcy and the issue of
Treasury notes to meet internal currency demands were all innovations for
Britain.

It might be said that little can be generalized from the 1914 stock market
episode, since its cause was so unusual and its aftermath, war, affects all
subsequent economic data. But that issue is taken up later, for, as will
emerge, comparative analysis of all the episodes considered here is very
useful. The next London 'crash' was in 1929.

LONDON IN 1929

The behaviour of the British stock market in 1929 was admittedly not a
'crash' – rather it was a gradual but very substantial decline. The economy
reached a cyclical peak in the middle of 1929, and its next trough came in
1932. The following upswing then lasted until 1937. From the 1929 peak to
the 1932 trough, real GDP fell by 6 per cent – a very mild recession by the
standards of those years. (Unemployment, it should be remarked, tells a
different story.)

How did the stock market behave? From a base of 100 in 1924 the market
peaked at 149 at the beginning of 1929. In September the index was at 144.
The low point came in June 1932, when the index reached 73. This, an

approximate fall of 50 per cent, is manifestly substantial. But it was not a crash. Such declines over a period of about three years were not unknown then (and are not now).

Why did the London market decline? There was nervousness with the return of a labour government in 1929. But the majority was small, and, within the labour party in parliament, most were what might be termed no more than moderately socialist. Nerves were not strained for long over the government. Much more alarming was a financial scandal, which broke in September 1929.

Clarence C. Hatry had for some years been a prominent financier and company promoter, particularly active during the post-First World War boom. Doubts developed about his business. The Committee of the Stock Exchange suspended dealings in shares in the Hatry group on 21 September 1929. The accountants Price Waterhouse investigated the group's affairs. Hatry resigned from the board of London Assurance and, on 23 September, it was reported that he and others were being charged with conspiracy to defraud. A number of brokers in both London and the country lost substantially through orders they had executed for the Hatry group. Confidence was understandably shaken, and fears spread to Amsterdam, Berlin and, it is often claimed, New York.

The market was thus in a fragile state. To this nervousness was added monetary tightness. The monetary base fell in the last quarter in 1928, and in three quarters in 1929. A broad measure of money, M3, started to fall in late 1928 and continued doing so throughout the first half of 1929.

Interest rates tell a similar story of monetary stringency. The Treasury Bill rate had been steady around 4.25 per cent in 1927, started a gentle climb in 1928, in February 1929 stood at 5.2 per cent, and in September was just over 6.1 per cent. The bank rate behaved likewise. It stood at 4.5 per cent in 1928, was raised early in 1929, and had reached 6.5 per cent, its peak in that cycle, in September 1929.

Now, as has already been remarked, the stock market declined, albeit substantially, rather then 'crashed'. The episode is nevertheless important, for, as will have been noticed from the above narrative, the movements of the stock market and the economy paralleled each other, 1929 being the peak and 1932 the trough for both. But again, we for the moment defer discussion of causality, and move to a much more dramatic episode.

THE GREAT CRASH, 1929

The Great Stock Market Crash of 1929 is of the greatest importance, and not only because of the subsequent economic contraction in the United

States. There is reason to believe that it also influenced all subsequent work on financial crashes and banking crises. For without that event, it seems likely that more heed would have been paid to the *lack* of connection between crashes and subsequent crises and recessions. But this point is developed further, and related to other episodes, below.

New York stock prices (as measured by the S&P90) reached their peak of 254 on 7 September 1929. There were then four weeks of uneventful decline to 228 on 4 October, after which the index climbed to 245 on 10 October. Decline turned into panic on 23 October. On 24 October, the index fell to 162, and about 16.5 million shares were traded – compared with a September daily average of just over 4 million. (After a brief recovery the index continued down, reaching its low in 1931.)

Did this crash have any direct effects on the economy? It is hard to make it the *culprit* for the downturn, for a cyclical peak occurred in August, before the peak of the market and well before the dramatic market fall.[2] Can it be blamed for the *severity* of the 1930s Depression? Some authors have claimed that it did at the least contribute to that severity, changing the atmosphere to one of gloom and making consumers and business cautious and reluctant to spend.[3] (Hansen 1932; Schumpeter 1939; Gordon 1952; Romer 1990).

Consistent with this claim, there was a decline in velocity (of M2). The velocity fall (of 13 per cent, 1929–30) was, however, in size only second-equal among the seven velocity falls between 1907–08 and 1929–30. The fall in 1913–14 was of the same size, and that of 1920–21 was 15 per cent. A 13 per cent fall in velocity, unless offset by a sustained monetary expansion, is nonetheless bound to be associated with a fall in nominal income. Unfortunately, the stock market crash had no *sustained* monetary consequences. There was a scramble to liquidate securities. This was accommodated by a substantial increase in loans to brokers and dealers by New York city banks. They were able to provide this accommodation because the Federal Reserve Bank of New York both opened its discount window to the banks and bought some $160 million of government securities in the market. These actions produced what Friedman and Schwartz (1971) call a 'sharp wiggle' in demand deposits and in high-powered money, but there was no sustained monetary growth to offset velocity's fall. Even if the economic slowdown had ended by late 1930 or early 1931, it would have been one of the more severe US contractions on record. By October 1930, industrial production had fallen 26 per cent, prices 14 per cent and personal income 16 per cent from the cyclical peak in summer 1929.

This severity cannot be ascribed solely to the crash and its effect on velocity. The money stock also fell, by just over 2.5 per cent from the August 1929 cyclical peak to October 1930. This is a larger fall than in all but four previous contractions, and these four were also severe contractions.

Nevertheless, the large velocity fall together with the speed of slowdown increasing with the crash do suggest that the crash may well have contributed to the severity of the 1929–30 recession.

But 1929–30 was not the 'Great Contraction'. There were a further three years of decline, until by 1933 money income had fallen by 53 per cent and real income by 36 per cent from the 1929 peak. Why? The pace of bank failures accelerated sharply from November 1930. In that month, Caldwell and Company of Nashville failed. It was the largest investment banking firm in the South. That undoubtedly affected confidence, and bank failures were widespread in agricultural areas. The pace of failures accelerated yet again in December, and on 11 December the Bank of United States failed. This New York bank was the largest (by value of deposits) ever to fail up to that time in the United States. It triggered the first of a series of liquidity crises that did not end until March 1933. The initial crisis was short-lived, and bank deposits rose from January to March 1931. In 1931, indeed, there were some signs that the downturn in activity was approaching an end. Industrial production rose from January to April, while the rate of decline of factory employment slowed sharply. But a second banking crisis broke in March. The public converted deposits to currency, and banks sold off assets to increase their liquidity. This again put downward pressure on the money stock, and was only partly offset by inflows from abroad. The Federal Reserve did not act to offset the squeeze. There was a resumption of drain abroad when Britain's leaving the gold standard in September 1931 caused fears the United States would do likewise. Domestic depositors started to withdraw currency from the banks. The Federal Reserve raised its discount rate sharply. While ending the external drain, this intensified domestic difficulties, for the Federal Reserve had raised the rate – half of Bagehot's prescription – but it neglected the other half and did not lend freely. Indeed, its net holdings of US government securities fell.

A large-scale bond purchase programme was eventually started in April 1932, but yet again relief proved temporary. In reaction to a further wave of bank failures and fears of a foreign drain – there were rumours (subsequently justified) that the incoming administration would devalue – the Federal Reserve acted as it had in September 1931. It raised its discount rate but took no action to offset the effects of either the external or internal drains from the banks.

The problem ended on 6 March 1933, when President Roosevelt closed all banks and suspended gold redemption shipments abroad. The banks did not reopen until Congress authorized emergency issues of Federal Reserve notes, and banks then gradually reopened over 13, 14 and 15 March.

Why were there successive waves of bank failures? There were uncertainties about the policies of the new administration, including conflicting rumours concerning its attitude to the gold parity. These uncertainties came at a time well into an economic downturn. The first was surely important, and the second certainly cannot have helped. All that said, the scale of the banking collapse is startling.

Two explanations have been advanced for the bank failures – banking practices of previous years, with banks getting into securities dealing through affiliates, and the behaviour of the Fed.[4] What is the evidence? White (1986) found that the presence of securities affiliates reduced the risk of bank failure; that affiliates dampened rather than increased fluctuations in combined bank-affiliate earnings; and that neither capitalization nor liquidity was adversely affected by the presence of an affiliate. Peach (1941) examined the behaviour of affiliates. He found the following. While some gave misleading information on high-risk securities this was not common; affiliates were used for the personal profit of bank directors, but on a scale trivial in comparison to the economy; and occasionally a parent bank was drawn into losses on a security floated by an affiliate, but also on a scale sufficient to threaten only a few institutions. Benston (1990) found only the first and second of these three charges to be supported; and Kroszner and Rajan (1994) concluded that in general, banks underwrote high quality securities. Losses on government bonds greatly exceeded losses through securities affiliates. It is possible that interest rate mismatching contributed to the problems, but the scale of the bond price collapse was such that the primary responsibility must rest with the Fed. There was a substantial and unrelieved pressure on bank liquidity, resulting from the conversion of deposits to cash and subsequent (and resulting) forced sales of bonds at deep discount, which the Federal Reserve did not relieve.[5]

The Federal Reserve had failed to act adequately as lender of last resort. Rather it acted exactly as the Bank of England had in 1866. It had lent 'hesitantly, reluctantly, and with misgiving'. That 1866 behaviour incurred the following criticism from Bagehot (1873): 'to make large advances in this faltering way is to incur the evil of making them without obtaining the advantage. . .[that] is the worst of all policies'. The consequence of that 'worst of all policies' was the worst of all depressions in the United States.

ANALYSIS AND APPRAISAL

So far, then, the facts of various stock market crashes have been reviewed. These crashes were undoubtedly disastrous for all those who lost wealth in them. But a key issue is whether damage spread beyond that group. Did the crashes cause recessions?

A striking and important point is that the timing relationship between falls in the market and declines in the economy is highly variable. In the United States, for example, sometimes market falls precede recession (40 per cent of the time) but sometimes the market coincides or even lags. Aside from that, how might the market cause decline? It could affect either consumption or investment. Consumption could be affected through the effect of the market on the wealth of individuals. However, most individuals hold shares indirectly, so may be little aware of the effect of fluctuations in their wealth. Those who hold shares directly, at least on a substantial scale, are usually fairly sophisticated investors, well aware that the market does fluctuate, and look through these fluctuations.

Investment spending could be affected by a variety of channels. The lower is the market, and thus (other things equal) the higher the yield, the more it costs firms to raise capital by new issues. Further, market falls may create uncertainty. Romer (1990) constructs a model in which increased uncertainty deters spending. A key distinction in the model is the degree of 're-saleability' of goods. The easier they are to resell, the less does uncertainty deter purchasers. She uses this model in the United States, and finds that, in the wake of the 1929 crash, spending on durables declined sharply, most notably when they had poor re-sale potential. As she points out, financial commentators at the time also said there was increased uncertainty.

What of 1931? Britain's abandoning of gold is often said to have been a crisis. But internally there was no crisis; indeed, all the consequences were benign. Schumpeter's (1939, 956) description is characteristically vivid: 'In England there was neither panic nor – precisely owing to the way in which the thing had been done or, if the reader prefer, had come about – loss of "confidence" but rather a sigh of relief'.

Nevertheless, despite the possibility of establishing a causal link, it is far from clear that, on the basis of the episodes reviewed, 'crashes' caused severe problems for the economy. In 1914 in London, the economy was of course affected by war; but the financial turmoil, even despite the problems overseas, was over so fast that it is hard to see how it could affect the real economy. The 1929–32 decline in the London market was substantial, although admittedly not sufficiently fast as to be called a crash. Here, too, there is an abundance of factors, even leaving aside the stock market, to explain the performance of the British economy. The defence of sterling's gold partly until 1931 is a major factor; and when that defence was abandoned, the British economy started to recover.[6]

What of the United States in 1929? As set out above, there were monetary factors working to produce economic contraction after 1929; and the Great Depression, which did not start immediately in the wake of the crash, was certainly very largely the result of the monetary squeeze produced by the Federal Reserve's inadequate actions.

It would seem reasonable to say, on the basis of these three episodes, that stock market crashes lead to recessions only if they are allowed to produce monetary contactions – for, in contrast to the United States after the 1929 crash, London was supplied with abundant liquidity in 1914, and again in 1931 the moment the struggle to stay on gold was given up. This position is set out very clearly in Anna Schwartz's (1986, 21) classic paper:

> The reasons may now be summarised, accounting for financial crises that did or did not occur in the past. In both cases the setting is one in which the financial distress of certain firms became known to market participants, raising alarm as creditors became concerned about the value of their claims not only on those firms but also firms previously in sound condition. Banks that were creditors of the firms in distress became targets of suspicion by the depositors. *When monetary authorities failed to demonstrate readiness at the beginning of such a disturbance to meet all demands of sound debtors for loans and of depositors for cash, a financial crisis occurred. A financial crisis per contra could be averted by timely predictable signals to market participants of institutional readiness to make available an augmented supply of funds* [emphasis added]. The sources of the funds supplied might have been inflows from abroad – attracted by higher domestic than foreign interest rates – or emergency issues of domestic currency. The readiness was all. Knowledge of the availability of the supply was sufficient to allay alarm, so that the funds were never drawn on.

A NINETEENTH-CENTURY DIGRESSION

As the above point is an important one, it is worth briefly looking outside the twentieth century at some nineteenth-century evidence, to see whether it provides support for that position.

Identifying whatever timing patterns there may be in the occurrence of crashes and crises is an essential first step towards seeing their relationship to business cycle fluctuations. In organizing the data it is useful to start with a well-established pattern at higher than business cycle frequency.

Seasonal regularity has been noted both by present-day and by nineteenth-century writers. Miron (1986, 125–40) observes that financial panics in the nineteenth century displayed a seasonal pattern in both Europe and the United States. For US data, a χ^2 test rejects at the 0.001 per cent confidence interval the hypothesis that crises were distributed randomly across the seasons (Miron 1986). An examination of Kemmerer's (1910) listing of 29 banking panics between 1873 and 1908 shows 12 to be in the spring (March, April, May) and a further ten in September or December. Kindleberger's (1978) enumeration of panics in Europe between 1720 and 1914 yields similar results. A χ^2 test rejects the hypothesis of uniform distribution across the year; as in the United States, a marked preponderance fell in the spring or the autumn (Miron 1986).

The still accepted explanation for this seasonality is that given by Jevons (1866). He observed a seasonal pattern in interest rates associated with the agricultural cycle in asset demands. Reserve/deposit ratios for banks fell in the spring and the autumn when there was a seasonal upturn in the demand for both currency and credit. So it was in spring and autumn that banking systems were at their most vulnerable. The seasonal pattern in interest rates largely vanished when central banks started smoothing the interest rate cycle.[7] Note as of crucial relevance the importance of monetary impulses in the seasonal cycle.

Was there a cyclical as well as a seasonal regularity in the occurrence of crises? Seasonal regularity certainly need not imply cyclical regularity; it is necessary to look afresh at the data. Numerous writers in the nineteenth century noted the regularity with which 'commercial crises' occurred. Palgrave (1894, 1896, 1898) lists 1753, 1763, 1772–73, 1783, 1793, 1815, 1825, 1836–39, 1897, 1866, 1875 and 1890. As he noted:

> An examination of recorded years of acute commercial distress suggests periodicity. During the 140 years trade and banking have been carried on in war and peace, with a silver standard, with a gold standard, under a suspension of cash payments, in times of plenty, and in times of want; but the fatal years have come round with a considerable approach to cyclical regularity. (Palgrave, 1894, 466)

Periodicity was also remarked on by Langton (1858), Jevons (1866), Mills (1868), and Chubb (1872), among others.

Table 7.1 shows the main 'commercial crises' listed by Palgrave, with a brief description of each from a contemporary or near-contemporary source.

Of these 'commercial crises', only that of 1847 was not at a business cycle peak according to the Burns and Mitchell (1946) chronology of British business cycles. This appears to suggest a close association with subsequent recessions.

But it is not clear how much weight that finding can bear. The reason for this arises from how Burns and Mitchell determined their cyclical chronology. Their method was to inspect a large number of series for different aspects of the economy, and, on the basis of this inspection, reach a judgement on the length of each cycle. This causes a problem because one of the series they examined was for financial panics, and they regarded the occurrence of one of these as suggesting the economy was at or around a business cycle peak. Further doubt about the finding is created by comparing

Table 7.1   Eighteenth- and nineteenth-century 'commercial crises'

1792–93	Followed 'investments in machinery and in land navigation. . .Many houses of the most extensive dealings and most established credit failed' (MacPherson 1805)
1796–97	'Severe pressure in the money market, extensive failures of banks in the North of England, great mercantile discredit' (Palgrave 1894)
1810–11	'the fall of prices, the reduction of private paper, and the destruction of credit, were greater and more rapid than were before, or have since, been known to have occurred within a short space of time' (Tooke 1838)
1825	'one of the most severe through which the commercial and banking systems of the country had ever passed' (Palgrave 1894). On this crisis, Palgrave also quotes Huskinson as saying 'that we were within a few hours of a state of barter' but does not give any source for that quotation. This crisis followed a steady and very substantial fall in yields. Palgrave gives the price of 3% public funds (prices in £ sterling per £100 of nominal stock):

1823	3 April	73½
	1 July	80¾
	3 October	82½
1824	1 January	86
	2 April	94½
	28 April	97¼ (the highest)
	November	96½
1825	January	94½
1826	14 February	73⅛ (the lowest)

	'Though the period of pressure in 1825 was so short, it had been preceded by considerable and extravagant speculations in foreign loans and shares of companies, mining and commercial' (Palgrave 1894)
1847	'a considerable period of speculative activity, fostered by a low rate for money, preceded this crisis also'. Palgrave (1894) also notes that Peel's Bank Act came into effect on 2 September 1844, and this 'took away from the directors [of the Bank of England] alike any power or any responsibility for the "regulation of the currency" so far as this consisted of their notes'. Interest rates fell, and there was, as in 1825, considerable speculation, this time in 'railways and other improvements at home'
1857	'it is very clear that during the years 1855 to 1856 the extension of credit was enormous and dangerous.. . .[in 1857] the reserve of the Bank of England may be said to be continually at a danger point' (Palgrave 1894)
1866	Failure of Overend, Gurney and Co.
1890	Baring crisis

Table 7.2   National banking era panics

NBER cycle (peak-trough)	Crisis date
Oct 1873–Mar 1879	Sept 1873
Mar 1882–May 1885	Jun 1884
Mar 1887–Apr 1888	No panic
Jul 1890–May 1891	Nov 1890
Jan 1893–Jun 1894	May 1893
Dec 1895–Jun 1897	Oct 1896
Jun 1899–Dec 1900	No panic
Sep 1902–Aug 1904	No panic
May 1907–Jun 1908	Oct 1907
Jan 1910–Jan 1912	No panic
Jan 1913–Dec 1914	Aug 1914

Source: Gorton (1988).

the Burns and Mitchell chronology with that which Capie and Mills (1991) developed by estimating a segmented trend model. Capie and Mills' work goes back only to 1870, but between that year and 1907 (their last peak) they differ from Burns and Mitchell in the timing of three (out of five) peaks and one (out of five) troughs.

Turning next to the United States, analysis has been carried out by Gorton (1988). His approach was to consider whether banking crises ('real' crises) are random events, 'perhaps self-confirming equilibria in settings with multiple equilibria', or alternately, whether they were systematic, linked to 'occurrences of a threshold value of some variable predicting the riskiness of bank deposits'. Table 7.2 provides the basic data for the early part of the period in the United States. Crises were usually at business cycle peaks, but were not by any means at every business cycle peak.

Deposit behaviour changed after 1914 (the founding of the Federal Reserve) and again after 1934 (the start of deposit insurance), but despite that, crises remained systematic, linked to the business cycle. According to Gorton (1988, 778): 'The recession hypothesis best explains what prior information is used by agents in forming conditional expectations. Banks hold claims on firms and when firms begin to fail, a leading indicator of recession (when banks will fail), depositors reassess the riskiness of deposits.'[8]

It might be thought that Gorton's result gives support for the similar Palgrave/Burns and Mitchell view. But caution is necessary, for the structures of the banking systems of the two countries differed (and still differ) greatly. Britain had a fully fledged central bank – one which, inter alia, knew the importance of injecting liquidity to prevent bank runs and was capable of doing so, by the last quarter of the nineteenth century. The United States did not have one at all until 1914, and in 1929 it carried out its duty somewhat inadequately. Further, Britain had before the end of the nineteenth century developed a system where banks were substantial in scale, and substantially diversified by region. They were thus robust in the face of the kind of shocks that brought down the smaller, often unbranched, US banks. Britain, in short, experienced monetary stability in the face of market 'crashes': the United States often did not.

OTHER EPISODES

But surely, it may be said, there have been other occasions when 'crashes' caused recessions. In fact, a careful examination of the evidence suggests that such episodes are hard to find. We have already examined two of the four biggest declines in the London market. The other two were in 1940, again wartime, and in 1974, after the oil price shock of that year. Soon after 1940, the British economy surged to a level of output above its long-term sustainable capacity (Capie and Wood 2002). Now, it may be argued that the 1940 episode, taking place as it did in wartime and indeed at a time when victory for Britain seemed in doubt, is so special that nothing can be learned from it about peacetime stock market crises. That may be so. But nevertheless the attitude of contemporary observers and policy-makers is of interest. There was no concern that the market fall would lead to a collapse in demand. Rather, insofar as there was any interest in the market, there was concern that it would *not* have a significant effect on private sector demand. All discussion was of how to contain the inflation that the war could produce. Keynes's 1940 contribution to this discussion is notable in this context. In *How to pay for the war* he outlined the ideas for the containment of excess demand that were adopted in Kingsley Wood's Budget of 1941 (Pollard 1962). Particularly noteworthy is that Keynes is identified with one aspect of a body of analysis that maintains that asset price falls *in conjunction with deflation* can cause or at the least exacerbate recession (see Capie and Wood 2004 for a discussion of this). His views in 1940 suggest that asset price falls without deflation were not expected to have a significant effect on demand, reinforcing the conclusions drawn so far in the chapter from pre-1940 episodes.[9]

The 1974 crash appears to have been triggered by the oil price shock that affected all developed countries. Stock market declines were quite similar everywhere, not surprising since a good number of companies by then had their shares traded in more than one market, thus producing mechanical linkages in addition to the effects of profit-seeking arbitrageurs (see Table 7.3).

Table 7.3   Stock prices in 1974

Stock market	High	Low
London	339.3	150.4
New York	891.7	557.6
Japan	342.5	252.0
Germany	609.2	520.0

Sources: Dow-Jones and Bloomberg.

But subsequent effects, despite the commonality of the shock, varied widely. This was certainly not due to the varying extents to which countries depended on imported fuel, as was sometimes claimed at the time when commentators, and of course governments, blamed the oil price rises for inflation. In Japan, for example, wholly dependent on imported fuel, inflation was lower than in either Britain or the United States, both of which were oil producers. What did seem to matter was the monetary policy response. The oil price rise initially was followed by a sharp contraction in output. Demand was transferred abroad, and the sharp rise in price of an input for which substitution was not easy led to cutbacks in aggregate supply. Different governments responded differently. Some, concerned to maintain employment regardless of the upward shock to prices, eased money. Notable in this group were Britain and the United States.[10] Others were more concerned about inflation, and either eased money very little, or not at all. Those countries that accommodated the shock by monetary ease subsequently had inflation (and then recession as they tacked inflation); those where there was little or no monetary accommodation had modest slowdowns and then recovered. Germany, Switzerland and Japan are examples of this latter group. Again, while not denying that market falls may have some economic effects, the accompanying monetary response seems the dominant factor.

Finally in our review of episodes we come to East Asia at the end of the twentieth century. While not identical in every country, there were certainly some major common features. There were asset price booms, followed by crashes, followed by major banking system problems and flight to foreign currencies. Just why the market crashes (which were in property markets as well as stock markets) led so rapidly to banking problems, and then to flights from the currency, has been very neatly summarized by McKinnon (2000, 34):

> Banks and other financial institutions were poorly regulated but their depositors were never the less insured – implicitly or explicitly – against bankruptcy

by their national governments. The resulting moral hazard was responsible for the excessive build-up of short-term foreign currency indebtedness.

The build-up of foreign currency indebtedness was encouraged by the pegged exchange rate regime. The guarantees led to undiversified lending as well as undiversified borrowing by banks. The substantial problems were, in many cases, further exacerbated by many of the banks having made loans on government direction rather than by market criteria. In short, the system could not have been worse designed either to provide stability or to facilitate the injection of liquidity by lender of last resort action. Hence, crash turned into crisis.

OVERVIEW AND CONCLUSION

Are stock market crashes disasters? Yes for those who lose wealth – there can be no doubt of that. But what of a more widespread sense? Are they inevitably catastrophic for the economy? Here the answer is a clear-cut no. They can be if they are allowed to lead to a sharp monetary squeeze, but not otherwise. That conclusion has emerged clearly from a study of some major twentieth-century market crashes, and was reinforced by a brief glance at the evidence on the importance of banking system stability in the nineteenth century. It is clear that although market crashes are undoubtedly inevitable from time to time, they turn into economic disasters not inevitably, but only as a consequence of banking and monetary system failures. Anyone who still doubts that should look at the market, monetary and economic aftermath to the terrorist attacks of 11 September 2001.

NOTES

1. I am greatly indebted to Kath Begley of the Bank of England Information Centre for her help in finding and confirming references.
2. A detailed examination of the explanations for the market decline can be found in White (1990).
3. A good bit of any effect must have been indirect; investment in stocks and shares was much less widespread than now.
4. The first was the justification for the Glass-Steagall Act.
5. The problem was shortage of liquidity, a problem lender of last resort action can cure, rather than shortage of capital, which such action cannot help. In the Great Depression the US banking system lost capital equal to about 3–4 per cent of 1930 US GNP. This should be contrasted with the 15–20 per cent of 1990 Japanese GNP that the Japanese banking system seems to have lost in its recent difficulties. (I am indebted to Charles Calomiris for these striking items of data.) The similarity of symptoms between the United States in the 1930s and Japan in the 1990s should therefore not disguise a fun-

damental difference in cause – in the United States a shortage of bank liquidity, in Japan a shortage of bank capital.
6. See Capie, Mills and Wood (1986) for an account of the defence and of subsequent economic performance.
7. This could not be done before 1914, as it was a worldwide interest rate cycle and would have required concerted worldwide action by central banks. This was not possible as the United States, a major agricultural producer, did not have a central bank until 1914.
8. Gorton also tests whether the Fed was an improvement on previous stabilizing devices – private clearing houses – by running his pre-1914 equations on post-1914 data and comparing the forecast outturn with events. The hypothetical outcome was much preferable.
9. There was also a market crash in the United States in 1940. The market decline in May of that year was the third largest negative monthly return in the years 1830–1988 (Wilson, Scylla and Jones 1990). But the economy was booming and interest rates were low, and the crash had absolutely no knock-on effects, even in financial markets. For example, the interest rate spread between low- and high-quality bonds hardly changed at all.
10. A vivid account of problems particular to Britain at this time can be found in Blakey (1997).

REFERENCES

Bagehot, W. (1873), *Lombard Street: a description of the money market*, London: Henry S. King.
Benston, George J. (1990), *The separation of commercial and investment banking: the Glass-Steagall Act revisted and reconsidered*, London: Macmillan.
Blakey, G.G. (1997), *The post-war history of the London Stock Market: 50 years of business, politics and people*, Chatford: Management Books.
Brown, W.A. (1940), *The international gold standard reinterpreted: 1914–1934*, New York: National Bureau of Economic Research.
Burns, A. and Mitchell, W. (1946), *Measuring business cycles*, New York: National Bureau of Economic Research.
Capie, F.H. and Mills, T.C. (1991), 'Money and business cycles in the US and the UK, 1870–1913', *Manchester School*, 59.
Capie, F.H., Mills, T. and Wood, G.E. (1986), 'What happened in 1931?', in F.H. Capie and G.E. Wood (eds), *Financial crises and the world banking system*, London: Macmillan.
Capie, F. and Wood, G.E. (2002), 'Price controls in war and peace: a Marshallian conclusion', *Scottish Journal of Political Economy*, 49.
Capie, F. and Wood, G.E. (2004), 'Price change, financial stability, and the British economy, 1870–1939', in C. Richard, K. Burdekin and Pierre L. Siklos (eds), *Deflation: current and historical perspectives*, Cambridge: Cambridge University Press.
Chubb, H. (1872), 'Bank act and crisis of 1866', *Journal of the Statistical Society of London*, 35.
Clapham, J. (1944), *The Bank of England: a history*, Cambridge: Cambridge University Press.
de Cecco, M. (1974), *Money and empire: the international gold standard, 1890–1914*, Oxford: Blackwell.
Friedman, M. and Schwartz, A.J. (1971), *A monetary history of the United States, 1867–1960*, Princeton, NJ: Princeton University Press.

Galbraith, J.K. (1955), *The great crash, 1929*, London: Hamish Hamilton.

Gordon, R.A. (1952), *Business fluctuations*, New York: Harper.

Gorton, G. (1988), 'Banking panics and business cycles', *Oxford Economic Papers*, 40, 751–81.

Hansen, A.H. (1932), *Economic stabilization in an unbalanced world*, New York: Harcourt, Brace and Company.

Hawtrey, R.G. (1933), *Trade depression and the way out*, London: Longmans, Green and Co.

Jevons, S. (1866), 'The frequent pressure in the money market', *Journal of the Statistical Society of London*, 29.

Kemmerer, E.W. (1910), *Seasonal variations in the relative demand for money and capital in the United States*, National Monetary Commission, Washington, DC: Government Printing Offices.

Keynes, J.M. (1914a), 'War and the financial system, August 1914', *Economic Journal*, 24.

Keynes, J.M. (1914b), 'The prospects of money, November 1914', *Economic Journal*, 24.

Keynes, J.M. (1921) *Activities 1914–1919: The Treasury and Versailles,* reprinted in *The collected writings of John Maynard Keynes Vol. XVI*, London: Macmillan.

Keynes, J.M. (1940) *How to pay for the war*, London: Macmillan.

Kindleberger, C.P. (1978), *Manias, panics and crashes: a history of financial crisis*, New York: Basic Books.

Kroszner, R.S. and Rajan, R.G. (1994), 'Is the Glass-Steagall Act justified? A study of the US experience with universal banking before 1933', *American Economic Review*, 84.

Langton, W. (1857–58), 'Observations on a table showing the balance of account between the mercantile public and the Bank of England', *Transactions of the Manchester Statistical Society*, read 30 December 1857.

MacPherson, D. (1805), *Annals of commerce, manufacturers, fisheries and navigation*, volume 4, London: Nichols and Son.

McKinnon, R. (2000), 'The East Asian dollar standard, life after death?', *Economic Notes*, 29.

Mills, J. (1868), 'On credit cycles and the origin of the commercial panics', *Transactions of the Manchester Statistical Society.*

Miron, J.A. (1986), 'Financial panics, the seasonality of nominal interest rates, and the founding of the Fed', *American Economic Review*, 26.

Morgan, E.V. (1962), *The stock exchange, its history and functions*, London: Eleu.

Palgrave, R.H.I. (1894, 1896, 1898), *Dictionary of political economy*, London: Macmillan.

Peach, W.N. (1941), *The security affiliates of national banks*, Baltimore, MD: The Johns Hopkins University Press.

Pollard, S. (1962), *The development of the British economy 1914–1950*, London: Edward Arnold Publishing.

Romer, D.D. (1990), 'The Great Crash and the onset of the Great Depression', *Quarterly Journal of Economics*, 105.

Sayers, R.S. (1976), *The Bank of England, 1891–1944*, Cambridge: Cambridge University Press.

Schumpeter, J.A. (1939), *Business cycles*, New York: McGraw-Hill Book Co.

Schwartz, A. (1986), 'Real and pseudo-financial crises', in F. Capie and G.E. Wood (eds), *Financial crises and the world banking system*, London: Macmillan.

Tooke, T. (1838, 1840, 1848), *History of prices*, London: Longman, Brown, Green & Longmans and Roberts.

White, E.N. (1986), 'Before the Glass-Seagall Act: an analysis of the investment banking activities of national banks', *Explorations in Economic History*, 23.

White, E.N. (1990), 'When the ticker ran late', in E.N. White (ed.), *Crashes and panics: the lessons from history*, Homewood, IL: Dow Jones-Irwin.

Wilson, J., Scylla, R. and Jones, C.P. (1990), 'Financial market volatility panics under the national banking system before 1914 and volatility in the long run, 1830–1988' in E.N. White (ed.), *Crashes and panics: the lessons from history*, Homewood, IL: Dow Jones-Irwin.

Withers, H. (1915), *War and Lombard Street*, London: Murray.

8.   The demise of the command economies in the Soviet Union and its outer empire[1]

Steven Morewood

On 25 April 2005 Vladimir Putin, President of Russia, gave the annual address to the Federal Assembly of the Russian Federation, which had emerged from the former Soviet Union:

> Above all, we should acknowledge that the collapse of the Soviet Union was a major geopolitical disaster of the [twentieth] century. As for the Russian nation, it became a genuine drama. Tens of millions of our co-citizens and compatriots found themselves outside Russian territory. Moreover, the epidemic of disintegration infected Russia itself. Individual savings were depreciated, and old ideals destroyed. Many institutions were disbanded or reformed carelessly. Terrorist interventions and the Khasavyurt capitulation that followed damaged the country's integrity. Oligarchic groups – possessing absolute control over information channels – served exclusively their own corporate interests. Mass poverty began to be seen as the norm. And all this was happening against the backdrop of a dramatic economic downturn, unstable finances, and the paralysis of the social sphere. Many thought or seemed to think at the time that our young democracy was not a continuation of Russian statehood, but its ultimate collapse, the prolonged agony of the Soviet system. (Putin 2005)

Such nostalgia heralded an effort to revive some elements of the Soviet monolith while paying lip service to democracy and capitalism. But there could be no reconstitution of the old system per se, no turning back to the old economic ways, centred on the command economy, which sowed the seeds of the disaster that engulfed the Soviet Union, bringing about an eventual implosion.

The command economy emerged in October 1928 when the Soviet leader, Josef Stalin, abandoned the New Economic Policy (NEP) and inaugurated state-directed economic planning and distribution with the First Five-year Plan. Thereby he established the template for his own and successor governments. Once Soviet dominance was extended to most of its neighbours in Eastern Europe (Bulgaria, Czechoslovakia, Hungary, Poland, East Germany and Romania) over 1944–49, so they too embraced versions of the original model. Collectively they became known as the Soviet bloc or the outer empire.[2] Persisted with throughout the Cold War, the command economy was the common denominator characterizing the United Soviet Socialist Republics (USSR) and its satellites when they collapsed, domino fashion, in the monumental three-year period 1989–1991, which ended the East–West ideological confrontation, stretching back to 1946–47.

It will be argued here that while the Soviet model and its variants suffered from inherent flaws, these were not the fundamental cause of collapse. The survival into the twenty-first century of China, Cuba, North Korea and Vietnam as stand-alone communist beacons demonstrates that, under certain circumstances, the species can defy extinction. What distinguished the Soviet Union and the intertwined bloc initially was their common destiny – military, political and economic. Increasingly this fractured, once the communist ideal portrayed by state propaganda failed to match the reality and the general population became ever more disillusioned. As command economies floundered, so tantalizing glimpses of Western capitalism seeped through via increasing trade and black marketeers, providing hope of a better future for downtrodden ordinary citizens, who eventually found their political voice. By the 1970s the leaderships felt compelled to strive to raise living standards beyond the mundane through an import-led growth strategy made possible by East–West détente but in the process saddled their economies with unsustainable external debt levels without delivering the hoped for transformation. The Soviet leadership escaped this fate initially but by the early 1980s woefully bad economic indicators forced it too to embrace more radical policies, leading to Gorbachev's election as the General Secretary of the Communist Party of the Soviet Union (CPSU). Under his over-confident stewardship the introduction of a heady mixture of political and economic reforms would fatally undermine the Soviet system and ensure its ultimate collapse. The de-escalation of the Cold War, allied to the fact that the Kremlin was no longer willing or able to make the economic sacrifices necessary to help sustain its dominance over its outer empire, brought the latter crashing down in 1989. Two years later the Soviet Union itself followed, together creating the greatest number of new states since African decolonization in the 1960s.

As Table 8.1 indicates, the road to economic disaster for the Soviet Union and its East European satellites was a shared experience. After achieving spectacular economic growth in the 1950s, slowdown set in during the 1960s, which accelerated in the 1970s, followed by recession and collapse in the 1980s and early 1990s. During the 'Golden Age' in the capitalist West, 1950–73, economic growth across Eastern Europe generally kept pace with,

Table 8.1   *Per capita growth performance in former USSR and Eastern Europe, 1950–98 (annual average per capita growth rate %)*

Country	1950–73	1973–90	1990–98
Former USSR	3.36	0.74	−6.86
Armenia		−0.04	−7.33
Belarus		−0.29	−9.35
Estonia		1.85	−3.71
Georgia		1.27	−0.73
Kazakhstan		−0.23	−5.09
Latvia		1.39	−0.58
Lithuania		0.73	−4.55
Moldova		0.85	−10.77
Russian Federation		0.98	−6.53
Tajikistan		−1.67	−8.88
Ukraine		1.15	−10.24
Uzbekistan		−1.17	−3.32
Total Eastern Europe	3.79	0.51	0.06
Albania	3.59	0.57	−0.41
Bulgaria	5.19	0.29	−2.36
Czechoslovakia	3.08	1.12	
Czech Republic			−0.36
Slovak Republic			−0.01
Hungary	3.60	0.85	0.05
Poland	3.45	−0.35	3.41
Romania	4.80	0.08	−2.45
Former Yugoslavia	4.49	1.60	−3.45
Croatia			−1.93
Slovenia			1.09
Other former Yugoslavia			−6.37

Source: Maddison (1997, 156).

and occasionally surpassed, that of Western Europe. The great change came between 1973–90: although aggregate per capita growth in Western Europe fell to 1.9 per cent per annum, reflecting the two oil shocks, the performance of Eastern Europe plunged to 0.5 per cent per annum, feeding the growing discontent that exploded with the 1989 revolutions (Madison 1997, 160). After 1990, although economic disaster lingered, the psychology had changed. Where before, recession reflected the failings of socialism to deliver tolerable living standards and pure egalitarianism, now dreadful economic indicators were seen as a price worth paying to achieve the transition to capitalism.

A FLAWED SYSTEM: THE COMMAND ECONOMY

The command economy left very little to chance: the state laboriously reviewed economic resources and allocated them according to its requirements. As the owner of the means of production (save for some inconsequential private enterprise), the state directed economic activity at the macro and micro level via the elaborate planning mechanism. Five-year and one-year plans, enunciated by the State Planning Committee (Gosplan), were implemented through a chain of command from ministry to factory floor with plan over-fulfilment the name of the game. Heavy industry (Sector A), was constantly favoured with the lion's share of resources at the expense of light industry (Sector B). This accorded with a pronounced emphasis on defence. Originally emanating from Stalin's well-founded conviction that Nazi Germany was intent on conflict and vindicated by the superior Soviet war economy, which ultimately out-produced the enemy during the Second World War, the defence orientation continued as the Cold War erupted and escalated thereafter. Indeed, a vast military-industrial sector was built on chemicals, energy, metallurgy, machine building and steel, providing the industrial base to service extensive armaments requirements. In time, around 5000 enterprises were directly engaged in the Soviet military sector. One calculation suggests that by 1988 it employed one-fifth of the total industrial labour force, generating 16 per cent of gross industrial output (Cooper 1993, 9, 12–13).

When considering the fraternal states that constituted the Soviet bloc a number of qualifications are in order. First, the Soviet Union and its satellites were at different junctures on the road to communism: the former was deemed to be at the 'developed socialism' stage while the latter were at the earlier phase of 'people's democracy' (Janos 2000, 244). Economically, with the exceptions of Czechoslovakia and East Germany, agriculture predominated. Second, although from 1948 onwards bloc countries introduced imitative five-year plans in industry and collectivization in agriculture, they did not exactly replicate the Soviet model because their circumstances were different. Accordingly, collectivization was not pursued in so draconian a fashion, being adopted piecemeal, as in Romania, or else it was cut back, after the initial impetus and generally not completed until the late 1950s or early 1960s (Swain and Swain 2003, 121). Again, popular resistance to economic reform erupted far more frequently in the satellites than in the Soviet Union and bloc leaders took due note. Recognizing this pressure, Moscow relinquished direct control through officials on the spot and only intervened as a last resort. Satellites could not be trusted with military forces and weaponry that might threaten their imperial master. Indeed, the Red Army remained stationed in several strategically vital spots even after communist

regimes became firmly established. Furthermore, their economies only produced light weaponry that was not critical to the Soviet military machine or
liable to pose a serious threat should a satellite attempt to break free from the
'prison of nations'. Nor were any nuclear weapons sited within the bloc lest
they fell into the wrong hands. By the 1970s, the USSR was carrying around
90 per cent of the defence burden of the Warsaw Pact (Bunce 1985, 21). The
Soviet obsession with armaments, then, was not echoed in its outer empire.
It is important to establish that all European communist states experienced
similar slowdowns, suggesting that it was a general failure of their economic
systems rather than military ambition and imperial overstretch, associated
with the Soviet case, that lay at the heart of the disaster that unfurled.

There were indeed shared characteristics between the Soviet model and
the bloc's. In macro political and economic terms little flexibility was
allowed. The recollections of a Czech economist, engaged in his country's
inaugural five-year plan, are enlightening:

> I remember that in 1950 we received the first guidelines for drafting the plan for
> Czechoslovakia according to Soviet methods. Actually it was nothing but a trans-
> lation of Soviet guidelines. The people in charge either had no time or could not be
> bothered to change things which had no validity whatsoever for Czechoslovakia.
> For instance, I remember that among the headings in the plan there was one
> stating. . .'fishing at sea',. . .something that did not apply to Czechoslovakia. Such
> things could, of course, be very easily removed and they did not appear in the
> guidelines the following year. But the more essential replicas of Soviet methods
> were there to stay for a very long time. (Quoted in Rupnik 1988, 178)

When deviant roads to socialism were pursued Moscow reacted furiously.
Hungary and Czechoslovakia, in 1956 and 1968 respectively, provoked military intervention to make them conform. Planning systems within the bloc
were comparable with the five-year plans at the heart of economic development. As in the USSR, there was a similar emphasis on heavy industry; the
nationalization of the 'commanding heights' of the economy was of the
same magnitude; and the urban population rose substantially as industrialization and collectivization took effect. In Poland, for example, over half the
industrial workforce of the 1960s originated in the countryside and massive
coal and steel complexes, on the Soviet scale, like Nowa Huta near Cracow,
sprang up. Similarly, East Germany, often seen as the exemplar of the bloc
economies, instigated massive heavy industry projects focused on energy
and steel, in the 1950s (Rupnik 1988, 179; Fowkes 2000, 46; Ross 2002, 71).

As Swain and Swain (2003, 122) remark, 'Identical models produced
identical problems'. Distortions and unbalanced growth resulted from
prioritizing some sectors above others, the feast or famine scenario. It was
ordinary citizens who paid the price with much lower average living standards than prevailed in the capitalist world. The blight of endemic shortage

was built in to the system and was a perennial feature regardless of whether command economies were doing well or in severe difficulties. Nevertheless, for much of the period under review acute shortages and rationing signified a worsening situation. The shortage economy provided a hostage to fortune once the lie of a West intent on conquest and exploitation ceased to ring true and helped fuel discontent.

Inefficiency and corruption increasingly corroded the system. It became virtually impossible for the centre to quantify precisely available resources, exactly how they were distributed and the resulting products. It was to be taken on trust that enterprise managers would endeavour to fulfil plan targets. What happened in practice was that where targets were not met, managers fudged their returns, creating a distorted picture of economic activity. In turn, false reporting generated extra resources that actual production did not merit. The later introduction of computerized planning failed to alter the picture because its efficiency depended on reliable data input. 'The command economy', one critic wrote (Rupnik 1988, 178), 'is a pyramid of lies in which each factory, each bureaucracy, lies to the levels above and below in the hierarchy about its performance and optimum plan targets'. The supreme irony was that the Soviet Central Committee came to rely on published Central Intelligence Agency (CIA) estimates of sector performances (CIA 1999, 20). Official Soviet and bloc growth figures therefore need to be treated with some scepticism.

The fixation with plan fulfilment and the absence of market signals produced several unfortunate consequences. In particular, a lack of quality control, the wasteful employment of resources, high-cost manufacture and a shortage of goods. The growth of a 'second economy', which evidenced a nascent entrepreneurial spirit suppressed by communism, added to the confused picture. Even Stalinism, with its punitive penalties, was unable to eliminate black marketeers and once punishments became less severe their number multiplied. Endemic thefts from state factories to service the unfulfilled demands of consumers, allied to a host of other underground activities, became widespread across the Soviet Union and its satellites from the early 1960s onwards. Indeed, communist regimes often deliberately turned a blind eye to evidence of the 'shadow economy' in the knowledge that it catered for demand that the state could not meet, thereby providing a welcome social outlet and political stabilizer (Fowkes 2000, 91).

Another inherent flaw was that state directives tended to supplant prices as signals for economic activity. As the Austrian economists von Mises (1947) and von Hayek (1935, 25) warned, central planners would always lack precise indicators to set relative prices, relative wages and relative factor costs. Furthermore, prices did not change according to supply and demand as they did in market economies. They were rarely altered and even when they were it was on the basis of crude cost-based accounting prices that more often than not were out of date, not to say absurd. By the 1980s, for example, it cost the equivalent of $10 for a taxi fare from Moscow Airport to the city centre but just $7 to fly with the national carrier, Aeroflot, over 4000 miles from Vladivostok to the capital! Moreover, the increasingly complex planning system remained cumbersome by Western standards and struggled to deliver commodities in the right quantities. Frequently some products were produced in abundance while others proved hard to come by. The Polish joke summed up the conundrum best: 'in a planned economy you ended up trying to assemble ten bicycles with nine screws' (Rupnik 1988, 181). East German planners and enterprises were compared to ancient mariners attempting to find a safe port caught in a fog and dangerous waters without the aid of a compass, coordinates or map (Ross 2002, 79).

Cynicism was one area in which East Europeans excelled. 'We pretend to work and they pretend to pay us' became a mantra of the disillusioned Soviet employee. An anonymous author composed a poem entitled 'The eight wonders of the socialist economy', which highlighted the absurdities of the system.

> There is no unemployment, but nobody works.
> Nobody works, but the plan is fulfilled.
> The plan is fulfilled, but there is nothing to buy.
> There is nothing to buy, but you can find anything.
> You can find anything, but everybody steals.
> Everybody steals, but nothing has been stolen.
> Nothing has been stolen, but it's impossible to work.
> It's impossible to work, but there is no unemployment.
> (Quoted in Rupnik 1988, 164)

These contradictions, over time, proved to be the harbingers of doom. The black economy grew out of control; the heavy industry lobby, the Frankenstein's monster of the command economy, used its political muscle successfully to resist any reduction in its role; the state continued to bankroll loss-making enterprise to maintain full employment. Most crucially, the failure of command economies to deliver acceptable living standards and sustained economic growth would also prove a harbinger of doom.

'REFORM FROM WITHIN'

By the early 1960s the bloc economies had largely achieved rapid industrialization, replicating the achievement of Stalin's pioneering five-year plans of 1928–41. In similar fashion, a mass proletariat was created as agricultural workers left the land in droves to work in city factories or the service sector. East-Central Europe exhausted the potential for extensive growth first by exploiting reserves of labour, raw materials and the mechanization of agriculture. In the more backward Balkans extensive growth continued for longer. This phase of development was the most successful and the one in which the socialist technocrats were most in control. However, 'the developmental model' (Newton 2004, 163) ran out of steam. The conundrum then became that of conceiving reforms that were effective while remaining true to socialist principles.

During the 1960s, as surplus labour ran out and industrialization was completed, there was a palpable slowdown in economic growth across the region. With it came the recognition by central planners of the need to move to intensive growth – the more efficient use of resources and raising productivity through maximizing existing technology and introducing new innovations. This proved a much harder nettle to grasp and was never satisfactorily achieved, notwithstanding a raft of reformist measures.

At the regional level efforts to create an engine of growth to rival the European Economic Community soon ran into difficulties. In January 1949 the Council for Mutual Economic Assistance (CMEA), or Comecon, was founded in Moscow between the Soviet Union and its satellites, the CMEA Six.[3] At first the new organization carried little more than propaganda value as an answer to the Marshall Plan. With its control at its most authoritative, Moscow thereby missed the best opportunity to insist on supranational planning. When, belatedly, in December 1961, the Basic Principles of the International Socialist Division of Labour were adopted it was too late. It sought to achieve:

> the maximum utilisation of the advantages of the socialist world system. . .the determination of correct proportions in the national economy of each country. . .the rational allocation of production. . .the effective utilisation of labour and material resources, and. . .the strengthening of the defensive power of the socialist camp. (Brabant 1989, 67)

In practice, however, Czechoslovakia, Hungary, Poland and Romania refused to comply. The Romanians were especially indignant at the Comecon council's suggestion that they abandon autarkic forced industrialization for agricultural specialization. There was no desire among satellites to extend Soviet dominance and a fear that the problems already apparent in domestic central planning would be replicated and magnified at supranational level. Two factors increased the disinclination to heed Khrushchev's November 1962 call for a common single planning organ.

First, Moscow's continued willingness to subsidize its satellites. An early instance of this was the ad hoc grant extended to Hungary in 1957 amounting to 1138 million roubles in grants and long-term credits to shore up its communist regime after the attempted revolution of the previous year (Janos 2000, 265). Thereafter a trading pattern was established whereby the richly endowed Soviet Union provided its CMEA partners, which generally lacked primary materials, with energy and raw materials at substantially below world market prices and accepted manufactures of indifferent quality at world market prices. Second, after 1960 there was a relaxation of the West's trading restrictions, especially by Western Europe, which offered access to technology, finance, management and marketing. Although this avenue only really opened up in the 1970s with dangerous consequences, the antecedents were established in the previous decade (Bideleux and Jeffries 1998, 559–61).

All the Central European members of the bloc, taking their lead from Moscow, pursued economic reform ('reform from within') to some degree during the 1960s. East Germany, which instigated its New Economic System in 1963, sought to maximize economic potential through stimulating economic levers, such as prices, credit and bonuses, but had abandoned the scheme by the decade's close (Ross 2002, 71). Hungary, with its New Economic Mechanism (NEM), introduced in 1968, was most successful. Compulsory plan indicators, the essence of the Soviet command economy, were eliminated and replaced by free market price signals. The reform was partial, however, extending to 65 per cent of factory prices. Energy and raw materials, where fixed prices were retained and sensitive mass consumer staples, which the state continued to subsidize, were excluded. The absence of a labour and capital market and the continued dominance of state-owned monopoly enterprises all mitigated against the effect of the NEM even if new life was injected into the system through reining back stifling over-bureaucratization. With the crushing of the Prague Spring (see below) providing a potent reminder of the need not to stray too far from the Moscow model, the next wave of intended reforms were postponed and by the mid-1970s an anti-reform group dominated the Hungarian Communist Party (Berend 1996, 150–51).

Czechoslovakia likewise tinkered with a mixed economy but combined this with radical political change, dismembering the police state and instigating freedom of the press. Very quickly a mass democratic movement emerged that threatened to overwhelm the Communist Party's authority. It was this dimension as much as the projected economic reforms, that led Moscow, fearing a domino-like effect throughout the bloc, to lead a Warsaw Pact invasion to suppress the Prague Spring and reintroduce a Red Army presence. Gustáv Husák, a Soviet loyalist, was brought in as Czech leader and proceeded to denounce 'right-wing opportunists and adventurers who sought to introduce anarchic market relations and transform collective ownership into group-ownership' (Berend 1996, 146). Thereafter the Brezhnev Doctrine prescribed it as their bounden duty that members of the alliance intervened militarily whenever socialism was deemed to be under challenge. Until 1989 this latent threat served to keep satellites in check and ensured that economic solutions to mounting problems conformed to a socialist framework. Therein lay a recipe for looming disaster.

A CATASTROPHIC DECADE: THE 1970s

There was a gradual recognition by the satellites' leaderships that they must pay more attention to increasing standards of living through adjusting resource allocation or else face rising discontent. Accordingly, capital accumulation fell from 25–35 per cent of GDP in the early 1950s, when forced industrialization was at its height, to 20–25 per cent in succeeding decades. However, the embedded distortions of the command economy remained and acted as a brake on an improved quality of life notwithstanding dramatic increases in consumption. The capitalist West, ironically, was turned to increasingly for succour and inspiration. It provided the lead for the turn towards modern engineering sectors, especially motor cars and electronics, which served to meet rising consumer expectations. Electrical appliances, such as washing machines, refrigerators and television sets, already commonplace in Western economies, became widespread across Eastern Europe during the 1960s. Motor car ownership, whilst not prevalent throughout the region, took off in Czechoslovakia, Hungary and Poland (Okey 2004, 20–21).

The East German leadership, ever conscious of competing with West Germany, elected, in 1971, to support a generous welfare system, a move emulated elsewhere (Ross 2002, 81). By Western standards, the social safety net of a developed welfare system was introduced prematurely across Eastern Europe as industrialization proceeded and proved a continuous drain upon limited state resources. Old-age pensions were rapidly rolled out to embrace virtually all sectors of society. By the mid-1980s substantial portions of the population were living off state pensions,[4] increasing the strain on government funding. Free medical insurance became widely available in the 1970s and was generous even by Western standards. A year's sick pay (sometimes two for certain illnesses) was not uncommon and disability retirement was proffered for those unable to return to work. Social services were expanded to incorporate extensive periods of paid maternity leave. Vacations (within the Soviet Union and bloc) were offered for a nominal fee, proving hugely popular. The state also heavily subsidized everyday living expenses, including transportation, pharmaceutical products and housing rents. Nor were health services neglected. There was a three-fold increase in the number of medical doctors per 1000 inhabitants, between the 1950s and 1980s, bringing four countries up to the West German level. Similarly, the figure for hospital beds multiplied over the same period, leaving Bulgaria, Czechoslovakia, Hungary and Romania almost on a par with West Germany (Berend 1996, 156–60).

The unspoken outcome of these arrangements was a social contract: in return for a raft of benefits, including jobs for life, the masses were expected to tolerate socialist regimes, at least paying lip service to their ideology in public, only venting their reservations in private. The fact remained, however, that beneath the seemingly impressive statistics, high-class services were not being delivered because adequate financial underpinning was lacking. Often hospitals could not afford modern Western equipment and while services might, in theory, be available to all, in practice this was not the case. As with the economy at large, a shadow economy in health provision developed, leading to underhand payments to procure better care and a hospital place (Berend 1996, 162–9).

The growing gulf between state propaganda boasting of an all-embracing welfare system and the reality bred frustration and resentment. Poland was the first bloc member to boil over, serving as a wake-up call, suggesting that the existing arrangements were no longer sufficient to sedate the people. In December 1970 the government announced drastic food price increases, prompting violent demonstrations in Baltic cities, strikes in Warsaw, the capital, and the threat of a general walkout, which brought down the Gomulka government. The action continued into February, acquiring dangerous political overtones, which prompted Moscow to step in with a special loan that enabled the new Gierek government to promise the fixing of prices at the old rate for two years. Edward Gierek recognized that much more was required to stave off another serious uprising. His solution lay in importing Western technology through borrowing from the West with the loans to be repaid through selling the resultant goods in the Free World (Swain and Swain 2003, 190–93).

This import-led growth strategy embraced by Poland quickly caught fire across the bloc, as it seemed to offer a canny solution to improving living standards. Instead, a spectacular own goal was scored as participants failed to turn around stuttering economies and made matters a good deal worse than before. Recession in the West made Western financial institutions more enthused about lending to the East, convinced that the Soviet Union would act as a guarantor of last resort. The outcome was a spectacular expansion of Western imports, which rose nine-fold between 1970

Table 8.2 *Destination by country of communist high-tech imports from the industrial West (%)*

Country	1970	1975	1981
USSR	34	35	31
China	9	13	19
Bulgaria	2	3	4
Czechoslovakia	8	6	6
GDR	4	2	4
Hungary	5	4	6
Poland	7	13	6
Romania	9	7	13
Yugoslavia	19	14	17
Other	3	3	2

Source: Aldcroft and Morewood (1995, 163).

and 1981 (Bunce 1985, 36). As Table 8.2 indicates, at the start of the 1970s, the Soviet Union was the leading recipient of high-tech imports from the West, a position it maintained throughout the decade. Next came Yugoslavia, conspicuous by its absence from the Soviet bloc and already in receipt of substantial Western aid. During the first half of the decade, which marked the high point of détente, Poland quickly attained the Chinese level before falling away in the latter half. Czechoslovakia, Hungary and the German Democratic Republic (GDR), the leading bloc economies, fluctuated to a lesser extent. In the Balkans, Bulgaria proved more hesitant, where Romania, under the reckless Nicolae Ceausescu, had no inhibitions, attaining the high point reached by Poland in 1981. As Table 8.3 indicates, the CMEA Six entered the 1970s with generally respectable levels of GNP, gross fixed investment and personal consumption, but by the middle of the decade these indicators were much reduced and in some cases negative growth was registered, a trend that persisted into the 1980s.

Whatever the scale of high-tech imports the end result was the same: abuse and misuse. Poland was by far the worst exemplar. Between 1971–80 it purchased 416 import licences, spawning a welter of grandiose projects, the majority of which were never completed. Even when they were finished failure still resulted due to massive cost overruns, the production of goods for which there was no great demand or else output fell way below production expectations. The Katowice steel plant turned out lower-grade steels when the demand was for higher-grade steels, which had to be imported. The lamentable output of the Massey-Ferguson-Perkins Ursus tractor and

Table 8.3   *Eastern Europe's annual growth by five-year plan period,*
            1971–85 (%)

Country	1971–75	1976–80	1981–85
Bulgaria			
Total GNP	4.7	1.0	0.8
Gross fixed investment	6.4	−9.1	−1.1
Personal consumption	3.9	1.6	2.1
Czechoslovakia			
Total GNP	3.4	2.2	1.1
Gross fixed investment	6.5	−0.6	−1.2
Personal consumption	2.7	1.5	1.1
East Germany			
Total GNP	3.5	2.3	1.7
Gross fixed investment	1.5	1.7	−10.0
Personal consumption	3.8	2.0	1.2
Hungary			
Total GNP	3.3	2.0	0.7
Gross fixed investment	2.3	0.3	−5.2
Personal consumption	3.2	2.2	0.4
Poland			
Total GNP	6.5	0.7	0.6
Gross fixed investment	14.1	−2.9	−1.0
Personal consumption	5.6	2.4	−0.2
Romania			
Total GNP	6.7	3.9	1.8
Gross fixed investment	10.4	6.9	−2.2
Personal consumption	5.1	4.7	0.2

Source: CIA (1988, 166).

diesel engine plant and the Berliet bus plant conspicuously failed to justify
the huge investment in them (Aldcroft and Morewood 1995, 163–4).

The fundamental flaw with the import-led growth strategy was that
neither the managerial nor the technological infrastructures necessary to
assimilate high-tech imports were properly in place. During the 1970s and
1980s a communications revolution occurred in the West founded on the
microprocessor, invented in California's Silicon Valley. This spawned the
proliferation of computers for industrial, service and private use. High-
technology industries, such as electronics, microelectronics and biotech-
nology emerged as the driving engines of the new computer age. In turn, a
post-industrial society, based on services, was developed, leading to a sharp

fall in blue-collar industrial employment and a countervailing rise in computer-related work. These trends passed the Eastern bloc by, leaving a chasm, which could not be bridged while the Cold War lasted. Accordingly, in key areas, such as semiconductor technology and computer-based production, the region made only a faltering start. One outcome was to perpetuate the gross waste associated with command economies together with much lower productivity. To quote Ivan Berend (1996, 198):

> The seventies and eighties became crisis-ridden years in Central and Eastern Europe when structural and technological renewal became impossible. The countries of the region thus continued marching, though gradually and at a slower and slower pace, still on their previous road of industrialisation, developing an economy which had already become obsolete.

The overarching emphasis on heavy industry meant that the service sector was starved of investment for decades. This neglect began to have a telling effect. In particular, the telephone network, so critical to the communications revolution, was not developed to anything approaching the Western norm. By 1980, the United States, Japan and the European Community (EC) boasted 79, 46 and 28 telephone lines respectively for every 100 citizens. Yet in the Soviet bloc the average was a meagre 7.4, wherein waiting times for the installation of a new telephone line could be as long as 10–15 years! (Berend 1996, 196–200)

The first oil shock of 1973–74, which ended the Long Boom in the West, failed to deter the Soviet satellites because their energy supplies derived not from the Middle East but from their sponsor, the Soviet Union, which possessed some of the largest oil reserves outside that volatile region. Over the first half of the 1970s they were paying prices that reflected the cheaper and more stable world market prices of the preceding five years, on the basis of the Bucharest formula. Indeed, some recipients of cheap Soviet oil, such as Bulgaria and East Germany, took advantage and recycled any surpluses to the West. But the situation proved a double-edged sword. In the West, the reverberations of the oil shock galvanized energy-saving efforts where in the East the opposite was true, compounding the growing problem of pollution, and generally failing to halt the shift from coal to oil burning. The end result was that the CMEA Six became more dependent on energy imports, with their ratio of net energy imports to primary energy consumption more than doubling from 11 to 24.4 per cent between 1970–80. Moreover, from 1975, Moscow altered the pricing formula for oil and other minerals, involving annual revisions, based on the world average price of the last three years. This meant that the first oil shock finally caught up with the satellites in the early 1980s when increased oil prices, plus the depressed economic environment, prompted a levelling off of their energy consumption. The effects of the second oil shock (1979) then hit home to accentuate the trend. What's more, Moscow now demanded that a proportion of the manufactured goods bartered for the oil should comprise those manufactured under foreign licence. As a consequence, the satellites were forced to increase their exports to the USSR by around 10 per cent (Aldcroft and Morewood 1995, 167–8; Pittaway 2004, 170–71).

From the mid-1970s the chickens were coming home to roost as the 'Western strategy' fell apart. Subsequently the Joint Economic Committee of the US Congress concluded (1989, xii):

> The strategy did not work in part because of excessive investment in import-intensive industries, neglect of modernizing the agricultural sector, and the use of government subsidies to raise living standards to artificially high levels. Decisions regarding the level and composition of imports were based more on considerations of ideology, political expediency, and excess demand than on cost or efficiency. . .The opportunities for development were squandered.

Corruption at the highest levels meant that much of the Western capital was diverted into providing luxury accommodation for leading officials while the heavy industry lobby also creamed off some funding to sustain its predominance. In any event, a protracted recession in the West severely limited export opportunities, a situation that was compounded by planners' woeful ignorance of Western consumer tastes. The Poles, for instance, produced heavy leather luggage suitcases when the current demand was for lighter plastic variety. Greater exposure to world commodity prices sucked in inflation as the cost of imported Western machinery went up astronomically. The terms of trade of the CMEA Six fell dramatically, both with the West and with the Soviet Union. This meant that exports needed to be increased to sustain the same volume of imports, which in turn resulted in greater shortages of consumer goods. Although there was an eight-fold increase in Western imports from the USSR and its satellites between 1970–81, the outcome was in fact disappointing. The expansion was achieved from a very low base, so was actually pitiful, and much of it comprised Soviet energy exports. In Western countries, with the exceptions of West Germany and Austria, Soviet bloc trade remained below 5 per cent of the total (Bunce 1985, 36). The situation was compounded by the hard currency foreign debts that were incurred through the misguided import-led growth strategy. As Table 8.4 indicates, Poland was the worst affected followed by the GDR whose largesse was facilitated by a bilateral clearing system with West Germany, which had guaranteed bank credits.

Bulgaria was unique within the bloc in boasting a hard currency balance of payments surplus by 1981. That year Poland was forced to seek a rescheduling of its hard currency debt, involving 500 banks and several

Table 8.4   *East European indebtedness in the 1970s: gross debt in billions of current US dollars*

Country	1971	1972	1973	1974	1975	1976	1977	1978	1979
Bulgaria	0.7	1.0	1.0	1.7	2.6	3.2	3.7	4.3	4.5
Czech.	0.5	0.6	0.8	1.0	1.1	1.9	2.6	3.2	4.0
GDR	1.4	1.6	2.1	3.1	5.2	5.9	7.1	8.9	10.1
Hungary	1.1	1.4	1.4	2.1	3.1	4.0	5.7	7.5	7.8
Poland	1.1	1.6	2.8	4.6	8.0	11.5	14.0	17.8	20.5
Romania	1.2	1.2	1.6	2.7	2.9	2.9	3.6	5.2	6.9
Yugoslav.	3.2	3.9	4.7	5.4	6.6	7.9	9.5	11.8	15.0
Total	9.3	11.3	14.4	20.8	29.6	37.4	46.2	58.7	68.7

Source: Aldcroft and Morewood (1995, 161).

Western governments, its debt-service ratio having reached 35 per cent, with over $4 billion falling due in 1982. Indeed, it was in no position to pay the interest, let alone the principal. The following year Romania followed suit, having become a net importer of oil from 1977. Out of favour with Moscow for its maverick line in foreign policy, Romania was forced to pay world market prices for Soviet oil after the Iranian Revolution put paid to a favourable oil supply deal with the Shah. By 1980, the year after the second oil shock, Romania was recording a deficit of $1.6 billion on its oil account (Aldcroft and Morewood 1995, 161, 169). East Germany managed to come through the 1970s relatively unscathed, but in the 1980s the Honecker leadership elected to develop the microelectronics sector. This proved a fatal choice, first because the West remained streets ahead in the technology, and second because the effort swallowed up huge amounts of investment and contributed to an escalating debt crisis, which had brought the prospect of insolvency by the end of the decade (Ross 2002, 81).

The close of the 1970s and start of the new decade caught the Soviet bloc between the devil and the deep blue sea. Debt-service repayments now consumed finite financial resources that would have been more productively invested in expanding Sector B. The greater contact with Western business people arising from the import-led growth strategy, which led to amenities catering for their needs, only served to increase the populations' growing taste for Western consumerism, particularly among the young, and to discredit further the banality of life under communism. Against this background most bloc economies were mired in deep recession from 1979 to 1983, setting the tone for the new decade, which was to culminate in a year of revolutions. Far from delivering improved living standards, the opposite was achieved, with the debt burden compelling governments to

Table 8.5   Percentage growth in per capita living standards, 1970–85

Country	1970–75	1980–85
Bulgaria	3.6	2.0
Czechoslovakia	2.5	1.4
GDR	4.9	1.6
Hungary	3.1	0.6
Poland	4.6	0.5
Romania	4.0	1.2

Source: Gati (1990, 108).

introduce austerity programmes. The result was that after reasonable growth in living standards over the first half of the 1970s the position was reversed by the opening of the 1980s with worse to follow (see Table 8.5). The seething discontent of the masses now became increasingly difficult to contain.

Already Poland evidenced signs of what was to come. When, in June 1980, the Babiuch government ill-advisedly attempted to raise retail food prices and exacerbated existing shortages by exporting more agricultural produce, it sparked a wave of protest strikes in the huge Baltic shipyards. From these emerged the free trade union Solidarity led by a marine electrician, Lech Walesa. Among the promises he extracted from the government was one to reform the economic system in consultation with Solidarity. Soon the union, which rapidly attracted 10 million members out of a population of 35 million, was threatening to wield its economic muscle to remove communism from power altogether. With the perturbed Soviet Union denouncing Solidarity as 'counter-revolutionary' and massing troops menacingly along the eastern border, the new Polish leader, General Wojciech Jaruzelski, cracked down hard on Solidarity to avert external intervention. Martial law was imposed in December 1981, leading to mass arrests and the outlawing of the dissident union altogether in 1982 (Bideleux and Jeffries 1998, 572–6). But the pressures that brought it into existence remained and would resurface. There was also an economic cost to Moscow. During 1981, to shore up the Jarulzelski government, it provided $6.7 billion worth of raw materials and energy supplies at half price, when it was charging other CMEA members 70 to 80 per cent of the Organization of Petroleum-Exporting Countries (OPEC) rate for oil. More widely, the burdens of empire were straining the creaking Soviet economy, with aid to its East European satellites totalling $133.8 billion between 1971 and 1980, almost double their total debt to the West (Bunce 1985, 17, 20).

THE SOVIET UNION: THE ROAD TO REFORM

During the 1970s, a crisis-torn period for its satellites, the Soviet Union exuded a supreme confidence, signifying that it considered it had at last arrived as a true superpower on a par with the United States. Having achieved nuclear parity, Moscow could now negotiate arms control agreements from strength. Internally, the stage of 'most highly developed socialism' was proclaimed. Soviet economists confidently informed the leadership that the 'crisis of capitalism' was at hand, prompting Leonid Brezhnev, the General Secretary since 1964, to pronounce that 'capitalism is a society without a future'. Rashly he authorized the expansion of Soviet influence into the Third World, believing it a fertile ground for the spread of communism, and continued to spend exorbitant amounts on defence with the mighty Soviet arsenal proudly shown off before the world at the annual May Day parade. Brezhnev also spoke of the Soviet Union and its East European satellites as a 'socialist community', a 'well-knit family of nations', which were the 'foundation of the future worldwide brotherhood of nations' (Brezhnev 1973, 93). The true picture within the 'prison of nations' was rather different.

By the 1980s there was no longer any credence to the fanciful notion, dating from Khrushchev, that the Soviet Union was catching up with, let alone overtaking, its rival superpower. The CIA began monitoring the economic performance of the command economies in the 1950s, seeking to pinpoint their strengths and weaknesses for political advantage in the Cold War. The CIA (1999, 19–20) estimated that the Soviet economy actually peaked in 1970, calculating that it then reached 57 per cent of American GNP. Thereafter the superpower development gap widened once more with the United States economy growing on average over 1975–85 by one percentage point per annum more than its rival. Brezhnev's final years, between 1979 and 1982, came to be known as 'the era of stagnation' with the ailing economy mirroring his declining health. The Eleventh Five-Year Plan (1976–80) sought growth of 4.1 to 5.1 per cent, the lowest ever, after the preceding plan (1971–75) failed to meet its target of 6.1 per cent by one percentage point. By the 1980s scrappage rates for machinery and equipment were ridiculously low at a time when labour force growth was falling, exacerbating declining productivity (Tompson 2003, 81). Only through the cushion of oil and gold exports to the free world and arms sales to the Arab world during the 1970s could superpower pretensions be sustained and economic reform postponed, but that was not an option that Brezhnev bequeathed to his successors.

What exactly went wrong? It has been suggested that the Soviet Union won the wrong race. By 1980 it out-produced the United States in coal, steel,

oil, tractors and selected machine tools. But in the crucial aspects associated
with the Third Industrial Revolution it was very much a laggard. Quality of
product, cost-effectiveness and technological innovation outside the military sector were three key areas where the Soviets failed badly. Even by 1987,
two years into the Gorbachev experiment, the USSR had only 200 000
microcomputers compared with over 25 million in the United States
(Strayer 1998, 57–60). More galling still was the fact that the Soviet Union
had even fallen behind some of its satellites in certain respects. By 1983 the
United States boasted 540 passenger cars per 1000 people against only 36 in
the USSR, where Hungary and Poland managed 118 and 76 respectively.
Telephones per capita told a similar tale: the United States recorded 76 telephone units per 100 population against just 9.8 in the Soviet Union, 21.1 in
East Germany and 22.6 in Czechoslovakia (Boettke 1993, 35). Per capita
output (Table 8.6) is revealing. It will be seen that Czechoslovakia turned
out more steel and (with Poland) coal than the Soviet Union; East Germany
generated more electricity and three times the fertilizer; Czechoslovakia,
East Germany and Romania made more machine tools; Bulgaria,

*Table 8.6   Per capita output of selected commodities in CMEA countries,
1978*

Commodity	Bulgaria	Czech.	GDR	Hungary	Poland	Romania	Soviet Union
Industrial commodities							
Steel (kg)	280	1010	416	363	550	539	580
Coal (kg)	796	4278	–	942	4885	479	1860
Electricity (kwh)	3572	4559	5727	2391	3301	2940	4600
Cement (kg)	584	674	747	446	618	636	486
Fertilizer (kg)	77.5	81.2	276.0	96.7	74.9	113.0	90.5
Machine tools (per 10 000 inhabitants)	17.4	22.6	11.5	11.9	7.9	12.4	9.1
Cars and lorries (per 10 000 inhabitants)	–	143.0	124.0	0.6	109.0	52.7	79.4
Agricultural commodities							
Grain (kg)	860	735	591	1266	623	873	908
Meat (kg)	82.4	101.0	108.0	143.0	89.5	70.0	58.8
Milk (kg)	227	377	442	220	488	256	362
Eggs	247	310	311	444	243	288	242

Source: Kux (1980, 70).

Czechoslovakia, East Germany, Poland and Romania produced greater quantities of cement; Czechoslovakia, East Germany and Poland manufactured more motor cars. In agriculture the disparities are yet more marked, with all bloc economies outstripping the Soviets in meat and egg production and Hungary in grain output (Kux 1980, 29).

The CIA was puzzled by the marked slowdown in the Soviet economy after 1975 and, following several in-house industry case studies, analysed what was happening in an overview paper produced in 1983. Among the more critical constraints identified were the escalating shortfalls of raw materials, growing labour shortages, increasing difficulties expanding energy supplies, rail transport bottlenecks and the priority accorded to defence (Noren 2003, 5). The failure to modernize the Soviet economy is illustrated by the dramatic increase in industrial employment growth from 1960–89 – the largest in the world – which reflected a continuing reliance on labour over machinery and the political need to offer secure work to the masses. Where, over the period, the Soviet Union increased its industrial workforce to 36.4 million the United States achieved a reduction to 18.4 million, reflecting its much greater use of labour-saving technology (Spulber 2003, 200–1).

In a rare moment of candour, Brezhnev conceded during a speech of 11 June 1971 that 'without major defence expenditure we should have moved our economy forward faster' (Miller 1971). In January 1968 the CIA's Director of Central Intelligence, Richard Helms, informed Congress that the Soviet Union had recently altered its resource allocation to favour defence even more than before at the expense of manufacturing industry and agriculture. He predicted that 'the cutback in investment is bound to affect economic growth adversely'. Three years later at a further Congressional briefing Helms considered that economic problems would not deflect the Kremlin from military projects or foreign adventures since the Soviet economy was 'now large enough that even low rates of growth mean a very substantial increase in output'. A CIA report of May 1976 estimated Soviet defence spending as rising from 40–50 billion roubles in 1970 to 55–60 billion roubles by 1975 (constant 1970 prices), with defence requirements now absorbing between 11–13 per cent of GNP as against under 8 per cent in 1969 (Noren 2003, 11).

Whatever the true figures (recent calculations range between a third and one half of GDP), the defence over-commitment explanation for Soviet economic decline can be pushed too far. As Mark Harrison (2002, 400) recognizes, 'it is sometimes overlooked that the Soviet defence industry was itself an important source of growth'. Certainly its workforce was more dedicated than usual and the sector was well administered given its importance to national security. At the same time, while excessive defence spending might have qualified the Soviet Union as a *military* superpower, the evidence is strong that it became an economic burden too great to bear. During the 1970s the Soviet Union was metamorphosed from a regional to a global superpower. It delved into Southeast Asia, Africa and the Middle East, developed a multi-ocean navy, maintained a formidable nuclear arsenal and boasted the biggest field army ever assembled in peacetime, with 170 divisions deployed in Eastern Europe with a lesser, but still formidable, force in the Soviet Far East facing rival China. The resulting economic strains and lost opportunity costs were considerable. 'The geopolitical effort', notes Janos (2000, 331), 'claimed the best 40 per cent of all machinery, 33 per cent of metal products, and 20 per cent of all the energy produced in the Soviet Union'. Indeed, in the non-military sector, civil firms generally escaped modernization, with some retaining equipment dating from the 1930s and 1940s or even earlier (de Tinguy 1997, 15). Again, client states proved more of a drain than an asset. The enormous foreign aid effort was consuming 2 per cent of GNP by the early 1980s. Wherever communism was established in the Third World, the Kremlin clung to the doctrine that it should be rendered irreversible and was prepared to squander resources to try to ensure the longevity of converts. In turn, the clients greedily exploited their patron for subsidies, which meant that their backward economies were never weaned off assistance. Cuba, a Kremlin ally since the early 1960s, was by far the largest recipient, claiming around $6 to $9 billion a year in Soviet aid. Nor, generally, did the Soviet Union pay any less than Western market economies for imports of raw materials from favoured Less Developed Countries. Indeed, by 1989 the Soviet Union was left to rue the fact that non-European socialist states owed it 45 billion transferable roubles while 'friendly' Third World countries owed a further $79 billion, most of which debt was not recoverable (Janos 2000, 332).

Unnerved by the Polish riots of 1970 the Soviet leadership, for the first time, prioritized consumer goods over capital goods in the Ninth Five-Year Plan, unveiled the following year. Brezhnev even proclaimed that a higher standard of living was an 'ever more imperative requirement of our economic development, one of the most important preconditions for the rapid growth of production' (quoted in Wilson 1971). In practice, the skewed emphasis on Sector A over Sector B continued, the former receiving the lion's share (95 per cent or more) of manufacturing investment between 1956 and 1985 (Spulber 2003, 204). The fact was that far from Soviet communism giving rise to a classless society it spawned a new ruling class, the *nomenklatura*, who used the CPSU's dominance for personal advantage. Under Brezhnev the upper 10 000 of Soviet officialdom enjoyed a privileged existence, which embraced hard currency accounts to access Western consumerism, luxury holidays and extravagant accommodation. Below them, around two million others wallowed in a middle class lifestyle, gaining subsidized housing, vacations and consumer goods from East Germany and Hungary. Such corruption was hidden from public view behind high-walled dachas and off-limit areas but nevertheless became common public knowledge, encouraging widespread disillusionment with the system. The depressing effects were apparent through increased alcohol consumption, which mushroomed alarmingly during the 1970s. By 1980 an estimated 37 per cent of workers had taken to the vodka bottle compared with 11 per cent in 1925. Not only men but also women became alcoholics, thereby raising infant as well as adult mortality rates. Beneath the froth of his routine rhetoric about creating the 'new Soviet man', Brezhnev hinted at deeper social problems at the Twenty-sixth Soviet Party Congress:

> Soviet man. . .has been educated by the party, by the country's heroic history, by our entire system; he lives the full-blooded life of the creator of a new world. This does not mean, of course, that we have already solved everything with the moulding of the new man. (British Foreign and Commonwealth Office 1981, 1)

The impact of inebriation was widespread. Mondays saw the lowest rate of productivity for any working day following a weekend of irresponsible bingeing; pay day resulted in more industrial accidents than any due to workers dipping into their wages to buy hard drink (Tucker 1987, 110).

Ever-lengthening queues for food were another irritant for the average citizen. To its deep consternation, from 1963 the Kremlin became reliant on grain and meat imports from its sworn ideological enemy, the United States. This was in stark contrast to the days of Tsarism when Russia, in the late nineteenth century, became the world's leading grain exporter. The dire performance of Soviet agriculture (Table 8.7) remained an Achilles heel that dogged successive leaders, creating a vulnerability to external pressure. By the 1970s the Soviet Union had become a net food importer, during which decade there was a ten-fold increase in food imports. Although there were a series of disastrous harvests, the situation was compounded by gross inefficiency in domestic agriculture. Tractors and other machinery took too long to produce and reach collective farms, around one-fifth of the grain harvest was routinely lost due to rotting or belated harvesting and a good proportion of the potato crop habitually disappeared through inadequate storage facilities and a disorderly distribution system. Moreover, Brezhnev's commitment to increase meat production to improve the diet of citizens proved a further strain. Although annual meat production rose from 8.3 to 14.9 million tons between 1964 and 1975, thereafter, until 1982, it stagnated at around 15 million tons. Over the same period, per capita consumption of meat, milk, milk products, meat and poultry rose

Table 8.7   Soviet agriculture, rates of growth, 1951–79 (average annual percentage rate of growth)

Commodity	1951–60	1961–70	1971–79
Grain	3.4	4.0	−0.3
Potatoes	−0.8	2.0	−0.5
Fruits and vegetables	6.5	5.3	3.3
Technical crops	4.6	4.0	1.3
Net crop output	2.6	3.7	0.7
Meat	6.1	3.5	2.7
Milk	5.7	3.0	1.3
Other	9.0	5.5	−0.9
Net livestock output	6.1	3.7	1.0
Net agricultural output	4.3	3.7	0.9

Source: Bialer (1986, 48).

significantly reflecting the huge subsidies for agricultural products on the official market. By 1980 Soviet agriculture employed 35.5 million people, double the amount of farm workers in the United States, Canada, Japan, France, West Germany and Italy combined. It was also absorbing around 27 per cent of total investments, despite which a change in fortune remained elusive (Bialer 1986, 47, 67).

After suffering two strokes and becoming dependent on medication to live, Brezhnev remained Soviet leader in name only. At the same time as he was rendered ineffective, so the factors that had enabled his regime to avoid meaningful reform disappeared. During the 1970s, the Soviet Union, like its satellites, took advantage of cheap short-term credits that became available from the West through the surge in petrodollars. But by the early 1980s, with interest rates on loans now in double digits, it became prohibitively expensive to repay existing debt through new borrowing. The first oil shock had seen the price of a barrel of oil shoot up from $3 to $40 while the plummeting dollar sparked a retreat to gold, whose guaranteed price per ounce rose from $35 to $180 and eventually to a peak of $840 at the close of the 1970s. As a major exporter of both commodities, the Soviet Union benefited hugely, using the extra revenue to purchase record amounts of grain from the United States, Canada and Argentina. The heavy reliance on hard currency earnings from oil exports (Table 8.8) was a mixed blessing, especially given the fluctuating prices on the world market.

From 1979, the year in which the Soviet Union triggered the 'New Cold War' by invading Afghanistan, the external environment dramatically turned against the Kremlin. Ronald Reagan, a former cowboy actor,

Table 8.8   *Hard currency earnings from Soviet oil exports, 1971–85 (nominal US$)*

Year	Foreign exchange earnings (millions of US$)	Expressed as a % of total hard currency earnings
1971	567	21.6
1972	556	19.6
1973	1248	26.1
1974	2548	34.1
1975	3176	40.5
1976	4514	46.4
1977	5275	46.5
1978	5716	43.4
1979	8932	45.7
1980	10803	46.7
1981	11222	58.3
1982	13747	61.4
1983	14085	64.2
1984	13669	61.6
1985	10867	53.8

Source: Considine and Kerr (2002, 138).

entered the White House and was soon openly denouncing the Soviet Union as the 'evil empire', ominously promising to consign it to 'the ash heap of history' and foreseeing a 'world without communism'. Reagan, the oldest president in American history, instinctively recognized that the USSR and its East European satellites were ripe for collapse. In similar vein, the CIA, with its accumulated knowledge of Soviet economic vulnerability saw this moment, along with right-wing hawks close to the administration, as opportune to apply pressure to the enemy. Recognizing how the Kremlin had survived the 1970s virtually unscathed, Washington acted to deny it the same line of retreat. The second oil shock, therefore, was not such a boon as the first to the USSR because the United States successfully pressured friendly oil producers, especially Saudi Arabia, to step up their production. Moreover, in March 1983, the Americans persuaded OPEC to cut its oil price for the first time since its inception in 1961. Simultaneously, the Reagan government pursued deflationary policies, one effect of which was substantially to reduce the price of gold to $250 an ounce. It is also now known that the CIA wrecked a pipeline transporting natural gas from Western Siberia to West Germany and France through planting 'Trojan horse' software via an elaborate sting against the KGB's Directorate T, which engaged in the acquisition of advanced Western technology.

Programmed to function normally for a time, the software then went haywire, producing a massive explosion that the Kremlin only kept quiet because of the remoteness of the location (Allen-Mills 2004).

Through its invasion of Afghanistan and subsequent deployment of mobile medium-range nuclear missile-launching systems targeted on Western Europe the Kremlin inadvertently provided hostages to fortune for its enemy to exploit. Reagan publicly abandoned any aspiration of a balanced budget and engaged in a $2 trillion armaments programme to overhaul American military capabilities at every level, thereby deliberately engaging the Soviet Union in a new arms race it was in no position to win. Washington recognized that with its much larger economy it needed to devote a much smaller proportion of its GNP (5.5 to 7 per cent) to defence than the Soviets. There was no contest. In 1982 the American State Department calculated the GNP of the United States and its rich allies at $7.5 trillion against the Soviet alliance's $2.1 trillion. Moreover, in its determination to spend what it took to achieve military supremacy, the United States could borrow at will – paying for around half of its armaments through German and Japanese investment in US Treasury bonds – which the USSR could not. Added to this, Reagan threatened to take the 'New Cold War' to a technological level the Soviets could not match – the Strategic Defence Initiative (1983) designed to provide a nuclear shield in outer space. Thoroughly alarmed, the Kremlin now sought a new course before its existing power position was eroded irrevocably (Janos 2000, 333–9).

Yuri Andropov, who succeeded Brezhnev after his third and fatal stroke in November 1982, could ill afford to ignore the growing economic problems that had produced stagnation. Soviet GNP growth averaged just 2.7 per cent per year from 1976–80 and actually fell by 1.4 per cent in 1980 (Bunce 1985, 21). Under his leadership the emphasis was placed on thrift, discipline and hard work, which were accompanied by laws to reward good workers and penalize slackers, including senior officials. Selected consumer prices were raised in an effort to reduce queues and discourage black marketeers. Five Leningrad factories were earmarked to resurrect the 'Scekino' experiment from 1967 permitting the sacking of workers, with savings in the wages fund utilized to introduce incentive payments. In agriculture, 'contract collective' methods, again harking back to the 1960s, were encouraged whereby a 'brigade' was made responsible for completing a task from start to finish, rather than piecemeal as hitherto. By 1983 150 000 such 'brigades' were cultivating one-fifth of the arable area, promising higher yields.

The overall aim was to improve productivity but critics sneered that Andropov was merely tinkering with the system and averting fundamental reform. David Ratford, the British Chargé D'affaires in Moscow, concluded that 'Andropov aims to extract the last percentage point of economic growth from the considerable reserves still untapped within the present system (itself no mean task) but that his ambition does not extend much further' (Ratford 1983, 7). A leaked official Soviet document, which became known as the 'Novosibirsk Report', surfaced in the West in 1984. Its author, who later became an adviser to Gorbachev, lamented an economy that had become immune to innovation, beset by a lazy workforce and rife with corruption. They regarded the continuance of a Stalinist industrial infrastructure as regressive, a view that chimed with the diagnosis of underground publications. It was during this period that the word *perestroika*, meaning reconstruction, first began to be used in official circles, even though Gorbachev later claimed it for his own (Hanson 2003, 167–8).

As far as it went, the 'Andropov effect' carried the promise if not the certainty of an economic turnaround. Deploying police to investigate truancy from work revived some of the fear associated with Stalinism, more especially given Andropov's KGB background. Unemployment (parasitism) was deemed a crime and the discipline campaign revealed the startling fact that in three towns the number of parasites was greater than the perceived labour shortfall in the vicinity, suggesting either that they were working in the black economy or else taking time off work to join the queues for everyday essentials. Although insisting that employees remained in their workplace during official working hours did not ensure that greater effort was applied, the limited evidence does suggest that supervisors, managers and branch-ministry officials imbibed the sense of fear and applied themselves more effectively. The net result, together with increased investment instigated by Andropov, was an improvement in economic performance in 1983 (Hanson 2003, 165–72).

Whether Andropov might have succeeded where Gorbachev later failed so calamitously can only be conjecture. 'While Andropov's ascension to power', concluded the CIA (1985, 2), 'gave a glimmer of hope for change, his tenure was too short and he had too little personal energy to reverse the decades of abuse and mismanagement tolerated by his predecessors'. It seems improbable that he would have unleashed the political freedoms associated with *glasnost* (openness), which so undermined Gorbachev's economic agenda. And while Andropov was unlikely to have cured the patent, it might have survived for some time longer rather than fall victim to the 'blundering surgeon' treatment that Gorbachev's critics accuse him of (Read 2001, 198).

In the end, Andropov's poisoned chalice turned out to be Gorbachev himself. Notwithstanding an unsuccessful period in charge of agriculture,

Gorbachev, at Andropov's urging, became the Politburo's youngest member in 1981. As Andropov's favoured successor, Gorbachev became acquainted with a group of freethinking intellectuals, from whom many of the impetuses for his reforms were drawn. All the same, Gorbachev had to bide his time: following Andropov's death in February 1984 he was promoted to number two behind the geriatric conservative Constantin Chernenko, favourite of the Brezhnevite old guard. It was only in March 1985, therefore, following his decrepit leader's expiry that Mikhail Gorbachev became, at 54, the youngest Soviet leader since Stalin. He would be the CPSU's sixth and final General Secretary.

RECIPE FOR DISASTER: *PERESTROIKA*

The debate over the demise of the Soviet economy centres on two key areas: whether the system was suffering from systematic malaise and as a result was doomed regardless of the actions of the leadership, or whether it faced severe difficulties but nevertheless remained workable but for the reforms introduced by Gorbachev. An argument can be made that central planning had malfunctioned for a long time and finally broke down under Gorbachev. Some analysts have suggested that the Soviet command economy was beyond reform and thus in the long term unsustainable. Both explanations have some validity but what can be said is that the timing of the débâcle was down to Gorbachev. 'That the collapse was inevitable', observes de Tinguy (1997, 29), 'does not mean that it was inevitable when it took place, in 1991'.

The state of the economy when Gorbachev came into office was not healthy but neither was it catastrophic. It retained the cushions of considerable oil, gas, gold and armaments exports even if the revenues were not constant due to world prices fluctuating. While the economy depended on food imports the grain embargo imposed by President Carter, following the invasion of Afghanistan, ironically hurt American farmers more, leading President Reagan, his successor, to lift it in April 1981. Again, unlike several satellites, Brezhnev had not embarked on a reckless import-led growth strategy in the 1970s. Indeed, when grain imports were above average, purchases of Western technology were cut back to compensate. So, although the USSR began to accumulate a hard currency deficit, it never reached crisis proportions and, provided the world energy prices remained reasonably buoyant, was easily manageable. What confronted Gorbachev, then, was not a disastrous position. In fact he spoke of a 'pre-crisis situation', which he dramatically encapsulated in mid-1986 as: 'If not us then who? If not now when?' (Acton 1995, 311).

Some reforms were clearly necessary but their nature and extent were matters for debate. There was a clear division within the Kremlin between radicals and conservatives. Had Gorbachev's more cautious rivals bested him for the leadership they would have shunned the combustible mixture of parallel economic and political reforms that he favoured, which, within six years, had brought the Soviet experiment to a shuddering and cataclysmic end. Gorbachev's recalibration of foreign, domestic and economic policies ('new thinking') marked him out from the typical Soviet leader. Styling himself as a 'man of the 1960s' from the generation that did not fight in the 'Great Patriotic War', Gorbachev was in fact acutely aware of the fate of Nikita Khrushchev, who was ousted in a Politburo coup in October 1964 after his economic reforms went badly wrong. The Politburo had only approved Gorbachev's succession by a narrow margin and he recognized that he needed to build up a political base of support outside the Kremlin to sustain his leadership. Thus Gorbachev shunned any notion of duplicating the Chinese reforms, begun in 1978, which aimed at a steady economic transformation whilst retaining an authoritarian political system. Again, this gradualist route, which commenced with agriculture, was not one that appealed to the new Soviet leader. Having failed once already with agriculture, for Gorbachev to hazard a repeat risked sharing Khrushchev's fate after the ignominious calamity of his ill-advised Virgin Lands scheme. In Gorbachev's defence, the Chinese economy, unlike the Soviet, was predominantly agricultural and could safely postpone tackling its under-performing large-scale enterprises where he could not (Gregory and Stuart 2001, 241; Chow, 2002).

Andrei Grachev, one of Gorbachev's advisers, considered him 'the last true believer in communism'. Gorbachev felt that if only communism's ideals were put into practice, transparently free from corruption, then the CPSU could become genuinely popular and not require violence and repression to retain power. His aim was to bring about 'revolution without any shot' and to 'give a second wind to socialism, on the basis of socialist values' (de Tinguy 1997, 32). Gorbachev's initial reforms were cautious and did not yet reveal their radical nature. Greater democracy, inside and outside the workplace, in Gorbachev's vision, would facilitate *perestroika* and galvanize the population into actively supporting rather than passively tolerating the communist regime. The Twelfth Five-Year Plan (1986–90) had as its core the goal to transform the machine-building complex (machine tools, instrument making, electronics and robotics) in order to modernize plants and make them competitive in world markets. The conversion of the defence industry, as resources became available from the peace dividend of a rapprochement with the United States, would transform the light and food industries. A new state committee, Gospriemka, was created to monitor quality and set about its business with vigour. The initial enthusiasm with which his reforms were received on the streets and in factories, where Gorbachev – in an unprecedented gesture for a Soviet leader – made himself accessible to ordinary people, and his ignorance of the limitations of the system, initially made him wildly optimistic: '80 per cent to 95 per cent of the total output of basic goods will correspond to world standards by 1990', he confidently informed the June 1986 Plenary Meeting of the Central Committee of the CPSU, 'with the figure for newly developed products reaching practically 100 per cent. It is planned to switch production entirely to top-quality articles between 1991 and 1993' (Geron 1990, 30).

Gorbachev's honeymoon period with the population lasted only until he unleashed his ill-considered anti-alcohol campaign in May 1985. There had been such campaigns before dating from Brezhnev. The issue perturbed Andropov but he went no further than exhorting people to moderate their drinking habits by consuming beers and wines rather than spirits. Gorbachev's campaign was much more draconian, quickly succeeding in curtailing the output of alcoholic beverages and reducing consumption, with some 67 per cent of liquor stores closed down. Gorbachev and his cohorts seriously miscalculated the impact of the campaign, which was the first in a series of trial-and-error initiatives. Productivity was not improved because addicts took more time off work to join the lengthy queues for what drink was still officially available. A fillip was given to underground production by criminals. They became notorious as the 'alcomafia', whose output not infrequently led to alcoholic poisoning! Gorbachev's popularity was damaged and he was derided as 'Lemonade Joe', 'Comrade Orange Juice' and the 'Mineral Water Secretary', an image that stuck and came back to haunt him once the vodka-loving Boris Yeltsin emerged as a rival from the wings. Worst of all, perhaps, the campaign deprived the state of tax revenues it could ill afford to lose, with 53 billion roubles raised in 1984, the year before the initiative started. Finally, in October 1988, the campaign was abandoned as a lost cause. Tax revenues never returned to their previous level (by 1990 *Pravda* was positing an annual budget shortfall of ten billion roubles as a consequence of the anti-alcohol campaign), inflationary pressure was stoked up, the state forever lost its previous monopoly on alcohol production and sugar remained in short supply as the bootleggers continued to prosper (Ligachev 1996, 335–39; Marples 2004, 27–9).

Aside from this catastrophic own goal, elsewhere Gorbachev at first trod carefully, emphasizing the need for 'further perfecting' the centralized system while he removed conservative opponents from the Politburo, meanwhile not even daring to evince the word 'market' (Nove 1992, 394). While, at the Twenty-seventh Party Congress of February 1986, he spoke of 'a radical reform' being necessary, not until the June 1987 plenary session of the Central Committee did he unveil significant underpinning legislation. The Law on State Enterprises gave managers more freedom to choose their products according to demand and reward their workforce. The Law on Cooperatives sought to legalize a raft of underground activities with a measure of private enterprise also allowed in agriculture. The term 'cooperative' cloaked capitalist activity in socialist dogma but there was no escaping the fact that, although they needed to be registered and their profits were subject to tax, cooperatives would operate outside the central planning system and were largely free to set their own prices. The move represented an attempt to reign in the black market. Although Gorbachev spoke of making the peasant 'the real master of the land' there was no intention of private land ownership outweighing collective farms. 'Allowing private enterprise on a small scale in selected activities', observes Hanson (2003, 215), 'was at this stage as far as he would go'.

It soon became clear that simply tinkering with the system was not enough. There were too many restrictions. Although the revival of commercial accounting, harking back to NEP, implied that enterprise managers could respond to the market, their prime responsibility remained plan fulfilment with over 80 per cent of their total output still devoted to state orders. State enterprises remained subject to a superior branch ministry, which accentuated the reluctance of managers, imbued with the servitude, not to mention the convenience, of taking state orders, to be adventurous. Cooperatives were not seen as a full-time occupation and niggling constraints hindered their freedom to attract workers. Official figures suggest that by 1991 over six million people worked in 245 356 cooperatives. But they were no substitute for the state's poor provision of goods and services, they were tainted in the public's mind through association with criminal gangs and the black market, and their prices were often beyond the average citizen's ability or willingness to pay. Similarly, the lend-lease land scheme failed to take hold. Local agricultural bureaucracies, with a vested interest in the status quo, frustrated the reform; unappealing short-term leases, rather than the 50-year terms permissible, were offered; available farm machinery was not designed for small holdings; and all-important fertilizer remained in short supply (Gregory and Stuart 2001, 235–36).

At the macro level, other initiatives also fell short of expectations. The machine-building programme failed to transform the industrial base. A shortage of high-quality steel undermined its scope while domestic producers, knowing they had a captive market, continued to turn out defective equipment. Although there was some improvement in production and computerization, a 1988 estimate suggested that half the machine tools suffered from a lack of sophisticated computers. Moreover, state orders still dominated the sector, thereby failing to inject competition to raise standards. The situation was not helped by the penalties applied by Gospriemka for late deliveries and poor quality, which saddled the sector with almost four billion roubles of debt between 1986 and 1988, retarding the intended transition to cost accounting. Indeed, Gospriemka provoked such resentment from central planners and enterprises at the scale of output rejected that it was eventually forced to close down (Considine and Kerr 2002, 191–2).

Likewise, the reorientation of the defence sector towards civilian production was not a roaring success. Enterprise managers resented the new responsibilities conferred on them to produce household appliances and spoke of 'falling under conversion' as if they had contracted a deadly disease. Used to returning healthy profits, defence enterprises were understandably 'unwilling to risk lower returns from making fruit juice squeezers' (Wolf 1990) and the like. Indeed, by 1991 conversion had become too expensive to contemplate on a mass scale, not least because it carried with it the threat of extensive unemployment with its dangerous political connotations. That spring Gorbachev openly conceded that the conversion programme had failed and was now prepared to contemplate an arms export drive as an interim solution (Cooper 1993, 32–3, 45, 48–9).

The political consequences of economic reform also stymied price reform. The initial intention was to introduce an industrial wholesale price system wherein centrally set prices were the exception rather than the norm. The rest would be determined through agreement between buyers and sellers, albeit according to guidelines laid down by central planners. There was also an intention to free up retail prices, thereby removing state subsidies. In the event, reform was minimal because of the feared political consequences that might flow from sudden price increases. The result was that official prices remained irrational and increasingly this was reflected in the free market.

Gorbachev sought to revisit the foreign variant of NEP and encourage joint ventures between domestic and foreign firms outside the Soviet bloc. Globalization, borne on the vine of multinational corporations, largely bypassed the USSR, because of the Cold War. Gorbachev was acutely conscious of this. 'By the early 1980s', he observed in February 1986, 'the transnational corporations accounted for more than one-third of industrial production, more than one-half of foreign trade, and nearly 80 per cent of the patents for new machinery and technology in the capitalist world' (Brooks and Wohlforth 2000–01, 38). Gorbachev overturned the stale portrayal of the West as 'imperialist' and sought a mutually productive economic relationship to fully integrate the Soviet Union into the world economy, thereby gaining greater access to Western capital and technology.

Membership of the International Monetary Fund (IMF), World Bank and the General Agreement on Tariffs and Trade (GATT), shunned by Stalin and his successors, was now sought.

The Ministry of Foreign Trade was abruptly abolished in January 1988. With it went a virtual monopoly on foreign trade. Its successor, the Foreign Economic Commission, was empowered to authorize enterprises to trade directly overseas. In the event, joint ventures did not take off as expected. For would-be foreign investors there were too many unanswered questions and objectionable arrangements. Major stumbling blocks included the legal ownership of assets if there was a falling out with the Soviet partner; the inability to dismiss employees; the domination of material inputs by central planners with no concern for joint ventures outside the plan; the repatriation of profits; majority Soviet equity. The taxing of supposedly duty-free imported materials also proved irksome. Nevertheless, the enormous potential market – approaching 300 million consumers – and greater Soviet willingness to relax some red tape had led to the establishment of 2905 joint ventures by the turn of 1990–91. Moscow even succumbed to its own branch of McDonalds, a status symbol of American capitalism. But the majority failed to reach the production stage or else were on too small a scale to make any difference, the lack of a proper market economy and consequent legal uncertainties leading most foreign firms not to go beyond registering their interest (Hanson 2003, 200–201).

In the end, the interaction with the world economy was of an altogether different ilk to that originally contemplated. As Soviet satellites had done, Gorbachev increasingly resorted to Western loans and credits, especially from West Germany, whose banks, in October 1988, extended a \$1.6 billion credit, principally to help modernize the food processing and consumer goods sectors (Desia 1989, 106). In May 1990, despite misgivings over the conditions, the USSR joined the EBRD as a prelude to eventual membership of the IMF and World Bank. The West, however, was in no hurry, sensing that the economic and political chaos that Gorbachev's reforms had by now engendered would not bring about full-blooded democracy and a free market economy. Thus a three-year transition period on entry into the EBRD was imposed, denying the Soviets full lending facilities. In turn, the United States and EC coalesced to block Soviet GATT entry, first mooted in 1986, until May 1990, following the Malta superpower summit, officially ending the Cold War. Even then admission was granted only on the basis of observer status. Again, the USSR acquired Most-Favoured-Nation (MFN) status in a trade agreement with the EC in December 1989 but the latter's quantitative restrictions were only to be gradually removed over the next six years. Brussels in turn made it abundantly clear that prospective EC membership, and the enticing subsidies that went with it, was not on the agenda. Gorbachev's vision of 'a common European home', therefore, was more pipe dream than reality in his time. Finally, the 1990 Houston Summit saw Western governments pass the buck to the IMF, which was given the remit of analysing Soviet economic problems, generating a huge report but no bailout (IMF 1990; Metcalf 1997, 125–7).

THE CMEA SIX, *PERESTROIKA* AND ECONOMIC MELTDOWN 1985–89

A good case can be made for suggesting that the satellites had already sealed their fate before Gorbachev's arrival on the scene, through their economic mismanagement of the 1970s. 'When Gorbachev assumed power in 1985', the CIA (1988, 158) reflected, 'Eastern Europe had endured nearly a decade of economic decline and stagnation'. The Soviet bloc's real GDP growth rate had plummeted from an average of 3.23 per cent over 1971–80 to 0.9 per cent between 1981–85, providing the prelude to a catastrophic negative value of –1.16 per cent in 1989, the year of revolutions (Brooks and Wolhforth 2000–01, 24). Those regimes that had partaken most enthusiastically in import-led growth were left to rue the consequences – continual financial crisis arising from the external debts accrued, falling trade with the West, the scarcity of new credits and a fresh peak in Soviet oil prices in 1982–83, as they caught up with the second oil shock.

A critical change now occurred as the Kremlin began signalling its dissatisfaction with the longstanding economic relationship with its satellites. Between 1972 and 1984 the USSR extended the equivalent of $114 billion in trade subsidies to the CMEA Six (Metcalf 1997, 2). By the 1980s there was a growing current of Soviet dissatisfaction, even resentment, at the sub-standard manufactures delivered by satellites in return. Behind the scenes there were sarcastic references to 'plant management with no plants', 'despoilers of the Soviet Union' and 'parasites'. The disquiet produced a CMEA summit in June 1984, attended by Gorbachev, whereby the CMEA Six undertook to double their output by the year 2000 and prioritize automation, electronics and biotechnology. When he became leader, Gorbachev attempted to galvanize bloc members into providing manufactured goods of world quality. When these efforts failed miserably, and a sustainable rapprochement was achieved with the West, the principle that Soviet interests came first became paramount. The terms of trade then moved decidedly against the satellites. By 1989 some 32 per cent of Soviet exports went to Western markets and the USSR was moving away from the transferable rouble to dollar pricing, notwithstanding objections from the CMEA Six. Moreover, the Kremlin was now insisting that any oil it provided above normal quotas be paid for in hard currency (US dollars), thereby compounding rather than easing the financial difficulties of the satellites. It will be seen that, with the exception of Romania, the millstone of hard currency debts worsened during the Gorbachev period.

Throughout the 1980s the satellites persisted with the command economy structure. The alternative of import-led growth via Western capital and technology as pursued in the 1970s was no longer viable. Poland, which had purchased 316 industrial licences over 1971–75, invested in just six between 1981–85, involving a mere 1.2 per cent of industrial output. Czechoslovakia plunged to forty-second place in world industrial production while East Germany, by the late 1980s, could manage only half of West Germany's living standard. There was now an air of unreality surrounding economic policies. The Polish five-year plan for 1986–90, for instance, looked to increase coal production by 14 million tons annually, ignoring an official report that energy conservation was preferable to greater extraction on cost grounds (Okey 2004, 35–6). The debts incurred in the 1970s preoccupied the minds of bloc leaders and limited their scope for manoeuvre. Unwisely the neo-Stalinist Ceausescu determined to repay Romania's external debts within a decade. Though he succeeded by 1989 (Table 8.9) the incredible deprivations this involved for ordinary citizens – whilst their detested leader and his grandiloquent wife led a conspicuously sumptuous lifestyle – built up a seething resentment that only the loyalty of security forces kept in check.

'In reality', a Politburo memorandum of October 1988 recorded of bloc regimes, 'all of them need changes, although we do not tell them this publicly to avoid criticism for trying to impose our *perestroika* on our friends' (quoted in Zubok 2003, 15). The previous April, on a visit to Hungary, Yegor Ligachev, the CPSU's ideology chief, had openly hinted at Moscow's changing stance towards its satellites. 'Each individual country', he pronounced, 'can act independently. In the past it used to be said that the orchestra was conducted by Moscow and that everybody listened. That is no longer the case' (quoted in Chafetz 1993, 71). Behind the scenes Gorbachev did in fact attempt to persuade satellite leaders to emulate his reforms but with decidedly mixed success. Hungary and Poland proved more receptive than recalcitrant East Germany and Romania, with Bulgaria and Czechoslovakia falling in between, paying lip service to *glasnost* and *perestroika* without really changing anything.

Nevertheless, the 'Gorbachev effect' stirred dissident movements across the bloc where before they had been hesitant and for good reason. Initially, there was some expectation that Gorbachev's heresy would not last long. By 1988 not only had he survived but he was about to light the torch paper

Table 8.9   Estimated hard-currency debt of the Soviet bloc, 1990 (US dollars, billions)

Country	1975	1980	1985	1986	1987	1988	1989
Bulgaria							
Gross	2.6	3.5	3.2	4.7	6.1	8.2	9.2
Net	2.3	2.7	1.2	3.3	5.1	6.4	8.0
Czech.							
Gross	1.1	6.9	4.6	5.6	6.7	7.3	7.9
Net	0.8	5.6	3.6	4.4	5.1	5.6	5.7
The GDR							
Gross	5.2	13.8	13.2	15.6	18.6	19.8	20.6
Net	3.5	11.8	6.9	8.2	9.7	10.3	11.1
Hungary							
Gross	3.9	9.1	14.0	16.9	19.6	19.6	20.6
Net	2.0	7.7	11.7	14.8	18.1	18.2	19.4
Poland							
Gross	8.4	24.1	29.3	33.5	39.2	39.2	40.8
Net	7.7	23.5	27.7	31.8	36.2	35.6	36.9
Romania							
Gross	2.9	9.6	6.6	6.4	5.7	2.9	0.6
Net	2.4	9.3	6.2	5.8	4.4	2.1	−2.2
Eastern Europe							
Gross	24.2	67.0	71.0	82.7	96.0	97.0	99.7
Net	18.8	60.5	57.4	68.1	78.2	79.9	NA

Source: Adopted from Comecon (1991, 11).

for the 1989 revolutions. During 1988 Gorbachev's advisors warned him of impending financial collapse in Bulgaria, Hungary, Poland and the GDR (Zubok 2003, 15). The Kremlin, even if it had so wished, was now in no position to bail out its politico-economic partners. To send in the tanks, as in 1956 and 1968, should the satellite populations revolt against socialist dominance, risked provoking economic sanctions and terminating Western credits. In any case, repression was against Gorbachev's nature and he would not hear of it. Already he had committed the Soviet Union to withdraw its forces from Afghanistan, curtailed or reduced military and economic aid to the Third World and slashed the military budget as verifiable nuclear arms limitation agreements were forged with Washington. As the image of an ailing superpower was transmitted to the satellite populations so they became increasingly restless. Soviet diplomats in Hungary and Poland, where Solidarity had revived, remitted alarmist reports on developments. The Kremlin took due note. 'Poland', Gorbachev informed the Politburo, was 'crawling away from us. . .And what can we do? Poland has a $56 billion debt. Can we take Poland on our balance sheet in our current economic situation? No. And if we cannot – then we have no influence' (Zubok 2003, 10–11).

It now became a matter of making political capital out of the situation to curry favour with the West and keep the credits flowing. In October 1988 Eduard Shevardnadze, Soviet Foreign Minister and close ally of Gorbachev, began drafting a keynote address intended as a belated riposte to Sir Winston Churchill's famous 'iron curtain' speech at Fulton, Missouri of March 1946, often seen as a declaration of the Cold War. Before a spell-bound United Nations General Assembly in New York, Gorbachev, on 7 December 1988, announced that Soviet armed forces would lose 500 000 military personnel and 5000 tanks from the bloc with the military budget set to fall by 14.2 per cent between 1989 and 1991. If ever a hint was given of non-interference with pending political change this was it. Further confirmation came during March 1989 with the first contested elections in the Soviet Union since December 1917, when the Congress of People's Deputies came into being. There followed the 'year of revolutions', commenced by Hungary and Poland, which ended with the bloody overthrow of Ceausescu. In fact, the more progressive of the satellites had already begun to reorient their trade towards the West, a trend the revolutions accelerated. The USSR, in turn, wanted to maximize its earnings potential in world markets. In July 1990 Moscow elected to reduce oil exports to East European members by 30 per cent and commence charging for its raw materials in hard currency at current world prices (Metcalf 1997, 124–5). The formal divorce came in June 1991 when the now moribund CMEA was formally wound up.

Events in the bloc were steered by Gorbachev's unwillingness to resort to violence. Although he gained enormous political kudos in the West, the course of events carried with them detrimental consequences for his position. First, transition economies emerged from the communist wreck-age with Poland in the vanguard through its 'shock therapy' approach. Overnight *perestroika* was made to seem pedestrian, especially as the increasingly hapless Gorbachev began back-pedalling, shifting politically to the centre ground. Second, far from retaining their 'socialist basis', as Gorbachev assumed, new governments in the former bloc, to varying degrees, sought to establish Western-style democracies. Finally, Gorbachev's passivity in the face of the revolutions influenced the already rest-less peripheral republics of the 'inner empire'. To his consternation the three Baltic States, incorporated into the USSR against their will in June 1940 under the terms of the secret clauses of the Nazi-Soviet

Non-aggression Pact, began clamouring for their economic and political independence. The writing was on the wall.

DENOUEMENT FOR *PERESTROIKA*, 1989–91

It was on the watch of Mikhail Gorbachev that economic disaster befell the Soviet Union. As Table 8.10 indicates, a manageable position at the time of his accession to power quickly escalated out of control.

Ultimately Gorbachev was hoist with his own petard. By 1989–90 his reforms had got out of kilter: the political initiatives of *glasnost* swept forward relentlessly, leaving the floundering *perestroika* trailing in their wake. In November 1990 the CIA judged that the situation was now critical:

> The USSR is in the midst of a historic transformation that threatens to tear the country apart. The old communist order is in its death throes. But its diehards remain an obstructive force and new political parties and institutions have yet to prove their effectiveness. The erosion of the center's influence, coupled with the republics' assertion of sovereignty, is creating a power vacuum. Gorbachev has amassed impressive power on paper, but his ability to use it effectively is in doubt. Meanwhile, economic conditions are slowly deteriorating. . .The question is not whether the economy will decline further but how steep that decline will be (CIA 1990, 87).

The increasing desperateness of the economic situation was revealed in mid-1989 when the chairman of Gosplan announced a 'crash programme' to increase the production of consumer goods by 12 per cent during 1990. Needless to say, it failed to deliver (Wolf 1990). By this point Gorbachev's reform initiatives were flagging on all fronts. The performance of agriculture in particular continued to be abysmal. During 1989 only sugar production rose significantly with butter, cheese and meat output barely

Table 8.10   Soviet economic performance under Gorbachev

Criteria	1986	1987	1988	1989	1990	1991
GNP growth (% year)	4.1	1.3	2.1	1.5	−12	−13
Internal debt as % GDP	20	22	36	43	55	NA
Budget deficit as % GDP	−2.4	−6.2	−8.8	−11	−14	−20
Balance of payments in convertible currencies ($US billions)	0.637	−2.3	−0.72	−3.7	−11.8	NA

Source: Brooks and Wohlforth (2000–01, 32).

registering increases and canned products actually falling. Although the grain harvest had actually exceeded 200 million tons in three of the last four years the dependence on substantial food imports remained. Again, housing starts, so promising in *perestroika*'s early years, were now at a virtual standstill (Peel 1990; Hanson 2003, 177–217).

In the past it would have been a case of 'grin and bear it' for the masses but by now *glasnost* gave them a critical political voice. After contested elections spread to the republics in 1990, local politicians curried favour with voters by putting regional concerns before the national interest. There quickly followed a critical breakdown in the longstanding economic relationship between the republics and central government, known as the 'war of laws', with the former no longer prepared to meet their national delivery obligations regardless of local consequences. Worse still, the republics withheld taxes from central government, with only 36 per cent of planned revenues received in the first quarter of 1991. That April, his patience finally exhausted, Gorbachev issued a decree giving republics a week to rescind their decrees obstructing exports to the centre. But without military intervention, which Gorbachev refused to countenance, his ultimatum was contemptuously ignored (Strayer 1998, 136–7). To make matters even worse, strikes, virtually unheard of before Gorbachev, became commonplace. Hitherto, strikes were hushed up and severely dealt with. Now they were allowed to fester and fed off the oxygen of publicity allowed by *glasnost*. Where, in 1989, a total of 7.3 million working days were lost, this figure had already been surpassed by February of the following year and the rising trend continued. Strikers' demands included higher wages, improved working conditions, job security, better housing, increased pensions and shorter hours. The litmus test of the government's crumbling authority was the damaging miners' strike of July 1989, which was only ended by injecting subsidies of eight billion roubles into the industry. Yet the miners, aggrieved by the ever rising cost of living, struck again, in March 1991, with their cause prompting sympathy strikes and public donations. The government responded this time by offering to double wages but the inflationary environment meant that even this gesture was not enough. Only greater concessions and Yeltsin's intervention, as leader of the Russian Republic, persuaded the miners to return to work, but only after the settlement added more fuel to the inflationary flames (Moskoff 1993, 183–225).

The farther *perestroika* went the more it turned into a quagmire. 1989 proved a pivotal year when several key indicators turned downwards. By then the domestic budget deficit had reached around 11 per cent of GNP, having more than quadrupled since 1985. Over the same period government debt rose from 16 to almost 45 per cent of GDP while gross hard currency debt on the external account doubled to reach around $22 billion (Wolf 1990). Gorbachev blamed extraordinary factors – falling world energy prices, the Chernobyl civilian nuclear reactor catastrophe (1986), the Armenian earthquake (1988) and lost tax revenues arising from the anti-alcohol campaign. The catalogue of excuses held some truth but the inexorable rise of the budget deficit was as much due to more enduring trends. Inefficient state enterprises continued to be subsidized by the state, which covered the difference between revenues and costs. Massive subsidies to keep food prices down (in 1989 consuming 110 million roubles) were judged politically expedient to avert widespread demonstrations (Moskoff 1993, 16). Once again, the fruits of *glasnost* served to make the situation much worse. The Congress of People's Deputies insisted on passing a new, but costly, pensions law and on returning 1.6 billion roubles to farmers to waive their electricity bills. Enterprise managers, who were now elected by their workforce, used their newfound freedom to set wages, helping to stoke up inflation, as earnings rose much faster than productivity. In 1989, for example, average wages rose by 10.9 per cent while industrial output grew by just 1.7 per cent (Wolf 1990). The belated increase in wholesale and retail prices, in January and April 1991 respectively, only exacerbated the inflationary spiral (see Table 8.11). As Alex Nove perceived (1992, 213), the price nettle was grasped 'far too late'. The collapsing value of the rouble against the American dollar led to a resort to the printing presses, which harked back to Weimar Germany's hyperinflation of 1923, with the currency in circulation skyrocketing from 4.1 billion to 28 billion roubles between 1985–89.

The situation was compounded by the decline in export earnings, thereby removing the counterweight to imports. Having reached $5.4 billion by 1989, the trade deficit surged to around $15 billion within a year. Oil and natural gas accounted for approximately 40 per cent of export revenue, but the twin perils of increasing extraction problems and declining world energy prices punctured the balloon. Imports, by contrast, continued to

Table 8.11   Soviet estimates on annual rates of inflation (%)

Year	Rate
1987	8.4
1988	8.4
1989	10.5
1990	56.5
1991	650–700

Source: Strayer (1998, 135).

surge, reflecting still inadequate food production and light industry's need to take 40 per cent of its inputs from abroad. Initially, the Gorbachev regime acted prudently, reducing Western imports by 28 per cent over 1985–87 to reflect lower oil revenues. The trend was, however, reversed between 1987–89 when Western imports rose by 43 per cent. In 1985, when Gorbachev entered office, external debt was around $16 billion. Within three years it rose to $42.3 billion, reaching as high as $90 billion, by some calculations, in December 1991, when he resigned. Inevitably, ever greater proportions of export earnings were consumed in servicing the debt, the debt service ratio rising from 22 to 50 per cent over 1988–91. Increasingly, gold reserves were denuded in order to earn desperately needed hard currency. As a consequence, little capital was available for direct investment into the moribund economy. The regime had abandoned financial rectitude in a vain effort to satiate the population with consumer desirables. In 1991 the financial crisis became so severe that a drastic curb on imports (of the order of 47 per cent in the first half) was imposed. From the laudable position of being considered a worthy creditor in international markets, the USSR was transformed, under Gorbachev, into an economic basket case (Nove 1992, 413; Moskoff 1993, 16–17).

Gorbachev and his reformers succeeded all too well in neutering the command economy without providing the cushion of a properly formed market economy to compensate. As the CIA's Office of Soviet Analysis concluded in April 1991:

> The centrally-planned economy has broken down irretrievably and is being replaced by a mixture of republic and local barter arrangements, some of which resemble a market, but which do not constitute a coherent system. . .The economy is in a downward cycle with no end in sight. (CIA 1991, 113)

In September 1988 Gorbachev abolished the Central Committee departments responsible for supervising economic ministries. *Perestroika*'s muzzling of ministerial powers was accompanied by a drastic reduction in central planning personnel from 1.6 million to 871 000 between 1986–89, representing a 46 per cent diminution. Such developments nullified Gosplan's traditional authority and created confusion. At the CPSU Plenum of February 1990 a leading official complained that 'the state's directing organs have lost control over many of the most basic aspects of economic development' (Nove 1992, 408).

'For citizens and visitors', an observer remarked (Wolf 1990), 'the nonavailability of almost any good one cares to name, except the rouble, has become the economy's salient characteristic'. By 1991, of 1100 types of consumer goods, only 20 were routinely available. Although shortages had also afflicted his recent predecessors, under them the population remained confident that its basic requirements would be met by the state and prices would stay stable. Such stoicism evaporated under *perestroika* and from 1988 people began hoarding, turning their flats into makeshift warehouses. The situation was worsened by cooperatives buying products from state shops to sell on at inflated prices. Excess demand, fuelled by inflationary wage rises from state enterprises, which, by early 1991, was estimated at 250 billion roubles, created an environment that was manna from heaven for bootleggers, who siphoned off state-produced consumer durables. Standing at an estimated 90 billion roubles by 1989, compared with only 5 billion roubles in 1960, the black economy was valued at around 130 billion roubles by early 1991, representing approximately 30 to 40 per cent of GNP, with no less than 20 to 30 million citizens actively involved. In 1989 the Department to Fight Organized Crime was established in the Interior Ministry, which also hosted the Department for Combating Speculation and the Embezzlement of Socialist Property. Both were fighting an uphill and unwinnable struggle. Between 1986–89 officially recorded cases of extortion rose from 1122 to 4621, increasing thereafter at an annual rate of 15 to 30 per cent. Moreover, these were only the tip of the iceberg, with most cases never reported. Not a particular problem before the Gorbachev era, extortion grew exponentially as the authority of the state crumbled. Very few cases came to court; of those that did, sporadic sentences were too lenient to deter; and corrupt party officials joined in protection schemes to line their own pockets (Moskoff 1993, 27–78).

Increasingly desperate, Gorbachev sought solutions but without ever finding them. The Abalkin programme of October 1989, approved by him, conceded that 'there is no worthy alternative to the market as the method of coordinating the activities and interests of economic agents' (Wolf 1990). All this was too drastic for the conservatives however, leading Prime Minister Nikolai Ryshkov to attempt to soothe them with a five-year transitional plan to a 'regulated market economy' (a contradiction in terms), wherein key prices would remain fixed to preserve jobs and there would be no rouble convertibility. Gorbachev rejected this approach as too gradual but equally he had no stomach for the '500-day plan' or 'Shatalin plan', inspired by Poland's 'shock therapy', which envisaged a rapid decontrol of prices, mass privatization and large budget cuts. Gorbachev's subsequent halfway-house 'Presidential plan', of October 1990, proffered only a partial commitment to the free market and left timing vague.

In any event, the impatient republics no longer had time to wait on the vacillating Gorbachev. By the start of 1991, five had declared themselves independent with more threatening to follow. Despite surviving a coup in August, Gorbachev was 'fatally' wounded as his seeming saviour, the populist Yeltsin, emerged as his natural successor, banning the CPSU in the Russian Federation and embracing a market economy. Earlier that month, the G7 members, meeting in London, denied Gorbachev the massive aid programme he craved, knowing that a more radical leader-in-waiting stood ready to sweep away all hesitations and deliver a true market economy. Yeltsin struck home when he derided the Gorbachevs as 'royalty': Mikhail in his Western designer suits and Raisa, his extrovert wife, notorious for her extravagant shopping sprees in the West, which were a world away from the dire situation at home. Yeltsin also took delight in humiliating Gorbachev in the televised debates of the Congress of People's Deputies. With his popularity fast evaporating, as opinion polls readily testified, Gorbachev became less accessible to the people but continued to spend time overseas as the West's reverence for him remained undimmed. When the Soviet people learnt that their leader had been awarded the Nobel Peace Prize for ending the Cold War it prompted the witticism that it would have been far better if it had been for economics! As it was, Gorbachev had become irrelevant. Already, on 24 August, he had resigned as General Secretary of the CPSU, clinging on to the new position of Executive President, created by him in March 1990. On Christmas Day 1991, with Yeltsin having outmanoeuvred his efforts to keep what republics remained together, Gorbachev also stepped down from this position, the USSR itself having ceased to exist since 9 December. The close of the momentous year saw the famous Hammer and Sickle flag lowered from the Kremlin for the final time.

AN ASSESSMENT

Gorbachev unleashed the last efforts to reform the Soviet system. But they were doomed to fail because they lacked rationality, consistency of application and fatally undermined the tacit political support that bound the USSR together. By removing, one by one, the pillars of the edifice, Gorbachev made eventual collapse inevitable. 'Mikhail Gorbachev', Hanson (2003, 117) wryly observes, 'was the first Soviet leader who, if one may judge by appearances, did not understand the Soviet system. He was therefore the last Soviet leader'. Critics of Gorbachev are at one in suggesting that he disengaged the command economy without first providing a market economy substitute. In truth, the process he began was beyond the career of any politician to accomplish and still continues to this day. There was no road map for him to follow and too many forces were ranged against him. The command economy created vested interests, which doggedly resisted change. Yet by introducing parallel political changes, partly intended to protect himself, Gorbachev unintentionally undermined his authority. Everyone in responsible positions, from factory managers to Congress members to republican leaders, now needed to be a populist to keep their positions. Economic prudence went out of the window. The central government's efforts to introduce a USSR-wide sales tax at the turn of 1990–91, for instance, proved an abysmal failure because of the regional resistance it encountered, which led to so many exceptions as to render it ineffective as a revenue generator. The situation was compounded by the competition that erupted between the central and republican governments from autumn 1990, to reduce tax rates to attract enterprises (Mau and Starodubrovsraya 2001, 234–5).

The sudden collapse of the USSR and its satellites over the period 1989–91 took the outside world by surprise. Reflection suggests that from the mid-1970s, at the latest, their economies were in severe difficulties. That decade provided the prelude to the denouement that followed. As well as the shortcomings of the command economies chronicled here, the changing relationship between politics and economics must be taken into account to understand the course of events. The astute Stalin had readily understood that the Soviet Union and its bloc must not on any account become entangled with the tentacles of the capitalist West. Accordingly, under his leadership, Czechoslovakia was denied permission to apply for Marshall Aid and neither the USSR nor its satellites became members of the multinational economic organizations that sprang up after the Second World War. In turn, the West, initially, was not keen to trade with the East. Both Western Europe and Japan applied quantitative restrictions (QRs) to their trade with the East while the United States exercised tariff discrimination through denying MFN status to East European countries. In 1951 the economic dimension of the Cold War intensified with the establishment of the Coordinating Committee for Multilateral Export Controls (CoCOM), comprising North Atlantic Treaty Organisation (NATO) members plus Japan, intended to deny any 'dual-use' technologies (military and civilian) to the East. Over time, however, disputes arose within its ranks as to what constituted 'strategic' goods and France and West Germany, in particular, broke ranks to take advantage of trading opportunities with the Eastern bloc.

It was the progressive coming together of the bipolar worlds that proved the harbinger of doom for communism across Eastern Europe. The process began in the late 1960s and accelerated with East–West détente. By the late 1970s the EC had lifted many QRs. Poland, Hungary and Romania became GATT members (albeit under special conditions) and were extended MFN status by the United States, seeking political more than economic advantage, during that decade. As they became embroiled in deepening economic crises, which carried with them the distinct prospect of the collapse of the bloc, so the West became eager to encourage the process. In 1988–89 the EC concluded trade and cooperation agreements with Hungary and Poland and subsequently, in the early 1990s, extended these to Czechoslovakia, Romania, the Baltic States and the Commonwealth of Independent States, successor to the Soviet Union. The full normalization of East–West trade relations followed the decision of former centrally planned economies to move to market-based systems. By November 1993 the United States had accorded MFN status to all former bloc members and ex-Soviet republics. That same month, CoCOM was abolished, at last giving the East full access to Western technologies. The European Union (EU) also began to relax its anti-dumping legislation vis-à-vis Eastern Europe, as a necessary prelude to extending membership to its nation states (Smolik 1995, 244–7). Western capital, from multinational, national and private sources, now poured into the region. This time, unlike the 1970s, the funds were properly managed and put to excellent use as the transition economies benefited from leading-edge technologies to transform their infrastructures and industries. With the money came Western management expertise to harness the immense potential that now existed.

The fatal wrong turn for the bloc came with the decision to adopt an import-led growth strategy. Based on floating interest rate loans, the moment chosen could not have been less opportune, and the end result was that they were saddled with a mountain of external debt. The gamble reflected the fact that in-house efforts to switch to intensive growth had palpably failed leading, ironically, to a turn to the capitalist West for a way out. The Soviet Union, aside from its military and space capabilities, resembled an undeveloped country, becoming the world's largest importer of grain and food and a considerable machinery importer. Its exports to the West comprised overwhelmingly of primary goods with only a tiny fraction deriving from manufactured products (Bialer 1986, 66). At the same time, it should be borne in mind that Soviet willingness to make 'foregone gains' in trade with the West in order to continue its dominance over its satellites helped to sustain their command economies for longer than might otherwise have been the case. Soviet trade data suggests that between 1974–84 Soviet exports to the bloc increased by only 35 per cent (comprising overwhelmingly of energy) while the volume of imports in return grew much more – machinery and equipment by 133 per cent, industrial consumer goods by 82 per cent and foodstuffs by 86 per cent (Smith 1992, 85–6). Only the last category was strictly necessary – the rest was politically motivated.

Once the Soviet Union itself ran into economic difficulties, so its leadership was compelled to question the value of the relationship with its satellites. There was, briefly, an effort to 'turn inwards' and transform the CMEA, which was seen as carrying the potential to render the Eastern bloc less susceptible to Western economic pressure with all its political overtones. When this failed, Gorbachev was given the ammunition to let the satellites drift away. Even had another Soviet leader been in place, the reality was that hard currency earnings from exports to Western markets were now all-important, meaning that repression, which risked provoking financial and economic penalties from the West, could no longer be entertained. In turn, Soviet energy exports were increasingly orientated towards Western markets because of their greater earnings potential and fuel subsidies to bloc members were gradually removed. Brezhnev began the trend; Gorbachev completed it.

THE AFTERMATH

It is important to recognize that economic disaster did not end with the collapse of communism, that there was an economic price to pay for political freedom. 'The declines in output in Eastern Europe and the Soviet Union', declared the United Nations Economic Commission for Europe (1991, 7–9) 'are now so large that it would be appropriate to speak of a depression'. Indeed, the fall in output in the transition economies was of a magnitude not seen since the Great Depression (see Tables 8.12–8.13). Poland, the earliest to instigate transition, experienced a fall in industrial output of 25 per cent and of GDP by 12 per cent in 1990 (Winiecki 2002, 5). The causes were manifold but at the heart of the continued economic collapse were the sudden withdrawal of Soviet demand and associated demise of the CMEA. Inevitably it took time to find new markets in the West, especially the EU, and produce quality products for them. In the meantime, a plethora of now unwanted socialist goods dominated, such as Ikarus buses (Hungary) and broad gauge railway locomotives (Czechoslovakia), produced specifically for the Soviet market. Such obsolete product lines constituted around 10 to 20 per cent of a typical socialist economy's GDP, with the private sector as yet too small to obviate against the decline. Moreover, the removal of state and Soviet subsidies rendered many goods uneconomic to produce (Aldcroft and Morewood 1995, 206–10). If anything, the initial economic performance of post-socialist countries was even more disastrous than under communism. The economies of Eastern Europe declined by an average of 7.6 per cent per annum between 1990–92. Even over the longer timeframe of 1989–98 average economic 'growth' for the region registered 1.0 per cent and were the former Yugoslav states, beset by ethnic strife, factored in then the figure would be lower still. Indeed, not until 1997 did light appear at the end of the tunnel when the region recorded positive growth of 1.4 per cent. By 1998 real GDP in Central and Eastern Europe attained, on average, 95 per cent of the 1989 figure, finally surpassing it in

Table 8.12   Real growth of GDP in Eastern Europe (%)

Country	1990	1991	1992	1993
Bulgaria	−9.1	−11.8	−11.0	−4.6
Czech Republic	−1.2	−14.2	−7.1	−1.6
Hungary	−3.3	−10.2	−5.0	1.7
Poland	−11.6	−7.6	1.2	5.0
Romania	−7.3	−13.7	−15.4	−5.1
Slovakia	−2.5	−15.8	−6.0	−7.1

Source: Aldcroft and Morewood (1995, 208).

Table 8.13   Aggregate industrial output fall from the start of transition (output change, %)

Country	Time period	Fall
Bulgaria	1991–93	−41.3
Czech Republic	1991–93	−31.3
Hungary	1990–92	−30.7
Poland	1990–92	−28.3
Romania	1991–94	−36.9
Lithuania	1992–94	−60.2
Belarus	1992–95	−46.1
Russia	1992–95	−46.1
Ukraine	1992–95	−44.7

Source: Winiecki (2002, 6).

2000 as the new century dawned (Bunce 1999, 763; Gros and Steinherr 2004, 107). At the same time, the immediate post-socialist economic performance should not be viewed too pessimistically. The continued growth of the black economy tended to magnify the official falls in output while the plunging indicators cannot be viewed as a conventional recession because of the clearing-out process involved in the switch from socialist to capitalist goods production (Grzegorz 1996, 16–33).

The transition phase was replete with difficulties. In essence, transition economies needed to overcome a number of hurdles before they could be considered market economies. These included macro-stabilization, currency reform, the establishment of an independent central bank and associated autonomous banking system, fiscal, price and market reforms, the creation of a legal system, financial and property markets and large-scale privatization. The sequencing was far from obvious and largely a matter of trial and error combined with either boldness or caution. The evidence supports the contention that those countries that adopted a 'big bang' or 'shock therapy' approach began to recover much sooner than those preferring gradualism. Without exception, the biggest falls in output were experienced in the year when price liberalization was introduced – for instance, Poland (1990), Czechoslovakia (1991), Russia (1992), Ukraine (1994) – which let loose an inflationary surge (Bunce 1999, 767; Gros and Steinherr 2004, 106–7). The evidence suggests that East European states performed better than most of the successor states in the USSR because their exposure to the command economy was over a shorter period, a trend repeated by the Baltic States. Moreover, Hungary and Poland, in particular, had begun removing the constraints of central planning *before* their political revolutions, giving them a head start in the post-communist transition period (Maddison 1997, 161).

Unlike Western Europe in the late 1940s, Eastern Europe in the 1990s was not rescued by a new version of the Marshall Plan to aid its recovery and transition to the market. While there was some forgiveness and restructuring of debt, the West was loath to risk its capital on a huge scale. The attitude of the United States and the European Bank for Reconstruction and Development (EBRD), founded in 1991 to aid the region, was that most funding for redevelopment must be internally generated from economic restructuring. Their indifference was shaped by the lesson of the 1970s when massive capital inflows were squandered and reforms retarded rather than advanced. There was also a tendency for the West to favour the new states of Central Europe over those further east since Hungary, Poland and the Czech Republic were more advanced and shared borders with West European countries. All three proved a magnet for foreign investors where Bulgaria and Romania did not. All three became full members of the Organisation for Economic Co-operation and Development first and were set to join the EU three years ahead of the two formerly communist Balkan States. Overall, the trio's situation was much more favourable, especially that of Hungary and Poland, which had already begun more far reaching economic reforms under communism and had the necessary mindset to fully embrace capitalism. Their economic turnaround therefore was achieved much sooner, beginning in 1992–93 (Okey 2004, 120–23).

In the post-communist period, economic performance was far from smooth even after the initially difficult immediate transition phase was endured. Poland, the fastest-growing economy by the late 1990s (see Table 8.14) following its 'shock therapy' approach, by 1997 had a GDP 11 per cent greater than 1989 before a slowdown from the year 2000 when unemployment rose to 16 per cent. Georgia, by contrast, recorded a GDP per capita in 1997 that was only just over a third of its 1989 level (Bunce 1999, 759; Okey 2004, 157–8).

Table 8.14 *Dynamics of basic economic categories, Poland 1989–94*
  (1988 = 100)

Categories	1989	1990	1991	1992	1993	1994
Gross domestic product	100.2	88.4	92.4	102.2	104.4	105.0
Industrial production	97.9	77.9	82.9	104.0	105.6	111.9
Agricultural production	100.9	99.7	106.8	87.2	101.5	–
Fixed capital formation	97.6	89.9	95.9	100.7	102.2	107.1
Consumption	104.9	84.6	98.6	105.0	105.0	–
Exports	100.2	113.7	97.6	97.4	113.5	118.3
Imports	101.5	82.1	137.8	113.9	115.8	113.4
Foreign investment	–	–	185.0	135.0	114.3	–
Working population						
Total	99.0	93.8	96.3	97.7	95.7	101.1
Public sector	–	88.9	85.5	93.7	91.7	96.1
Private sector	–	99.4	107.0	100.9	103.5	104.6
Inflation	332.0	586.0	170.3	143.0	137.6	132.0

Source: Grzegorz (1996, 7).

The mixed and fluctuating economic performance of Central and Eastern Europe demonstrates that a 'once. . .coherent area representing an alternative world order, this region has become – and very quickly – a microcosm of the larger world within which it resides' (Bunce 1999, 760). Not only was Eastern Europe now fully integrated into the world economy and its attendant economic cycles, but the political continuity provided by communism had also disappeared. Dependence on foreign capital also proved a mixed blessing, with large swathes of Czech, Hungarian and Polish industry and banking now controlled by outsiders which Robin Okey (2004, 164) equates to 'the interwar situation of foreign dependency'. In turn, the arrival of democracy meant that governments were often short-lived (Latvia headed the field with over a dozen regimes in a decade) and vulnerable to the whims of the electorate. Generally governments with too callous an approach have not long survived and socialism, albeit in a different guise allied to liberalism, was able to make a comeback.

In parts of Eastern Europe, especially the former Soviet Union, many have suffered extreme poverty and resent the emergent affluent entrepreneurs who took advantage of the sale of state assets at bargain basement prices. In Russia, for example, the average wage by 2004 was only £40 a week, which contrasted starkly with its billionaires' opulent lifestyles. The Russian state is ironically less caring than under communism, with its generous welfare system in the process of dismantlement by 2004, to the dismay of the many citizens still dependent on it. At the turn of the new millennium most Romanians were, in many ways, actually worse off than in 1989, receiving monthly incomes not much above $100. In Hungary, by 1999, the average income of the top tenth of the population was eight times greater than the bottom tenth compared with 5.8 times in 1988 (Okey 2004, 158, 165). At the same time, the legacies of the command economy have not been shaken off entirely.

In some key areas, therefore, Central and East European systems remain different from the Western norm. Post-communist economies generally feature a higher proportion of manufacturing industry than services; more workers are employed than are strictly necessary; productivity is lower; and collecting tax revenues remains a major problem as the black economy continues to prosper (Gros and Steinherr 2004, 121–27). 'The biggest task', rued the Australian managing director of Russia's most up-to-date aluminium plant at Krasnoyarsk, Western Siberia, 'has been trying to make the workers understand that it is not their boss who is the most important person, but the customer. It has been hard to get people to understand that they must work to the demands of the market' (Armitstead 2004).

In May 2004 the first tranche of transition countries from the former Soviet bloc, including the three Baltic States, were admitted into the EU with more set to follow.[5] The enlargement increased the EU's area and population by a fifth, giving it one-and-a-half times the citizens of the United States. Its borders now run up to the Russian Federation, Belarus and Ukraine and it is no longer inconceivable that one day they too might join the EU. In that event, Gorbachev's dream of a 'common European home' will have finally been realized. Yet there is also the prospect that the EU may expand no farther east, a possibility that he recognizes. 'Today', he wrote (Gorbachev 2004), 'a great deal hinges on where Europe goes from here. It can head towards new dividing lines or towards a truly united Europe that includes Russia'. Putin's inclination to revere his former master, Andropov, and by turns to court or ostracize the West suggests that for the foreseeable future the ever extending borders of the EU will not embrace Russia or its allies. The fact that Russia has become an 'energy superpower' buoyed up by rising gas and oil prices and able to curry favour with European or Asian customers, gives the Kremlin room for manoeuvre. The collapse of the rouble in 1998, rendering Western imports prohibitively expensive, together with a growing aversion by many Western firms to establish themselves in Russian markets, created an opportunity for domestic entrepreneurs to seize opportunities without fear of outside competition. Consequently, the big Russian cities, especially Moscow and St Petersburg, are thriving on home-grown consumerism and, to a certain extent, their growing wealth is gradually radiating outwards. That said, poverty remains widespread among former Soviet citizens who had become dependent on the generous Soviet welfare system that has virtually disappeared.

The collapse of communism across Eastern Europe is still too recent for firm conclusions to be drawn. Nevertheless, it is already apparent that the outcome is not as clear-cut as American triumphalists thought when the Cold War ended, especially once the economic dimension is considered. For Western companies, the economic disaster presaging the fall of the Soviet Empire heralded a golden opportunity to make profits in the land that time forgot. Western technology, for example, has revived Western Siberia's oil potential to the extent that in May 2004 Russian output rose to 9.2 million barrels per month, a post-Soviet record, around two-thirds of which is exported. Above all, it was the ability of the Russians to maximize their oil sales revenue that produced a surplus on their trade balance and current account. To the West the situation is a blessing as OPEC's supplies of around 23 million barrels a month from the turbulent Middle East become more uncertain and expensive with global consumption rising much faster than new discoveries (Appenzeller 2004, 97, 102). Conversely the West's exertions in helping to bring about Soviet communism's collapse have not been without their downside. Under the combative Reagan, the United States became a debtor nation for the first time in its history, a situation that was exacerbated during the presidency of George W. Bush and his resolute pursuit of a 'war on terror'. Ironically, it was the CIA's unprecedented effort to thwart the USSR in Afghanistan by arming religious zealots to harass Soviet forces that helped to spawn Osama Bin Laden and al-Qaeda. Despite the former West Germany pumping 5 per cent of its GNP annually into the former East Germany the economic rewards were slow in coming and contributed to the marked slowdown in German growth (Okey 2004, 158). The EU has been brave in taking on transition economies of varying quality, which for generations will be net recipients rather than net contributors to its ever-burgeoning budget and may never make the quantum leap. Per capita GDP of the ten new members on joining was only 20 per cent of the EU average. For the moment, their capacity to undermine the financial stability of the EU has been contained by the decision of the Copenhagen summit to limit enlargement-related expenses to only £40 billion. In 2006 endemic corruption in Bulgaria and Romania provided the excuse to postpone their accession into the EU until it is contained, delaying entry by a year until January 2007.

The implosion of the USSR, Yugoslavia and Czechoslovakia created a plethora of new nations whose economic viability and performance is hugely variable. Nationalism gave rise to some successor states after the First World War that ultimately proved unsustainable in a hostile political and economic environment. The EU's embrace and NATO's protection should avoid any repeat this time. Equally, the rules and regulations that come with EU membership may obviate the economies of scale promised to new members, many of whom bring with them an economic dynamism that was so lacking under communism but also an economic baggage of uncertain dimensions. As Niall Ferguson (2004) warned, the attractions of the transition economies – low wages, longer hours and competitive corporation tax – are likely to disappear at the insistence of the EU's established members like Germany and Belgium. 'The dynamic new boys', predicts David Smith (2004), 'will make a lot of noise, but the EU's old codgers will draw the curtains and carry on as before'. Politically, then, there is little doubt that the collapse of Soviet-style communism was a blessing, bringing about the end of the Cold War and the threat of a nuclear holocaust. Economically, there is much more room for argument and it very much depends on the perspective taken. Only time will tell.

NOTES

1. The author would like to record his debt to the editors and Professor Philip Hanson for their helpful comments and suggestions on the original draft.
2. A fellow communist state in Eastern Europe, Yugoslavia was never formally part of the Soviet bloc. It was expelled from Cominform for ideological deviance in 1948 and subjected to economic sanctions orchestrated by the Kremlin, becoming reliant on American aid. Its alternative socialism, with Tito creating communism's first 'market economy', proved equally disastrous in the long term, presaging the disintegration of the early 1990s and descent into civil war and economic dislocation. Albania withdrew from the Soviet orbit in 1961 but remained the poorest economy in Europe, with its communist regime departing office in March 1992. Because neither Yugoslavia nor Albania were aligned with Moscow they do not form part of the analysis here.
3. Bulgaria, Czechoslovakia, East Germany, Hungary, Poland and Romania.
4. Some 25 per cent in Bulgaria, 22 per cent in Hungary, 18 per cent in Poland and 14 per cent in Romania.
5. Cyprus, Czech Republic, Estonia, Hungary, Latvia, Lithuania, Malta, Poland, Slovakia, Slovenia. Bulgaria and Romania were set to join in 2007.

REFERENCES

Acton, E. (1995), *Russia. The Tsarist and Soviet legacy*, 2nd edn, Harlow: Longman.
Aldcroft, D.H. and Morewood, S. (1995), *Economic change in Eastern Europe since 1918*, Aldershot, UK and Brookfield, US: Edward Elgar.
Allen-Mills, T. (2004), 'Reagan sting blew up pipeline the West built', *The Sunday Times*, p. 25.
Appenzeller, T. (2004), 'The end of cheap oil', *National Geographic*, 205.
Armitstead, L. (2004), 'Western firms strike out into the wastes of Siberia', *The Sunday Times*, 27 June, Business Section 3: 11.

Berend, I.T. (1996), *Central and Eastern Europe, 1944–1993. Detour from the periphery to the periphery*, Cambridge: Cambridge University Press.

Bialer, S. (1986), *The Soviet paradox. External expansion, internal decline*, London: I.B.Tauris.

Bideleux, R. and I. Jeffries (1998), *A history of Eastern Europe. Crisis and change*, London: Routledge.

Boettke, P. (1993), *Why Perestroika failed. The politics of socialist transformation*, London: Routledge.

Brabant, J. (1989), *Economic integration in Eastern Europe*, London: Harvester Wheatsheaf.

Brezhnev, L. (1973), *On the policy of the Soviet Union and the international situation*, New York: Doubleday.

British Foreign and Commonwealth Office (1981), 'Background brief: problems in Soviet society', The National Archives, Kew, London, FO 973/203.

Brooks, S.G. and Wohlforth, N. (2000–01), 'Power, globalization and the end of the Cold War: re-evaluating a landmark case for ideas', *International Security*.

Bunce, V. (1985), 'The empire strikes back: the evolution of the Eastern bloc from a Soviet asset to a Soviet liability', *International Organization*, 39.

Bunce, V. (1999), 'The political economy of post-socialism', *Slavic Review*, 58.

Central Intelligence Agency (1985), 'Gorbachev's economic agenda: promises, potentials and pitfalls', September, https://www.cia.gov/, accessed 23 December 2003.

Central Intelligence Agency (1988), 'Soviet policy towards Eastern Europe under Gorbachev', 12 September, https://www.cia.gov/csi/books/19335/art-1.html, accessed 23 December 2003.

Central Intelligence Agency (1990), 'The deepening crisis in the USSR: prospects for the next year', November, https://www.cia.gov/csi/books/19335/art-1.html, accessed 23 December 2003.

Central Intelligence Agency (1991), 'The Soviet cauldron', April, https://www.cia.gov/csi/books/19335/art-1.html, accessed 23 December 2003.

Central Intelligence Agency (1999), 'At Cold War's end: US intelligence on the Soviet Union and Eastern Europe, 1989–1991', https://www.cia.gov/csi/books/19335/art-1.html, accessed 23 December 2003.

Chafetz, G. (1993), *Gorbachev, reform, and the Brezhnev doctrine. Soviet policy toward Eastern Europe, 1985–1990*, Westport: Praeger.

Chow, C.G. (2002), *China's economic transformation*, Oxford: Blackwell.

Comecon (1991), *Comecon Data 1990*, Basingstoke: Macmillan.

Congress, Joint Economic Committee (1989), *Pressures for reform in the East European economies*, Washington DC: US Government Printing Office.

Considine, J.I. and Kerr, W.A. (2002), *The Russian oil economy*, Cheltenham, UK and Northampton, MA, USA: Edward Elgar.

Cooper, J. (1993), *The Soviet defence industry. Conversion and reform*, London: Royal Institute of International Affairs.

Desia, P. (1989), *Perestroika in perspective. The design and dilemmas of Soviet reform*, London: I.B.Tauris.

de Tinguy, A. (1997), 'Collapse or suicide?' in A. de Tinguy (ed.), *The Fall of the Soviet Empire*, Boulder, CO: East European Monographs.

Ferguson, N. (2004), 'Let no one doubt it: this is one of history's good things', *Independent on Sunday*, 2 May.

Fowkes, B. (2000), *Eastern Europe 1945–1969. From Stalinism to stagnation*, Harlow: Pearson Education.

Gati, C. (1990), *The bloc that failed: Soviet–East European relations in transition*, London: I.B.Tauris.

Geron, L. (1990), *Soviet economic foreign policy under Gorbachev*, London: Royal Institute of International Affairs.

Gorbachev, M. (2004), 'A United Europe needs an integrated Russia', *Financial Times*, 30 April.

Gregory, P.R. and Stuart, R.C. (2001), *Russian and Soviet economic performance and structure* (7th edn), London: Addison Wesley.

Gros, D. and Steinherr, A. (2004), *Economic transition in Central and Eastern Europe*, Cambridge: Cambridge University Press.

Grzegorz, G. (1996), *The regional dimension of transformation in Central Europe*, London and Bristol, Pennsylvania: Jessica Kingsley Publishers.

Hanson, P. (2003), *The rise and fall of the Soviet economy. An economic history of the USSR from 1945*, Oxford: Oxford University Press.

Harrison, M. (2002), 'Coercion, compliance, and the collapse of the Soviet command economy', *Economic History Review*, LV.

International Monetary Fund (IMF) (1990), *The economy of the USSR. A study undertaken in response to a request by the Houston Summit*, New York: IMF.

Janos, A.C. (2000), *East-Central Europe in the modern world. The politics of the borderlands from pre- to post-communism*, Stanford: Stanford University Press.

Kux, E. (1980), 'Growing tensions in Eastern Europe', *Problems of Communism*, XXIV.

Ligachev, Y. (1996), *Inside Gorbachev's Kremlin. The memoirs of Yegor Ligachev*, Boulder: Westview Press.

Maddison, A. (1997), *The world economy: a millennial perspective*, New York: OECD.

Marples, D. (2004), *The collapse of the Soviet Union 1985–1991*, Harlow: Longman.

Mau, V.A. and Starodubrovskaya, I. (2001), *The challenge of revolution. Contemporary Russia in historical perspective*, Oxford: Oxford University Press.

Metcalf, L.K. (1997), *The Council of Mutual Economic Assistance. The failure of reform*, New York: Columbia University Press.

Miller, D.I. (1971), 'Miller to Fall', 16 June, The National Archives, Kew, London, FCO 28/1576.

Mises, L. von (1947), *Planned chaos*, New York: Foundation for Economic Education.

Moskoff, W. (1993), *Hard Times. Impoverishment and Protest in the Perestroika Years. The Soviet Union 1985–1991*, Providence, Rhode Island: Brown University.

Newton, S. (2004), *The global economy 1944–2000. The limits of ideology*, London: Edward Arnold.

Noren, J. (2003), *CIA's analysis of the Soviet Economy*, https://www.cia.gov/csi/books/19335/art-1.html, accessed 23 December 2003.

Nove, A. (1992), *An economic history of the USSR 1917–1991*, final edn, London: Penguin.

Okey, R. (2004), *The demise of communist East Europe. 1989 in perspective*, London: Edward Arnold.

Peel, Q. (1990), 'Farmers' woes', *Financial Times Survey*: Soviet Union, 12 March.

Pittaway, M. (2004), *Eastern Europe 1939–2000*, London: Edward Arnold.

Putin, V. (2005) 'Annual address to the Federal Assembly of the Russian Federation', 25 April 2005, http://kremlin.ru/eng, accessed 8 June 2006.

Ratford, D. (1983), 'Andropov's economic policy', The National Archives, Kew, London, FO 972/110.

Read, C. (2001), *The making and breaking of the Soviet system*, Basingstoke: Macmillan.

Ross, C. (2002), *The East German dictatorship. Problems and perspectives in the intepretation of the GDR*, London: Edward Arnold.

Rupnik, J. (1988), *The other Europe*, London: Weidenfeld & Nicolson.

Smith, A. (1992), 'Economic relations', in A. Pravda (ed.), *The End of the outer empire. Soviet–East European relations in transition, 1985–90*, London: Royal Institute of International Affairs.

Smith, D. (2004), 'Will new blood revive Europe?', *The Sunday Times*, 2 May.

Smolik, J.E. (1995), 'The transformation of East–West trade relations', in C.T. Saunders (ed.), *Eastern Europe in crisis and the way out*, Basingstoke: Macmillan.

Spulber, N. (2003), *Russia's Economic Transitions. From late Tsarism to the new millennium*, Cambridge: Cambridge University Press.

Strayer, R. (1998), *Why did the Soviet Union collapse? Understanding historical change*, New York: M.E. Sharpe.

Swain, G. and Swain, N. (2003), *Eastern Europe since 1945* (3rd edn), London: Palgrave Macmillan.

Tompson, W. (2003), *The Soviet Union under Brezhnev*, London: Pearson Longman.

Tucker, R.C. (1987), *Political culture and leadership in Soviet Russia: from Lenin to Gorbachev*, New York: W.W. Norton & Co.

United Nations (1991), *Economic Commission for Europe Bulletin*, 43, New York: United Nations.

von Hayek, F. (ed.) (1935), *Collectivist economic planning: critical studies of the possibilities of socialism*, London: Routledge.

Wilson, A.D. (1971), 'Wilson to Sir Alec Douglas Home', 7 May, The National Archives, Kew, London, FCO 28/2053.

Winiecki, J. (2002), 'An inquiry into the early drastic fall of output in post-communist transition: an unsolved puzzle', *Post-Communist Economies*, 14.

Wolf, M. (1990), 'Death rattle of the Stalinist war economy', *Financial Times, Financial Times Survey: The Soviet Union*, 12 March.

Zubok, V.M. (2003), 'New evidence on the end of the Cold War. New evidence on the "Soviet factor" in the peaceful resolutions of 1989', *Cold War International History Project Bulletin*, 12/13.

9.   The fatal inversion: the African growth disaster[1]

Derek H. Aldcroft

The wind of change is blowing through the African continent. Whether we like it or not, this growth of national consciousness is a political fact. (Harold Macmillan, Cape Town, South Africa, 3 February 1960)

Disaster, tragedy, crisis, chaos: all words that have been used to describe the economic experience of Africa, especially Sub-Saharan Africa (SSA), since decolonization (see Ravenhill 1986; Onimode 1988; Ayittey 1998). 'Africa's economic history since 1960 fits the classical definition of tragedy: potential unfulfilled with disastrous consequences' (Easterly and Levine 1997, 1203). Africa's growth performance has been described as the largest economic disaster of the twentieth century (Artadi and Sala-i-Martin 2003, 18). And not without justification. Broadly speaking, there was very little material progress on average in the post-colonial period; per capita incomes were generally no better by the end of the twentieth century than they had been in the early 1960s, and in some cases they were a good deal worse. 'For many Africans, conditions of life are scarcely better, and possibly worse, than they were when their colonial rulers departed' (McCarthy 1990, 35). While poverty worldwide has declined over the past half century, the numbers living in poverty in Africa have skyrocketed. They now make up around one half the population of the African continent as a whole and the proportion is even higher in SSA. Furthermore, nearly one half of the world's poor now live in Africa. This is indeed a remarkable state of affairs. At a time when the world economy was expanding rapidly, albeit more slowly in the last quarter of the century, Africans actually became poorer relatively and in some cases absolutely. No other region can match this disastrous economic record.

Ironically, African countries set out with high hopes as they threw off the colonial yoke, which most of them did from the later 1950s onwards. Kwame Nkrumah no doubt reflected the view of many African leaders when he made his famous prophecy in 1949: 'If we get self-government, we'll transform the Gold Coast into a paradise in ten years' (Fieldhouse 1986, 89–90). At the time many development economists were also fairly optimistic about the future potential of the African continent; indeed, more so than they were about Asia, including East Asia, which later became a very dynamic zone of development. In fact, some African countries were deemed possibly to be better placed than those in East Asia. In the early 1960s economic conditions and levels of income, especially in Korea and Taiwan, were not very different from those in many African countries (Maddison 1989, 15; World Bank 1993b, 39, 219). Korea's per capita GDP in 1960, for example, was the same as that of the Sudan, while Taiwan's was very similar to that of Zaïre (Morris 1995, 2). Income and exports per capita in Ghana, on the other hand, were higher in 1965 than those in Korea, and the same could be said of Nigeria and Indonesia (Landes 1999, 499; World Bank 2000, 19). In fact in the post-war period, that is, straddling the last years of colonial rule and early independence, most African countries recorded quite respectable rates of economic growth. So, why were their initial hopes so rudely shattered?

The features and characteristics of African development have spawned many studies and there would be little point in traversing in detail the same territory. Likewise, the explanations of failure now read like a laundry list, and a very long one at that. More appropriate would seem to be to pinpoint some of the underlying causes of long-term failure by drawing on the experience of the development process of the past.

Successful development in the past, especially in the West, has been predicated, inter alia, on the following factors: a long preparatory period before modern economic growth took hold; the containment of population pressure so that it never really became a threat to the resource base; the expansion of agriculture including some increase in productivity to cope with growing food needs; reasonable education levels at the point of departure to modern economic growth and strategic improvements to the human capital stock thereafter; and state institutions, political systems and structures that were generally favourable to development (see Aldcroft 1995 for a general review).

In all respects African countries, with few exceptions, have been deficient with respect to the above criteria. They have tried to compress modern development into decades rather than centuries as was the case in the past. There are of course exceptions in this respect, notably the East Asian success stories, but they score highly on the other counts. Second, population has exploded in Africa at the worst possible time, that is, before the development process could really get under way and in the absence of the requisite response from agriculture. Education levels were also low at the point of departure and despite considerable input into educational facilities the quality of the human capital stock has remained poor. Finally, the deficiency in statecraft: state institutions, political systems, bureaucracies and administrative systems and legal frameworks have often been anything but favourable to development and they tended to deteriorate over time.

There are a lot of factors that can be said to have arrested African development, but many are symptoms rather than underlying causes. Looking through the European mirror one can see how African countries have failed to measure up to the standards of the past. But first a brief review of the economic record is in order.

AFRICA'S GROWTH FAILURE

Since the Second World War Sub-Saharan Africa has had the poorest economic performance of any region in the world. This is even more so since the 1970s when, in the words of Collier and Gunning (1999b, 4), Africa experienced 'a chronic failure of economic growth'. It is true that in the late colonial and early independence years – the boom years of the world economy – Africa recorded quite respectable growth even on a per capita basis. For this period, statistics are far from comprehensive, but estimates suggest that per capita growth may have been of the order of between 1.8 to 2.5 per cent per annum (Fieldhouse 1986, 71; Maddison 1995, 80–83). After the mid-1970s there was rapid deterioration. While it is true that most regions of the world grew more slowly than previously in the last quarter of the twentieth century, at least growth was positive. By contrast, for many Sub-Saharan African countries, per capita growth was negative through to the 1990s. Thus, on average, Africa was no better off by the latter date than it had been in the early 1960s. Though gross domestic product (GDP) grew on average by some 2.9 per cent a year between 1960–94, this was swamped out by a population growth of similar magnitude so that per capita income remained more or less static for the bulk of the population (World Bank 1992, 1997; Crafts 2000, 17–18). There was some recovery in growth from the mid-1990s but this barely kept pace with population expansion and certainly did nothing to make an indent on the mass of poverty, with two-thirds of the population subsisting at or below the absolute poverty line (United Nations 1997, 1–3).

As Table 9.1 demonstrates, over the long haul (1965–97) more than one half the countries in the region had negative or very low growth, while only Botswana, Mauritius and Lesotho recorded strong performances. A cross-section sample of countries in Tables 9.2 and 9.3 shows clearly how poorly Africa performed compared with other regions. Accounting for growth using a standard Cobb-Douglas function produces the results listed in Table 9.4. The collapse in growth since 1973 is largely attributable to the decline in physical capital accumulation, which was actually negative between 1984–94,

Table 9.1   SSA: income and population growth (% per annum)

Country	Date of independence	GNP per capita growth 1965–97	Population 1960–92
Angola	1975	–	2.3
Benin*	1960	−0.1	2.5
Botswana	1966	7.7	3.2
Burkina Faso	1960	0.9	2.4
Burundi	1962	1.1	2.2
Cameroon*	1960	1.4	2.6
Cape Verde	1975	–	2.1
Central African Republic	1960	−1.2	2.3
Chad	1960	0.1	2.1
Comoros	1975	–	3.2
Congo Democratic Republic	1960	−2.2	3.0
Congo Republic	1960	1.7	2.8
Côte d'Ivoire	1960	−0.9	3.9
Djibouti	1977	–	–
Equatorial Guinea	1968	–	1.2
Eritrea	1993	–	–
Ethiopia	–	−0.5	2.5
Gabon	1960	0.4	3.0
Gambia	1965	0.5	3.0
Ghana	1957	−0.9	2.7
Guinea	1958	–	–
Guinea–Bissau	1974	0.1	2.0
Kenya	1963	1.3	3.5
Lesotho	1966	3.2	2.4
Liberia	1847	–	3.1
Madagascar	1960	−1.9	2.8
Malawi	1964	0.5	3.4
Mali	1960	0.5	2.6
Mauritania	1960	−0.2	2.4
Mauritius[†]	1968	3.8	1.0
Mozambique	1975	−0.1	2.2
Namibia	1990	0.7	2.8
Niger	1960	−2.5	3.2
Nigeria	1960	0.0	2.7
Rwanda	1962	0.1	3.2
São Tomé & Principe	1975	–	2.1
Senegal	1960	−0.5	2.8
Seychelles	1976	–	1.7
Sierra Leone	1961	−1.4	2.1
Somalia*	1960	−0.1	2.8

Table 9.1　(continued)

Country	Date of independence	GNP per capita growth 1965–97	Population 1960–92
South Africa	1910	0.1	2.6
Sudan	1956	−0.2	2.8
Swaziland	1968	–	2.8
Tanzania*	1963	−0.2	3.2
Togo	1960	−0.6	2.9
Uganda*	1962	−2.4	3.3
Zambia	1964	−2.0	3.2
Zimbabwe	1980	0.5	3.2
SSA	–	0.2	2.8

Note:　* GNP per capita 1965–90; † population 1980–97.

Sources:　Collier and Gunning (1999b, 5); World Bank, *World development reports*, various issues.

Table 9.2　*Growth performance by region 1950–92/94 (annual average compound growth rates)*

Region	GDP growth		GDP growth per capita	
	1950–73	1973–92/94	1950–73	1973–92/94
W. Europe (12)	4.6	2.0	3.8	1.7
Southern Europe (5)	5.8	3.0	4.8	1.9
United States	3.9	2.5	2.4	1.5
Eastern Europe (7)	5.0	−0.4	4.0	−0.8
Africa (10)	4.5	2.6	1.8	−0.4
Latin America (7)	5.2	2.7	2.4	0.6
Asia, ex. Japan (10)	5.2	5.7	2.6	3.6
Japan	9.2	3.8	8.0	3.0
Hong Kong	9.6[a]	6.5[b]	6.8[a]	5.4[b]
Singapore	8.6[a]	6.9[b]	7.5[a]	6.1[b]
South Korea	7.6	8.3	5.2	6.9
Taiwan	9.3	7.8	6.2	6.2

Note:　[a] 1960–80; [b] 1980–93. Figures in brackets are number of countries in sample.

Source:　Maddison (1995, 80–83); World Bank (1992, 1995).

Table 9.3   Per capita income levels and growth rates by region 1960–94

Region	Per capita income*		Growth rates 1960–94	
	1960	1990	GDP	Population
China	0.6	1.3	6.8	1.8
East Asia	0.9	3.6	6.8	2.2
South Asia	0.8	1.1	4.2	2.3
Africa	0.6	0.7	2.9	2.8
Middle East	1.9	3.0	4.5	2.9
Latin America	2.4	4.1	4.2	2.4
Industrial countries	6.4	14.9	3.5	0.9

Note: * Thousands of 1985 dollars.

Source: Collins and Bosworth (1996, 136).

Table 9.4   Growth decomposition for SSA and other developing countries, 1960–94

	Growth in real GDP per worker	Contribution of		
		Physical capital	Human capital	Factor productivity
21 SAA countries				
1960–94	0.39	0.60	0.23	−0.44
1960–73	1.76	1.05	0.18	0.53
1973–94	−0.44	0.33	0.26	−1.02
45 other developing countries				
1960–94	3.14	1.44	0.33	1.34
1960–73	2.07	1.19	0.39	0.46
1973–94	1.65	1.45	0.49	−0.30

Source: Ndulu and O'Connell (1999, 45).

together with the sharp deterioration in factor productivity, which alone accounted for nearly two-thirds of the decline in the growth in real GDP per worker. As can be seen, the African record was much worse than that in other developing countries; the growth in output per worker was the lowest on record and it was the only region, with the exception of the Middle East, to have had a negative total factor productivity value for the whole period, 1960–94 (Collins and Bosworth 1996, 158–9).

Thus Africa has retrogressed in the past half century compared with other regions of the world, including other less developed countries (see the illustrative graph in World Bank 1994, 19); its share of world trade has dwindled, as has that of global manufacturing production; productive resources have remained in low-tech activities, while exports have become even more concentrated in primary commodities. As one writer commented: 'Its extremely low level of industrialization combines with the atypically weak institutions, human capital and infrastructure to make Africa (with the notable exception of a minority of countries) the world's only region that has intensified its position as a pre-industrial society' (Soludo 1998, 278, 287–8).

THE GHOST OF MALTHUS

Population explosion, on initial inspection, would appear to be Africa's number one problem. Recall that in the past few countries, apart from regions of recent settlement, moved into the modern economic growth phase (sustained per capita income increase) with population increasing much in excess of 1 per cent per annum (Bairoch 1975, 204). Much of the Third World has had population growth rates two to three times this figure in the post-war decades, though several countries, China and the East Asian, have successfully striven to control their burgeoning numbers. Africa, however, has been in a class of its own. Most of the 50-odd countries of Sub-Saharan Africa (SSA) have had population growth rates around 3 per cent a year over recent decades and the average is also very close to this figure. Effectively, much of the gain in absolute gross domestic product expansion has been wiped out by the growth in numbers. It is significant that Mauritius, one of the few outstandingly successful economies in SSA (of which more below), has managed to contain its population growth within reasonable bounds, at around 1 per cent per annum.

The relationship between population growth and development is of course a very complex one and the suggested implication drawn here between peoples and poverty will appear too simplistic to mature scholars. This is undoubtedly true: some countries, notably Brazil and Malaysia, have experienced extensive development with rapid population growth. Moreover, the structure of the population change needs to be considered: whether it is indigenous or largely migratory and how this effects dependency ratios. Briefly, the African case suggests negative rather than positive qualities stemming from structural characteristics. But before discussing these let us glance through the European mirror.

The distinctive feature or contrast is that, contrary to general impressions, Europe (or more precisely Western Europe) was never really swamped by a population explosion. True it experienced temporary

Malthusian setbacks in the pre-modern period, and it had continuous population growth in the modern period, but these never scuppered the development process. Western Europe was in fact in a uniquely favourable position in that it was never suffocated by extreme population pressures that affect many Third World countries today, or retarded some Eastern civilizations, for example Ming China, in the distant past. Though in pre-industrial times Europe's population did sometimes outstrip the capacity to maintain it, at least in the short term, population pressure was never so acute as to upset radically the balance of the environment in the long term. In fact, Western Europe's ability to stave off the Malthusian devil in the longer term was crucial to easing the way to modernity.

This favourable outcome can be explained by the unique family life-cycle pattern, whereby abstinence from marriage (high proportion of celibates) and a later age of marriage for women combined to restrain fertility levels. This pattern appears to have prevailed in England, France, the Low Countries, Scandinavia, Germany and Switzerland, and also, significantly in the light of later achievements, in Japan (Laslett 1988, 235–8; McNeill 1996, 25, 34).

Checking population expansion was only one side of the equation, however. The other side was Western Europe's ability to improve its supply capability in the early modern period to a point whence it could cope with population-driven expansion from the eighteenth century onwards (Komlos 1989a, 247–8, 1989b, 204–5). In much of Western Europe both agrarian and non-agrarian sectors had been responding positively for some time so that when the population revolution took place it could be accommodated (van der Woude 1992, 247–8). The improving food supply situation, through extension of the cultivated area and enhanced agricultural productivity, albeit slow and irregular at times, meant that domestic food supplies, supplemented from time to time with imports from the Baltic and elsewhere, were at least able to keep pace with population growth (Mokyr 1976, 23–4; Grigg 1992, 2). Bairoch's study (1989) of the delivery potential of agrarian systems suggests that Western Europe was capable by the eighteenth century of matching population expansion, not necessarily by raising overall living standards initially, but by preventing them from falling away as had happened under earlier though less vigorous population expansions. It was this ability to match food to population that unlocked the door to modern development. Of added significance in the light of later experience in Third World countries, non-agrarian output and employment were expanding simultaneously, thereby enabling surplus agrarian labour to find alternative employment so that the primary sector was never swamped with labour to a point where zero or negative marginal labour productivity took hold.

Thus the moral of Western experience 'is not the rates of growth that were achieved but the fact that for the first time many European societies escaped the Malthusian trap' (Komlos 1989a, 205). A combination of restrained fertility and long-term improvements in supply capability ensured that population never became a serious constraint to development, as it was to do in many countries in the twentieth century.

One could argue that many Third World countries, and especially those of SSA, have suffered the penalty of lateness; they have become trapped by late entry into the development race. That is, the forces that worked to bring down death rates (for example, medical improvements, better hygiene etc.), while birth rates remained high, meant that populations exploded before these countries were in a position to accommodate the enlarged numbers. The previous equilibrium between population and supply potential that had prevailed in previous centuries of lower population growth was shattered in the post-war era as Western health measures were applied rapidly and more widely.

Population pressures did not always generate a pure Malthusian situation, whereby any initial uplift in income or output was quickly swamped by population expansion, resulting in incomes (per capita) stagnating or even falling, as had happened from time to time in previous centuries. In fact, the majority of less developed countries (LDCs) were able to increase their output sufficiently in the post-war period to offset population gains so that per capita income growth remained positive. But the important point to note is that in order to overcome the population handicap, LDCs had to grow that much faster in absolute terms even to maintain their relative position in the world economy, and still faster if they were to have any hope of improving their relative income levels vis-à-vis those of the developed world. In actual fact they have been unable to achieve that goal so that on average the Third World's share of world income tended to decline during the twentieth century.

Sub-Saharan Africa has been by far the worst Malthusian victim. As rates of economic growth slowed down dramatically in the less favourable global climate of the last quarter of the twentieth century, while population growth remained stubbornly high, negative per capita income change became common, so much so that many countries returned to the post-colonial departure point in terms of income and welfare levels.

The population problem in SSA has much wider implications. Two in particular merit special attention: one the question of feeding ever-growing numbers from indigenous resources when agriculture fails to respond (see below); second, the strain placed on infrastructure facilities and social overhead capital such as education, housing, health and welfare, at a time of limited capital resources. The problem in the latter respect is especially acute since the population expansion is overwhelmingly home-grown (as opposed say to immigration of able-bodied, productive workers to the

United States in the nineteenth century). This means that the age structure of the population is heavily skewed towards young dependants, whose needs in terms of education, health and medical provision put a large strain on the limited welfare and social services. No less than 45 per cent of the population in Africa was below the age of 15 in 1990 compared with only 15 per cent in developed countries (Colman and Nixson 1994, 109). Nor does this heavy age-dependency augur well as far as the future containment of the population is concerned.

Whatever eventually happens to fertility, the population problem is going to loom large in Africa for many years to come. Though relatively sparsely populated, Africa has not been able to cope with a population growth far exceeding that experienced by most successful developing countries of the past. The failure to give special priority to policies designed to moderate population expansion has been one of the signal failures of post-colonial development strategy. The same may be said of the lack of attention to feeding the people.

AGRICULTURE AND FOOD SUPPLY

Since agriculture tends to be the dominant sector in less developed or pre-industrial societies, it is generally acknowledged that it has a critical role to play in the process of modernization (Reynolds 1985, 406; World Bank 1993a, 109–10). Western experience suggests that it has fulfilled several functions to a greater or lesser extent, including that of a source of labour and capital accumulation, earning foreign exchange for the purchase of imports and, most importantly in the early stages of modernization, providing food for an expanding population. It is true that agriculture may not have been the fastest growing sector in the transition to modern economic growth, but most writers on development would no doubt agree that it is vital that it responds in a way that facilitates economic modernization. 'The history of economic development shows that few countries have achieved sustained economic growth without first, or simultaneously, developing their agricultural sector. . . .without an efficient agricultural sector, a country is severely constrained in its ability to feed itself or import foreign products for domestic consumption and development' (Birkhaeuser, Everson and Feder, 1991, 607).

But in many Third World countries agriculture has failed to live up to these expectations. For much of the twentieth century the productivity record has been very poor in many parts of the Third World, though only in Africa has labour productivity actually declined (Bairoch 1989, 345). Food output has therefore struggled to keep pace with population expansion within the confines of extendable cultivation. The worst scenario has undoubtedly been the African continent, the only region in the world to experience a marked decline in food output per capita. Sachs (1996, 25–7) suggests a drop in per capita food production of 11.6 per cent between 1961–95, though some estimates are higher especially over shorter periods (Kelley 1988, 174; Grigg 1992, 132). This has meant an increasing depend-ence on imports of basic foods with a consequent drain on scarce foreign exchange reserves. Once self-sufficient, and indeed a net exporter of foodstuffs, Africa by the first half of the 1980s was barely 80 per cent self-supporting (Grigg 1992, 133).

Though food imports had been rising steadily in the 1960s, it was not until the following decade that the food situation really became serious. Food production was increasing at only about half the rate of population growth. In many countries per capita food output was falling and by the early 1980s it was only around four-fifths of the level in 1970 (Lofchie 1986, 3).

As can be seen from the data in Table 9.5, a large number of countries suffered severe declines in per capita food production during the 1970s. Only a few such as the Ivory Coast and Tunisia and Libya in North Africa managed to record a significant increase. The result was that around one half the countries in SSA were experiencing major food emergencies in the early 1980s, which were only partially relieved by food imports and food aid (Bates 1986, 49).

Many factors, both external and internal, contributed to the food crisis of the 1980s. One stands out above all others and that is the relative neglect of agriculture, especially the food production sector as opposed to cash crop export production, in both the colonial and post-independence eras. Forbes Munro (1984, 72) for instance, argues that the main deficiency of the British presence in Tropical Africa was 'the absence of any noticeable breakthrough in the productivity of food supply', which acted as a serious constraint on African growth and development. There was a remarkable consistency in the neglect of agriculture from colonialism through inde-pendence. At the root of the problem was the peasant farm sector, which accounted for the bulk of food production for domestic use. This sector was not only neglected but it was also squeezed by successive administrations with the result that its structure and efficiency changed very little over time, while the incentive to improve performance was notably absent. As Lofchie (1986, 13) writes, 'the most conspicuous feature of African agriculture when independence occurred was the glaring discrepancy between the modernity of export agriculture and the almost completely undeveloped state of the food-growing regions'.

The immediate problem would seem to be the sheer weight of numbers on the land, which inhibited structural transformation, in conjunction with, in varying degrees, land shortages, poor fertility, primitive techniques,

Table 9.5   Percentage decline in per capita food output in selected countries 1969–71–82

Country	% decline
Angola	30
Benin	3
Burundi	4
Cameroon	3
Ethiopia	32
Ghana	35
Madagascar	19
Mali	31
Mozambique	28
Niger	28
Nigeria	16
Senegal	24
Sierra Leone	10
Sudan	18
Tanzania	12
Togo	21
Uganda	21
Zaire	8
Zambia	17
Zimbabwe	18
SSA	12
SSA (excl. South Africa)	14

Source: Calculated from data in Christensen and Witucki (1986, 22).

lack of capital resources and technical knowledge, and in some cases hostile climatic conditions. But overall, Africa is by no means an infertile or barren continent, and the failure in food production can be attributed to the lack of an effective strategy in official policy programmes. As Eicher (1986, 156) notes, 'the food production crisis stems from a seamless web of political, technical and structural constraints which are a product of colonial surplus extraction strategies, misguided development plans and priorities of African states since independence, and faulty advice from many expatriate planning advisers'. Since independence the majority of African governments have regarded agriculture as a backward and low-priority sector; politicians have been content to continue the old colonial practice of pumping the surplus out of agriculture through negative pricing and taxation and using the proceeds to promote primitive industrialization, build prestige projects such as airports, dams and hotels, or for more nefarious purposes (Eicher 1986, 161–5). African farmers have been the most heavily taxed in the world, explicitly through producer price-fixing, export taxes and taxes on agricultural inputs, and implicitly through overvalued exchange rates and high levels of industrial prices, which raised the price of farmers' own consumption and inputs. High rates of taxation undoubtedly contributed to the dramatic decline in the rate of growth of agricultural production, from 2.2 per cent between 1965–73 to 0.6 per cent in the first half of the 1980s (World Bank 1994, 76–7). Meanwhile, little was done to modernize agriculture, to encourage small farmers or to improve infra-structure facilities such as marketing, technical instruction and transport. In many parts of the continent, transport costs accounted for over one half of total production and marketing expenses, while about one-third of per-ishable products are wasted due to transportation difficulties (African Development Bank 1998, 41). It is not surprising therefore that the African Development Bank made a plea for 'back to basics' in one of its recent reports. It argued that agriculture would remain the potential engine of growth for most African countries for the foreseeable future and stressed that a more consistent agrarian strategy was vital in order to eliminate food deficits, generate more foreign exchange and eventually provide the where-withal for industrialization (African Development Bank 1998, 41–2).

Neglect of agriculture is not unique to Africa. Other LDCs have been culpable, so too have East European countries and the Soviet Union to their great cost. The situation in Africa is more acute partly because of the very low levels of productivity, which Bairoch (1975, 40–41) reckoned were only about one half those in today's developed countries at the start of their modernization. The other big contrast is that the latter achieved the break-through with relatively stable agrarian populations since development outside the primary sector siphoned off surplus labour on the land. This helped to raise agricultural productivity and generate surpluses, which in turn provided savings for use elsewhere.

As long as population pressure and poor agricultural performance persist, it is difficult to envisage an easy escape from this trap. Further industrialization would help, but to soak up the excess labour reserves would require impossible rates of industrial expansion, while agriculture cannot provide the resources to achieve this. Nor is there any large and prosperous mercantile sector, as in earlier Western societies, to provide the means for accumulation. In fact, in the present state of the art it is as much as agriculture can do to maintain levels of output, hence the increasing depen-dence on food imports and food aid. Though the latter were necessary to avoid starvation, ironically, greater dependence on food imports tends to have negative effects on indigenous economies leading to greater external indebtedness, while doing little or nothing to tackle the fundamental problems of agriculture.

EDUCATION AND HUMAN CAPITAL DEVELOPMENT

A common feature of nearly all past developed countries seems to have been a relatively high level of literacy or educational attainment at the dawn of modern economic growth and sustained educational provision to improve the human capital stock subsequently. In North America, Western Europe, Japan and later, the East Asian countries, this has generally been found to be the case, while it has been suggested that literacy levels at a given point in time are a good predictor of future per capita income levels (see Easterlin 1981, 10–14; Sandberg 1982, 687–97; Aldcroft 1998, 240–43). A study by Barro (1991) covering 98 countries over the period 1960–85 found the real per capita growth rate to be positively correlated with the initial stock of human capital (proxied by 1960 school enrolment ratios) and negatively related to initial (1960) levels of real GDP per capita. In other words, poor countries had the potential to catch up with richer countries providing they initially had high human capital provision (per capita) relative to their level of per capita GDP, but not otherwise (Barro 1991, 437).

Though it is generally recognized that the relationship between education and economic growth is a complex one, nevertheless it is also widely believed, and the historical evidence seems to lend some support to the contention, that countries deficient in educational provision will face great difficulty in unlocking the door to modern economic growth. This sets the scene for the African context. At the time of independence no African country could boast well-established educational systems, nor for that matter, health services and housing programmes. South Africa apart, the continent was largely illiterate with the lowest educational provision in the world. Only about 16 per cent of adults were literate. The proportion of the population between the ages of 5 and 19 receiving some form of formal education was of similar magnitude, compared with 44 per cent in South-east Asia, 50 per cent in Latin America and 76 per cent in Scandinavia. Secondary, tertiary and technical education were a rarity. Thus the bulk of the population was receiving no proper schooling even at the primary level. The average years of schooling amounted to a mere 1.48 years whereas in East Asia and the Pacific it was already 2.26 years (Adedji 1984, 225; Fieldhouse 1986, 34–5; Barro and Lee 1993, 383).

During the next several decades, Africa, in common with many other LDCs, launched massive educational programmes, with budgetary

Table 9.6   Public expenditure on education

Country	As % of GNP		Per inhabitant ($)	
	1980	1993	1980	1993
World total	4.9	5.1	129	229
Africa	5.3	6.2	48	38
America	4.9	5.4	310	597
Asia	4.4	4.3	41	92
Europe	5.1	5.2	417	782
Oceania	5.6	6.0	467	743
Developing countries	3.8	4.1	32	43
Sub-Saharan Africa	5.1	5.7	41	28

Source: UNESCO, 1995, Table 2.11.

expenditure on education (as a percentage of GDP) ranking quite respectably by international standards. Unfortunately, such quantitative indicators give rather a false impression of achievement. Take spending for example: when converted to a per capita basis, educational spending was minuscule compared with that of the Western world, and Africa was the only region in which it actually fell over time (see Table 9.6). By 1993 educational spending per inhabitant in SSA was only 3.6 per cent that of European countries (UNESCO 1995, Table 2.11). Differences in purchasing power parities do not improve the situation since, due to low efficiency of resource use, unit costs of education tended to be very much higher in Africa than in Asia or Latin America, not to mention than in the developed countries of the West (World Bank 2000, 114–15). The efficiency of educational spending in Africa, especially in terms of delivery, is also low compared with that in Asia and the western hemisphere (Gupta and Verhoeven 2001, 452–3). Not surprisingly therefore, in absolute terms SSA recorded the lowest improvement in educational provision of any region between 1960–85; years of schooling rose from 1.5 to 2.7, whereas over the same period they increased from 2.3 to 5.2 years in East Asia and the Pacific (Barro and Lee 1993, 383–5).

The World Bank, which has often extolled the virtues of human capital development, was somewhat puzzled by the protracted economic decline in some Third World countries, especially Africa, given the increased provision of education (rising enrolments) since independence (World Bank 1994, 25). It need not have been. Quantity indicators such as enrolments, expenditure ratios, numbers of schools and teachers, are all very well but they tell us little about the quality and delivery of the final service. When we look more closely at these aspects it becomes much clearer why the educational advances achieved so little.

The large educational programmes of the post-war period have been criticized frequently by educational commentators. Simmons (1979, 1005) found them to be 'expensive, inefficient and inequitable', with the result that they often failed to promote the well-being of the majority of the population. In fact in terms of quality and delivery the record has been very poor. In part this has been due to financial constraints coupled with the huge increase in numbers requiring education, which has meant that spending per head has been very low. This has naturally affected the delivery system adversely, which is reflected in shortages of books, teaching materials, equipment and the quality of teachers. The appalling conditions under which tuition and instruction take place in many Third World primary schools has been graphically illustrated by Graham-Brown's study (1991).

Transparent defects apart, the educational strategies were often misconceived in terms of the needs of the countries in question, and sometimes they were frustrated by political and social subversion. Educational programmes were all too often modelled along Western lines by planners incapable of appreciating the nuances of local requirements. Hence the content of curricula was ill-adapted to local conditions, the quality of the teaching was poor and the equipment and textbooks tended to reflect the interests and aptitudes of pupils in the metropolitan centres of the West. The colonial heritage was only partly to blame for this situation since many indigenous politicians were only too eager to adopt the styles of the West in the belief that they held the key to modernization (Watson 1982, 199).

These factors, coupled with straitened family circumstances that raised the opportunity costs of schooling dependants, meant that enrolments and attendance at schools were low, while failure and drop-out rates were high. Even as late as the 1990s, some 50 per cent of school-age children in Africa were not in regular attendance, while only two-thirds of those actually enrolled in primary schools reached the final grade five (African Development Bank 1998, 148–9, 171). Thus the average male received less than three years of schooling and the average female about one year. No doubt poor facilities and the unattractive nature of the tuition system explain some of the wastage, but by far the most important factor, especially in rural areas, was the simple fact that parents could not afford to let their children go to school (Luthra 1984, 57).

Given the general inadequacy of educational provision it is not surprising that illiteracy rates in Africa have remained the highest in the world, at over 50 per cent in the 1990s. But literacy scores give a distorted view of reality. Due to underfunding, poor delivery, low attendance and high drop-out rates, many school leavers could scarcely be regarded as literate or numerate in the internationally accepted sense. One estimate suggests that less than half of primary school graduates were able to read a newspaper (Simmons 1979, 1007), while Psacharopoulos (1988, 4) reckoned that the level of reading comprehension in poorer countries was probably no more than one-third that of Western nations. Clearly, attending school was no guarantee of success.

The degree of educational backwardness is well illustrated by the fact that even by 1990 the stock of human capital in Africa was reckoned to be far below the level in East Asia *in 1965* (African Development Bank 1998, 128). This means that a large proportion of the labour force has not been well-prepared to contribute to development. Comparisons are often made with the East Asian economies where there has been strong emphasis on educational attainment, which is considered to have been an important factor in their economic success (African Development Bank 1998, 126; Griffiths and Wall 2001, 804–6). The crucial element in these countries seems to have been initial concentration on basic education or primary schooling, the pay-off from which is substantial. It not only makes people more productive, acquisitive and socially aware, but it also facilitates other objectives, including fertility control, improvements in health, nutrition and personal hygiene, literacy and general communication, and in some cases a strengthening of cultural and national pride (Colclough 1980, 19; Aldcroft 2000, 176, 179). From a purely economic point of view the private and social rates of return are generally higher than those from any other form of education, while unit costs are appreciably lower (Psacharopoulos 1985). However, Barro in his study of growth determinants over a large cross-section of countries did find that the main positive influence on growth came from male secondary and higher education, though he acknowledged that primary education was essential in preparation for more advanced study. Also noted was the fact that female education did little to enhance growth though there was found to be a strong negative correlation between female primary education and fertility (Barro 1997, 19–22).

If we take the lesson of the East Asian countries as a guide then the first priority would seem to be to concentrate resources on basic education, at least in the initial stages. Yet many countries in the Third World have eschewed this strategy. In fact there has been a lack of clear strategy and too large a share of resources has been devoted to secondary and tertiary education to the detriment of primary education and equity (Mingat and Tan 1985, 305). Governments, it seems, pandered to those with social clout. They have acknowledged the demands of elitist groups who have been subsidized at the expense of the bulk of the population. The cost of tertiary education is extremely high in SSA; in 1990, government spending per student on higher education was 44.1 times as large as that on primary school students, a very much larger gap than in Asia and the West. Yet the social rate of return to primary education was more than twice that of the return to tertiary education, which suggests a costly misallocation of resources (Gupta and Verhoeven 2001, 456–7). As Gannicott (1990, 43) noted with reference to SSA, 'It is governments themselves that foster a costly over-expansion of higher education through massive subsidy to tertiary students. Meanwhile, the prospects for universal primary education, on which the social rate of return is very high, recede beyond the turn of the century'.

While the returns to basic education are high in Africa compared with those in more mature economies, the quantity and quality of educational provision, especially the latter, has nowhere near matched that of past developers. Unlike the more recent newly developing East Asian countries, many Third World countries, it is claimed, have missed out on the human capital revolution (Mehmet 1995, 127–8). Furthermore, they have failed to develop a home-grown educational strategy, as in East Asia, but continued for many years to follow slavishly the Western pattern of education (Simmons 1979, 1015).

The deficiency in human resource development has been singled out by the African Development Bank (1998, 126) as one of the key factors in the differential growth performance between SSA and East Asia. There are many ways in which it has impinged adversely on development, for example in the diffusion of new skills, techniques and methods of production, in general efficiency improvements and structural change, and in terms of its influence on fertility. But the ramifications of educational advance can be very wide-ranging as Núñez (1990, 135) recognized in her case study of Spain, and one of the frequently overlooked contributions, she argues, could be 'a better disposition towards change and social mobility in a very general sense'.

But all may not finally be lost, even though Africa has much ground to make up. In a cogent analysis of human resource strategies in developing countries, Wheeler (1984, 8, 10, 78–81) argued that only if educational provision was frozen at current levels would a low-level development trap emerge. 'If the poor African and South Asian societies follow the human resource path which has already been blazed in Latin America and East/South-east Asia, the predicted future is promising'. This conclusion is based on the following premises: (1) that output and investment respond favourably to enhanced educational inputs; (2) income gains arising therefrom react favourably on nutrition, health and hygiene; (3) improved educational opportunities and a rise in per capita income lead to a moderation in fertility and population expansion; and (4) educational strategies address basic needs (and quality especially) in the first instance and then build upwards. All this pre-supposes a competent and efficient statecraft to which we now turn.

STATE AND INSTITUTIONAL CONSTRAINTS

Government and institutions, or what Hall and Jones (1999, 84) refer to as 'social infrastructure', have come to be regarded as important attributes for successful economic development. The relevance of institutional change to economic progress has long been recognized. A century ago Cunningham (1904), for example, touched upon many of the key issues, which were later elaborated in more detailed and rigorous form in the works of North and Thomas (1970, 1973) and North (1981). In order that economic enterprise may thrive it is essential that the institutional and legal frameworks protect individual property rights, enforce contracts, minimize the costs of economic transactions and facilitate resource flows. In addition, social institutions should be such that they protect citizens from excessive diversion of the product of their labour, either by the state itself or by private agents through thievery, protection rackets and the like. Since the state or its government is best equipped for this purpose it is important that it does not fall into the hands of a self-chosen elite, which can often degenerate into 'negative sovereignty', states in name only, inefficient, illegitimate, corrupt and frequently unstable. The antithesis, 'positive sovereignty' is more likely to flourish under pluralistic democratic regimes, producing a social infrastructure more conducive to economic development (Jackson 1990, 1–21).

Positive sovereignty, along with modern states and appropriate infrastructures, did not happen overnight. They evolved gradually and erratically and it was to be many centuries before they crystallized in their modern form. But when they did they provided an environment conducive to economic enterprise and personal endeavour since graft, corruption, thievery, exaction and confiscatory taxation had been reduced to a minimum, while the legal framework upheld economic and commercial transactions. This of course was only true of Western Europe and North America by the nineteenth century. Eastern Europe and much of the rest of the world still laboured under negative sovereignty reminiscent of the Dark Ages in Europe.

The modern Western legacy was not passed on to the ex-colonial regimes of Africa, or at least if it was, then only very briefly and in a weakened form. This is perhaps scarcely surprising since democracy rarely featured in the bureaucratic and autocratic administrations of the colonial period, even though they were reasonably efficient, fairly incorrupt and impartial. Thus the successor states, like their counterparts in Eastern Europe after the First World War, had little experience of pluralistic democratic governance. They were anxious to claim legitimacy based on national identity and for a time to flirt with democracy and institutional systems based on Western models. But, as Landes (1990, 10) pertinently observes, they tried to create the whole panoply of institutions and infrastructures in a matter of years or decades, something that had taken Europe centuries to accomplish. Very soon, therefore, through the pressures of claims upon them, they degenerated into something quite different. In the words of Fieldhouse (1986, 57),

> They were encumbered with layers of claimants to power and wealth whom they could not satisfy. They were saddled with promises of rapid economic and social development which were unrealizable. The common result was fundamental political instability usually concealed under monopolistic or oligopolistic authoritarian regimes.

According to Ndulu and O'Connell (1999, 47), by the mid-1970s most of the newly independent African states had cast off the trappings of democracy to be replaced by authoritarian structures of one sort or another. A decade or so later only five countries in SSA (Botswana, Gambia, Mauritius, Senegal and Zimbabwe [the last very questionable]) had multi-party systems with meaningful political representation. The rest could be classified as follows: 11 military oligarchies, 16 plebiscitary one-party systems, 13 competitive one-party systems and two 'settler oligarchies' (Namibia and South Africa). Tilly (1992, 209–13) reckoned that two-thirds of African states were under military control in 1986. Since the late 1980s, possibly under the influence of IMF and World Bank pressures, there has been a trend towards greater democratization in several countries, notably Benin, Malawi, Mali, Mozambique, Niger and Zambia; by contrast, Gambia went the other way following the coup of 1994 (Barro 1997, 84). But one should be wary of reading too much into these positive shifts; democratic features were often cosmetic or skin-deep, Zimbabwe providing the classic illustration of perverted democracy.

In many Third World countries, political institutions and social infrastructures have been less conducive to economic progress than those that served the Western world in the nineteenth and twentieth centuries. But the drift to political and institutional disintegration has been deeper and more pervasive in Africa than anywhere else in the world. African finance ministers admitted that by the end of the twentieth century the majority of countries in SSA had a lower state capability than at the time of independence (Hawkins 1997, 26). Many commentators have highlighted the general collapse of statecraft. The World Bank (1993a, 22) described the situation in these terms: 'In many African countries the administrations, judiciaries, and educational institutions are now mere shadows of their former selves. . . .Equally worrying is the widespread impression of political decline. Corruption, oppression, and nepotism are increasingly evident'. Fernández Jilberto and Mommen (1996, 10), were even more forceful in their condemnation of political degeneration:

> The most appalling aspect of Africa's decline is the decay of Africa's institutional capacities. Corruption, criminality, nepotism and oppression are common features of all African countries. Some regimes and their bureaucratic rulers have been extremely brutal and have regarded their dominance as an occasion for pillage. Routinely used torture and murder became their instruments when they tried to stay in power and their successor regimes have often had just as little respect for human rights and liberties. Most of these regimes have failed in their attempts to construct a nation state or to cope with the legacy of their colonial past. Military regimes have been the outcome of economic failure and most African regimes rely on ethnic support and bureaucracies in order to control the population. Growing violence and instability have accompanied and induced a process of state disintegration in many an African country.

Once this sort of situation arises the whole body politic becomes rotten and the upshot is a system of governance and administration that runs counter to best practice as far as development and human welfare are concerned. There is no longer a positive role for the state and its institutions in terms of law, order, human welfare, enterprise and the protection of property and political rights of the populace at large since government, if one can call it that, is by elite groups for elite groups. The majority of the population, including the important small-scale entrepreneurial class, is effectively marginalized by the political process.

In other words, the state in any real sense of the term, had almost ceased to exist in many African countries. Effectively it had been captured by tiny groups of predatory leaders intent largely on perpetuating their position and enriching themselves. Questions of poverty, education, housing and the promotion of economic growth were the least of their worries. The elite groups thrived by exploiting the majority (mainly the peasantry) and they were essentially a parasitical vampire class. But it was basically an unstable situation as rival groups jockeyed for position at the top and inevitably this led to strife and institutional breakdown. Thus until the state vehicle is reformed it is unlikely that African countries will move far along the development path (see Ayittey 1998, 343).

Having said that, it should be noted that the instabilities and incongruities in the political and social structure could well of course be a symptom or reflection of the stage of development, and may not therefore remain continuously a barrier to progress. After all, it took many centuries before European states resolved their inner conflicts and power struggles, and, even by the nineteenth century, Eastern and Southern European countries retained many of the vestiges of traditional society, including acute tribal and religious conflicts. It may therefore take some time before Third World countries can adapt their state structures to those approaching Western Europe in the nineteenth century.

Many commentators do believe, however, that bad government and poor social infrastructure have had a significant role to play in the economic degeneration of Africa. To quote Wallace (1999, 133): 'it is not an exaggeration to argue that the failure of the state institutions is a major determinant of the limited progress in the improvement in human development indicators'. Jones (1996, 85) sees institutional failure as the main cause of Africa's economic predicament and suggests that government policies (which he refers to as macroeconomic populism) made it virtually impossible to experience agrarian-led growth following independence. Hall and Jones in their wide-ranging cross-country analysis (127 countries) of differing levels of productivity conclude that differences in social infrastructure are sufficient to explain the major variations in capital intensity, human capital per worker and productivity (Hall and Jones 1999, 110). They found a close and powerful relationship between levels of output per worker and measures of social infrastructure such that observed differences in social infrastructure between say Niger and the United States could explain most of the 35-fold difference in labour productivity between the two countries (Hall and Jones 1999, 84–5). Freeman and Lindauer (1999) came to a similar conclusion: that given a stable political and institutional environment that enables individuals to reap the rewards of their investments, then many of the alleged barriers to growth – education, trade, inequality, the handicaps of geography and climate – will prove to be surmountable. Ayittey (1998, 343) believes that the state vehicles currently in existence in many African countries are totally unsuited to the 'development journey' of the twenty-first century. On the other hand, Barro (1997, 119) is a little more circumspect about the influence of regime structures, but recognizes the importance of the rule of law and an improvement in democratic rights up to a certain point.

Some authors have personalized the matter, blaming directly the unscrupulous leaders who have captured the organs of power and used them for their own purposes. Thus Collier and Gunning (1999a, 100) argue that 'Africa stagnated because its governments were captured by a narrow elite that undermined markets and used public services to deliver employment patronage. These policies reduced the returns on assets and increased the already high risks private agents faced. To cope, private agents moved both financial and human capital abroad and diverted their social capital into risk-reduction and risk-bearing mechanisms'. Even more forthrightly, some writers attribute the African mess largely to its leaders, who have presided over declining economies while carefully enriching themselves and their cronies, the governments of most poor countries being controlled by rich and influential people (Ramsay 1984, 393; Rotberg 2000, 47–52):

> kleptocratic, patrimonial leaders [like Mugabe of Zimbabwe] give Africa a bad name, plunge its peoples into poverty and despair, and incite civil wars and bitter ethnic conflict. They are the ones largely responsible for declining GDP levels, food scarcities, rising infant-mortality rates, soaring budget deficits, human rights abuses, breaches of the rule of law, and prolonged serfdom for millions – even in Africa's nominal democracies. (Rotberg 2000, 47)

The question here is the line of causation. Did bad institutions throw up bad leaders or was it the latter who were directly responsible for the degeneration of the social infrastructure? And, in turn, how much feedback is there from slower growth to political instability and institutional degeneration? These are questions that we cannot explore here but have been the subject of recent analysis (see Guillaumont, Jeanneney and Brun 1999; Gyimah-Brempong and Traynor, 1999).

There are many ways in which states and institutions have distorted market incentives and thereby deterred enterprise and investment in African countries. Widespread economic regulation and the imposition of exacting demands on private producers seriously weakened economic incentives. The proliferation of administrative controls and licences, bureaucratic inefficiency and red-tape, the imposition of various exactions (including taxes) and the distortion of normal market forces by regulatory decrees, not merely discouraged enterprise but gave rise to corruption, bribery and nepotism and set the individual against the system (Reynolds 1986, 129; McCarthy 1990, 26). Mauro's study of corruption and bureaucratic inefficiency suggests that there is a negative relationship between corruption and investment and growth and that bureaucratic efficiency is conducive to growth and investment (Mauro 1995, 705–6). Administrative control and regulation, often reminiscent of wartime conditions, has done much to increase insecurity and stifle enterprise and investment, especially among small-scale producers in both agriculture and industry. This type of climate does not favour the growth of a strong, acquisitive and market-orientated bourgeoisie, operating by and within the rule of law, which was the hallmark of nineteenth-century Western development. When the risk and reward patterns so clearly favour the politically astute and those with the right connections at the expense of individuals of enterprise and initiative, who in their right mind would risks their assets (Landes 1990, 10; Batou 1990, 465)?

The state has had a much higher presence in economic affairs than was the case with most European governments in the nineteenth century. Budgetary outlays have accounted for up to a third of national income, which may be no bad thing providing budgetary systems are efficient. Unfortunately, this has not generally proved to be the case. There has been a general lack of transparency in budgetary accounting, expenditure patterns are often distorted, while revenue-raising exactions have been inequitable. On balance the system favoured the rich and those with power at the expense of the population at large.

For the majority of African countries, budgets have been described as 'a figment of the imagination' (Wallace 1999, 32). There is a lack of direct correspondence between allocations and deliveries and only a few countries have been able to produce audited accounts within a year of the completion of the relevant fiscal period. Deviations from planned or allocated expenditure have been frequent, such that funds for, say, school textbooks mysteriously get diverted into ministerial limousines (ibid., 132). These aberrations apart, there are grounds for arguing that the structure of budgetary outlays is inappropriate. Something like two-thirds of budgetary expenditures on average is devoted to defence (spending on which is high by past Western standards), and 'other sources'. The latter consist mainly of expenditure on general administration, including employee compensation. By comparison, spending on social services tends to be very modest, while the remaining outlays are devoted to economic services, the benefits from which are far from apparent.

The military budget is worth exploring in a little more detail since this is the one that has really burgeoned in the post-colonial period. On average, for SSA, it leapt from 0.7 per cent of GDP in 1960 to 3.8 per cent in 1990 and is now more than health and education spending combined (Deegan 1996, 191). Since African countries have few major external foes, much of the expenditure is devoted to training and equipping soldiers in the art of fighting and killing domestic enemies, rather than in the skills of law enforcement and the security of resources, in order to preserve the power and privilege of military and other rulers. The problems have of course been compounded in many cases by severe internal conflicts, civil wars and border conflicts in which a regime's soldiers often end up fighting each other. Civil wars and political turmoil have been endemic in Africa – at any one time probably about a quarter to one-third of the continent is embroiled in some form of internal conflict – a situation arising more through poverty and polarization of society than from ethnic fragmentation (note, however, that the existence of over 2000 different ethnic groups in Africa has not helped matters in this respect), though no doubt sometimes instigated by rulers themselves to serve their own purposes (Collier and Hoeffler 1998, 563–73). Be that as it may, vulnerability to internal conflict has not only absorbed scarce resources in military spending, but civil war itself has had disastrous effects on economic performance. Collier (1999, 175–81) estimates that civil wars resulted in per capita GDP declines of over 2 per cent a year, and that in a prolonged civil war of some 15 years (for example, Uganda 1971–86) the GDP loss could be as high as 30 per cent. Instability and disturbance discourages inward investment and few African states have been able to guarantee freedom from political turbulence to reassure multinational corporations, as has been the case in East Asian countries (Higgott 1986, 294).

On the revenue-raising side of state accounts, tax regimes tend to be highly regressive and discriminatory and often benefit a small minority of people. This situation has been a common feature of less developed countries in the past and one from which few lessons have been learned. Agricultural producers especially are often heavily taxed (compare the situation in nineteenth-century Eastern Europe), while benefit systems tend to favour the well-paid professional classes (often government employees) with little protection afforded to the bulk of the population. In consequence, fiscal policies tend to strengthen the already unequal distribution of income and wealth, compounded in some cases by excessive concentration of land ownership due to the absence of land reform. The result is that the majority of the population, and especially the small-scale entrepreneurial class, is marginalized by the political and economic system.

One by-product of societies with deficient social infrastructures and institutions and corrupt practices among the ruling oligarchies is a notable lack of trust among individuals and organizations. Research by neuroeconomic theorists suggest that trust or lack of it may be a significant factor in how societies develop. Where trust expectations are low and the level of deceit is high then people outside the ruling elite will be wary about engaging in economic and financial transactions, and this in turn will react adversely on economic growth. The level of trust varies a great deal between countries but it appears to be especially low in many lesser developed nations, often falling below the critical level of 30 per cent. Persaud (2004, 24) believes that 'countries where trust is lower than a critical level of about 30 per cent, as with much of South America and Africa, are at risk of remaining in a suspicion-locked poverty trap'.

We may assume that the politico-institutional structure has been responsible for the restrictive economic policies of many African countries, which have, it is argued, damaged African growth prospects. Sachs and Warner (1997) reckon that Africa is not incapable of generating fairly robust economic growth despite geographic, demographic, resource and climatic handicaps. However, they argue that African countries have been held back since independence as a result of highly distorted trade policies and non-market-orientated institutions. Had Africa followed growth policy strategies similar to those of East Asian countries, it is estimated that it could have achieved a per capita growth averaging 4.3 per cent a year over the period 1965–90. The emphasis is very much on the gains to be had from trade liberalization and trade openness and the prospects for trading on a global basis (see also Sharer 1999, 93; Basu, Calamitsis and Ghura 2000, 9), but one wonders whether this would have been enough, or indeed whether it could have been realized without significant political and structural reforms first having taken place.

MAURITIUS: BEACON OF LIGHT

Very few countries in SSA have managed to achieve sustained per capita income growth and structural change sufficient to give them relatively high levels of income. There have been a number of countries that recorded high growth rates for a time but most petered out in the oil and debt crises of the 1970s and 1980s, and those that did not were based on insecure foundations, as in the case of Botswana with its heavy reliance on its minerals. The World Bank and other key international organizations have frequently spotlighted success stories, though most of these have been ephemeral and short-lived (Ayittey 1998, 11). But one country at least stands out: Mauritius, a small island economy that was originally seen as destined for failure because of its monocrop culture, rapid population growth, ethnic tensions and susceptibility to exogenous shocks (Subramanian and Roy 2001, 4). Here is an example that suggests that all is not lost for African countries.[2]

Forty years on from this original description of Mauritius, a United Nations Conference on Trade and Development report on Mauritius had a very different story to tell (United Nations 2001, 1):

> Mauritius is an economic success story. The economy has sustained high 6 per cent annual growth for two decades – first driven by sugar, then textiles and clothing, and tourism, and most recently by financial services. Economic growth and structural change were achieved while maintaining national stability and social cohesion. A generation of Mauritians has enjoyed a rise in living standards that few countries can match, reaching an income per capita of $4000 today. What was once only another commodity producer, today is the leading manufactures exporter in Sub-Saharan Africa.

In the latter part of the twentieth century, Mauritius had one of the fastest growths in living standards in the world (Hodd 1994, 798). It is in fact the only African country to have experienced sustained real income growth along with significant structural change such that the country is no longer dependent on one or two staple export commodities in international trade, as is the case with the majority of SSA countries (Bloom and Sachs 1998, 212). The share of manufactures in total exports was no less than 68 per cent in 1990, twice the figure for South Africa.

The first thing to note about Mauritius is that it came to grips with the demographic time-bomb at an early stage. Family planning measures, using a wide variety of techniques, were implemented in the 1960s, which brought down fertility levels, while emphasis on basic education and increasing participation of women in the workforce led to later marriage and lower fertility. By 1990 adult literacy, at 86 per cent, was more than twice that for Africa as a whole, as a result of heavy concentration on primary and then secondary education as opposed to tertiary education. In the 1980s population growth was down to 1.4 per cent a year, and in the following decade it was little more than 1 per cent as against 3 per cent in the 1950s (Bowman 1991, 51, 115). In other words, the Mauritian demographic and human resource model is in keeping with those of past developers.

The second main point to emphasize is the open political culture and the reasonable degree of social harmony despite a considerable ethnic diversity. Mauritius has not been wracked by civil war and ethnic strife; nor has it lapsed into dictatorship but has had open pluralistic government under a multi-party system, which has allowed the development of institutions, legal systems and government policies that have been conducive to enterprise and development. Graft, corruption and violence to persons and property have been relatively rare compared with many other African countries. Macroeconomic policies have won high praise from multilateral organizations and external debts have been modest (Bowman 1991, 163; African Development Bank 1998, 85–9).

Mauritian governments have generally been favourable to enterprise and development, and in this respect they are following the pattern of the East Asian countries. The strategy has been to foster exports and stimulate structural change in order to wean the economy away from the traditional heavy dependence on sugar. Thus manufactures (textiles, clothing), tourism and financial services have now replaced agriculture and sugar as the main source of employment and exports. But in the process agriculture has not been neglected and nor has it been squeezed to death by penal taxes as in many other African states. In particular, unlike many African countries that have taxed their resource-rich primary sectors (shades of Eastern Europe again), Mauritius did not kill its main cash cow, sugar, which was largely in the hands of the French minority community (Subramanian and Roy 2001, 37).

The latest strategy in the diversification process is to turn Mauritius into the financial and communications hub of the Southern African Development Community (SADC), in which fund management, investment, trading, shipping, banking and information become an integral part of the economy (African Development Bank, 1998, 85–9). Thus by the turn of the century Mauritius had an economic structure that resembled that of many mature economies, with the primary sector accounting for a small part of output and employment, manufacturing for a quarter or more, while services accounted for over half of all economic activity (Europa Publications 2001, 2679). As Bloom and Sachs (1998, 212) note, no other African country has made a similar structural transition. After many years of structural adjustment reform programmes under the auspices of international agencies, the majority of African countries still remained heavily dependent on primary commodity exports, though according to Deaton (1999, 38–9) international commodity price trends are not the root cause of the continent's poor economic performance.

By way of stark contrast, it is instructive to look briefly at Guinea-Bissau, one of the poorest countries in the world, where 88 per cent of the population are said to live on less than a $1 a day. It is a small country (population 1.34 million in 2000) situated on the west coast of the African continent just below Gambia and Senegal. Agriculture accounts for four-fifths of employment and the major crop is cashew nuts, most of which are exported in shell form and account for 95 per cent of the country's exports.

Yet Guinea-Bissau probably has as much potential for modern development as Mauritius were it to be harnessed effectively. Its population is small and not growing as rapidly as in most other African nations and its ethnic problems are manageable. The rainfall is ample and fairly reliable and there are some rich primary resources including fisheries, untapped mineral resources such as bauxite and phosphates, the potential for large-scale tropical fruit production for export, the prospects of offshore oil reserves and of course the lure of spectacular tropical islands to entice tourists (*Financial Times*, 2003).

Sadly very little has been done to exploit these opportunities since the country gained its independence from Portugal in 1974. Neither the command economy that followed independence and the subsequent shift to pseudo-capitalism under the Liberation Party made much difference. Then the 11 months' civil war of 1998–99 only made matters much worse. The growth of gross domestic product declined by no less than 28.2 per cent in 1998 (compared with a 6.5 per cent increase in the previous year) and it has never really recovered from the shock since. The political instability that followed the assumption of presidential powers by Koumba Yalá does not

seem to have helped matters since he appears from reports to be more inter-
ested in building his own power base than in ensuring the survival of democratic institutions and processes.

The neglect of the opportunities for development are very evident.
There has been little diversification in agriculture towards producing high-
value tropical fruits. Cashew nuts remain the major crop and most are
exported in untreated form to India, thus losing the value added and
employment creation of processing at home. When processed and packed
they fetch more than twice the price paid to the native cultivators. The rich
fisheries are exploited either by pirates or EU fishers operating under
licence and most of the fish goes abroad for processing and packing since
there is virtually no fish exporting industry in Guinea-Bissau. This again
means a loss for the domestic economy. Mineral and oil resources remain
largely unexploited and tourism is still very much in its infancy. Until
Guinea-Bissau addresses these issues it is likely to remain a very underdeveloped economy.

THE ROLE OF THE WEST

One final issue needs to be addressed before closing this chapter, and
that is the role of the West in African development. While a good part of
the blame for the African predicament can be laid at the door of the
Africans themselves, especially their leaders, one is also conscious that
the Western developed countries have not always followed strategies that
are in the best interests of Africa, or for that matter the Third World in
general.

As might be expected, the colonial legacy is a subject that crops up frequently. African leaders and officials have been ardent critics of the colonial legacy, but partly no doubt to conceal their own mismanagement.
Admittedly, colonialism may not have bequeathed a great deal to Africa,
but not infrequently the post-colonial rulers squandered or failed to retain
that limited inheritance. Ayittey (1998, 41–2) demonstrates, with concrete
examples, their failure on this score: 'in many African countries, the leadership could not maintain, let alone augment, the little that was inherited
from colonialism. In fact, they destroyed it. The inherited infrastructure –
roads, bridges, schools, universities, hospitals, telephones, and even the civil
service machinery – are in a shambles.'

One cannot of course live on sunk costs indefinitely and perhaps more
pertinent than the colonial legacy from the point of view of African development are Western policies and strategies in the post-colonial period.
In a recent study Mehmet (1995) has accused Western planners and

institutions of trying to impose a Eurocentric version of development on Third World countries, which has often proved unsuitable for their purposes. There is some validity in this argument, evident especially in educational policies, though it should be noted that many African leaders were quite eager to adopt the trappings of Western civilization. On a wider plane, the major international organizations such as the IMF and the World Bank have often forced the implementation of policies that have sometimes run counter to the best interest of the LDCs. It is true that at some point structural adjustment programmes and greater economic liberalization have become necessary, but often the strategies have been applied so fiercely and harshly that they have, not surprisingly, bred resentment in the countries on which they have been imposed. Moreover, such programmes were usually implemented following a period in which countries had been allowed, even encouraged, by the West to run up huge debts, with disastrous consequences for their economic welfare.

The debt issue is worth examining in a little more detail since in the 1970s and 1980s Third World debts escalated alarmingly giving rise to a global debt crisis, which at one point threatened to engulf the Western financial world (Aldcroft 2001, 174). Before the early 1970s Sub-Saharan Africa had been a modest and fairly prudent borrower but very soon it joined the ranks of the heavily indebted countries. Total external debt rose from an estimated $6 billion in 1970 to $136 billion in 1988. Over the same period the ratio of external debt to gross domestic product rose from 14.6 per cent to 78 per cent, while the ratio of that debt to exports of goods and services rose from 67.5 to 366.7 per cent. The debt-service ratio (that is, the ratio of debt-service payments to the exports of goods and services) rose from 7.8 per cent in 1970 to a peak of almost 34 per cent in 1985. However, this latter ratio somewhat underestimates the true burden of debt-service obligations since it reflects the payments that were actually made rather than scheduled obligations before taking account of debt relief measures and rescheduling of debts. By the late 1980s more than half of African countries had arrears on debt services and were actively seeking a rescheduling of their debts. If these are allowed for then the debt-service ratio may have been close to 50 per cent (Greene 1989, 839–44).

Dornbusch and Fischer (1986, 837) have neatly summed up the origins of LDC debt crisis: 'Imprudent borrowing policies in the debtor countries and imprudent lending by commercial banks had a chance encounter with extraordinarily unfavourable world macroeconomic conditions that exposed the vulnerability of the debtors and creditors.' It is true that both creditors and debtors can be held responsible for the debt plight of many countries. 'There is' as Cuddington (1989, 38) notes, 'lots of blame to go round' and the debtors have come in for a good share of it. The main allegations may be listed as follows:

1. Government spending spree on the back of a commodity price boom leading to overborrowing in relation to carrying capacity.
2. Funds received were often used unwisely to finance consumption, budgetary deficits, show projects or the like, rather than invested in productive activities that would generate foreign exchange earnings.
3. Macroeconomic policies were inappropriate for good economic management, tending to be restrictive, inward-looking and protective.
4. Regime structures were prone to corruption and political favour rather than economic efficiency.

Part of the borrowing was of course occasioned by the oil price explosion of the 1970s, which hit non-oil producing LDC countries hard. Cline (1984, 8–11) sees this as the most important exogenous cause of the subsequent debt burden. Unfortunately the second wave of heavy borrowing occurred at the turn of the decade when, soon after, the commodity price boom broke and export earnings of non-oil producers declined and real interest rates rose.

Much of the debt held by SSA countries was non-commercial, that is, it was granted on concessional terms by various international agencies and donor governments, with only about 21 per cent owned by commercial financial institutions. One might therefore have expected better appraisal and monitoring techniques than practiced by commercial banks, but this does not seem to have been the case. The World Bank roundly condemned the deployment of funds, some of which had gone to finance large public show projects that had contributed little to economic growth and foreign exchange earnings. It referred to the excessive number of 'white elephants', too many show projects selected either on the basis of political prestige or through inadequate regard for their likely economic and financial rate of return (World Bank 1984, 24, 1985, 51–4).

Unwittingly the World Bank was condemning its own inability to monitor the use of funds properly. As Jones (1996, 90) points out, the World Bank's experience in Tanzania highlighted the failure of responsible international institutions to control recipient governments and their tacit acceptance of endemic government corruption. He quotes an illuminating report in *The Economist* of 24 August 1991 which was highly critical of Western aid donors who in effect had caused much suffering to indigent populations by financing dictatorships and uneconomic projects, by helping to destroy once viable economies and by assisting bankrupt and corrupt governments to remain in power.

While Western donors must clearly share some of the blame for SSA's debt burden, many academic commentators have been highly critical of the borrowers themselves. The problem, it is argued, is not simply one of excessive borrowing but seemingly one of the sheer misuse of resources through mismanagement. Schuker (1988, 136) has been one of the most strident critics of Third World debtors. He castigates the activities of governments of many debtor countries who have frittered away resources on show projects, on arming against aggressors, on over-consumption, and for the misappropriation of funds by local elites who conveniently blurred the distinction between public assets and private ones for their own gain. Similar assertions, though less stridently, have been made by Greene (1989) who argues that domestic policies were a major factor in debt accumulation in Sub-Saharan Africa. The combination of over-ambitious development programmes partly financed by external sources and misguided economic policies left many African states with severe financial problems once the commodity price boom broke.

By the final decade of the twentieth century Third World indebtedness, and especially that of SSA, was running out of control. External debts were not far short of the whole of the gross domestic product of SSA and interest and payments on past debt were similar to the inflow of loans and grants from lending countries (Brown 1995, 85, 89). Many African countries were overwhelmed by debt burdens and no amount of tinkering through rescheduling and structural adjustment policies was going to erase the burden. The only solution appeared to be that of outright cancellation.

However, there are grounds for concern over the whole issue of aid and debt, which raises serious questions for the future. There are critics (though relatively few in number since it is now non-pc to query the utility of aid) who question the whole structure of the international aid machine run primarily by governments and international organizations, which has given rise to 'a gigantic system of outdoor relief for poor nations' (author's words). Bauer (1981) is one who is highly critical of the methods and criteria of the massive aid programme and doubts whether it has been in the best interests of Third World countries. There are several reasons why one should take a sceptical view of external aid:

- It is not necessarily good for developing countries if they become hooked on aid or become aid-dependent to such an extent that it adversely affects indigenous enterprise. Bauer (1981, 113–14) quotes the case of the US trust territory of Micronesia in the Pacific, which has been so lavishly provided with handouts that even the most elemental enterprises were abandoned. The end result is immiseration and pauperization.

- International aid has become something of an organized racket, which benefits anyone but the poor in the Third World. It has become a veritable gold mine for middle class liberals in the West and the elites in Third World countries. Academics, the staff of international organizations, the politicians and bureaucrats in the Third World, the media and entertainment industry, Western exporters, and no doubt quite a few more, have a vested interest in keeping the aid programmes rolling irrespective of whether or not there are tangible benefits for the poor in the Third World. As Bauer (1981, 148) notes: 'The powerful and articulate groups behind aid have created an effective claque which has managed to silence discussion of the subject, including worthwhile reform of aid. This claque has also helped to divert attention from the evident anomalies of aid, and from its far-reaching consequences.'
- Much aid is wasted or diverted from good use because of corrupt practices, poor monitoring and the absence of a transparent price mechanism. Aid, especially in the form of grants and on concessional terms, distorts the free market and the price mechanism.
- It is questionable whether aid can significantly promote development if the conditions are not right for it. If in fact the right conditions are present then capital will be forthcoming on sound commercial terms.
- Bauer (1981, 134) in fact argues that the reduction in Western trade barriers to Third World products would do more to promote development than even the most enlightened aid policies.

However, when all is said and done, and wherever the blame lies, the fact remains that Africa has not made the best use of its external funding and yet in the process it has become saddled with a heavy debt burden. Even more telling is the fact that over the past half century or so Africa has had the equivalent of Marshall Aid several times over and yet has little to show for it. Debt relief and rescheduling have sought to ease the burden, but Western governments, now conscious of the continued plight of Africa and other LDC countries, are urging each other to provide more generous aid to poorer countries to relieve their poverty. But whatever the form in which the aid materializes, it will serve little useful purpose if it is not monitored much more closely by donors and receivers than has been the case in the past.

A second area of contention has been the West's attitude to imports of agrarian/primary products and low-tech manufactures from underdeveloped countries. These constitute a very large share of African exports and it is important that secure markets can be found abroad. This, however, has been increasingly difficult in a world dominated by agrarian protection and farm subsidization. OECD subsidies to agriculture at the end of the twentieth century amounted to some $300 billion a year, which is approximately the value of Africa's total GDP (*Financial Times*, 1 June 2000). A liberalization of Western trade policy with respect to farm products would probably be more beneficial to the revitalization of African agriculture than any amount of overseas aid. The same applies to Western protection for non-agrarian products, especially clothing and textiles. The major Western markets have been insulated from Third World products by increasing protection (Fortress Europe) to the detriment of indigenous industries in Africa and elsewhere (see Roarty 1990, 33–4). Africa is a very small participant in world trade (less than 2 per cent and declining) and therefore has little clout in global negotiations shaping world trading systems. As the United Nations pertinently observed in one of its reports, the rules of global free trade have been designed to favour the world's richest countries. Trade in which the less developed countries have a relative advantage, that is, agricultural products and labour-intensive manufactures such as clothing and textiles, is heavily protected, whereas trade barriers are low for sophisticated manufactures and services in which rich countries specialize (United Nations 1997).

Even more serious for African and other Third World countries is the damage done to indigenous activity as a consequence of subsidized farm exports and food aid from the United States and Europe. Insofar as subsidies or credits undercut world prices this acts as a disincentive to local farm production. The same adverse effect is also produced when food aid is rendered in kind as in the case of much of the American contribution (Monbiot 2003, 19).

Greater economic integration and globalization among the rich trading nations have probably been detrimental to African development. The institutions and strategies of the major players tend to be designed to enrich the rich and expose the poor, and hence are of little benefit to emerging economies (see Hopwood 1998, 252–4). Paradoxically, the Third World has lost out through decolonization and globalization. Whereas before the war some 15 per cent of the foreign trade of the European colonial powers was conducted with their overseas possessions, today trade with former colonial possessions is but a few per cent. The bulk of foreign trade and direct foreign investment now takes place within and among the developed nations. In other words, globalization has by-passed Third World countries that previously had a flourishing trade with the colonial powers (see Etemad 2000).

The rich nations of the West blithely assume that the march of industrial progress, or 'catch-up' and 'convergence', to use more modern terminology, will eventually take place within an integrated and globalized world economy, and that then all will be well. Unfortunately, this view presupposes a perfect world and a level playing field, neither of which obtains. In which case convergence will not take place; the world economic system is so riddled with imperfections, often put in place by the Western nations themselves, that there is little likelihood that the gap between rich and poor nations will be narrowed, at least in the foreseeable future. If anything the poor nations are likely to get relatively poorer. As the Secretary General of the United Nations Economic Commission for Africa observed, Africa's place in the global economy is now at the periphery of the periphery (quoted in Hopwood 1998, 249). You cannot get much lower than that.

At what point will the West react to the rich-poor divide? Probably when Africa becomes a serious security threat to the Western democracies as a result of the export of people, drugs, disease, violence and the like, all of which are already becoming evident (Landes 1990, 12; Holman 1994).

REFLECTIONS

African economic experience ranks as a major disaster of modern times, but one which many people prefer to forget in the disturbed and violent times of the present. By the end of the twentieth century most African countries had entered a low-level equilibrium development trap, not unlike that of their Asian counterparts in the early 1960s when Africa's growth potential was said to be ahead of that of East Asia. But unlike the spectacular record of some East Asian countries, the African experience provides a superb exemplar of how not to 'do' economic development. The irony is that many of the newly independent states had high hopes and expectations of success once released from the colonial yoke: that they would be able to emulate the Western model and move quickly from rags to riches, a decade at most according to Nkrumah, but reality proved to be very different. Though many African countries have potential, and Mauritius has shown the way in this respect, the post-colonial leaders have for the most part failed to harness that potential.

Unfortunately the Western model was misread and inverted (*the fatal inversion*) by the new governments along the way. Hobsbawm (1994, 200) argues that there was no real operational model other than 'Westernization' or 'modernization' or whatever one chooses to call it. This was adapted to suit their own purposes so that Rome could be built in a day, and bigger, better and more quickly:

> the new governments had their own schemes of economic development and
> social engineering, inspired by a new world of peripatetically eager experts and

technicians – eager to spend money, to do good, to wield power. These doers, be it said, had no trouble imagining schemes, the bigger the better (Landes 1999, 504).

And when the schemes failed who better to blame than the West?

The problem was that there was no easy short-cut to development. It had taken the West many centuries to reach economic maturity and high-income status, which involved, inter alia, the development of an appropriate statecraft and institutional/social infrastructure, agrarian modernization, controlled population expansion and investment in the human capital stock. All of which took much time, but time was not on the side of the African leaders. They were not prepared to wait and the consequence of their subsequent actions was the 'poisoning of development efforts in the direction of haste, waste and corruption' (Landes 1991, 19).

They therefore abandoned the prerequisites of the Western model and tried to telescope modern development into decades by their own methods, but with disastrous results. The strategy was not so much forced upon them from below by recalcitrant populations, but imposed from above by power-hungry bosses who saw the prospects of enriching themselves at the expense of the masses, while blaming the West for the resulting predicament of their countries. Landes (1999, 504) in his inimitable style explains how the story unfolds and is worth quoting at length:

> Much of the gap between expectation and realization came from unprepared-ness. The post-colonial Africans had no experience of self-government, and their rulers enjoyed a legitimacy bounded by kinship networks and clientelist loyal-ties. Abruptly, these new nations were pressed into the corset of representative government, a form alien to their own traditions and unprepared by colonial paternalism. In some instances, this transition had been preceded by a war of liberation, which mobilized passion and identity. But the legacy was rule by a strongman, autocratic embodiment of the popular will, hence slayer of democ-racy. Stability depended on one man's vigor, and when he weakened or died (or was helped to die), the anarchy of the short-lived military coup followed.

> The governments produced by this strongman rule have proved uniformly inept, with a partial exception for pillage. In Africa, the richest people are heads of state and their ministers. Bureaucracy has been inflated to provide jobs for henchmen; the economy, squeezed for its surplus. Much (most?) foreign aid ends in numbered bank accounts abroad. These kleptocrats have much to gain by living in Switzerland, near their banks. But maybe money alone is not enough.

No doubt post-war Africa inherited adverse legacies from the past and experienced unfavourable influences along the way, but these cannot fully explain the dismal record. While African nations may not have had a great inheritance, one cannot but feel that their leaders very soon squandered what little there was. It may be argued that many Asian countries were in the same boat in the early post-war years – indeed they showed less promise than many African nations – yet some were able to surmount the difficulties and shorten the time-frame of the development process. Mauritius demonstrates that Africans could do it given the will and the strategy to succeed. Thus the long Western run-in that Landes emphasizes as essential may not be so crucial if the right strategies are in force. Barro (1997, 44–6) in his projections of winners and losers places South Korea at the top of the list because of its high educational attainment, strong rule of law, low fertility, low government spending, high investment and low inflation. Many of the losers are in SSA; taking Sierra Leone as the prototype one can see why: weak rule of law, low school attainment, high fertility, low life expectancy, no political freedom, high government consumption and very little investment. Being poor therefore is not sufficient to generate catch-up and convergence and hence for some countries, but not all, it does not pay to be late.

It could of course be argued that the comparison with East Asian countries is somewhat unjust since the latter had a stronger national identity and civil consciousness stemming from their greater ethnic homogeneity. By contrast, some of the most ethnically heterogeneous societies of the world are located in Africa. Easterly and Levine (1997, 1204–5, 1233) estimate that a quarter to two-fifths of the East Asia-Africa growth differential can be attributed to ethnic diversity, which works indirectly on economic performance through public policies, institutions and infrastructures and political instability.

When all is said and done, the prospects for SSA and the Third World in general are not very promising, at least if one thinks in terms of catch-up and convergence. Even with a fair wind, it would take a very long time to get anywhere near the income levels of the West. The best scenario would be one where the West stayed still (nil per capita growth) and poor countries achieved per capita income growth of 3 per cent or more a year. On this wildly improbable trajectory it would take well over a century for many low-income countries to get even within spitting distance of the income levels of the rich nations. On a rather more realistic note, though still an optimistic one, namely a marginal relative advance in growth performance (per capita) over that of the West, it would take many centuries to catch up. Thus, we can say confidently that, short of a miracle, the prospects for most of the very poor nations, and especially the SSA group, will continue to remain very bleak indeed.

NOTES

1. My grateful thanks to Dr Steven Morewood for reading and commenting on this chapter and for making several corrections. This chapter is part of a larger study on the development of post-colonial Africa. Because of space limitations some of the sections in this chapter have had to be abbreviated.
2. It turned out to be a great success story and the complete antithesis to Nicholas Monsarrat's fictitious Pharamaul, an island on the opposite side of the continent. In his novel *Richer than all his tribe* (Monsarrat 1968), a sequel to Monsarrat (1956), the author foreshadowed the future decline of Africa with remarkable accuracy.

REFERENCES

Adedeji, A. (1984), 'The economic evolution of developing Africa', in M. Crowder (ed.), *The Cambridge history of Africa, vol. 8 from c.1940 to c.1975*, Cambridge: Cambridge University Press.

African Development Bank (1998), *African development report 1998: human capital development*, Oxford: Oxford University Press.

Aldcroft, D.H. (1995), 'Rich nations-poor nations: a long run view', *The South African Journal of Economic History*, 10.

Aldcroft, D.H. (1998), 'Education and development: the experience of rich and poor nations', *History of Education*, 27.

Aldcroft, D.H. (2000), 'Education and development: the experience of the four little tigers' in A.J.H. Latham and H. Kawakatsu (eds), *Asia Pacific dynamism 1550–2000*, London: Routledge.

Aldcroft, D.H. (2001), 'The twentieth-century debt problem in historical perspective', *Journal of European Economic History*, 30.

Artadi, E.V. and Sali-i-Martin, X. (2003), 'The economic tragedy of the xxth-century growth in Africa', *National Bureau of Economic Research Working Paper*, No. 9865.

Ayittey, G.B.N. (1998), *Africa in chaos*, New York: St Martin's Press.

Bairoch, P. (1975), *The economic development of the Third World since 1900*, London: Methuen.

Bairoch, P. (1989), 'Les trois révolutions agricoles du monde développé: rendements et productivité de 1800 à 1985', *Annales*, 44.

Barro, P. (1991), 'Economic growth in a cross-section of countries', *Quarterly Journal of Economics*, 106.

Barro, R.J. (1997), *Determinants of economic growth*, Cambridge, MA: The MIT Press.

Barro, R.J. and Lee, J.W. (1993), 'International comparisons of educational attainment', *Journal of Monetary Economics*, 32.

Basu, A. Calamitsis, E.A. and Ghura, D. (2000), *Promoting growth in Sub-Saharan Africa*, Washington DC: IMF.

Bates, R.H. (1986), 'The regulation of rural markets in Africa', in S.K. Commins, M.F. Lofchie and R. Payne (eds), *Africa's agrarian crisis: the roots of famine*, Boulder, Colorado, Lynne Rienner Publishers.

Batou, J. (1990), *Cent ans de résistance au sous-développement: l'industrialisation de l'Amérique latine et du Moyen-orient au défi européen, 1700–1870*, Geneva: Droz.

Bauer, P.T. (1981), *Equality, the Third World and economic delusion*, London: Weidenfeld and Nicolson.

Birkhaeuser, D. Everson, R.E. and Feder, G. (1991), 'The economic impact of agricultural extension: a review', *Economic development and cultural change*, 39.

Bloom, D.E. and Sachs, J.D. (1998), 'Geography, demography and economic growth in Africa', *Brookings Papers on Economic Activity*, 2.

Bowman, L.W. (1991), *Mauritius: democracy and development in the Indian Ocean*, Aldershot: Dartmouth Publishing Company Limited.

Brown, M.B. (1995), *African choices: after thirty years of the World Bank*, Harmondsworth: Penguin Books.

Christensen, C. and Witucki, L. (1986), 'Food policies in Sub-Saharan Africa', in S.K. Commins, M.F. Lofchie and R. Payne (eds), *Africa's agrarian crisis: the roots of famine*, Boulder, Colorado, Lynne Rienner Publishers.

Cline, W.R. (1984), *International debt: systematic risks and policy response*, Washington DC: Institute for International Economics.

Colclough, C. (1980), 'Primary schooling and economic development: a review of the evidence', *World Bank Staff Working Paper*, No. 399, Washington DC: World Bank.

Collier, P. (1999), 'On the economic consequences of civil war', *Oxford Economic Papers*, 51.

Collier, P. and Gunning, J.W. (1999a), 'Explaining African economic performance', *Journal of Economic Literature*, 37.

Collier, P. and Gunning, J.W. (1999b), 'Why has Africa grown so slowly?', *Journal of Economic Perspectives*, 13.

Collier, P. and Hoeffler, A. (1998), 'On economic causes of civil war', *Oxford Economic Papers*, 50.

Collins, S.M. and Bosworth, B.P. (1996), 'Economic growth in East Asia: accumulation versus assimilation', *Brookings Papers on Economic Activity*, 2.

Colman, D. and Nixson, F. (1994), *Economics of change in less developed countries*, Hemel Hempstead: Harvester Wheatsheaf.

Crafts, N. (2000), 'Globalization and growth in the twentieth century', in IMF, *World economic outlook: supporting studies*, Washington: IMF.

Cuddington, J.T. (1989), 'The extent and causes of the debt crisis of the 1980s', in I. Husain and I. Diwan (eds), *Dealing with the debt crisis*, Washington DC: World Bank.

Cunningham, W. (1904), *An Essay on Western Civilization in its Economic Aspects*, Cambridge: Cambridge University Press.

Deaton, A. (1999), 'Commodity prices and growth in Africa', *Journal of Economic Perspectives*, 13.

Deegan, H. (1996), *Third Worlds: the politics of the Middle East and Africa*, London: Routledge.

Dornbusch, R. and Fischer, S. (1986), 'Third world debt', *Science*, 234, 14 November.

Easterlin R.A. (1981), 'Why isn't the whole world developed', *Journal of Economic History*, 41.

Easterly, W. and Levine, R. (1997), 'Africa's growth tragedy: policies and ethnic divisions', *Quarterly Journal of Economics*, 112.

Eicher, C.K. (1986), 'Facing up to Africa's food crisis', in J. Ravenhill (ed.), *Africa in economic crisis*, Basingstoke: Macmillan.

Etemad, B. (2000), 'L'Europe et le monde colonial. De l'apogée des empires à l'après-décolonisation', *Revue Economique*, 51.

Europa Publications (2001), *The Europa world year book 2001*, Vol. 2, London: Europa Publications.

Fernández Jilberto, A.E. and Mommen, A. (1996), 'Setting the neo-liberal development agenda: structural adjustment and export-led industrialization', in Fernández Jilberto, A.E. and Mommen, A. (eds) (1996), *Liberalization in the developing world: institutional and economic changes in Latin America, Africa and Asia*, London: Routledge.

Fieldhouse, D.K. (1986), *Black Africa: economic decolonization and arrested development*, London: Allen & Unwin.

Financial Times (2003), *Guinea-Bissau, Special Report*, 25 June.

Freeman, R.B. and Lindauer, D.L. (1999), 'Why not Africa', *National Bureau of Economic Research Working Paper* No. 6942, Cambridge, MA.

Gannicott, K. (1990), 'The economics of education in Asia-Pacific developing countries', *Asian-Pacific Economic Literature*, 4.

Graham-Brown, S. (1991), *Education and the developing world: conflict and crisis*, London: Longman.

Greene, J. (1989), 'The external debt problem of Sub-Saharan Africa', *IMF Staff Papers*, 36.

Griffiths, A. and Wall, S. (2001), *Applied economics*, 9th edn, Harlow: Pearson Education.

Grigg, D. (1992), *The transformation of agriculture in the West*, Oxford: Blackwell.

Guillaumont, P., Jeanneney, S. and Brun, J.-F. (1999), 'How instability lowers African growth', *Journal of African Economies*, 8.

Gupta, S. and Verhoeven, M. (2001), 'The efficiency of government expenditure: experiences from Africa', *Journal of Policy Modeling*, 23.

Gyimah-Brempong, K. and Traynor, T.L. (1999), 'Political instability, investment and economic growth in Sub-Saharan Africa', *Journal of African Economies*, 8.

Hall, R.E. and Jones, C.I. (1999), 'Why do some countries produce so much more output per worker than others?', *Quarterly Journal of Economics*, 114.

Hawkins, T. (1997), 'Gloom starting to lift', *Financial Times World Economy and Finance Survey*, Part II, 19 September.

Higgott, R. (1986), 'Africa and the new international division of labour', in J. Ravenhill, (ed.) (1986), *Africa in economic crisis*, Basingstoke: Macmillan.

Hobsbawm, E. (1994), *Age of extremes: the short twentieth century 1914–1991*, London: Michael Joseph.

Hodd, M. (1994), *East African handbook 1995*, Bath: Trade & Travel Publications.

Holman, M. (1994), 'The sounds of a continent cracking', *Financial Times*, 23 July 1994.

Hopwood, I.G. (1998), 'Africa: crisis and challenge', in K. Booth (ed.), *Statecraft and security: the Cold War and beyond*, Cambridge: Cambridge University Press.

Jackson, R.M. (1990), *Quasi-states: sovereignty, international relations and the Third World*, Cambridge: Cambridge University Press.

Jones, S. (1996), 'Macroeconomic populism and economic failure in Africa since 1960', in D.H. Aldcroft and R.E. Catterall (eds), *Rich nations – poor nations: the long-run perspective*, Cheltenham, UK and Brookfield, USA: Edward Elgar.

Kelley, A.C. (1988), 'Economic consequences of population change in the Third World', *Journal of Economic Literature*, 26.

Komlos, J. (1989a), *Nutrition and economic development in the eighteenth-century Habsburg monarchy: an anthropometric study*, Princeton, NJ: Princeton University Press.

Komlos, J. (1989b), 'Thinking about the Industrial Revolution', *Journal of European Economic History*, 18.

Landes, D.S. (1990) 'Why are we so rich and they so poor?', *American Economic Review, Papers and Proceedings*, 80.

Landes, D.S. (1991), 'Does it pay to be late?, in C. Holmes and A. Booth (eds), *Economy and society: European industrialisation and its social consequences*, Leicester: Leicester University Press.

Landes, D.S. (1999), *The wealth and poverty of nations: why some are so rich and some are so poor*, London: Abacus.

Laslett, P. (1988), 'The European family and early industrialisation', in J. Baechler, J.A. Hall and M. Mann (eds), *Europe and the rise of capitalism*, Oxford: Blackwell.

Lofchie, M.F. (1986), 'Africa's agricultural crisis: an overview', in S.K. Commins, M.F. Lofchie and R. Payne (eds), *Africa's agrarian crisis: the roots of famine*, Boulder, Colorado, Lynne Rienner Publishers.

Luthra, K.L. (1984), 'Human resource development in Asia: achievements and tasks ahead', *Asian Development Review*, 2.

Maddison, A. (1989), *The world economy in the 20th century*, Paris: OECD.

Maddison, A. (1995), *Monitoring the world economy, 1820–1992*, Paris: OECD.

Mauro, P. (1995), 'Corruption and growth', *Quarterly Journal of Economics*, 110.

McCarthy, S. (1990), 'Development stalled: the crisis in Africa: a personal view', *European Investment Bank Papers*, 15.

McNeill, J.R. (1996), 'The reserve army of the unmarried in world economic history: flexible fertility regimes and the wealth of nations', in D.H. Aldcroft and R.E. Catterall (eds), *Rich nations – poor nations: the long-run perspective*, Cheltenham, UK and Brookfield, USA: Edward Elgar.

Mehmet, O. (1995), *Westernizing the Third World*, London: Routledge.

Mingat, A. and Tan, J.-P. (1985), 'On equity in education again: an international comparison', *The Journal of Human Resources*, 20.

Mokyr, J. (1976), *Industrialization in the Low Countries, 1795–1850*, New Haven, CT: Yale University Press.

Monbiot, G. (2003), 'Africa's scar gets angrier', *The Guardian*, 3 June.

Monsarrat, N. (1956), *The tribe that lost its head*, London: Cassell.

Monsarrat, N. (1968), *Richer than all his tribe*, London: Cassell.

Morris, P. (1995) 'Education and development: an introduction', in Morris, P. and Sweeting, A. (eds), *Education and development in East Asia*, New York: Garland Publishing.

Munro, J.F. (1984), *Britain and tropical Africa 1880–1960: economic relationships and impact*, London: Macmillan.

Ndulu, B.J. and O'Connell, S.A. (1999), Governance and growth in Sub-Saharan Africa', *Journal of Economic Perspectives*, 13.

North, D.C. (1981), *Structure and change in economic history*, New York: Norton.

North, D.C. and Thomas, R.P. (1970), 'An economic theory of the growth of the Western world', *Economic History Review*, 23.

North, D.C. and Thomas, R.P. (1973), *The rise of the Western world*, Cambridge: Cambridge University Press.

Núñez, C.-E. (1993) 'Literacy and economic growth in Spain, 1860–1977', in G. Tortella (ed.), *Education and economic development since the Industrial Revolution*, Valencia: Generalitat Valenciana.

Onimode, B. (1988), *A political economy of the African crisis*, London: Zed Books Ltd.

Persaud, R. (2004), 'The animal urge', *FT Magazine*, 28 August, 70.

Psacharopoulos, G. (1985), 'Returns to education: a further international update and implications', *Journal of Human Resources*, 20.

Psacharopoulos, G. (1988), 'Critical issues in education: a world agenda', *International Journal of Educational Development*, 8.

Ramsey, R. (1984), UNCTAD's failures: the rich get richer', *International Organization*, 33.

Ravenhill, J. (ed.) (1986), *Africa in economic crisis*, Basingstoke: Macmillan.

Reynolds, L.G. (1985), *Economic growth in the Third World*, New Haven, CT: Yale University Press.

Reynolds, L.G. (1986), *Economic growth in the Third World: an introduction*, New Haven, CT: Yale University Press.

Roarty, M.J. (1990), 'Protectionism and the debt crisis', *National Westminster Bank Quarterly Review*, February.

Rotberg, R.I. (2000), 'Africa's mess, Mugabe's mayhem', *Foreign Affairs*, 79.

Sachs, J.D. (1996), 'Growth in Africa: it can be done', *The Economist*, 29 June.

Sachs, J.D. and Warner, A.M. (1997), 'Sources of slow growth in African economies', *Journal of African Economies*, 6.

Sandberg, L.G. (1982), 'Ignorance, poverty and economic backwardness in the early stages of European industrialization. Variations on Alexander Gerschenkron's grand theme', *Journal of European Economic History*, 11.

Schuker, S.A. (1988), *American 'reparations' to Germany, 1919–33: implications for the Third-World debt crisis*, Princeton NJ: Princeton University.

Sharer, R. (1999), 'Liberalizing the trade system', in L. Wallace (ed.), *Africa: adjusting to the challenge of globalization*, Washington DC: IMF.

Simmons, J. (1979), 'Education for development', *World Development*, 7.

Soludo, C.C. (1998), 'Africa: industrialization strategy in the context of globalization', in Z. Iqbal and M.S. Kahn (eds), *Trade reform and regional integration in Africa*, Washington DC: IMF.

Subramanian, A. and Roy, D. (2001), 'Who can explain the Mauritian miracle: Meade, Romer, Sachs, or Rodrik?', *IMF Working Paper*, WP/01/116, International Monetary Fund.

Tilly, C. (1992), *Coercion, capital and European states, AD990–1990*, Oxford: Blackwell.

UNESCO (1995), *Statistical yearbook 1995*.

United Nations Conference on Trade and Development (1997), *Trade and development report 1997*, New York: United Nations.

United Nations Conference on Trade and Development (2001), *Investment policy review: Mauritius*, New York: United Nations.

United Nations/Economic Commission for Africa (1997), *Report on the economic and social situation in Africa*, Addis Ababa: United Nations.

van der Woude, A.M. (1992) 'The future of west European agriculture: an exercise in applied theory', *Review, Fernand Braudel Centre*, 15.

Wallace, L. (ed.) (1999), *Africa: adjusting to the challenge of globalization*, Washington: IMF.

Watson, K. (1982), *Education in the Third World*, London: Croom Helm.
Wheeler, D. (1984), *Human resource policies, economic growth and demographic change in developing countries*, Oxford: Oxford University Press.
World Bank (1984), *Toward sustained development in Sub-Saharan Africa*, Washington DC: World Bank.
World Bank (1985), *World development report 1985*, Oxford: Oxford University Press.
World Bank (1992), *World development report 1992*, New York: Oxford University Press.
World Bank (1993a), *Annual report*, Washington DC: World Bank.
World Bank (1993b), *The East Asian miracle: economic growth and public policy*, New York: Oxford University Press.
World Bank (1994), *Adjustment in Africa: reforms, results and the road ahead*, New York: Oxford University Press.
World Bank (1995), *World development report 1995*, New York: Oxford University Press.
World Bank (1997), *World development report 1997*, Oxford: Oxford University Press.
World Bank (2000), *Can Africa claim the 21st century?*, Washington DC: World Bank.

Index